Improving Large-Scale Assessment in Education

Large-scale assessments (LSAs) are playing a growing role in education policy decisions, accountability, and education planning worldwide. This book focuses on central issues that are key components of the successful planning, development, and implementation of LSAs. The book's main distinction is its focus on practice-based cutting-edge research. This is achieved by having chapters co-authored by world-class researchers in collaboration with measurement practitioners. The result is a how-to book whose language is accessible to practitioners and graduate students as well as academics.

No other book so thoroughly covers current issues in the field of LSA. An introductory chapter is followed by 15 chapters that each focus on a specific issue. The content is prescriptive and didactic in nature but based on the most recent scientific research. It includes successful experiences, exemplary practices, training modules, interesting breakthroughs or alternatives, and promising innovations regarding large-scale assessments. Finally, it covers meaningful topics that are currently taking center stage, such as motivating students, background questionnaires, comparability of different linguistic versions of assessments, and cognitive modeling of learning and assessment.

This book is suitable for graduate-level assessment courses in both education and psychology, for LSA designers and users, as well as for a wide range of academics who share an interest in the advancement and use of large-scale assessments.

Marielle Simon is Professor in the Department of Psycho-education at the University of Ottawa, Canada.

Kadriye Ercikan is Professor of Measurement and Research Methods in the Department of Educational and Counseling Psychology and Special Education at the University of British Columbia, Canada.

Michel Rousseau is Professor of Education at the Université du Québec à Trois-Rivières, Canada.

Improving Large-Scale Assessment in Education

Theory, Issues, and Practice

Edited by Marielle Simon, Kadriye Ercikan, and Michel Rousseau

NEW YORK AND LONDON

First published 2013
by Routledge
711 Third Avenue, New York, NY 10017

Simultaneously published in the UK
by Routledge
2 Park Square, Milton Park, Abingdon, Oxon OX14 4RN

Routledge is an imprint of the Taylor & Francis Group, an informa business

© 2013 Taylor & Francis

The right of the editor to be identified as the author of the editorial material, and of the authors for their individual chapters, has been asserted in accordance with sections 77 and 78 of the Copyright, Designs and Patents Act 1988.

All rights reserved. No part of this book may be reprinted or reproduced or utilised in any form or by any electronic, mechanical, or other means, now known or hereafter invented, including photocopying and recording, or in any information storage or retrieval system, without permission in writing from the publishers.

Trademark notice: Product or corporate names may be trademarks or registered trademarks, and are used only for identification and explanation without intent to infringe.

Library of Congress Cataloging in Publication Data

Improving large-scale assessment in education : theory, issues and practice / edited by Marielle Simon, Kadriye Ercikan, Michel Rousseau.
   p. cm.
   Includes bibliographical references and index.
   1. Educational tests and measurements—Methodology.   I. Simon, Marielle.   II. Ercikan, Kadriye.   III. Rousseau, Michel, 1971–
   LB3051.I467 2012
   371.26—dc23
   2012009731

   ISBN: 978–0–415–89456–2 (hbk)
   ISBN: 978–0–415–89457–9 (pbk)
   ISBN: 978–0–203–15451–9 (ebk)

Typeset in Minion
by Apex CoVantage, LLC

Printed and bound in the United States of America
by Edwards Brothers, Inc.

Contents

List of Illustrations   xi
Preface   xv
Acknowledgments   xvii

1 Introduction   1
MARIELLE SIMON, KADRIYE ERCIKAN, AND MICHEL ROUSSEAU
Brief History of LSA   1
Key Issues Related to LSAs   4
Conclusion   7
References   8

PART I: ASSESSMENT DESIGN, DEVELOPMENT, AND DELIVERY

2 Large-Scale Assessment Design and Development for the Measurement of Student Cognition   13
JACQUELINE P. LEIGHTON
Introduction   13
Traditional Procedures for Large-Scale Test Item Development   15
Examples of Testing Programs With "Cognition in Mind"   20
Conclusion   24
References   25

3 Role and Design of Background Questionnaires in Large-Scale Assessments   27
RUTH A. CHILDS AND ORLENA BROOMES
Introduction   28
An Example: Who Is Failing Ontario's Literacy Test and Why?   28
What Information Do We Need?   29
How Should We Ask the Questions?   34
Prioritizing the Information Needed   34
Writing the Questions   35
Testing the Questions   38

Creating the Final Questionnaire 40
Resources 40
Conclusion 41
References 41

4 Student Motivation in Large-Scale Assessments 43
CHRISTINA VAN BARNEVELD, SHERRI-LYNNE PHARAND,
LORI RUBERTO, AND DAPHNE HAGGARTY
Introduction 44
Theories of Motivation 44
Measuring Motivation 45
Self-Report Measures of Motivation 45
Student Test-Taking Behaviors as Measures of Motivation 46
What Is the Proportion of Students Who Are Not Motivated? 48
The Impact of Low Motivation on Large-Scale Assessment Results 48
Minimizing the Impact of Low Motivation on Large-Scale Assessment Results 49
Multiple Perspectives 50
Framework for Improving Research, Policy, and Practices 58
Agenda for Future Research 58
Conclusion 59
References 60

5 Computer-Based and Computer-Adaptive Testing 62
RICHARD M. LUECHT
Introduction 62
A Brief History of CBT 63
CBT Venues and Platforms 64
Item Types and Interfaces 67
Test Designs for Delivering CBT 71
Conclusion 80
Notes 81
References 82

PART II: ASSESSING DIVERSE POPULATIONS

**6 Academic Assessment of English Language Learners:
A Critical, Probabilistic, Systemic View** 87
GUILLERMO SOLANO-FLORES AND MARTHA GUSTAFSON
Introduction 87
Population Misspecification and the Definition of English Language Learners 90
Measurement Error, Sampling, and the Testing of English Language Learners 92
Measurement Error and Overgeneralization in Test Adaptation
  for English Language Learners 96
Probabilistic Approaches for Improving Assessment Systems
  for English Language Learners 100

	Conclusion	104
	Notes	105
	References	105

7 Score Comparability of Multiple Language Versions of Assessments Within Jurisdictions — 110
KADRIYE ERCIKAN, MARIELLE SIMON, AND MARÍA ELENA OLIVERI

Introduction	110
Review of Research on Comparability of Multiple Language Versions of Tests	112
Current Practices Within Canadian Jurisdictions	113
Challenges and Solutions to Ensuring Score Comparability Within Jurisdictions	116
Conclusion	121
References	121

8 Accommodating Special Needs for Large-Scale Assessments — 125
LEILANI SÁEZ, ELISA JAMGOCHIAN, AND GERALD TINDAL

Introduction	125
Accommodation Appropriateness	127
Research on the Effectiveness of Accommodations	129
Determining Accommodation Appropriateness to Examine Effectiveness	131
Practical Implications	132
Upgrading Practice	136
Conclusion	137
References	138

PART III: SCORING, SCORE REPORTING, AND USE OF SCORES

9 Scoring Issues in Large-Scale Assessments — 143
MARÍA ELENA OLIVERI, BRITTA GUNDERSEN-BRYDEN, AND KADRIYE ERCIKAN

Introduction	143
Overview of Provincial LSAs Administered in British Columbia	144
Scoring in LSAs of Educational Achievement	146
Diverse Models Used to Score the Foundation Skills Assessment	150
Conclusion	151
References	152

10 Standard Setting: Past, Present, and Perhaps Future — 154
ROBERT W. LISSITZ

Introduction	154
Performance Level Descriptors	156
Traditional Standard-Setting Methods	159
The Big Picture	166
Expected Future of Standard Setting	167
Issues of Reliability and Validity for Standard Setting	171
Conclusion	172
References	173

11 **From "Here's the Story" to "You're in Charge": Developing and Maintaining Large-Scale Online Test- and Score-Reporting Resources** 175
APRIL L. ZENISKY and RONALD K. HAMBLETON
Introduction 175
A Brief Overview of Online Reporting Resources 176
Guidelines for Static, Results-Oriented Online Documents 179
Guidelines for Interactive Results-Oriented Tools 180
Guidelines for Programmatic/Informational Web Pages 181
Guidelines for Test- and Score-Reporting Website Home Pages 182
Developing Score-Reporting Resources: The Hambleton and Zenisky Model 183
Conclusion 184
References 185

12 **Making Value-Added Inferences From Large-Scale Assessments** 186
DEREK C. BRIGGS
Introduction 186
Value-Added Models 188
How Well Do VAMs Estimate the Effects of Teachers or Schools on Student Achievement? 190
Value-Added Inferences and Shoe Leather 193
The Stability of Value-Added Indicators 197
Implicit Assumptions About Large-Scale Assessments 198
Conclusion 200
Notes 201
References 201

PART IV: PSYCHOMETRIC MODELING AND STATISTICAL ANALYSIS

13 **Complex Person and Item Sampling: Implications for Analysis and Inference** 207
JESSICA L. MISLEVY, LAURA M. STAPLETON, AND ANDRÉ A. RUPP
Introduction 208
Sampling and Statistical Inference 208
Types of Sampling Designs for Students and Items 209
Motivating Example 211
Impact of Sampling Design on Estimation and Inference 214
Accommodating Complex Sampling Designs of Students in Analyses 218
Accommodating Complex Sampling Designs of Items in Analyses 226
Conclusion 228
Note 230
References 230

14 **Taking Atypical Response Patterns Into Account: A Multidimensional Measurement Model From Item Response Theory** 238
GILLES RAÎCHE, DAVID MAGIS, JEAN-GUY BLAIS, AND PIERRE BROCHU

	Introduction	238
	Formulation of Logistic Models	239
	Person-Characteristic Curves	246
	Multidimensional Models of Person-Characteristic Curves	246
	Estimation of Person Parameters	248
	Examples of Application	249
	Example of the Application to the PISA Data (2003)	251
	Conclusion	254
	Notes	255
	References	255
15	**Missing Data: Issues and Treatments**	**260**
	MICHEL ROUSSEAU	
	Introduction	260
	Definition, Classification, and Mechanisms	261
	Prevention	262
	Diagnosis	264
	Treatment	265
	Conclusion	274
	References	275
16	**Measurement and Statistical Analysis Issues With Longitudinal Assessment Data**	**276**
	BRUNO D. ZUMBO, AMERY D. WU, AND YAN LIU	
	Introduction	276
	Measurement Issues	277
	Statistical Analysis Issues	280
	Conclusion	287
	References	288

Index   291

List of Illustrations

Figures

4.1	Teacher Description of the Moment When Her Perceptions Regarding the Importance of Large-Scale Assessment Changed	53
4.2	Teacher Description of the Process of Using Large-Scale Assessment Data for Educational Decision Making	54
4.3	A Successful "Literacy Night" for Families	57
4.4	An Example of Exceptional Teaching at an Inner-City School	57
5.1	A Template Mock-Up for a Choose-Two Selected-Response Item	71
5.2	The Basic CAT Process	73
5.3	Panels With 15-Item MILs for a 1–3–4 ca-MST Template Configuration	76
5.4	Eight TIF Targets for 15-Item MILs With Good Separation (1–3–4 ca-MST Panels)	78
5.5	Eight TIF Targets for 15-Item MILs With Marginal Separation (1–3–4 ca-MST Panels)	79
6.1	Linguagrams of Four Hypothetical ELL Students	91
6.2	An Example of an Item Whose Linguistic Features May Be Biased Against ELL Students	94
6.3	The Lunch Money Item	96
10.1	*From left to right*: Distribution for Basic, for Proficient, and for Advanced Y-Axis Is Frequency of Each Standard Score	161
10.2	Item Information Summary Sheet	163
10.3	Sample Answer Sheet for Standard Setting Bookmarks Using the Ordered Item Bookmark System	165
10.4	Time and Effort to Complete Standard Setting	168
10.5	Sample Ready to Judge Form	169
12.1	Plots of School-Level Achievement and Growth, Boulder Valley School District, 2011	194
13.1	SAS Analysis of Variance Output from Example Dataset with School as Between-Subjects Factor	217
13.2	SAS Syntax for Obtaining Traditional Sample Statistics in a Regression of Y on X	221
13.3	SAS Syntax for Obtaining Weighted Sample Statistics in a Regression of Y on X	221

13.4	SAS Syntax for Obtaining Weighted Sample Statistics and Linearized Standard Error Estimates in a Regression of Y on X	223
13.5	Flow Chart for Analyzing Complex Survey Data	229
14.1	Examples of Item Characteristic Curves for the One-, Two-, Three-, and Four-Parameters Logistic Models Resulting from IRT (Dichotomous Responses)	240
14.2	Functions of Likelihood of Patterns of Response Without A Priori Distribution	241
14.3	Functions of Likelihood of Patterns of Responses With A Priori Distribution	243
14.4	Persons Characteristic Curves as Per Four Profiles	247
14.5	Distribution of the Four-Person Parameters in a Sample of Results Obtained in Mathematics From PISA in 2003 in Canada	252
16.1	A Path Diagram for the 3-Phase MIML Model	285

Tables

6.1	Judgmental and Empirical Evidence of Language Bias in the Lunch Money Item	95
6.2	Examples of Sources of Randomness in the Testing of ELLs	101
6.3	Dimensions for Evaluating ELL Large-Scale Assessment Systems	102
6.4	Confusion Matrix for Assessing the Accuracy of Classifications of Students as ELLs or Non-ELLs	102
7.1	Verification of Comparability of Assessment and Development Procedures	115
7.2	Procedures Conducted to Verify Comparability of Assessments	115
8.1	Universal Design for Assessment (UDA) and Test Development	135
10.1	Performance Level Descriptors for Grade 11 Literacy	157
10.2	Proficiency Growth Summary Based on Action Verbs for 11th Grade Literacy	158
11.1	Summary of Guidelines for Static, Results-Oriented Online Documents	179
11.2	Summary of Guidelines for Interactive Web-Based Reporting	181
11.3	Summary of Guidelines for Programmatic/Informational Web Pages	182
11.4	Summary of Guidelines for Test- and Score-Reporting Homepages	183
13.1	Summary of Sampling Designs	212
13.2	Population and Sample Considered in Example	213
13.3	Sampling Design Characteristics and their Prototypical Design Effects and Impact on Estimates	216
13.4	Steps for Calculating Sampling Weights	219
13.5	Linear Regressions of English Reading Proficiency (Y) on Minutes of Reading (X)	221
13.6	Example using Plausible Values to Estimate Effect of Minutes of Reading on English Reading Proficiency	228
14.1	Example of the Estimation of Person Parameters When the Personal Parameters of Fluctuation, Pseudoguessing, and Inattention Are All Equal to 0	250
14.2	Example of the Estimation of Person Parameters of When the Personal Fluctuation Parameter Is Equal to 0.5	250
14.3	Example of the Estimation of Person Parameters When the Personal Pseudoguessing Parameter Is Equal to 0.3	251
14.4	Example of the Estimation of the Persons Parameter When the Personal Inattention Parameter Is Equal to 0.3	251
14.5	Example of the Estimation of the Person Parameters from Results in Mathematics Achieved at the 2003 PISA in Canada. (First 10 observations without missing data from a total of 2,182 observations)	252

14.6	Descriptive Statistics and Pearson Correlations Between the Estimated Values of the Person Parameters From the Results in Mathematics Achieved by 2003 PISA in Canada (Solely Observations With No Missing Data Where n = 2,182)	253
15.1	Descriptive Statistics and Regression Coefficients for the Entire Sample	265
15.2	Descriptive Statistics and Regression Coefficients Obtained via the Listwise and Pairwise Deletion Methods	266
15.3	Descriptive Statistics and Regression Coefficients Obtained by Mean Imputation and Regression Imputation	268
15.4	Regression Coefficient Average	271
15.5	Intraimputation Variance	271
15.6	Interimputation Variance	271
16.1	Equations for the Three-Phase MIML Model	284

Appendices

13.A	Simple Example Dataset	231
13.B	SAS Code for Generating and Applying Jackknife and Bootstrapping Techniques	235
14.A	*R* Source Code Used to Produce the Results of Four Examples	257
14.B	*R* Source Code Used to Produce the Results of the Example From the PISA	258

Preface

The publication of a book on large-scale assessment (LSA) and how to improve on persistent issues that still take center stage, such as student motivation, accommodations, standard-setting and background questionnaires is timely. The book combines a mix of conceptual, methodological, technical, and statistical aspects that researchers, practitioners, and policy makers deal with in LSA contexts. Given its orientation and its content, it is at times prescriptive and didactic and, in some instances, descriptive and instructive in nature. It is one of few current resources that explicitly present detailed descriptions of successful experiences, exemplary practices, important breakthroughs or alternatives, promising innovations and recommendations regarding key topics related to LSAs.

This book is particularly suitable for graduate level courses on educational assessment in Education and Psychology. At this level of studies, students have been made aware of the many dimensions and issues associated with LSA and have enough theoretical and statistical background to understand the technical aspects of some of the more advanced chapters. Needless to say, LSA designers, developers and users, as well as a wide range of academics who share an interest in the advancement and use of LSAs will also find the book useful particularly as they are called to apply the latest methods and approaches.

Although at the time the book was written most of the contributing authors were professors at various American, Canadian, and European universities, some were practitioners within various educational settings, and others were doctoral students or post-doctoral research fellows. Practitioners included government officials, members of associations responsible for the development and administration of LSAs, and school board members. The team of co-authors of one of the chapters even includes a high school student.

Another unique feature of this book is that each of its chapters was peer-reviewed, using a double-blind process by a pair of experts working within academia or in practice and policy contexts. The referees were encouraged to be critical of the chapter under review by filling out a detailed 5-point appraisal scale that focused on 16 items such as articulation of issue, theoretical implications, practical implications, supporting illustrations/examples, clarity, validity of conclusions, overall flow, respect of targeted audience and instructional aspects. Their respective ratings and comments were then sent anonymously to the author(s) when minor or major modifications were recommended.

The international collaborative nature of the book is also significant. The international contributions add diverse perspectives to discussions of different issues in LSA. They also provide opportunities for the reader to gain insights about LSA contexts in different countries. Authors and reviewers from Canada, the United States and Europe worked together to ensure highly relevant, complete and coherent chapters on timely and popular themes solicited by a variety of readers. This is reflective in the universality of examples across the chapters, in the extensive literature reviews and in the consistency of terminology throughout. In Canada, experts from both English and French communities contributed to the volume. In fact, the chapters by Raîche, Magis, Blais and Brochu and by Rousseau were initially written in French and translated to English.

The book is divided into five sections. The introductory chapter starts with a brief historical background of LSAs which is followed by a description of the book's organizing framework and a short description of each of the four sections and related chapters. Finally, the last section offers a discussion of the future of LSA. The four other sections group three or four chapters together in terms of their conceptual, pragmatic and psychometric nature. Each chapter however presents the theory, issues and practice associated with its theme.

Acknowledgments

We wish to take this opportunity to convey our heartfelt gratitude to everyone who has assisted in the development of this book. These include the contributing authors, Ronald K. Hambleton who provided suggestions in the conceptualization of the book, Christopher L.S. Coryn at Western Michigan University and Audrey Beardsley at Arizona State University who reviewed the book proposal for Taylor and Francis and who steered us in the direction of expanding the book to include a wide range of topics, and an international cast of experts who provided thoughtful and thorough reviews of the chapters. The names of each reviewer and his or her affiliation at the time are given in alphabetical order in the following list:

Serge Boulé, Conseil des Écoles Publiques de l'Est de l'Ontario (School Board)
Louise Bourgeois, University of Ottawa
Krista Breithaupt, Canadian Medical Council
Pierre Brochu, Council of Education Ministers, Canada
Christopher Coryn, University of Western Michigan
Robert Crocker, Memorial University
Jean Dumais, Statistics Canada
Richard Duran, University of California
Lorna Earl, Aporia Consulting Ltd and formerly from OISE/University of Toronto
Daniel Eignor, Education Testing Service
Victor Freiman, University of Moncton
Éric Frenette, Université Laval
Marthe Graig, Council of Educational Ministers, Canada
Claude Houssemand, University of Luxembourg
Maciej Jakubowski, Organisation for Economic Co-operation and Development
Hong Jiao, University of Maryland
Richard Johnson, Saskatchewan Ministry of Education
Don Kligner, Kingston University
Michael Koslow, Education Quality and Accountability Office
Benjamin J. Lovett, Elmira College
Jean Moreau, Canton de Vaud
Paul Nichols, Pearson
Christian Nidegger, République et Canton de Genève
Denis Savard, Université Laval
Elizabeth Stone, Education Testing Service
Linda Sturman, National Foundation for Educational Research

Charles Ungerleider, University of British Columbia
Donald Zimmerman, formerly from Carleton University
Bruno Zumbo, University of British Columbia

It is also our great pleasure to express our sincere thanks to Lilia Simões Forte, a doctoral candidate at the University of Ottawa, for ensuring that the entire book manuscript met the formatting expectations and guidelines.

1
Introduction

Marielle Simon, Kadriye Ercikan, and Michel Rousseau

> *Brief History of LSA*
> *Key Issues Related to LSAs*
>   *Part I: Assessment Design, Development, and Delivery*
>   *Part II: Assessing Diverse Populations*
>   *Part III: Scoring, Score Reporting, and Use of Scores*
>   *Part IV: Psychometric Modeling and Statistical Analysis*
> **Conclusion**

Large-scale assessments (LSAs) play an important role in education policy decisions, accountability, and education planning worldwide. They are also the object of a very active area of research regarding the planning, development, and implementation of LSAs and dissemination of their results. The *Standards for Educational and Psychological Testing* (1999) defines assessment as "Any systematic method of obtaining information from tests and other sources, used to draw inferences about characteristics of people, objects, or programs" (p. 172). LSAs are standardized assessments conducted on a regional, national, or international scale involving large student populations. In this book, the focus is primarily on assessments of learning and achievement. In this chapter we provide a brief historical background to LSAs and a description of the unique contribution of each chapter, concluding with a word on the future of LSAs.

Brief History of LSA

Of all the historical developments that have helped shape LSA, at least three stand out. One is the influence of the scientific paradigm in the 1900s, which focused on psychology and on the measurement of human behavior, sensory processes, and mental abilities (Thorndike & Thorndike-Christ, 2010). The era of mental testing started as early as 1905, with the works of influential researchers such as Charles Spearman, Alfred Binet, Lewis Terman, and Arthur Otis. As a result of World Wars I and II, there was an even greater surge in measurement and testing for military recruitment purposes. Another major development that paralleled the mental measurement movement was an interest in comparative education, which can be traced back to the 1800s with philosophers such as Marc-Antoine Jullien and, later, in universal public education with American educational reformers such as Horace Mann, Joseph Kay, and Matthew Arnold, who traveled abroad to develop the concept (Cowen & Kazamias, 2009). A third influential era was student assessment in education. As late as the early 1900s, only the best students were admitted into public school systems, and testing was used to select the brightest minds (Cowen & Kazamias, 2009). By the mid-1900s, however, the civil rights movement in the United States led to access for all, which was soon followed by the period of accountability in order to determine whether government-funded programs were achieving their goals (Cowen & Kazamias, 2009; Thorndike & Thorndike-Christ, 2010, p. 6). The accountability movement evolved from the program level in the 1960s, to the school and district levels in 1980s, and to standards-based accountability systems in the 1990s (Linn, 2000) and into the 2000s.

Some of the earliest initiatives of LSAs that are still ongoing date back to 1958 with the birth of what was to later become the International Association for the Evaluation of Educational Achievement (IEA). During the period of 1959–1962, the IEA implemented the Pilot Twelve Country Study of samples of 13-year-old students' achievement in five subjects: mathematics, reading comprehension, geography, science, and nonverbal ability (Lafontaine & Simon, 2008). This led to the launch, in 1964, of the First International Mathematics Study (FIMS), which also tested samples of 13-year-olds and preuniversity students from 12 countries. Similar efforts were deployed in the 1970s with the First International Science Study (FISS). The second rounds of the IEA-led LSAs (SIMSS) occurred in the 1980s in up to 20 countries. In the 1990s, the IEA administered two parallel LSAs: the Trends in Math and Science Study (TIMSS) and the Program for International Reading Literacy Study (PIRLS). Between 1995 and 2011, TIMSS was administered five times and the PIRLS, three times. Over 60 countries participated in the TIMSS 2011 and 55 in the PIRLS 2011.

In 2000, another major player, the Organisation for Economic Co-operation and Development (OECD), administered the Programme for International Student Assessment (PISA). That year 32 countries participated in PISA, which measured 15-year-old students' literacy in reading, mathematics, and science. In 2009, PISA was administered to samples of students from 70 countries (OECD, 2010). Although the purpose of both IEA and OECD was to provide the participating educational jurisdictions (countries, states, provinces, districts) with comparative data, IEA favored a decentralized, cooperative management model of decision making and implementation, whereas OECD members formed an official coalition of participants that planned long-term objectives for cyclical testing (Lafontaine & Simon, 2008).

One of the main impacts of these two major organizations was contribution to a culture of standardized assessments to support educational public policy and reform within participating educational jurisdictions. This culture of data-driven public policy and reform was particularly evident in the United States, as Crundwell (2005) explains:

The publication of the 1983 National Commission of Excellence in Education document, *A Nation at Risk,* brought to the forefront the issue of educational accountability in the United States (U.S.)....More recently, the passing of the Elementary and Secondary Educational Act (ESEA) has placed increased emphasis on the role of the U.S. federal government in education. ESEA, better known as No Child Left Behind (NCLB), places increased emphasis on standards-based accountability and mandates large scale assessment from grade 3 to grade 8 to ensure continued progress towards academic proficiency and standards (MASP, 2004). Within the NCLB legislation, the performance of a school or district on the assessment can result in either incentives or severe sanctions for schools that meet or fail to meet predetermined levels of proficiency. Schools that fail to meet the predetermined threshold of proficiency may lose funding or be taken over by the federal government.

This quotation also reflects distinct shifts in LSAs' goals and use over the years. Since the 1960s, census testing has been conducted regionally (i.e., by school districts and school boards) under mandated conditions (e.g., Title 13) or on a voluntary basis. Whereas the LSAs administered in the 1980s and 1990s randomly sampled groups of students to provide data for monitoring overall student achievement, in the 2000s state or province-wide LSAs were being used to test all students for high-stakes accountability purposes from institutional and governmental perspectives but with low stakes for students. Later, in the 2000s, LSAs were also used for gatekeeping purposes, with higher stakes for the students (Nagy, 2000). Increasingly, students' LSA scores were being partially or fully integrated in their course final grades for promotion or graduation purposes.

Throughout the implementation of LSAs, whether at the international, national, or state/provincial levels, a number of conceptual, technical, and pragmatic issues became the subject of intense debate, discussion, and research. One of the main concerns during the Pilot Twelve Country Assessment was test translation. Over the years, a number of concerns related to validity and reliability of results arose. These included, for instance, opportunity to learn, test accommodations, and bias. Other issues were related to student and item sampling, test equating, standard setting, communication of results, and security of tests items. A great deal of scientific literature on these topics allowed researchers and practitioners to solve many of the problems and concerns involved in designing and implementing LSAs.

Interestingly, in speculating about the future of LSAs, Bennett (1997, p. 3) claimed that despite major advancement in that field over the years, in practice, they had still undergone very little change:

Although there has been much recent intellectual ferment and experimentation in educational assessment, the practice of large-scale testing is much the same today as it was twenty years ago. Most large-scale tests still serve only institutional purposes, are administered to big groups in single sittings on a few dates per year, make little use of new technology, and are premised on a psychological model that probably owes more to the behaviorism of the first half of this century than to the cognitive science of the current half.

Nearly 15 years later, it appears that today's LSAs, particularly those conducted within educational jurisdictions, tend to lean toward a common and universal format that closely follows the measurement model, with its emphasis on reliability, on the use of a combination of multiple-choice and short open response items, and on speedy, cost-effective, and objective scoring methods (Crundwell, 2005). The cognitive and constructive models of learning, which favor the development of "big ideas" in reading, mathematics, and sciences, thus continue to take a back seat (Lane, 2004; Suurtamm, Lawson, & Koch, 2008). Since the publication of *Knowing What Students Know* (Pellegrino, Chudowsky, & Glaser, 2001), there has been greater emphasis on assessments to capture complex thinking, to be more closely aligned with learning and instruction, and to provide information that can guide student learning. Even though there have been great improvements with respect to these goals (Ercikan, 2006), there is evidence that LSAs may not be sensitive to instruction and may even contribute to narrowing it to the teaching of superficial contents (Wiliam, 2007). Thus an often heard principle associated with contemporary assessment is that decisions should be based on the results of more than one assessment.

Key Issues Related to LSAs

The previous summary brings to light a number of issues that were the subject of intense discussion, debate, and research across several decades. Despite intellectual advancements, many of these problems continue to plague today's LSAs and are constantly revisited by leading authors and experienced practitioners who are currently involved in these respective areas. This book features many of these issues in four sections: (a) assessment design, development, and delivery; (b) assessment of diverse populations; (c) scoring, score reporting, and the use of scores; and (d) psychometric modeling and statistical analysis.

Part I: Assessment Design, Development, and Delivery

This first section deals with the processes of planning, reviewing existing options, and organizing all aspects of LSAs prior to their administration. It features four chapters specifically dealing with such issues as investigating conceptual frameworks and designs for the measurement of student cognition and learning; developing background questionnaires to collect contextual data from students, teachers, school principals, and parents; motivating students to be fully engaged in LSAs; and adopting computer-based or computer-adaptive testing as a delivery option for LSAs.

The first chapter in this section, by Leighton, offers a thorough discussion of some of the latest research and practice for designing and developing LSAs of student knowledge and skills based on cognitive-psychological and learning principles. The author uses examples from operational testing programs to demonstrate key assessment design and development issues.

In their chapter, Childs and Broomes explore ways to improve background questionnaires typically associated with LSAs. These questionnaires are often administered to students, teachers, principals, and parents. They constitute an essential component of LSAs to produce contextual information that can serve to interpret students' achievement results. Resulting data are the object of primary and secondary descriptive or inferential analyses whose findings often contribute to the advancement of learning theories. Using examples from LSAs administered in Canada, this chapter outlines the types of information that can be collected using background questionnaires. The authors offer practical guidance for designing background questionnaires and writing questionnaire items.

The chapter on student motivation—with Van Barneveld as the lead author and developed in collaboration with Pharand, Ruberto, and Haggarty—stresses the importance of having students participate fully in responding to LSA tests and background questionnaires. It contains a summary of research evidence regarding the relationships between examinee motivation, examinee behaviors, and key elements of the assessment context. Personal perspectives provided by these authors—one a superintendent, one a teacher, and the other a student—highlight the variation and complexity of individual motivation orientations related to LSAs. Finally, guidelines are offered for motivating individuals to engage in the various LSA activities.

A fourth chapter by Luecht offers a number of assessment design, development, and implementation considerations when LSA is computer-based or computer-adaptive. His chapter provides information regarding venues, platforms, interfaces, item types, and delivery designs that are relevant for testing in various sectors, such as medicine, health sciences, accounting, and more specifically education. The chapter also refers to computer-based testing (CBT) options for end-of-grade and end-of-course assessments. Given CBT's complex designs, related security issues, and financial costs, it is not surprising that common regional, national, and international large-scale assessments have not yet implemented CBT. Although the reader is warned about the complicated nature of CBT, sufficient details, explanations, and corresponding examples are offered in the chapter for graduate students and practitioners with minimal knowledge of advanced measurement principles—such as item design and item banking and psychometric theory such as item response theory (IRT)—to apply these to the context of LSA.

Part II: Assessing Diverse Populations

This section focuses primarily on the assessment of diverse populations such as English language learners (ELLs), students in minority language contexts, and students with special needs, such as those with cognitive disabilities. It features three chapters. The chapter by Solano-Flores and Gustafson examines the limitations of current practices in the assessment of ELLs. According to these authors, there is a need to adopt a probabilistic view of language and to address (a) the dynamic nature and heterogeneity of language groups and (b) the multiplicity of categories of English proficiency. The capacity of assessment systems to deal with randomness in language and linguistic groups and to model language variation as a source of measurement error is raised as critical to improving assessment systems for ELLs.

In their chapter, Ercikan, Simon, and Oliveri examine issues, challenges, and potential solutions regarding comparability of scores resulting from a minimum of two linguistics versions of LSAs. It is intended to inform educational jurisdictions where resources for establishing and verifying comparability of multiple language versions of tests are not always available and when student samples are small. Some educational jurisdictions around the world, in particular those serving small numbers of students, may not have linguistic, curricular content area, or sophisticated measurement expertise to ensure linguistic comparability of results. Moreover, some linguistic minority groups may have such small sample sizes that they prohibit using the recommended statistical and psychometric analyses for establishing comparability. The chapter offers options for these limited contexts.

With in-depth knowledge, experience, and expertise in LSA accommodation, Sáez, Jamgochian, and Tindal offer a chapter on ways to improve accommodations strategies (a) to assist persistently low-performing students or students with significant cognitive disabilities and (b) to increase accessibility for all students.

Part III: Scoring, Score Reporting, and Use of Scores

This section covers four key aspects related to LSA scores. The main outcome of LSAs is performance results of students and inferences based on these results. The first chapter in this section reviews different issues in scoring student results; the second chapter focuses on performance-level descriptors and standard setting. Among the many methods of reporting LSA scores, web-based reporting is becoming one of the most popular. Such a trend calls for the development of models, which are featured in the third chapter in this section. Finally, given the widespread use of LSA results for making inferences about school quality and teaching effectiveness using value-added models (VAMs), the fourth chapter in this section is dedicated to discussing VAMs.

Scoring involves the interpretation of examinees' responses or performances and transforming them into numeric or alphanumeric codes representing levels of completion or correctness. Scoring is often based on scoring rubrics, and the chapter by Oliveri, Gunderson-Bryden, and Ercikan offers a discussion of two important topics regarding the scoring process: appropriate application of scoring rubrics and consistency across scorers. The authors use an example from the province of British Columbia to illustrate several aspects that must be taken into account in the scoring process.

The scoring process yields results that reflect student performance on LSAs. Standard-setting processes assist in the interpretation of that performance by classifying students on different levels of competency. In his chapter, Lissitz presents the conceptual and practical aspects of standard setting. The first step is to determine performance-level descriptors (PLDs). Those descriptors serve to capture differences in examinee competencies measured by the test. Once those PLDs have been developed, the cut score for each category can be determined in various ways. Widely used standard-setting methods for establishing cut scores are presented. Some aspects of the future of standard setting, such as promising new models or models used within a computer-adaptive testing (CAT) context, are also addressed in this chapter.

It is more and more common for LSA administrators to use the Internet as a viable venue for reporting their results. Many stakeholders are interested in student performance and use the results to make various comparisons. Web-based reporting is an efficient way to disseminate results among a large community and to assist stakeholders in the use of LSA data. The third chapter in this section, by Zenisky and Hambleton, distinguishes among three categories of online score reporting resources: static, interactive, and programmatic/informational. It provides many examples of websites that fall into each category and proposes guidelines for building efficient websites for online score reporting. The authors also suggest a model consisting of steps to follow in the development process of online score reporting.

Many stakeholders infer effectiveness of schools and teachers based on the students' performances on LSAs using value-added models (VAMs). In his chapter, Briggs defines the concept of VAMs and presents two of the most common ones. The author emphasizes that the ability of VAMs to infer causal effects of teachers or schools is still being debated among researchers. Based on an example from epidemiology, Briggs proposes using the results of VAMs as descriptive indicators to identify schools or teachers that yield greater or lesser gains than expected. The last section of this chapter raises issues related to the assumptions associated with VAMs.

Part IV: Psychometric Modeling and Statistical Analysis

The four chapters in this section describe a variety of complex psychometric and statistical issues researchers and practitioners encounter in large-scale assessments. These chapters cover item and student sampling, item response modeling, item and person parameter estimation, modeling growth and change, and issues related to missing data.

Sampling is at the core of large-scale assessment design. The chapter by Mislevy, Stapleton, and Rupp addresses complexity and challenges in sampling designs used in large-scale assessments. The chapter discusses how sampling designs for students and items in these assessments affect estimation resulting from the application of statistical models applied to student response data. For correcting the impact of the sampling design for students, both design- and model-based perspectives are presented. For complex sampling of items, the plausible values person parameter estimation is described. Limitations in the suggested approaches for correcting the sampling issues are examined and estimation procedures are elaborated using multiple concrete examples.

Psychometric modeling of examinee responses in most large-scale assessments is largely based on item response theory and models. The chapter by Raîche, Magis, Blais, and Brochu presents a variety of item response theory–based options for modeling item functioning and person behavior in large-scale assessments using dichotomous item response data. The authors describe a unique four-parameter logistic model for the unidimensional modeling of responses. In addition, a variety of multidimensional models that include more than one person parameter to capture person inattention, fluctuation in performance, and pseudoguessing are also introduced. Methods such as maximum likelihood, marginal maximum likelihood, and Bayesian estimation—which are used for estimating item and person parameters in the models presented in the chapter—are closely examined. The final part of the chapter provides models and estimation procedures using sample data from PISA.

LSAs typically produce considerable databases on which primary and secondary statistical analyses are conducted. Missing data constitute a common obstacle in quantitative and mixed-methods research and are equally problematic in LSAs, given their reliance on the participation of students, despite their relatively low stakes. In his chapter, Rousseau presents three ways to deal with missing data: (a) planning the research, (b) analyzing the research context, and (c) applying appropriate treatment methods. It focuses particularly on the third aspect, which currently benefits little from a sound knowledge base.

Measuring change and growth in education is one of the ultimate purposes of large-scale assessments. Zumbo, Wu, and Liu's chapter addresses measurement and statistical analysis issues in measuring growth and change in longitudinal assessments. Among the key measurement issues, temporal measurement invariance, standardization, and vertical scaling are featured. The section on statistical issues distinguishes between issues that arise when longitudinal data are collected at two time points versus data collected over more than two time points. With regards to data collected over two time points, the discussion focuses on the appropriateness of use of difference scores as indicators of change. Three statistical modeling approaches are presented when data are collected over more than two time points: hierarchical linear, structural equation, and multiple indicators latent growth models.

Conclusion

Although this book covers a number of current key issues related to LSAs, not present in this volume despite their highly sensitive and relevant nature are topics such as the politics surrounding the various purposes given to LSAs; consideration of alternative item formats (e.g., interactive items); and achieving balance among test security (cheating), transparency, and fairness, to name only a few. A number of recent papers have been written on such themes and on the future of LSAs (e.g., Black & Wiliam, 2007; Decker & Bolt, 2008). We offer a brief reflection on some of these.

In addition to serving accountability and comparability purposes, LSA is often expected to support student learning and contribute to the calculation of students' final grades (Black & Wiliam, 2007). Such purposes serve to ensure buy-in of key stakeholders to ensure full participation from students and their teachers. However, these multiple purposes lead to confusing and sometimes contradictory messages. To meet all these goals, ideally LSAs would measure student performance, processes, and products using diverse and creative assessments. They would also be administered in a fully transparent way and inclusive of teacher and student input. In reality, however, owing to financial costs and tight timelines, most current LSAs continue to rely on standardized and centralized means that measure primarily products and performance (Huff, Steinburg, & Matts, 2010). The channeling of limited resources into the assessment of measureable knowledge and skills, in turn, leads to standardization of the curriculum content, teaching, learning, and student assessment at the classroom level. In the context of accountability, teachers feel pressured to align their teaching to such LSA models at the expense of following student progress in their development of reasoning and complex thinking (Black & Wiliam, 2007).

As alluded in the chapter on CAT, increased use of computers in many aspects of the lives of the students, including in their classrooms, will undoubtedly have direct impact on item formats. Alternative item formats, which may include multimedia, are expected to gradually transform the existing model of multiple-choice and open-ended items. In the near future, a great number of students across the globe will know how to deal with video segments, podcasts, or animations, with or without sound, and to use touchscreens. In order to maintain the relevance and authenticity of LSAs, items will need to integrate such technology and invite greater interaction between the student and the test items. In turn, this will likely foster increased student motivation, engagement, and participation. However, such desirable changes are not without complexity. A gradual adoption of such alternative items will require an eye for how item formats affect student thinking and performance.

Alternative item formats that may present students with interactive tasks or assessments that utilize the opportunities computer- and Internet-based assessments provide will result in potentially every student taking a different test. In such assessment contexts, the key definition of LSAs—that is, the simultaneous large-scale administration of tests in standardized settings—will no longer hold. This raises challenges for the measurement field in creating scores that are comparable across students and current notions of fairness. Furthermore, when assessments engage students in a small number of interactive tasks, the possibilities of students remembering the tasks and possible violation of the security of the test increase. As technological developments promise better assessments of complex thinking, faster feedback, improved score reporting, and closer alignment with student learning, they also present LSAs with new challenges as well as enhanced versions of some of the older challenges.

Finally, perhaps the most promising and exciting research areas regarding LSAs will be found in the investigation of interactions among the various themes explored in this book. These include, for example, the study of the impact of CAT on item formats and on test security and the role of item formats on student motivation. The issue of missing data in background questionnaires is already the subject of investigation by Rutkowski and Rutkowski (2010). In fact, such research possibilities become limitless in considering all existing and potential conceptual, practical, and technical issues associated with LSA.

References

American Educational Research Association, American Psychological Association, & National Council on Measurement in Education. (1999). *Standards for educational and psychological testing.* Washington, DC: American Educational Research Association.
Bennett, R. E. (1997). *Speculations on the future of large-scale educational assessment.* Princeton, NJ: Educational Testing Service, pdf. Retrieved from http://www.ets.org/Media/Research/pdf/RR-97-14
Black, P., & Wiliam, D. (2007). Large-scale assessment systems design principles drawn from international comparisons. *Measurement, 5*(1), 1–53.
Cowen, R., & Kazamias, A. M. (2009). *International handbook of comparative education* (Vol. 22). New York: Springer.
Crundwell, R. M. (2005). Alternative strategies for large scale student assessment in Canada: is value-added assessment one possible answer? *Canadian Journal of Educational Administration and Policy, 41,* 1–21.
Decker, D. M., & Bolt, S. E. (2008). Challenges and opportunities for promoting student achievement through large-scale assessment results: research, reflections, and future directions. *Assessment for Effective Intervention, 34*(1), 43–51.
Ercikan, K. (2006). Developments in assessment of student learning and achievement. In P. A. Alexander & P. H. Winne (Eds.). *Handbook of educational psychology* (2nd ed., pp. 929–953). Mahwah, NJ: Erlbaum.
Huff, K., Steinberg, L., & Matts, T. (2010). The promises and challenges of implementing evidence-centered design in large-scale assessment. *Applied Measurement in Education, 23,* 310–324.
Lafontaine, D., & Simon, M. (2008). Évaluation des systèmes éducatifs. *Mesure et évaluation en éducation, 31*(3), 95–123.
Lane, S. (2004). Validity of high-stakes assessment: Are students engaged in complex thinking? *Educational Measurement: Issues and Practice, 23,* 6–14.
Linn, R. L. (2000). Assessments and accountability. *Educational Researcher, 29*(2), 4–14.

Nagy, P. (2000). The three roles of assessment: Gatekeeping, accountability, and instructional diagnosis. *Canadian Journal of Education, 25,* 262–279.

OECD (2010). *PISA 2009 Results: What students know and can do. Student performance in Reading, Mathematics and Science* (Vol. 1). OECD.

Pellegrino, J. W., Chudowsky, N., & Glaser, R. (2001). *Knowing what students know: The science and design of educational assessment.* Washington, DC: National Academy Press.

Rutkowski, L., & Rutkowski, D. (2010). Getting it "better": The importance of improving background questionnaires in international large-scale assessment. *Journal of Curriculum Studies, 42*(3), 411–430.

Suurtamm, C., Lawson, A., & Koch, M. (2008). The challenge of maintaining the integrity of reform mathematics in large-scale assessment. *Studies in Educational Evaluation, 34,* 31–43.

Thorndike, R. M., & Thorndike-Christ, T. (2010). *Measurement and evaluation in psychology and education* (8th ed.). New York: Pearson.

Wiliam, D. (2007, September). *Sensitivity to instruction: the missing ingredient in large-scale assessment systems?* Paper presented at the annual meeting of the International Association for Educational Assessment, Baku, Azerbaijan.

Part I
Assessment Design, Development, and Delivery

2

Large-Scale Assessment Design and Development for the Measurement of Student Cognition

Jacqueline P. Leighton

> *Introduction*
> *Traditional Procedures for Large-Scale Test Item Development*
>   Generating a Test Philosophy and Being Clear About Its Purpose
>   Establishing the Validity Evidence Foundation Required for
>   Test Design
>   Generating Test Specifications
> *Examples of Testing Programs With "Cognition in Mind"*
>   The College Board's SAT Reasoning Test
>   Development of the 2003 Programme for International
>   Student Assessment (PISA)
>   Berkeley Evaluation and Assessment Research (BEAR) System
> *Conclusion*

Preparation of this chapter was supported by a grant to the author from the Social Sciences and Humanities Research Council of Canada (SSHRC Grant No. 410–2007–1142). Grantees undertaking such projects are encouraged to express freely their professional judgment. This chapter, therefore, does not necessarily represent the positions or the policies of the Canadian government, and no official endorsement should be inferred. Correspondence pertaining to this chapter should be directed to Jacqueline P. Leighton by airmail at 6–110 Education North, Centre for Research in Applied Measurement and Evaluation (CRAME), Dept. of Educational Psychology, Faculty of Education, University of Alberta, Edmonton, Alberta, CANADA T6G 2G5 or email at jacqueline.leighton@ualberta.ca.

Introduction

The purpose of this chapter is to discuss some of the latest research and practice for designing and developing large-scale student assessment of knowledge and skills based on cognitive-psychological and learning principles. The assessment of student learning is attracting tremendous attention and undergoing substantial analysis. Why so much interest and analysis at this time? Efforts to improve the delivery of instruction and assessment of learning seem warranted given pressures to produce an increasingly literate workforce to keep pace with shifting labor force demands (Goldenberg, 2006). From an economic perspective, it is well documented that there is a strong positive relationship between years of schooling, productivity, income, and economic growth (Hanushek, 2003). Manski and Wise (1983) have found that students who perform well on standardized tests, many of which are large-scale assessments, tend to acquire more years of schooling than those students who do not perform well. In particular, investigations have produced strong evidence of a relationship between measured cognitive achievement and labor market outcomes (Bishop, 1989; Murnane, Willett, Duhaldeborde, & Tyler, 2000). The incentives to invest in "human capital" and leverage economic growth have led to increased government funding for primary, secondary, and tertiary education, including large-scale student assessment such as the Programme for International Student Assessment (PISA) (Organisation for Economic Co-operation and Development, 2003) to evaluate progress.

The United States and other countries are spending money to invigorate and in some cases refurbish educational systems that are out of date (Hanushek, 2003). The Canadian landscape shows that provinces have also made investments in their educational systems; for example, the Alberta investment in K–12 education was more than $6.3 billion in 2008–2009, an increase of almost 10% from 2007 to 2008 (Alberta Education, 2009). Likewise, in British Columbia, the Ministry of Education claims that the level of funding for K–12 education is at its highest level, a 34% increase since 2001, despite declining student body enrolment (British Columbia Ministry of Education, 2009). Increases in education spending, designed to improve school quality by focusing in part on teaching higher-level knowledge and skills, are expected to lead to payoffs similar to what has been observed with increases in length of schooling—a more literate workforce and greater economic growth.

But do we have the assessment tools to measure the types of learning, including innovative changes in instruction, that will lead to a more literate workforce? In other words, do we have the assessment tools to measure higher-level learning in students? Although education funding has increased, it is difficult to acquire exact data for how much of this funding is going toward the development and administration of assessment tools designed to measure innovative changes in instruction and, by implication, improvements in student learning. We do know that large-scale test scores, often administered by governments, have become one of the primary indicators of a nation's overall school quality and educational performance (Hanushek, 2003). But the issue is whether many of these large-scale assessments are presently designed to measure innovative changes in instruction and associated learning outcomes. Hanushek (2005, p. 270) identifies the issue well:

> One of the challenges in understanding the impact of school quality differences in human capital has been simply knowing how to measure quality. Much of the discussion of quality—in part related to new efforts to provide better accountability—has identified cognitive skills as the important dimension. And, clearly, much of the concern over PISA results and other international test scores implicitly assumes this is an appropriate measure. The question here is whether this proxy for school quality—students' performance on standardized tests—is correlated with economic outcomes including individuals' performance in the labor market and the economy's ability to grow. Until recently, little comprehensive data have been available to show any relationship between differences in cognitive skills and any related economic outcomes. Such data are now becoming available.

Investing in education is often a popular policy decision. However, a serious concern is whether our assessment instruments are currently designed to measure the knowledge and skills that governments are desperately trying to cultivate. There is understandably much governmental interest in taking account of how well investments are yielding the expected returns.

For decades, educational test developers and psychometricians have been grappling with the theoretical and practical problem of how to design and develop standardized, large-scale measures of higher-level knowledge and skills (Mislevy, Steinberg, & Almond, 2003; Snow & Lohman, 1989). Higher-level knowledge and skills, such as the ability to perceive the fundamental structure of one knowledge domain (e.g., macroeconomic systems) and transfer it to new domains (e.g., health care reform) for the purpose of solving problems in adaptive ways is expected to be essential for continued growth in knowledge-based economies. Many critics of large-scale standardized tests claim that so far this problem has not been solved (see Koretz & Hamilton, 2006, for a review). Critics continue to maintain that many large-scale tests that rely on the multiple-choice format measure primarily lower-level knowledge and skills such as students' ability to memorize isolated facts without much transfer to everyday practice (e.g., Resnick & Resnick, 1992; for additional viewpoints see Simon, Roberts, Tierney, & Forgette-Giroux, 2007; see also Gierl & Cui, 2008; Leighton, 2008; Rupp & Templin, 2008). One aspect of the problem that is generally agreed on is that educational test items—whether multiple-choice or constructed-response—should be viewed as problem-solving tasks requiring examinees to show their understanding by applying knowledge and/or skills (Snow & Lohman, 1989). Viewing test items as problem-solving tasks implies that (a) they can be designed to measure higher-level knowledge and skills associated with cognitive-psychological and learning principles, and (b) validity arguments can be developed to support test-based inferences about examinees' problem solving (Kane, 2006).

Viewing test items as problem-solving tasks has led to innovative research and practice in test design and development. The purpose of this chapter is to discuss some of the latest research and practice for designing and developing large-scale student assessment of higher-level knowledge and skills based on cognitive-psychological and learning principles. The road map for the present chapter is as follows: The first section provides a review of established procedures for test item development. Alongside a review of these procedures, commentary is offered for ways in which test item development could accommodate cognitive-psychological and learning principles to improve measures of knowledge and skills. The second section offers operational examples of testing programs that have begun to implement cognitive-psychological and learning approaches to test design. Finally, the third section concludes with an eye to future direction.

Traditional Procedures for Large-Scale Test Item Development

Psychometricians have had a long and successful tradition of developing tests to measure student-based behaviors. This long and successful tradition can be described as a well-oiled machine with a predictable assembly flow, a part of which includes the design of multiple-choice and constructed-response items that meet rigorous standards of reliability and validity. Schmeiser and Welch (2006; see also Downing & Haladyna, 2006) highlight the major phases of test design: (1) generating a test philosophy and being clear about its purpose, (2) specifying the intended examinee population, (3) accounting for administrative constraints, (4) recognizing legal considerations, (5) establishing the validity evidence foundation required for test design, (6) generating test specifications, and (7) reviewing, refining, and reaffirming the validity evidence for test design.

Should all seven phases of test design be altered to accommodate cognitive-psychological and learning principles? No, because some of the phases have more to do with sampling and test administration (e.g., phases 2, 3, and 4) than with the actual design of the tasks that will be included in the assessment tool. The four phases that can be most readily adapted to accommodate cognitive-psychological and learning principles for measuring higher-level knowledge and skills are primarily those that involve the objective of the test and its item design: that is, phases 1, 5, 6, and 7. For example, in phase 1, in generating a test philosophy and purpose, test developers can actively consider the *psychological substance* of the inferences they wish to generate from a test and not just the content and/or domain of inferences. In establishing the validity evidence required for test design, including its review and reaffirmation (phases 5 and 7), test developers can actively seek evidence of the knowledge and skills examinees are using to respond to test items. Also, in generating test specifications in phase 6, think-aloud interviews can be used to develop and inform the specifications and, by extension, provide a source of validity evidence for test design and test-based inferences. Although there is overlap among these phases, they will be considered in order.

Generating a Test Philosophy and Being Clear About Its Purpose

Schmeiser and Welch (2006, p. 308) define test philosophy as referring to "an explicit linkage between test purpose and the criterion that defines the test domain, that is, what will and will not be measured." It is recommended that the test domain be outlined explicitly indicating the content, tasks, knowledge and skills, and situational context for the assessment. At this phase in particular, decisions are made about the type and complexity of knowledge and skills to be measured. Although decisions are made about the type and complexity of knowledge and skills, often these decisions are made largely based on content than on cognitive-psychological and learning principles, as the following illustrates.

There are many established schemes for helping test developers define the purpose of the assessment they are designing (e.g., Millman & Greene, 1989). For example, Millman and Greene suggest a two-dimensional scheme that involves first deciding the type of test-based inference to be made about examinees—individual attainment, individual mastery, or group attainment; and second, deciding the type of domain onto which the inference is projected; that is, whether it will be projected to the here-and-now for a given context or to a future performance in an upcoming situation. This scheme and others like it are useful for facilitating thought and action about the purpose of a test. For example, a test developer generating a Grade 12 achievement exam in theoretical physics can use this scheme to decide that the test will measure examinee mastery and that the inference will be projected to the here-and-now for the domain of theoretical physics. However, in order to incorporate cognitive-psychological and learning principles, this scheme and others like it need to advance one step further. For example, this scheme could include questions that focus on the psychology of higher-order thinking, such as what are the indicators of emerging expertise or competence in theoretical physics? Does mastery involve being able to produce the correct answer to a specific question, or does it involve being able to produce the correct answer by applying a specific sequence of thought? These questions initiate a train of thought for test developers to consider not only the type of inference and the domain of the inference, which are mainly based on content, but also the *psychological substance* of the inference desired; that is, what does it mean to say that a student can perform X within content Y on the test? Does it mean that the student can do Z outside of the classroom because he or she possesses certain trains of thought? What about how well performance transfers to a practical environment or on a novel set of tasks because the student has abstracted structural features within the domain instead of surface features? If strong claims about the ways students know and solve problems are wanted, tests and test-based inferences must be developed to answer these questions. Also, these questions initiate a mind set for deciding the knowledge and skills to include in the test specifications and the kinds of evidence that will comprise validity arguments. The point here is that if test developers want to measure higher-level knowledge and skills, two decisions must be made at the outset—first, that measuring higher-level knowledge and skills must be the central purpose for the test and, second, that the psychology of learning must be incorporated in test design, which is normally initiated by asking questions about the psychological substance of the intended inferences.

Establishing the Validity Evidence Foundation Required for Test Design

Test-based inferences need to be validated with evidence. In traditional test development, the evidence normally considered involves content-related validity evidence. In fact, Downing (2006, p. 7) indicates that "the validity of inferences for achievement test scores rests primarily and solidly on the adequacy and defensibility of the methods used to define the content domain operationally, delineate clearly the construct to be measured, and successfully implement procedures to systematically and adequately sample the content domain." Schmeiser and Welch (2006) explain that there exists a continuum of content-related evidence that can be gathered to support test-based inferences. One end of the continuum is more subjective and represents the test developer's judgment about whether the test, including the collective of items, will support test-based inferences. The other end of the continuum is more objective and represents research studies conducted to verify that the test supports test-based inferences. The middle of the continuum, according to Schmeiser and Welch (2006), reflects a mixture of subjective and objective means for providing content-related evidence, such as reviewing existing information in the form of textbooks, curriculum guides and frameworks, published standards, and course descriptions.

It is accurate to say that at the time of this writing, the validity evidence considered under most test design frameworks focuses primarily on content (Ferrara & DeMauro, 2006; Koretz & Hamilton, 2006). Although it may be true that test developers do consider the psychological underpinnings of the construct being measured, this consideration has yet to transfer to changes in test development practices, since most constructs are operationalized with content-based arguments and not cognitive-psychological and learning-based evidence (Ferrara & DeMauro, 2006). This is changing, however, as I will show in the second section of this chapter. The point to be made here, however, is that cognitive-psychological and learning principles must have a larger role in guiding test design and the collection of construct-related validity evidence to the extent that test-based inferences are expected to have a cognitive-psychological dimension.

Although content-related evidence must continue to be important, since knowledge and skills are measured within a content domain, this evidence could be buttressed with verification of the response processes examinees use to answer test items. For example, a test item designed to assess an examinee's ability to synthesize knowledge about historical warfare and economic systems can be viewed as measuring the skill of synthesis within the content domain of history and politics. A content-related analysis might establish that the historical and political narrative of the item is adequate for the test because it is part of the program of studies. But this content analysis does not provide reason to believe that the student used the skill of synthesis to respond. A common assumption among test developers is that establishing the content of a test item somehow translates or reveals the knowledge and skills an examinee will use to respond to or solve the item (Leighton, 2004). This is a tenuous assumption. As Kane (2006, p. 135; italics added) points out, "content-related evidence, broadly conceived, can provide justification for content-based score interpretations, and it can provide essential support for more ambitious interpretations (e.g., in terms of latent attributes) *but cannot fully evaluate these more ambitious interpretations.*" More ambitious interpretations involve inferences about the psychological substance of examinees' understanding and problem solving, normally involving higher-order knowledge and skills (e.g., Jane can apply knowledge about World War II to explain the current troubles in the Middle East). What can provide an evaluation of these more ambitious interpretations? There needs to be evidence that examinees are engaging higher-level knowledge and skills in responding correctly to items that, on the surface, purport to measure these forms of understanding. This evidence can be acquired in part by conducting think-aloud studies or cognitive labs at the time the items are being field-tested (Leighton, 2004). Think-aloud studies are described further in the following sections.

Generating Test Specifications

The purpose of test specifications or "blueprints" is to provide direction for test construction (Schmeiser & Welch, 2006). Test specifications are based on test philosophy, purpose, and audience. Moreover, in principle, test specifications are supposed to be based on a strong base of empirical validity evidence gathered for the test (e.g., empirical evidence that the skills included in the specifications can be measured with the item formats indicated). Test specifications guide item development, item reviews, field testing, test delivery and assembly, and the final test evaluation.

Test specifications outline the content domain of an assessment, which involves the knowledge and skills targeted for measurement. A variety of methods are used to ensure that the knowledge and skills included in the test specifications match the learning experiences of students in the classroom, including surveying teachers as well as reviewing course objectives, syllabi, and class assignments. For example, for a provincial, large-scale test designed to measure the knowledge and skills students have learned at the end of a senior course in biology, empirical methods such as surveys can be used to collect information from representative samples of biology teachers about the standards, topics, and skills taught at the grade level targeted by the science test. These methods are implemented to ensure that test developers understand the structure of the domain being assessed, including the relations among topics and the levels of student mastery over time. Ultimately the goal is to have the assessment provide an accurate reflection of the breadth and/or depth of the content material students are learning and the knowledge and skills students are expected to have mastered by the time the course terminates.

Validity evidence is gathered to back the measurement of the knowledge and skills included in the test specifications. However, it has proven to be more challenging for test developers to gather validity evidence to support claims about sophisticated levels of understanding and problem-solving skills (e.g., critical thinking, problem solving, and causal reasoning). Schmeiser and Welch (2006, p. 316) indicate that "no current cognitive taxonomy seems to be supported by documented validation evidence." Schmeiser and Welch further state (2006, p. 316) that since "we have no way of empirically determining what students are actually doing when they respond to an item," test developers could learn about what students ought to be able to do on test items by surveying teachers about the level or sophistication of knowledge and skills taught in a classroom. Schmeiser and Welch are mistaken in their statement that we do not have empirical methods for determining what students are actually doing when they respond to test items. In fact, cognitive-psychological methods, described in the next paragraph, can be used to generate these data (e.g., Ercikan, Law, Arim, Domene, Lacroix, & Gagnon, 2004; Leighton, 2004). These data are needed because, although surveying teachers about the sophistication of knowledge and skills taught in the classroom may be useful for determining what students *should be able* to do, such surveys will tell us little about what students are actually doing or, more importantly, thinking when they respond to a test item.

Lohman and Nichols (2006) explain that using adult judgments about what students are thinking may not be helpful because adults think differently from children and often have a different knowledge and skill base than children. Leighton (2004, see also Ercikan et al., 2004) suggests using cognitive methods to inform what students are actually doing (and thinking) when they respond to a test item. For example, think-aloud interviews can be used to generate verbal reports about students' thoughts as they answer or solve a test item. Think-aloud interviews have been used extensively by cognitive and educational psychologists to investigate the semantic networks and information-processes participants have and use to solve problem-solving tasks (Ericsson & Simon, 1993; Leighton & Gierl, 2007). Conducting think-aloud interviews usually involves sitting down with a student one on one and having the student "think aloud" about his or her plans, ideas, strategies, and solutions as related to answering or solving the item. Although these interviews are time-consuming to conduct, the amount and quality of information about the thinking processes students have applied can be informative. For example, Hamilton, Nussbaum, Kupermintz, Kerkhoven, and Snow (1995) used the interviews to help uncover the thought processes students were using to answer items on the National Educational Longitudinal Study of 1988 (NELS:88 as cited in Hamilton et al., 1995) science assessment. These investigators found that students often did not respond to items using the skills test-developers expected them to use. Hamilton et al. (1995) recognized the limitations of using item content to infer students' thinking processes in their statement that "the interviews also helped identify several items in which the knowledge and reasoning that led students to correct answers seemed quite different from what item writers must have intended" (p. 564). Moreover, Ercikan et al. (2004) used think-aloud interviews to investigate the sources of differential item functioning (DIF) between English and French students on the School Achievement Indicators Program (SAIP) math and science tests. The results of the interviews suggested that content experts were correct on the sources of DIF for some of the items but not for others. In both the Hamilton et al. (1995) and Ercikan et al. (2004) studies, the authors concluded that inferring the thoughts students will engage as they respond to test items from adult judgments did not prove to be consistently accurate.

Think-aloud interviews can be helpful not only as a check of whether higher knowledge and skills included in test specifications match those used by students to answer items but also in interviews intended to help test developers understand the structure of learning from a test taker's perspective. That is, think-aloud interviews can provide data about the knowledge and skills that successful students have mastered in relation to the knowledge and skills of less successful students. The psychological study of novice and expert performance differences indicates, for example, that experts are better problem solvers than novices in part because experts have automated basic skills (Ericsson, Charness, Feltovich, & Hoffman, 2006). By interviewing students of the same grade but at different points in the learning cycle, test developers could outline the types of basic skills that more successful students have mastered in relation to less successful students. For example, a math item designed to measure multiplication of whole numbers (e.g., 3×9) may be solved by more successful students using the skill of recall, whereas less successful students may begin to apply basic addition skills (e.g., $9 + 9 + 9$). Both skills may lead to the correct answer, but use of the latter skill may indicate that these less successful students have yet to automate their multiplication knowledge.

Two other areas of test development worth mentioning, because they are natural extensions of the three phases already identified, include item writing and field testing. Item writers normally undergo extensive training to generate high-quality items that capture the knowledge and skill levels outlined in the test specifications (Downing & Haladyna, 2006). In addition to the training many item writers attain to produce technically sound items, writers could also be informed of the results from think-aloud interviews. By exposing writers to these data and results in addition to the content requirements for the test, writers could be encouraged to generate items that incorporate the learning structures distinguishing students who have mastered lower versus higher levels of knowledge and skills. Finally, field-testing items provides another opportunity to incorporate cognitive-psychological and learning principles for test design. Field testing allows test developers to check not only whether the items they have created elicit appropriate statistical indices (i.e., difficulty and discrimination) but also whether the items elicit the expected knowledge and skills in students. The think-aloud interview is only one method among others for investigating whether the expected knowledge and skills are being elicited in students (see Gorin, 2006). In the next section, examples of testing programs that have adopted one or more of the evidence-based cognitive-psychological guidelines mentioned in this section are presented.

Examples of Testing Programs With "Cognition in Mind"

The title of this section is borrowed from an article called "Test Design With Cognition in Mind," by Joanna Gorin. Gorin discusses three aspects of test development that can be improved with cognitive-psychological principles: construct definition, validation, and item writing. The three aspects outlined by Gorin overlap to a substantial degree with the three phases I have outlined in the previous section—namely, generating a test philosophy and being clear about its purpose, establishing the validity evidence foundation required for test design, and generating test specifications. Gorin describes the ways in which cognitive psychology can be infused in the test development process, particularly with the use of a *cognitive model* at the outset of test design. A cognitive model is essentially an evidence-based representation of the interrelated knowledge and skills students are expected to apply to answer and solve educational test items. The cognitive model, according to Gorin (2006; see also Leighton & Gierl, 2007), can direct the definition of the construct of the test, validation, and overall test development. However, it is necessary to acknowledge that there are still many unanswered questions about the types and the number of cognitive models to use for test design. Some have suggested a single model is required, whereas others indicate that multiple models are needed to reflect distinct achievement levels (Leighton & Gierl, 2007).

However, this should not discourage test developers. Even in the absence of a cognitive model, important steps can be incorporated in the test design process to accommodate cognitive-psychological principles as outlined in the previous section. In fact, the most important step at this juncture is for test developers to recognize that basic changes in the test development process can bring about a closer alignment with cognitive-psychological principles. Three examples are shared in this section reflecting the different phases outlined in the previous section. The first example involves the College Board's inclusion of the critical thinking component to the SAT and reflects a basic change in test philosophy and purpose. The second example involves the development of the 2003 Programme for International Student Assessment (PISA) and reflects a change in the type of validity evidence secured to support test item design. The third example involves the design of ordered multiple-choice test items based on the Berkeley Evaluation and Assessment Research (BEAR) center system and reflects a change in test specifications.

The College Board's SAT Reasoning Test

The College Board's SAT Reasoning Test is a standardized large-scale test for college admission in the United States. The original SAT was rooted in early intelligence testing, but its philosophy and objective evolved to better reflect student learning and achievement in the classroom. The SAT Reasoning Test is a good example of how test philosophy and purpose can be brought in line with cognitive-psychological principles because over the years the SAT has morphed into a test that is more closely aligned with what it purports to measure—readiness for college success. Given the accumulating educational and psychological research about the correlates of success in college (e.g., Harackiewicz, Barron, Tauer, & Elliot, 2002), the SAT has responded with numerous changes and updates since its early version in 1926 (Lawrence, Rigol, Van Essen, & Jackson, 2002). An important correlate of success in any academic domain is reading proficiency, since for most individuals reading becomes the main vehicle for learning new material independently.

The original SAT contained nine subtests, seven of which involved verbal content (i.e., definitions, classification, artificial language, antonyms, analogies, logical inference, and paragraph reading) and two of which involved mathematical content (i.e., number series and arithmetical problems). These nine subtests were slowly modified in line with an increasingly well-articulated test philosophy and purpose. The verbal content of the SAT is a good example of how the test has been adapted to reflect a growing understanding of the philosophy and objective of the SAT, which includes the targeted construct. Between 1936 and 1946, the verbal section of the test included various combinations of antonyms (100 questions), analogies (50 questions), double definitions (50 questions), and paragraph reading (50 questions). However, a variety of changes have been made to the verbal section since 1946 to bring it more in line with measures of higher-level reading. For example, after careful consideration, antonyms were removed from the test in 1994. Antonyms were found to encourage rote memorization and were not considered to measure meaningful verbal performance, as they were normally presented in the absence of context. In addition to the removal of antonyms, there was an increase in the percentage of items requiring passage-based reading material. According to Lawrence et al. (2002), between 1974 and 1994, the percentage of passage-based reading questions increased from 29% to 50%. This increase was in part implemented in order to send a signal to the schools about the importance of reading for college readiness. A summary of the major changes made to the verbal test in 1994 included (a) emphasis on critical reading and reasoning skills, (b) reading material that is accessible and engaging, (c) passages ranging in length from 400 to 850 words, (d) use of double passages with two points of view on the same subject, (e) introductory and contextual information for the reading passages, (f) reading questions that emphasize analytical and evaluative skills, (g) passage-based questions testing vocabulary in context, and (h) discrete questions measuring verbal reasoning and vocabulary in context. In particular, College Board officials (Commission on New Possibilities for the Admissions Testing Program, 1990, p. 5; Lawrence et al., 2002, p. 6) saw the inclusion of critical reading and reasoning skills as a demonstration of their attempt to bring the philosophy of the SAT in line with college readiness:

> The 1994 redesign of the SAT took seriously the idea that changes in the test should have a positive influence on education and that a major task of students in college is to read critically. This modification responded to a 1990 recommendation of the Commission on New Possibilities for the Admissions Testing Program to "approximate more closely the skills used in college and high school work."

Development of the 2003 Programme for International Student Assessment (PISA)

The Organisation for Economic Co-operation and Development (OECD) administers PISA every 3 years to 15-year-old students in 41 countries. PISA is a standardized international assessment that measures student knowledge and literacy skills in reading, math, science, and problem solving. The objective of the PISA is not simply to measure student mastery across these four academic domains but rather to measure student application of knowledge and skills to meet future challenges. This idea is articulated in the PISA 2003 technical report (Organisation for Economic Co-operation and Development, 2003, p. 8):

> The assessment is forward-looking: rather than focusing on the extent to which these students have mastered a specific school curriculum, it looks at their ability to use their knowledge and skills to meet real-life challenges. This orientation reflects a change in curricular goals and objectives, which are increasingly concerned with what students can do with what they learn at school.

Over 250,000 students wrote the PISA in 2003, a paper-and-pencil test that included both multiple-choice and open-ended response items. Unlike the development of the initial PISA in 2000, the test development and design of PISA 2003 reflects the incorporation of cognitive-psychological and learning principles, especially as it pertains to the validity evidence secured for test item design and, by extension, test-based inferences.

An international consortium—led by the Australian Council for Educational Research (ACER) in conjunction with the National Institute for Educational Measurement (CITO) in the Netherlands, Westat and the Educational Testing Service (ETS) in the United States, and the National Institute for Educational Research (NIER) in Japan—was responsible for the development and implementation of PISA 2003. Test developers of PISA 2003 were interested in using the results of the assessment to (a) create a profile of knowledge and skills among 15-year-olds, (b) understand this knowledge base for students across the different countries, and (c) track trends showing how the results are changing over time. Given the primary objective of PISA, test developers in 2003 sought for the first time to collect verbal reports via think-aloud interviews (i.e., the cognitive lab) to support the item design of the assessment and ensure that items measured the knowledge and skills that students were expected to acquire. Although a description of the full development and design of PISA 2003 is beyond the scope of this chapter (the interested reader is referred to *PISA 2003: Technical Report*), the focus here is on a description of the think-aloud method used to design PISA 2003. As mentioned previously, the think-aloud interview represents a cognitive method used to identify and validate the knowledge and skills individuals use to answer and solve problem-solving tasks (Ericsson & Simon, 1993). The addition of this method to secure validity evidence for item design and, by extension, test-based inferences is a major change reflecting the influence of cognitive-psychological and learning principles.

In the *PISA 2003: Technical Report* (Organisation for Economic Co-operation and Development, 2003, p. 19), the following reasons are stated for using cognitive laboratory procedures to develop test items:

> Different from the first survey cycle, the contractor shall also be expected to use new techniques and methods for the development of the item pool. For instance, cognitive laboratory testing of items may be useful in filtering out, even prior to the field test, poorly functioning items....

The contractor shall provide evidence from cognitive laboratories that student responses to items on the assessment are indeed reflective of the cognitive activities they were designed to sample. The contractor shall develop protocols for collecting input from students that reflects their approaches to the problems and which gives evidence about how they approached and solved the various problems. Without such information, interpretations of student response data may reflect a high level of inference.

The inclusion of the cognitive laboratory was implemented in the design of PISA 2003 by reviewing the literature associated with think-aloud interviews and cognitive laboratories in light of existing test item practices. In response to this review, a methodology was developed that included the following key elements (Organisation for Economic Co-operation and Development, 2003, p. 19):

1. Cognitive walk-through (otherwise known as item paneling, or item shredding)
2. Cognitive interviews (including individual think-aloud methods involving the recording of reports from individual students as they worked on items, cognitive interviews with individual students, and cognitive group interviews)
3. Cognitive comparison studies (including pre-pilot studies and other pilot testing of items with groups of students)

According to the technical report, these cognitive methods were applied to the development of almost all PISA 2003 items. For example, the cognitive walk-through, which involves expert analysis of the knowledge and skills expected to be elicited by an item, was employed on all items developed. Cognitive interviews, which require conducting one-on-one think-aloud interviews with students and are more time-intensive, were employed on a significant proportion of items. Finally, a cognitive comparison study, which essentially appears to involve field-testing items after item attributes have been refined, was used for all items.

Berkeley Evaluation and Assessment Research (BEAR) System

The BEAR system originated at the University of California at Berkeley as a comprehensive framework for measuring student academic performance in classrooms (Wilson & Sloane, 2000); however, its framework has recently been recommended for large-scale testing (Briggs, Alonzo, Schwab, & Wilson, 2006). The objectives of the BEAR system include (a) assessing student academic performance on key knowledge and skills identified in the curriculum, (b) setting standards of student academic performance, (c) tracking student progress over the years on these key knowledge and skills, and (d) providing feedback to students, administrators, parents, and other stakeholders about student learning progress and on the effectiveness of instructional materials and classroom instruction. The BEAR system is an example of how test specifications can be changed to accommodate cognitive-psychological and learning principles. How does the BEAR system do this? The system achieves this by designing assessments that are guided by four principles intended to ensure that (a) assessments reflect a developmental perspective on how students learn, (b) assessments match instructional content, (c) assessment results are informative for teachers and allow teachers to use the information to manage and take responsibility for the instruction of new knowledge and skills, and (d) assessments are evaluated by evidence that intended knowledge and skills are being measured. Although the BEAR system was first implemented for a specific middle school science curriculum called the Science Education for Public Understanding Project (SEPUP) at the Lawrence Hall of Science (see Wilson & Sloane, 2000, for a full description), its influence on the design of the Ordered Multiple-Choice (OMC) item (Briggs et al., 2006) provides evidence for its relevance to large-scale testing.

Briggs et al. (2006) illustrate the development, analysis, and interpretation of the OMC, a novel item format, which provides more diagnostic information than typical multiple-choice items. OMC items are designed to provide diagnostic information about student learning because each alternative is linked to a developmental stage of knowledge and skill. In this way, the development of the OMC exemplifies the first principle of the BEAR system; that is, assessments reflect a developmental perspective of how students learn. The alternatives of the OMC are based on construct maps of how students progress in their learning of a given topic. Construct maps are akin to cognitive models of student knowledge insofar as they represent the hierarchical stages through which students pass as they gain increasingly more sophisticated understanding of a given concept (knowledge and/or skill). Just like a cognitive model, construct maps need to be supported with evidence that show students passing through the proposed stages of knowledge and skill. This evidence may already be available in the form of cognitive or educational studies showing the progression of knowledge or skill for a topic (e.g., see Vosniadou & Brewer, 1994, for the Earth in the solar system). Alternatively, this evidence needs to be gathered by the test developer. Briggs et al. (2006) illustrate a construct map designed to show the range of understanding associated with the science content standard "properties of light." The construct map shows that at the lowest level of knowledge, students define light in relation to darkness and do not understand light apart from its effects; at the next level of knowledge, students have a limited cause-and-effect understanding of a light's source (bulb), state (brightness), and effect (patch of light); at the next level of knowledge, students understand light as a distinct entity in space, which travels in a straight line; however, they fail to understand how light interacts with objects. Finally, at the highest, most sophisticated level of understanding, students continue to understand that light is a distinct entity in space, but they now also understand the relationship between a light's source, its motion and path, and the effect it produces. The best answer to the OMC is the one associated with the most sophisticated form of understanding about properties of light, with each alternative reflecting a lower level of understanding and in some cases outright misconceptions.

The BEAR system along with the OMC provide examples of how test specifications can be changed to accommodate cognitive-psychological and learning principles. Test specifications based on the BEAR system reflect not only the correct or key intersection of knowledge and skills that must be measured by an item, but also differing stages of knowledge and skills, including misconceptions, that informs the level of learning a student has acquired. By linking test specifications to a cognitive model or construct map, every aspect of the item is cross-referenced to an aspect of student learning, from the item stem to each alternative.

Conclusion

This chapter has presented how cognitive-psychological and learning principles can be accommodated within current test development practices so as to improve measurement of knowledge and skills. Given the strides made in the study of cognition, there is great incentive for test developers and psychometricians to begin to devise ways in which this research can inform the measurement of student knowledge and skills. There is motivation to adapt test design in this way in order to begin to evaluate the investments in education that are taking place. Hanushek (2005) indicates that to better understand how economic outcomes and changes in quality of school instruction are related, there must be better measures of student knowledge and skills. There must be a way to measure the sophisticated changes taking place in the classroom to build student proficiency. At this moment, there are three ways in which current test development can accommodate cognitive-psychological and learning principles: generating a test philosophy and being clear about its purpose; establishing the validity evidence foundation required for test design, including reviewing, refining, and reaffirming it; and generating test specifications.

Ferrara and DeMauro's (2006) state-of-the-art review of standardized assessment of individual achievement in K–12 concludes that there is little evidence to suggest that advances in cognitive psychology and the learning sciences have influenced the current design and operation of K–12 assessments. However, there is reason to be hopeful. Ferrara and DeMauro (2006, p. 604) indicate that

> recent advanced work may be setting the stage for explicit approaches to achievement assessment design, development, and validation that may be practically feasible. These explicit approaches attempt to integrate cognitive and psychometric principles into the design of achievement assessments, development of assessment items and tasks, and validation of interpretation of examinee performance in relation to cognitive models of examinee achievement.

This is good news. We need to develop the best measures of student learning not only to take pride in the accomplishments of children and ensure that investments in education are paying off but also to prepare our citizenry to perform on what is going to be a highly competitive global economic stage.

References

Alberta Education (Government of Alberta). (2009). *Annual Report 2008–2009*. Retrieved from http://education.alberta.ca/department/annualreport/archive/2008–2009.aspx

Bishop, J. (1989). Is the test score decline responsible for the productivity growth decline? *American Economic Review, 79*, 178–197.

Briggs, D. C., Alonzo, A. C., Schwab, C., & Wilson, M. (2006). Diagnostic assessment with ordered multiple-choice items. *Educational Assessment, 11*(1), 33–63.

British Columbia Ministry of Education. (April, 2009). *The facts on declining enrolment in B.C. schools*. Retrieved from http://www.gov.bc.ca/fortherecord/enrolment/en_k12.html?src = /k12/en_k12.html

Commission on New Possibilities for the Admissions Testing Program. (1990). *Beyond prediction*. New York: College Entrance Examination Board.

Downing, S. M. (2006). Twelve steps for effective test development. In S. M. Downing & T. M. Haladyna (Eds.), *Handbook of test development* (pp. 3–25). Mahwah, NJ: Erlbaum.

Downing, S. M., & Haladyna, T. M. (Eds.). (2006). *Handbook of test development*. Mahwah, NJ: Erlbaum.

Ercikan, K., Law, D., Arim, R., Domene, J., Lacroix, S., & Gagnon, F. (2004, April). *Identifying sources of DIF using think-aloud protocols: Comparing thought processes of examinees taking tests in English versus in French*. Paper presented at the Annual Meeting of the National Council on Measurement in Education (NCME), San Diego, CA.

Ericsson, K. A., Charness, N., Feltovich, P. J., & Hoffman, R. R. (Eds.). (2006). *The Cambridge handbook of expertise and expert performance*. Cambridge, UK: Cambridge University Press.

Ericsson, K. A., & Simon, H. A. (1993). *Protocol analysis*. Cambridge, MA: MIT Press.

Ferrara, S., & DeMauro, G. E. (2006). Standardized assessment of individual achievement in K–12. In R. L. Brennan (Ed.), *Educational measurement* (4th ed., pp. 579–621). Westport, CT: National Council on Measurement in Education and American Council on Education.

Gierl, M.J., & Cui, Y. (2008). Defining characteristics of diagnostic classification models and the problem of retrofitting in cognitive diagnostic assessment. *Measurement, 6*, 263–268.

Goldenberg, M. (2006). *Employer investment in workplace learning in Canada*. Ottawa: Canadian Policy Research Networks.

Gorin, J. S. (2006). Test design with cognition in mind. *Educational measurement: Issues and practice, 25*(4), 21–35.

Hamilton, L. S., Nussbaum, E. M., Kupermintz, H., Kerkhoven, J. I. M., & Snow, R. E. (1995). Enhancing the validity and usefulness of large-scale educational assessments: II. NELS:88 Science Achievement. *American Educational Research Journal, 32,* 555–581.

Hanushek, E. A. (2003). The failure of input-based schooling policies. *Economic Journal, 113,* 64–98.

Hanushek, E. A. (2005). The economics of school quality. *German Economic Review, 6,* 269–286.

Harackiewicz, J. M., Barron, K. E., Tauer, J. M., & Elliot, A. (2002). Predicting success in college: A longitudinal study of achievement goals and ability measures as predictors of interest and performance from freshman year through graduation. *Journal of Educational Psychology, 94,* 562–575.

Kane, M. T. (2006). Validation. In R. L. Brennan (Ed.), *Educational measurement* (4th ed., pp. 17–64). Westport, CT: National Council on Measurement in Education and American Council on Education.

Koretz, D. M., & Hamilton, L. S. (2006). Testing for accountability in K–12. In R. Brennan (Ed.), *Educational Measurement* (4th ed., pp. 531–578). Washington, DC: American Council on Education.

Lawrence, I., Rigol, G. W., Van Essen, T., & Jackson, C. A. (2002). *A historical perspective on the SAT 1926–2001* (Research Report No. 2002–7). The College Board.

Leighton, J. P. (2004). Avoiding misconceptions, misuse, and missed opportunities: The collection of verbal reports in educational achievement testing. *Educational Measurement: Issues and Practice, Winter, 1*–10.

Leighton, J. P. (2008). Where's the psychology? A commentary on "Unique characteristics of diagnostic classification models: A comprehensive review of the current state-of-the-art." *Measurement, 6,* 272–275.

Leighton, J. P., & Gierl, M. J. (Eds.). (2007). *Cognitive diagnostic assessment for education. Theories and applications.* Cambridge, MA: Cambridge University Press.

Lohman, D. F., & Nichols, P. (2006). Meeting the NRC panel's recommendations: Commentary on the papers by Mislevy and Haertel, Gorin, and Abedi and Gándara. *Educational Measurement: Issue and Practice, 25,* 58–64.

Manski, C. F., & Wise, D. A. (1983). *College choice in America.* Cambridge, MA: Harvard University Press.

Millman, J., & Greene, J. (1989). The specification and development of tests of achievement and ability. In R. L. Linn (Ed.), *Educational Measurement* (3rd. ed, pp. 335–366). American Council on Education and Macmillan.

Mislevy, R. J., Steinberg, L. S., & Almond, R. G. (2003). On the structure of educational assessments. *Measurement: Interdisciplinary Research and Perspectives, 1,* 3–67.

Murnane, R. J., Willett, J. B., Duhaldeborde, Y., & Tyler, J. H. (2000). How important are the cognitive skills of teenagers in predicting subsequent earnings? *Journal of Policy Analysis and Management, 19,* 547–568.

Organisation for Economic Co-operation and Development. (2003). *PISA 2003* (Technical Report). Author.

Resnick, L.B., & Resnick, D. P. (1992). Assessing the thinking curriculum: New tools for educational reform. In B. R. Gifford & M. C. O'Connor (Eds.), *Changing assessment: Alternative views of aptitude, achievement, and instruction* (pp. 37–75). Boston: Kluwer.

Rupp, A. A., & Templin, J. L. (2008). Unique characteristics of diagnostic classification models: A comprehensive review of the current state-of-the-art. *Measurement, 2,* 219–262.

Schmeiser, C. B., & Welch, C. J. (2006). Test development. In R. L. Brennan (Ed.), *Educational measurement* (4th ed., pp. 307–353). Westport, CT: National Council on Measurement in Education and American Council on Education.

Simon, M., Roberts, N., Tierney, R., & Forgette-Giroux, R. (2007). Secondary analysis with minority group data: A research team's account of the challenges. *Canadian Journal of Program Evaluation, 22,* 73–97.

Snow, R. E., & Lohman, D. F. (1989). Implications of cognitive psychology for educational measurement. In R. L. Linn (Ed.), *Educational measurement* (3rd ed., pp. 263–331). New York: American Council on Education and Macmillian.

Vosniadou, S., & Brewer, W. F. (1994). Mental models of the day/night cycle. *Cognitive Science, 18,* 123–183.

Wilson, M., & Sloane, K. (2000). From principles to practice: An embedded assessment system. *Applied Measurement in Education, 13,* 181–208.

3

Role and Design of Background Questionnaires in Large-Scale Assessments

Ruth A. Childs and Orlena Broomes

Introduction
An Example: Who Is Failing Ontario's Literacy Test and Why?
What Information Do We Need?
   Students
   Classrooms
   Schools
   Community
How Should We Ask the Questions?
Prioritizing the Information Needed
   Is Some Information Available From Other Sources?
   Does All the Information Need to Be Gathered
     From Every Student?
   Does All the Information Need to Be Gathered
     Every Year?
   Which Information Is Most Important?
   Which Sources Are Most Cost-Effective and Feasible?
Writing the Questions
Testing the Questions
   Which Questions Are Understood as Similar?
   Do Respondents Give the "Right" Answer?
   What Do the Experts Think?
   What Are the Respondents Thinking?
Creating the Final Questionnaire
Resources
Conclusion

Introduction

Large-scale assessments provide important information about what students know and what they know how to do. However, this information alone is rarely enough. It tells us nothing about which students are performing well and which are struggling—or, more importantly, why. What learning opportunities have the students had? What resources are available to them inside and outside of school? What are their interests? What are their aspirations? What do their teachers and principals believe they can do? And how are these things related to the students' performance on the assessment? Background questionnaires—the questionnaires that students, teachers, principals, and sometimes parents are asked to complete when students take part in a large-scale assessment—can help us answer these questions.

We begin this chapter with an example, in which we ask: What information do educators need when trying to understand the results of the test? Next, we discuss the background information that can help teachers, principals, and educational policy makers interpret the results of large-scale assessments. This can range from information about students' social identities to the availability of resources in classrooms, schools, and communities. Finally, we discuss how to design background questionnaires to collect this information.

An Example: Who Is Failing Ontario's Literacy Test and Why?

Imagine we wanted to understand which Grade 10 students in Ontario were failing the Ontario Secondary School Literacy Test (OSSLT), a high school graduation requirement in Ontario, and why. The Education Quality and Accountability Office (EQAO), which develops and administers the test, publishes a provincial report of the results. According to its 2008 report (Education Quality and Accountability Office, 2008), of the 156,151 Grade 10 students who were eligible to sit the English-language version of the test in 2007–2008, 122,324 students passed, 23,279 failed, 4,357 were absent, and 6,191 received permission to defer taking the test. These numbers tell us nothing about who is failing the test (or is absent or deferred taking the test) or why.

The report also provides the numbers of students by gender with each test outcome. We know that, of the students who failed, 8,809 were female (12% of eligible females) and 14,466 were male (18% of eligible males). The numbers of absent students were similar for males and females (3% of each); however, many more males received deferrals: 3,711 males (5% of males) versus 2,480 females (3% of females). This information begins to tell us who is failing the test but not why they are failing. Are students failing *because* they are male? That seems unlikely. To better understand the results, we can go to the student background questionnaire that was administered with the OSSLT. The student background questionnaire does point to some gender differences in reading preferences: more females than males report reading fiction outside of school most weeks (79% versus 55%) and fewer say they read manuals and instructions (34% versus 52%). These numbers tell us that there are indeed some differences but that female and male students are still more alike than different in their reading habits. After all, more than half of both male and female students report reading fiction outside of school most weeks. Even if it turned out that the students who failed the test reported reading less often than those who passed the test, we would need to interpret this carefully. We could not, for example, conclude that reading infrequently *causes* students to fail the OSSLT; more likely, failing the test and reading infrequently are both symptoms of other factors, such as weak literacy skills. Finding such a relationship in the data from a large-scale assessment could, however, suggest hypotheses for researchers to test in further studies.

The students' language backgrounds may suggest other hypotheses about why students are failing the test. For example, of the 156,151 Grade 10 students who were eligible to take the test, 6,121 were identified by their schools as English language learners. Of these students, 38% passed the test, 26% failed (compared with 15% of all students), 3% were absent, and 33% received deferrals. A possible interpretation is that, although these students may be literate in other languages, many of them do not yet have the English language skills to pass the test. Perhaps more of these students should have been given deferrals so as to allow them time to strengthen their language skills.

Another area for consideration in interpreting the students' OSSLT results is programming. Ontario high schools offer three types of English courses in Grade 10: academic (incorporating "the study of theory and abstract problems"), applied (focusing on "practical applications and concrete examples"), and locally developed courses (Ontario Ministry of Education, 2007, p. 9). About 66% of Grade 10 students in 2008 were enrolled in an academic course, 25% in an applied course, and 4% in a locally developed course. Course does seem to matter: 94% of those taking academic courses but only 56% of those in applied courses and 13% of those taking locally developed courses passed the test. This does not mean that students are failing the test *because* they are taking an applied or locally developed course: They may be taking these courses because their literacy skills are weak. However, it does suggest where schools might focus their efforts to develop the literacy skills needed to pass the test.

For us, this example highlights two important points about the use and interpretation of large-scale assessment results. The first is that we have a responsibility to try to understand *who* the students are who are succeeding or failing on large-scale assessments and *why* they are succeeding or failing. The second is that we must not accept *who* as a substitute for *why*.

What Information Do We Need?

In this section, we describe the information that, ideally, educators should have to help them best use the results of large-scale assessments to improve education for all students. There are different ways of categorizing this information. For example, the Programme for International Student Assessment (PISA) seeks to collect data about antecedents, processes, and outcomes at each of four levels: individual learners, instructional units, educational institutions, and the educational system (Organisation for Economic Co-operation and Development, 2009). Some of the data from the individual learners (students) are combined to provide information about the instructional units (classrooms), educational institutions (schools), and educational system; for example, what is the average achievement of the students? Other data must be collected from other sources, such as school administrators (in 2006, PISA also offered countries the option of administering a parent questionnaire). In general, the antecedents, such as community and school resources and teachers' preparation, are assumed to affect the processes, such as how teachers teach and assess students' learning, which in turn affect the outcomes, including performance on large-scale assessments. The PISA model is based on one developed more than 20 years ago for the precursor of the Trends in International Mathematics and Science Study (TIMSS).

The Progress in International Reading Literacy Study (PIRLS) also develops its background questionnaires based on a hierarchical model. In that model, national and community contexts affect the home, school, and classroom environments where literacy instruction and experiences happen; these literacy instruction and experiences affect students' reading achievement, behaviors, and attitudes (Mullis, Martin, Kennedy, Trong, & Sainsbury, 2009). Most of the data for this model are collected using questionnaires for students, parents, teachers, and school administrators; in addition, each country provides a written description of its national context and approach to literacy education.

What these frameworks have in common is a recognition that contexts matter: Students' own attitudes and beliefs may affect their achievement (and their achievement may affect their attitudes and beliefs), but this occurs within larger contexts, both inside the school and beyond it. In discussing the information educators need, we begin with the students, followed by their classrooms, schools, and communities. We realize that, in any one assessment, it will probably not be possible to collect all this information. This, then, is a sort of "wish list." Later in this chapter, we discuss how to choose which information to collect and which questions to ask.

Students

Walk past teachers or parents talking about the performance of a student and you might hear, "She always finishes her math homework, but try getting her to read a book." "He does okay in school, but he's really interested in music." "If only she had more confidence!" "I assume he plans to go to university, so I'm going to push him harder." "She had great math instruction in her old school but hasn't yet figured out the math vocabulary in this curriculum." The information about students that helps teachers and parents interpret their school performance is also important for making sense of large-scale assessment results. Particularly important are students' social identities, experiences, attitudes, beliefs, and goals.

SOCIAL IDENTITIES

Analyzing how students' results relate to their social identities—for example, their gender, race, or ethnicity—can help us understand whether educational policies are differentially effective. Further relating students' social identities to information about the contexts in which they study and live may suggest possible reasons for these differences. Barton (2003), observing that the average scores on large-scale assessments for White students in the United States are consistently higher than scores for Black or Hispanic students, compared students' educational experiences and health and home factors. He found, for example, that schools with many Black and Hispanic students had more inexperienced teachers. Given that other studies have relationships between achievement and teacher experience, these findings suggest that educational opportunity is not equitably distributed.

Schools have long recorded students' gender. Although other countries, such as the United States and Britain, have long histories of collecting data about students' and teachers' race and ethnicity, Canadian schools are only beginning to collect these data. An example of social identity information being collected in Ontario is the Toronto District School Board's 2006 census of secondary students, which asked students to voluntarily answer questions that included not only their race/ethnicity but also their sexual orientation and whether they had been bullied based on their social identity. For several years, the Halifax Regional School Board has also collected data about students' race, ancestry, and language spoken at home.

EXPERIENCES

Information about students' previous educational experiences can also help educators to understand assessment results. For example, knowing whether students have been identified as having special learning needs is especially important. Also relevant are disruptions in schooling, such as changing schools, changing the language of instruction, or moving between school systems with different curriculums. This information is most likely in a school's records. Schools will also have information about students' prior achievement on large-scale assessments and their class marks. However, it can be useful to ask students for their perceptions of their previous achievement and of what they have experienced in the classroom.

A study of immigrant and nonimmigrant students by Elgie (2008) illustrates the insights that information about previous experience can provide. Based on an analysis of the students' results from the 2004–2005 Ontario Secondary School Literacy Test, she found that students who had been in Canada fewer than 3.5 years fared worst in schools with high percentages of students taking academic courses. These students also performed more poorly when they were in schools with many other new immigrants. Having this information, teachers and principals can investigate the possible causes—such as school climate, teachers' expectations, community and school resources, and social patterns of interaction among the students—and direct their resources accordingly.

Of course, school is only a part of students' lives, and how they spend their time outside of school can affect their success in school. Klinger, Rogers, Anderson, Poth, and Calman (2006) found that students who spent more time reading on the Internet and reading novels were more likely to pass the 2003–2004 OSSLT than those who spent less time. Intriguingly, students who spent more time in creative literacy activities, such as reading poetry and writing songs, were less likely to pass the test than those who spent less time on these activities—certainly this is an area for more research.

ATTITUDES AND BELIEFS

Numerous studies (see Pajares, 1996, for a summary) have shown that students' self-efficacy—that is, what they believe they can do—is an important predictor of their academic performance. This relationship was supported by Lawson, Penfield, and Nagy's (1999) investigation of data from Ontario's 1996–1997 Grade 3 assessment of reading, writing, and mathematics. For Grade 3 students, "I am a good reader" and "Reading is fun for me" were strongly related to reading scores; similarly, "I am good at mathematics" and "For me mathematics is easy" were strongly related to math scores. For writing, the pattern was different, however: "I am a good writer" was strongly related to writing scores, but "I like to write" was only weakly related. This last illustrates the importance of distinguishing beliefs, such as self-efficacy, from attitudes, such as liking something—and of measuring both.

Also important is students' motivation and what they believe causes them to succeed or fail. Some answers can be surprising. Bouchamma and Lapointe (2008) analyzed the responses of French-speaking students across Canada on the 2002 School Achievement Indicators Program (SAIP) writing assessment and found that those students who lived in communities where French was a minority language blamed their academic failures on luck, on their teachers' marking, and on their failure to study. Students in French majority environments, in contrast, blamed their failures on the difficulty of the course.

GOALS

Whether students think that what they are learning in school will matter when they are adults is also important. Jodouin (2002) did a study investigating why Ontario students in English-language schools scored better than those in French-language schools on the 1999 SAIP science assessment. He found that about 90% of English-language students but only about 55% of French-language students believed that many good jobs required knowledge of science. The students' educational plans were also very different: 86% of the English-language students but only 58% of the French-language students planned to go to university (however, 21% of the French-language students wanted to attend college, compared with 6% of the English-language students). Interpretation of these patterns is complicated by differences in geographic distribution: A greater proportion of Ontario's French-language students than English-language students live in rural areas, which may account in part for the differences in educational goals. However, it is worth further investigating the possibility that at least some of the students are not doing well in science because they do not believe it will be useful to them after high school.

Classrooms

It is also important to know about the teachers and classrooms. We may want to know who the teachers are and what their experiences are. The teachers can also give us important information about what happens in the classroom and the school and why. They can tell us how they teach and assess their students and what they believe they and their students can do. In short, we are interested in teachers' social identities, experiences, instruction and assessment practices, and beliefs. Teachers are also likely the best sources of information about the educational resources available in their classrooms.

SOCIAL IDENTITIES AND EXPERIENCES

Although much has been written about the importance of teachers' social identities, researchers have found it difficult to study the relationship among teachers' identities, students' identities, and students' performance because, especially in the United States, educational resources vary dramatically across schools and are often related to the socioeconomic status and social identities of the teachers and students (Dee, 2004). There is more research on the effect of teachers' experiences, including their educational training. For example, Golhaber and Brewer (2000) found that, in the United States, students whose high school mathematics teachers had university degrees in mathematics scored slightly better on a standardized mathematics test than students whose teachers did not have mathematics degrees. Darling-Hammond (2000) found that states with higher percentages of teachers with a major in their field and full teaching certification had significantly better student scores in reading and mathematics on the 1990, 1992, 1994, and 1996 National Assessment of Educational Progress (NAEP) in Grades 4 and 8.

INSTRUCTION AND ASSESSMENT PRACTICES

Teachers can also tell us about how they teach and assess students as well as more generally about their teaching style and philosophy of teaching. An example of the use of teachers' responses is provided by Dénommé (2006), who used the 2001 Progress in International Reading Literacy Study (PIRLS) data to compare teachers' practices in Ontario's English-language and French-language schools. She found that more teachers in Ontario's French-language schools used multiple-choice questions in language arts at least once a month (68%) than teachers in the English-language schools (52%). However, 39% of English-language teachers and only 16% of French-language teachers asked for paragraph-length responses at least once a week. Interestingly, the students in the English-language schools did better than students in the French-language schools on the PIRLS questions that required a paragraph-length response. Although finding this relationship in a sample of students and teachers does not prove that the teachers' practices influenced the students' test performance, it suggests that this is a hypothesis worthy of further study.

BELIEFS

Just as students' beliefs about what they can do are important, so too are teachers' beliefs about their own abilities. Numerous studies have found a relationship between teachers' self-efficacy and their students' achievement (see Tschannen-Moran, Woolfolk Hoy, & Hoy, 1998, for a summary). The relationship between teachers' beliefs about their students' abilities and those students' academic performance is less clear (Jussim & Harber, 2005): In particular, do teachers' beliefs affect students' performance, or does students' performance affect teachers' beliefs? Whichever the direction of effect, there is substantial research suggesting that some teachers have different expectations for students of different races (Tenenbaum & Ruck, 2007).

RESOURCES

Finally, teachers are well positioned to report on the resources—for example, textbooks, computers, manipulatives, curriculum experts, and special education supports—available to them and to their students. They can also report how often and in what ways they use the resources available to them.

Schools

Much of the information we need about schools is simply a matter of aggregating information about their students and classrooms—for example, what percentage of students achieve a certain standard of proficiency on a provincial assessment? However, research about school effectiveness (see Luyten, Visscher, & Witziers, 2005, for a summary) suggests that it can also be important to gather data about a school's leadership and culture. In particular, what are the social identities, experiences, and beliefs of the schools' leaders—usually, the principal of each school? Also important are how the school is organized (e.g., which grades, how many students in each grade), how it presents itself to the community (e.g., how does the principal communicate with parents, what opportunities or resources does the school offer parents), and how it accesses and distributes resources (e.g., textbooks, sports and music equipment, library resources and staffing, teacher professional development).

Community

Communities matter. Students' beliefs about what they can do and their aspirations for themselves as adults are affected by the beliefs and goals of the adults around them. It is important that educators understand those beliefs and goals. It is also important to understand how the community views the school and what roles it sees as appropriate for the school and community. This may depend in part on the social norms of the community and on the adults' own experiences of schooling.

Parents' involvement in their children's schooling is viewed by many educators as critically important, and many studies have shown that, indeed, higher levels of parental involvement are related to higher student achievement (e.g., Sui-Chu & Willms, 1996; see Cairney, 2000, for a review). However, it is also important to recognize that there may be many forms of parental involvement; volunteering in the classroom or on school trips or baking for school events are *not* the only ways for parents to support their children's learning. Background questions need to reflect the many different ways in which parents engage in their children's schooling. How parents and community members become involved with the school may depend on the amount of time the adults have available outside of work, on whether they are comfortable speaking the language in which their children are being educated, on the degree of their own confidence about their abilities to understand what their children are learning, and on their cultural norms. Some cultures discourage them from questioning schools' decisions. Teachers and principals need to understand how parents and community members view the school and what they believe to be the appropriate roles of the school and the community. They also need to know what cultural and other resources are available in the community.

This is not the only important information, of course. Buchmann (2002), in her review of questions about family background in large-scale international assessments, recommends asking questions about the size and structure of the family, parents' involvement in their children's education, educational resources (e.g., books) in the home, and whether the family engages in educational activities, such as going to museums. The challenge in creating questions about family background, we believe, is that such questions often assume a North American middle-class norm; communities, however, may be very diverse, with many different cultures and norms. Whereas museums, for example, may be a cultural resource for many communities, by asking only about museums we risk overlooking other valuable cultural resources that may be more common in other communities.

How Should We Ask the Questions?

Up to this point, we have talked generally about *what* information educators need if they are to make sense of the results of large-scale assessments. In the final section of this chapter, we discuss *how* to collect that information—that is, how to create the background questionnaires that are part of many large-scale assessments. We present this discussion in five parts:

- Prioritizing the information needed
- Writing the questions
- Testing and revising the questions
- Creating the final questionnaire
- Resources

Prioritizing the Information Needed

As we mentioned earlier, little time is available for background questionnaires in most large-scale assessments, meaning that hard decisions must be made about what information is most important to collect and when. We recommend asking the following questions.

Is Some Information Available From Other Sources?

For example, some information about the student's social identity (e.g., gender) and their previous educational experiences (e.g., whether they need or are using special education services) may be available in the school's records or in a central provincial database. Other information may be available from surveys administered by the school board (e.g., parents' involvement) or from the Canadian census (e.g., the socioeconomic status of the school's neighborhood). In deciding whether information from other sources will be useful, two additional questions need to be asked:

1. Is the information at the right level? For example, census data might be available for a neighborhood but not for individual students.
2. Can the information be matched with students, classrooms, schools, or communities? Some information about students, classrooms, or schools may be available only for groups or with identifiers removed because of privacy laws.

Does All the Information Need to Be Gathered From Every Student?

In most large-scale assessments, the background questionnaires are intended to provide general insights into which students are performing poorly and why. It may be possible to observe important patterns without asking the same questions of every student. For example, if only a randomly selected third of the Grade 10 students in a province were asked about their goals for future education, this would likely provide sufficient and appropriate data for investigating whether, in general, students' goals were related to their test performance.

Does All the Information Need to Be Gathered Every Year?

PISA is an example of a large-scale assessment that focuses on different subject areas (reading, mathematics, or science) in different years. Questions about students' perceptions of their mathematics knowledge and skill and teachers' instructional practices related to mathematics are assessed in the same years that most of the assessment items are related to mathematics. When dividing information across students or years, it is, of course, important to remember to measure at the same time and with the same students any information we want to correlate.

Which Information Is Most Important?

One of the most comprehensive reviews of what affects students' learning was conducted by Wang, Haertel, and Walberg (1993). Combining the results of meta-analyses, content analyses, and expert reviews, they concluded that "the actions of students, teachers, and parents matter most to student learning; policies at the program, school, district, state, and federal levels have limited effect compared to the day-to-day efforts of the people who are most involved in students' lives" (p. 279). Applying their conclusion to background questionnaires suggests that, if we must choose, we would do best to focus on the things closest to the students, such as what they do inside and outside the classroom, what their teachers do in the classroom, and what their parents do to support their learning. Because students' and teachers' social identities may affect how others view them and consequently how they act toward them, we also recommend including questions about social identity.

Which Sources Are Most Cost-Effective and Feasible?

Most large-scale assessments include questionnaires for students. Because the students are already answering the test questions, adding a background questionnaire is usually easy, although time constraints are, of course, a consideration. Many also include questionnaires for teachers and principals, who are typically already involved in administering of the assessment and are able to provide important information about the classroom and school contexts. A few include parent questionnaires; for example, Ontario's Grade 3 assessment of reading, writing, and mathematics, in its first few years, included a parent questionnaire with questions about parents' interactions with their children and about the resources in the home. The cost and logistics of having students take questionnaires home and then return them after their parents had filled them out can be daunting, however.

Writing the Questions

Much of what we now know about how to write good questions comes from research by cognitive psychologists and survey researchers. Over the past three decades, they have shown that many common intuitions about how people understand and answer questions are wrong—or, at least, very incomplete. As Schwarz (1999) writes, the problem is that "As researchers, we tend to view our questionnaires as 'measurement devices' that elicit information from respondents" (p. 103). We assume that the information is already known to the respondent and that the person needs simply to understand the words in our question, access the appropriate memory, and provide an answer. However, numerous studies (many of them summarized by Schwarz) have shown that, except when answering the very simplest factual questions (e.g., What is today's date?), respondents spend time actively developing a response based on the wording of the question, the distribution of the response options, the ordering of the items in the questionnaire, their understanding of the purpose of the question, and so on. Their experience of answering questions may even cause them to change how they think about themselves.

Tourangeau, Rips, and Rasinski (2000), in *The Psychology of Survey Response,* outline 13 steps respondents may go through in answering a question:

1. Attend to the questions and instructions.
2. Understand the meaning of the words.
3. Identify what information is being sought.
4. Link key terms to relevant concepts.
5. Generate a retrieval strategy and cues.
6. Retrieve specific and generic memories.
7. Fill in missing details.
8. Assess the completeness and relevance of the memories.
9. Draw inferences based on accessibility of the memories.
10. Integrate the material retrieved.
11. If the material retrieved is partial, make an estimate.
12. Map the judgment onto the response categories.
13. Edit the response.

Their point is not that *every* question will require all of these steps but that, in developing questions, we often make overly simplistic assumptions. For example, when we ask a student, "Do you agree with the statement 'I am a good writer'?," we may be assuming that she has already thought about whether she is a good writer and has only to retrieve an already-formed belief from her memory. However, it is very possible that she has never thought about it before. In trying to answer the question, the student may ask herself, "Have I gotten good marks in writing?" "Have other people told me I'm a good writer?" "Does it count more if it's my grandmother or my friends or my teacher?" "Do they mean writing for fun or writing in school or writing on this test?" "Is writing stories more or less important than writing poetry or writing essays?" "Do I think I did well on the writing part of this test?" Clearly which questions she asks herself will affect how she answers. If she has answered questions like this before, however, she may use a completely different strategy: instead of searching her memory for evidence on which to base a response, she may simply try to remember how she answered last time.

People answering questions also pay attention to whether the questions are consistent with the general rules or norms of communication. For example, research by Schwarz, Strack, and Mai (1991) has found that people responding to questionnaires assume that all the information included in the question will be relevant and important. In addition to trying to understand the *literal* meaning of the question (i.e., the words used), they also try to understand the *pragmatic* meaning of the question (i.e., what the questioner intended to ask). For example, when two similarly worded questions are asked together, respondents will interpret them as being more different than when they are asked separately—after all, if the questions are not asking for different information, why would the questionnaire developer include both of them?

In the response options, questionnaire respondents also look for clues about what they are being asked and why. Numerous studies, summarized by Schwarz (1999), showed that respondents assume that questionnaire developers create response options to represent the typical range of responses. They assume that the middle option is what the developer thinks will be the median response. For example, if the question asks how many hours they read novels each week and the response options are less than 1 hour, 1–2 hours, 2–3 hours, 3–4 hours, and more than 4 hours, respondents will tend to assume that 2–3 hours is the median response and that answering less than 1 hour or more than 4 hours would mean that their reading habits are very unusual. These assumptions can have a big effect on the answers respondents give, especially if, like most people, they cannot remember every time they have read a novel, when, and for how long and so are making estimates. The research has repeatedly shown that respondents are not good at remembering and distinguishing specific instances and remembering when they happened. Trying to be cooperative, respondents will try to estimate how often and when things happened. This can be difficult, and whether respondents are willing to work hard to make a good estimate may depend on how important they think the question is.

Response options can also tell respondents something about why we are asking. For example, Gerber (1999) describes a study in which she and her colleagues asked respondents their race. They found that respondents "paid close attention not only to the category that applied to their own group, but to the categories available for others as well," wanting to "make sure that the categories were evenhanded, and did not give preferential treatment to specific groups" (p. 230). For example, they noticed when groups were described with different levels of specificity.

Questions about respondents' social identities are not the only ones that require careful review. All questions should be reviewed by a panel of educators and community members whose range of experiences and perspectives is similar to that of the intended respondents. This is important to check that questions will be similarly understood by all respondents. Respondents who find a question confusing or offensive may choose not to respond to that question or the entire questionnaire.

In summary, in writing questions:

1. Use the simplest possible vocabulary and define any words that might be ambiguous.
2. Write from the respondent's point of view (e.g., labeling to a set of questions "Self-Efficacy" may indicate how researchers will categorize the questions, but not how the respondent will view the questions—much better to label the section "My Beliefs" or "What I Believe").
3. Explain why the questions are important—answering some questions can be hard work, and respondents are more likely to put forth the required effort if they believe that their answers matter.
4. Consider how the respondents will decide how to answer—will they first think of an answer or read the response choices? If the latter, it is especially important to make sure that the response options represent the typical range of responses.
5. If not all respondents are likely to know the answer to a question, include a "Don't know" response option. While it is possible that some people who do know the answer will choose this option, it avoids the worse alternative, which is that people who do not

know the answer will be forced to leave the question blank (becoming indistinguishable from people who left the question blank for other reasons) or will guess (providing inaccurate information).

6. Think ahead to how the data will be analyzed. This is especially important when response options are ranges (e.g., ages 21–25, 26–30, and so forth). If in doubt, it is usually better to include too many categories, which can always be combined for analysis, than too few; however, care must be taken not to make the number of response options overwhelming.
7. Consider the assumptions that may be implicit in the questions. For example, do the response options suggest that some family structures are better than others? Will students answer differently if we ask them how much they like to read (which implies that they do like to read) or whether they like to read? It may be worth trying out different versions of the questions about reading enjoyment and comparing the results.
8. Have the questions reviewed for sensitivity.

Testing the Questions

Even if we base our questions on the most recent research, how can we be sure our respondents will understand and answer them the way we expect? Tourangeau, Rips, and Rasinski (2000) describe several ways to find out: card sorts, vignettes, expert review, and cognitive interviewing.

Which Questions Are Understood as Similar?

In a card sort, respondents are asked to sort cards printed with statements or questions into piles by similarity. An analysis of how respondents grouped the statements or questions can provide insights into how the respondents understand them. If the groupings vary widely across respondents, this may also suggest that respondents vary widely in their interpretations. The statements or questions can describe attitudes or behaviors (e.g., "I like to read," "I spend at least an hour a day writing") or even resources (e.g., "a teacher-librarian," "at least one computer in each classroom").

Do Respondents Give the "Right" Answer?

In asking students, teachers, principals, or parents questions about themselves, it can be impossible to tell how much of the variation in their responses stems from real differences in what they are describing and how much occurs because they are interpreting the questions differently. With vignettes, respondents are asked to respond not about their own situation but about a hypothetical situation. For example, we might present respondents with a detailed description of a school and then ask them to answer the questionnaire as though they were answering as the principal of that school. If their responses differ from what we know to be the "truth" of our fictitious situation, we know we need to make the questions clearer.

What Do the Experts Think?

Review by experts of possible questions—and of the ordering of the questions—can also be very useful. For background questionnaires, it is important to include both experts in general survey development and educators who understand the appropriate language difficulty for students of various ages, the terminology used by teachers and principals, and the contexts of the communities in which the students and parents live.

What Are the Respondents Thinking?

Cognitive interviewing is a way to get at what respondents are thinking as they try to answer the questions. There are several variations: (a) respondents "think aloud" as they are answering the questions or afterwards (sometimes the interviewer will prompt the respondent or use verbal probes to get a more detailed description of their thinking—see Willis, DeMaio, & Harris-Kojetin, 1999, for a discussion of advantages and disadvantages of think-alouds), (b) groups of respondents discuss their interpretations of the questions in a focus group, and (c) respondents restate the questions using their own words. Tourangeau et al. (2000) caution against relying on cognitive interviewing alone, as the expense of the interviews usually requires limiting them to a very small number of respondents. However, cognitive interviews, especially with children, may provide information about respondents' thinking that is not obtainable any other way.

Levine and colleagues have used cognitive interviewing to investigate the background questionnaires that accompany the National Assessment of Educational Progress. In the first study (Levine, Huberman, Allen, & DuBois, 2001), they had Grade 4 and 8 students sit with a researcher in a room, while the parent sat outside with another researcher, watching the children through a one-way glass and listening over a speaker. The children answered the questions and explained their reasoning while the parents watched and confirmed or disconfirmed the accuracy of the children's answers. As Levine et al. (2001, p. vi) report:

> There was a 25 percent error rate to an item which asked, "Does either your father or your stepfather live at home with you?"... Some children reported that their fathers didn't really live at home with them since they work almost all the time, and confusion about how to interpret the conditional "or." That is, since the child didn't have a stepfather, the child responded "No."

Even eighth graders did not know their parents' education level; 17% were wrong about their fathers and 67% about their mothers. Levine et al. (2001, p. vi) note other confusions:

> Some children who knew their parents brought books into bed or into the bathroom would not consider these behaviors as "seeing" their parents read. A child who talked about things he studied in school with his father on the ride to and from school did not include this behavior as an example of "talking about things...studied in school with an adult at home."... At least three children counted their pets as "family members."

Questions about race and ethnicity were particularly confusing for children:

> Fourth and eighth grade students' responses to two items asking about their race/ethnicity were investigated. Both items listed the standard five racial/ethnic categories; a sixth category ("multiracial") was included in one of the versions. Using the standard five categories, 87 percent of the fourth and eighth graders were able to describe their own race/ethnicity accurately. When a multiracial option was provided, the accuracy of self-identification was 65 percent. Only 57 percent of the students could correctly define multiracial.

Five out of 12 eighth grade students misread "multiracial" as multicultural. An eighth grader described himself as multiracial "because my mother is Irish and my father is Italian." (p. vii)

With regard to questions about race and ethnicity, accuracy was not the only concern: Almost a quarter of the parents felt at least moderately uneasy about having their child answer such questions.

In a second study (Levine, Huberman, & Buckner, 2002), Levine's team asked students about their teachers' instructional practices. They found that (a) students had a hard time estimating how frequently their teachers did things; (b) teachers usually assumed questions referred to the current school year, whereas students might assume the time was longer or shorter; (c) teachers were not sure if "students in your class" meant any, all, or typical students; (d) students tended to focus on the examples given in a question; and (e) in long lists of items, students sometimes forgot the instructions or the question stem. As these examples illustrate, even carefully written questions may not work as intended. Card sorts, vignettes, expert review, or cognitive interviewing—or a combination of these approaches—not only provide information about whether items are measuring what they are intended to measure but also, if they are not, often will suggest how to revise them.

Creating the Final Questionnaire

Creating the final questionnaire or questionnaires is more than just listing the questions. As discussed earlier, respondents consider the context in which each question appears in answering it. After testing and revising the individual questions, it is important to test the questionnaire in the format and order in which the questions will appear.

In creating the questionnaires, we also need to think about confidentiality. Teachers, for example, may not be comfortable answering questions about their practices or beliefs if they believe their principal may see the information; similarly, students and parents may not want teachers to see their answers. When the questionnaires will be administered, how they will be collected, and when they will be returned for analysis must be carefully planned and clearly specified. Most large-scale assessment programs also have rules about reporting information. For example, EQAO does not report teachers' responses to their schools or boards. If a group of students is very small—for example, girls who identify themselves as First Nations and are also taking a particular high school course—most assessment programs will not report aggregated responses in order not to compromise students' confidentiality.

Resources

For more advice on developing background questionnaires, we recommend consulting Fink's *How to Ask Survey Questions* (2003), which provides a simple list of guidelines. Please do not stop there, though. For a more detailed analysis of wording order and the complexity of questions, question structures, and response options, see Saris and Gallhofer's excellent *Design, Evaluation, and Analysis of Questionnaires for Survey Research* (2007). The psychology behind survey design is explored in *Answering Questions: Methodology for Determining Cognitive and Communicative Processes in Survey Research* (Schwarz & Sudman, 1996), *Thinking About Answers: The Application of Cognitive Processes to Survey Methodology* (Sudman, Bradburn, & Schwarz, 1996), and *The Psychology of Survey Response* (Tourangeau, Rips, & Rasinski, 2000). Finally, many large-scale assessment programs publish their questionnaires, along with the frameworks on which the questionnaires are based. For example, PISA's technical report (Organisation for Economic Co-operation and Development, 2009) is an excellent resource.

Conclusion

Educators need the information from background questionnaires to fully interpret the results of large-scale assessments. In this chapter, we began by exploring *what* information educators need and *why*. We then discussed *how* to develop background questionnaires. Choosing what questions to ask, of whom, and how requires careful thought, time, and effort. Supporting the success of all students is worth it.

References

Barton, P. E. (2003). *Parsing the achievement gap: Baselines for tracking progress* (Policy Information Rep.). Princeton, NJ: Educational Testing Service.

Bouchamma, Y., & Lapointe, C. (2008). Success in writing and attributions of 16-year-old French-speaking students in minority and majority environments. *Alberta Journal of Educational Research, 54,* 194–209.

Buchmann, C. (2002). Measuring family background in international studies in education: Conceptual issues and methodological challenges. In A. C. Porter & A. Gamoran (Eds.), *Methodological advances in cross-national surveys of educational achievement* (pp. 150–197). Washington, DC: National Academy Press. Retrieved from http://www.nap.edu/catalog.php?record_id = 10322

Cairney, T. H. (2000). Beyond the classroom walls: The rediscovery of the family and community as partners in education. *Educational Review, 52,* 163–174.

Darling-Hammond, L. (2000). Teacher quality and student achievement. *Education Policy Analysis Archives, 8*(1). Retrieved from http://epaa.asu.edu/epaa/v8n1

Dee, T. S. (2004). Teachers, race, and student achievement in a randomized experiment. *Review of Economics and Statistics, 86,* 195–210.

Dénommé, F. (2006). *Determinants of educational achievement of Francophone students in Ontario* (Unpublished Ed.D. thesis). University of Toronto, Toronto.

Education Quality and Accountability Office. (2008). *Ontario student achievement: EQAO's provincial report on the results of the 2007–2008 Ontario Secondary School Literacy Test (English-language students).* Toronto: Author.

Elgie, S. (2008). *Achievement on the Ontario Secondary School Literacy Test: A focus on immigrant students* (Unpublished master's thesis). University of Toronto, Toronto.

Fink, A. (2003). *How to ask survey questions* (2nd ed.). Thousand Oaks, CA: Sage.

Gerber, E. R. (1999). The view from anthropology: Ethnography and the cognitive interview. In M. G. Sirken, D. J. Herrmann, S. Schechter, N. Schwarz, J. M. Tanur, & R. Tourangeau (Eds.), *Cognition and survey research* (pp. 217–234). New York: Wiley.

Golhaber, D. D., & Brewer, D. J. (2000). Does teacher certification matter? High school teacher certification status and student achievement. *Educational Evaluation and Policy Analysis, 22,* 129–145.

Jodouin, H. (2002). *Analysis of Ontario French-language contextual data from the School Achievement Indicators Program 1999 Science assessment* (Unpublished master's research paper). University of Toronto, Toronto.

Jussim, L., & Harber, K. D. (2005). Teacher expectations and self-fulfilling prophecies: Knowns and unknowns, resolved and unresolved controversies. *Personality and Social Psychology Review, 9,* 131–155.

Klinger, D., Rogers, W. T., Anderson, J. O., Poth, C., & Calman, R. (2006). Contextual and school factors associated with achievement on a high-stakes examination. *Canadian Journal of Education, 29,* 771–797.

Lawson, A., Penfield, R., & Nagy, P. (1999). *Relating attitudes, gender and student achievement in Grades 3 and 6* (EQAO Research Series No. 1). Toronto: Education Quality and Accountability Office.

Levine, R., Huberman, M., Allen, J., & DuBois, P. (2001). *The measurement of home background indicators: Cognitive laboratory investigations of the responses of fourth and eighth graders to questionnaire items and parental assessment of the invasiveness of these items* (NCES Working Paper Series No. NCES-WP-2001–19). Washington, DC: National Center for Education Statistics.

Levine, R., Huberman, M., & Buckner, K. (2002). *The measurement of instructional background indicators: Cognitive laboratory investigations of the responses of fourth and eighth grade students and teachers to questionnaire items* (NCES Working Paper Series No. NCES-WP-2002–06). Washington, DC: National Center for Education Statistics.

Luyten, H., Visscher, A., & Witziers, B. (2005). School effectiveness research: From a review of the criticism to recommendations for further development. *School Effectiveness and School Improvement, 16,* 249–279.

Mullis, I. V. S., Martin, M. O., Kennedy, A.M., Trong, K. L., & Sainsbury, M. (2009). *PIRLS 2011 assessment framework*. Boston: TIMSS & PIRLS International Study Center, Lynch School of Education, Boston College.

Ontario Ministry of Education. (2007). *The Ontario curriculum: Grades 9 and 10 English, revised*. Toronto: Author.

Organisation for Economic Co-operation and Development. (2009). *PISA 2006 technical report*. Paris: Author.

Pajares, F. (1996). Self-efficacy beliefs in academic settings. *Review of Educational Research, 66*, 543–578.

Saris, W. E., & Gallhofer, I. N. (2007). *Design, evaluation, and analysis of questionnaires for survey research*. New York: Wiley.

Schwarz, N. (1999). Self-reports: How the questions shape the answers. *American Psychologist, 54*, 93–105.

Schwarz, N., Strack, F., & Mai, H.-P. (1991). Assimilation and contrast effects in part-whole question sequences: A conversational logic analysis. *Public Opinion Quarterly*, 55, 3–23.

Schwarz, N., & Sudman, S. (Eds.). (1996). *Answering questions: Methodology for determining cognitive and communicative processes in survey research*. San Francisco: Jossey-Bass.

Sudman, S., Bradburn, N., & Schwarz, N. (1996). *Thinking about answers: The application of cognitive processes to survey methodology*. San Francisco: Jossey-Bass.

Sui-Chu, E. H., & Willms, J. D. (1996). Effects of parental involvement on eighth-grade achievement. *Sociology of Education, 69*, 126–141.

Tenenbaum, H. R., & Ruck, M. D. (2007). Are teachers' expectations different for racial minority than for European American students? A meta-analysis. *Journal of Educational Psychology, 99*, 253–273.

Tourangeau, R., Rips, L. J., & Rasinski, K. (2000). *The psychology of survey response*. New York: Cambridge University Press.

Tschannen-Moran, M., Woolfolk Hoy, A., & Hoy, W. K. (1998). Teacher efficacy: Its meaning and measure. *Review of Educational Research, 68*, 202–248.

Wang, M. C., Haertel, G. D., & Walberg, H. J. (1993). Toward a knowledge base for school learning. *Review of Educational Research, 63*, 249–294.

Willis, G. B., DeMaio, T. J., & Harris-Kojetin, B. (1999). Is the bandwagon headed to the methodological promised land? Evaluating the validity of cognitive interviewing techniques. In M. G. Sirken, D. J. Herrmann, S. Schechter, N. Schwarz, J. M. Tanur, & R. Tourangeau (Eds.), *Cognition and survey research* (pp. 133–153). New York: Wiley.

4

Student Motivation in Large-Scale Assessments

Christina van Barneveld, Sherri-Lynne Pharand, Lori Ruberto, and Daphne Haggarty

Introduction
Theories of Motivation
Measuring Motivation
Self-Report Measures of Motivation
    Questionnaire
    Interviews
Student Test-Taking Behaviors as Measures of Motivation
    Item Response Time
    Pattern Marking
    Item Nonresponse
    Guessing
    Detecting Guessing or Item Nonresponse by Examining
        the Relationship Between Item Parameter Estimates
        and Item Position
What Is the Proportion of Students Who Are Not Motivated?
The Impact of Low Motivation on Large-Scale Assessment Results
Minimizing the Impact of Low Motivation on Large-Scale
    Assessment Results
    Raise Motivation
    Identify Unmotivated Students
    Statistical Models of Motivation
Multiple Perspectives
    A Student Perspective: Daphne
    A Teacher Perspective: Lori
    An Administrator Perspective: Sherri-Lynne
Framework for Improving Research, Policy, and Practices
Agenda for Future Research
Conclusion

Preparation of this chapter was supported by a grant to the first author from the Social Sciences and Humanities Research Council of Canada (SSHRC Grant No. 410–2009–1471). Grantees undertaking such projects are encouraged to express freely their professional judgment. This chapter, therefore, does not necessarily represent the positions or the policies of the Canadian government, and no official endorsement should be inferred. Correspondence pertaining to this chapter should be directed to Christina van Barneveld by airmail at 955 Oliver Road, Faculty of Education, Lakehead University, Thunder Bay, Ontario, Canada, P7B 5E1 or mail at cvanbarn@lakeheadu.ca.

Introduction

The word *motivation* is used frequently in daily conversation. We tend to use it when referring to our enthusiasm to engage in an action. Similarly, in the field of education, we use the word *motivation* when referring to enthusiasm or reasons behind our actions or behaviors. In the context of large-scale education assessment, however, this commonly used word takes on a specific meaning.

When professionals in the field of large-scale assessment speak of motivation, they refer to specific outcomes related to an individual's personal beliefs, goals, and engagement in the assessment. For example, if students are motivated to engage in the tasks related to a large-scale assessment, we might expect them to prepare for and respond to assessment items to the best of their ability. Students may not engage with the assessment as expected, however, if their personal beliefs or goals are not aligned with the outcome of the assessment. Instead, students may not prepare for the assessment, and, during the assessment, they may opt to skip questions, guess randomly, mark patterns, fail to review their answers for accuracy before handing in their work, or quit answering assessment items entirely. The outcome of these test-taking behaviors is the underestimation of students' abilities, which may affect the interpretations and effective use of large-scale assessment results to inform education policy and practice. How can we explain and predict the interactions of individuals' motivation and their engagement in large-scale education assessment in order to maximize the usefulness of such efforts?

Theories of Motivation

Scholars propose theories of motivation to explain observed interactions between an individual's motivation and his or her engagement with tasks (e.g., Deci, Koestner, & Ryan, 1999; Eccles & Wigfield, 2002; Elliot & McGregor, 2001; Elliot, McGregor, & Gable, 1999). Eccles and Wigfield (2002) categorized theories of motivation into four groups: (a) theories focused on expectancy, (b) theories focused on reasons for engagement, (c) theories integrating expectancy and value constructs, and (d) theories integrating motivation and cognition.

In this chapter we focus on a theory of motivation titled *expectancy-value theory,* which integrates expectancy and value constructs (Atkinson, 1964; Cole, Bergin, & Whittaker, 2008; Eccles & Wigfield, 2002; Pintrich, 2004; Wigfield & Eccles, 2000). We chose to focus on expectancy-value theory because it is the system of ideas guiding much of the current research on motivation and large-scale assessment (Eklof, 2006; Sundre & Moore, 2002; Wolf & Smith, 1995; Wolf, Smith, & Birnbaum, 1995). We acknowledge that there are other theories also related to this chapter (e.g., achievement goal theory and theories that include metacognition); we suggest reading Eccles and Wigfield (2002) and Deci, Koestner, and Ryan (1999) for overviews of motivation theories and Ryan, Ryan, Arbuthnot, and Samuels (2007) for an overview of motivation theories applied to large-scale education assessment.

Expectancy-value theory links achievement performance, persistence, and choice directly to individuals' expectancy-related and task-value beliefs. Expectancy-related beliefs are individuals' beliefs about how well they will do on an upcoming task, either in the immediate or longer-term future (Eccles & Wigfield, 2002). Task-value beliefs are defined by four components: (a) attainment value—the personal importance of doing well on a task; (b) intrinsic value—the enjoyment the individual gets from performing the task; (c) utility value—how well the task relates to current and future goals, such as career goals; and (d) cost—negative aspects of engaging in the task, such as fear of failure. Eccles and Wigfield (2002, p. 118) describe the theory:

> In this model, choices are assumed to be influenced by both negative and positive task characteristics, and all choices are assumed to have costs associated with them precisely because one choice often eliminates other options. Consequently, the relative value and probability of success of various options are key determinants of choice....Expectancies and values are assumed to directly influence performance, persistence, and task choice.

Applied to large-scale assessment, expectancy-value theory states that an individual's motivation to engage in activities related to large-scale assessment depends on two things:

1. Expectation for success: This is related to an individual's belief about experiencing success that is related to the large-scale assessment. Note that the definition of success varies by individual, by the subject matter of the assessment, and by the assessment context.
2. Value: The value that an individual places on large-scale assessment typically refers to the individual's perceptions of interest, usefulness, and importance of the content, process, and/or outcomes of the large-scale assessment.

If individuals believe that they will experience success on the large-scale assessment and values outcomes related to it, they are more likely to be motivated, make an effort on tasks, and engage with the tasks to the best of their ability.

Measuring Motivation

Measurement professionals try to identify observable behaviors that they think represent individuals' motivation to engage in large-scale assessment for a given context. Then they propose methods of measuring these observable behaviors. Finally, they interpret measurements of the observable behaviors with respect to motivation.

In recent work, researchers have measured motivation using two approaches: self-report measures and observable student test-taking behaviors. These approaches, described in the next section, should be considered along with information about the assessment context and format as pieces of evidence for developing an argument about motivation and large-scale assessment. One of these approaches alone may not be sufficient evidence of motivation.

Self-Report Measures of Motivation

Questionnaire

Some researchers use self-report questionnaires as measures of student motivation. For example, Cole, Bergin, and Whittaker (2008) studied student motivation for low-stakes tests by examining the relationship between task value, effort, and student achievement on a low-stakes standardized general education test. To measure task value and effort, they used a 26-item paper-and-pencil questionnaire that was adapted from items from the Motivated Strategies

Learning Questionnaire (Duncan & McKeachie, 2005; Pintrich, Smith, Garcia, & McKeachie, 1991) and from the Student Opinion Scale (Sundre & Moore, 2002), which was adapted by Sundre and Kitsantas (2004). They found that perceived usefulness and importance of the assessment significantly correlated with test-taking effort and test performance. When students did not perceive a test to be important or useful, their effort suffered, and so did their test scores.

Other self-report questionnaires have been developed and used as measures of motivation. O'Neil, Abedi, Miyoshi, and Mastergeorge (2005) used an adaptation of the State Thinking Questionnaire (O'Neil, Sugrue, Abedi, Baker, & Golan, 1997) to measure motivation. Roderick and Engel (2001) used the Reynolds Adolescent Depression Scale (Reynolds & Mazza, 1998) to cross-check interview data of students' descriptions of their motivation. Eklof (2006) developed the Test-Taking Motivation Questionnaire. To learn more about these questionnaires, including their psychometric qualities, see the research articles cited.

Interviews

Some researchers use interviews to obtain information about motivation (Hong, Sas, & Sas, 2006; Roderick & Engel, 2001; Ryan, Ryan, Arbuthnot, & Samuels, 2007). For example, Ryan et al. (2007) used semistructured personal interviews with 33 eighth-grade moderate- to high-achieving math students to examine their motivation for standardized math exams. In the semistructured personal interviews, students were asked to talk about their experiences with mathematics test taking. Students reported beliefs and values that were not always consistent with the notion of "an ideal test taker" (p. 11)—one whose goal is to maximize test performance.

Student Test-Taking Behaviors as Measures of Motivation

Item Response Time

The use of item response time—the time it takes for a student to respond to an item—as a measure of motivation is based on the hypothesis that when administered an item, unmotivated students will respond before reading and considering the question (Wise & Kong, 2005); that is, unmotivated students will guess rapidly. The amount of time that determines rapid guessing is sometimes referred to as the response time threshold. The response time threshold varies from item to item and person to person. Both the speed at which the test taker operates and the time the items require should be considered when using item response time to identify unmotivated students. Recent work by Kong, Wise, and Bhola (2007), Wise and DeMars (2006), Wise and Kong (2005), and Yang (2007) proposes methods using item response time.

It is important to note that rapid guessing on items can also be an indicator of item preknowledge—that is, some students may know the assessment items in advance of the assessment (Van der Linden & Guo, 2008). Multiple sources of evidence are required to support the interpretation that rapid guessing is due to a lack of motivation.

In current practice, the capture of item response time data requires that the large-scale assessment be administered on a computer. In the future, it is possible that emerging technologies (e.g., digital pen, digital paper) or innovative uses of existing technologies (e.g., video) may allow the capture of such data on paper-and-pencil large-scale assessments.

Pattern Marking

The use of pattern marking as a measure of motivation is based on the hypothesis that an unmotivated student will respond to test items according to some pattern. Nering, Bay, and Meijer (2002, p. 183) describe an example:

> Suppose a test consists of multiple choice items and for each item there are four alternatives, A, B, C, and D. Assuming the correct answers are randomly distributed across the items as is often the case, examinees responding with a pattern such as ABCDABCDABCD...are clearly not taking the test seriously.

Nering et al. (2002) developed a pattern-marking (PM) index to detect pattern marking using datasets from large-scale assessments of mathematics for Grades 3, 6, and 10. They found that their PM index detected more students who were pattern marking than the other indexes studied. See their paper for examples of pattern marking detected at the different grade levels.

Item Nonresponse

The use of item nonresponse as a measure of motivation is based on the hypothesis that an unmotivated student will not respond to some items on the assessment, especially when items (a) do not count (DeMars, 2000; Wolf & Smith, 1995), (b) require a constructed response (DeMars, 2000), (c) appear toward the end of the test (Stocking, Steffen, & Eignor, 2001), and (d) several are linked to a common stem (Stocking et al., 2001). If the assessment context is such that the personal stakes of the assessment are low for students and the assessment format includes constructed response items, there may be a relatively high level of nonresponse to assessment items (Badger, 1989; Freund & Rock, 1992; Wainer, 1993). Constructed response items may be perceived by students as more "work" (Wolf et al., 1995), and an unmotivated student may opt to not do the work.

Item nonresponse has implications for the estimation of individual and group-level scores on large-scale assessment. Researchers have studied methods to accurately estimate individual and group abilities in the presence of missing data (e.g., De Ayala, Plake, & Impara, 2001; Finch, 2008). We encourage you to read Chapter 7 for methods used to address missing data in large-scale assessments.

Guessing

Using evidence of guessing as a measure of motivation is based on the assumption that unmotivated students will guess on some items instead of responding to the best of their abilities. It is important to note that guessing due to lack of motivation, guessing due to lack of time, and guessing due to lack of ability are different and require different strategies to minimize their impact on the results of large-scale assessments. Guessing for any reason, however, has the potential to introduce bias in the assessment results.

The methods used to collect evidence of guessing due to lack of motivation depend on the mode of testing. On a computer-administered assessment, evidence of rapid guessing can be collected through item response times. On assessments that are administered via paper and pencil, evidence of guessing has been collected by analyzing item statistics (e.g., item difficulty) and differential item functioning (DIF) between groups of students in high- and low-stakes assessment conditions. Guessing is related to item difficulty such that as guessing increases, the estimated item difficulty increases. DIF occurs if people in different groups, in spite of their same underlying true ability, have a different probability of giving a certain response on a test item (Bolt & Gierl, 2006; Kim, Cohen, Alagoz, & Kim, 2007; Penfield, 2007; Penfield & Algina, 2006). For example, Wolf et al. (1995) considered item difficulty, task exertion, and item position as predictors of DIF between students in high- and low-stakes testing conditions. They found that DIF between the low- and high-stakes groups was predicted by item difficulty and task exertion. For items that were more difficult and/or required more exertion, there was a difference in the probability that students would provide a given response (for example, the correct response) depending on whether the assessment was high stakes or low stakes for the student. The probability that students would provide the correct response is related to whether they are guessing.

Detecting Guessing or Item Nonresponse by Examining the Relationship Between Item Parameter Estimates and Item Position

The relationship between item parameter estimates and item position as a measure of motivation is based on the hypothesis that unmotivated students do not persist in applying their abilities throughout the test and may choose to randomly guess or omit items that are positioned toward the end of the assessment. Item parameter estimates, like item difficulty, are affected by student guessing or omitting behaviors. If some students randomly guess on items placed toward the end of the test, affected items may appear to be more difficult than if they were placed earlier in the test. The relationship between item parameter estimates and the item position can therefore be used as an indicator of student motivation (Wise, 1996).

If we attribute observable test-taking behaviors, such as guessing and omitting, to student motivation, it is necessary to demonstrate that other potential explanations for these behaviors are less likely. For example, if the large-scale assessment is speeded, then the attribution of random guessing or omission of items toward the end of the test might be explained by students running out of time. In order to attribute observable test-taking behaviors to student motivation, students must have adequate time to complete the assessment, and other potential explanations should be considered. Assessment context is an important part of understanding the motivation of students.

What Is the Proportion of Students Who Are Not Motivated?

The proportion of students who are not motivated to engage in a large-scale assessment depends on the assessment context, assessment format, and the students. For example, on a low-stakes, unspeeded, 60-item multiple-choice test administration with university students, researchers found that about 75% of test takers were engaged throughout the test, about 20% were engaged for over half the test items, and about 5% were engaged for less than half the test (Wise & DeMars, 2006). In another example, when a low-stakes, unspeeded, 45-item multiple-choice test was *easy*, more than 75% of the students remained engaged throughout the test. When the items were *difficult*, however, less than half of the students remained engaged throughout the whole test (Van Barneveld, 2007; Wise, 1996).

The Impact of Low Motivation on Large-Scale Assessment Results

Low motivation can introduce bias in the results of large-scale assessment. Determining the amount of bias resulting from student motivation is usually done by administering two counterbalanced test forms to students and manipulating motivation using incentives (e.g., having the results count toward grades). Research studies using this design found that student scores ranged from 0.26 to 0.60 standard deviations higher when incentives were used than when they were not used (Kim & McLean, 1995; Sundre & Kitsantas, 2004; Wolf & Smith, 1995; Wolf et al., 1996), whereas other studies found mixed results regarding the impact of incentives (O'Neil et al., 1996, 2005). For a review of literature describing the bias in results of large-scale assessment resulting from low motivation, we encourage interested readers to see the work of DeMars (2007).

Minimizing the Impact of Low Motivation on Large-Scale Assessment Results

Three approaches to minimizing the impact of low motivation on large-scale assessment results are reflected in recent research literature. The first approach is to raise the motivation of those engaged in the process of large-scale assessment. The second approach is to identify and remove unmotivated students from the large-scale dataset. The third approach is to include measures of motivation into the item response models used to account for the factors contributing to students' scores.

Raise Motivation

Strategies for raising the motivation of those engaged in the process of large-scale assessment include providing support and incentives. For example, Roderick and Engel (2001) studied the motivational responses of 102 low-achieving Grade 6 and Grade 8 students to a policy that ended social promotion and increased funds to schools in order to extend instructional time for students at risk of failing. The premise of this policy was that high-stakes testing combined with extra funds would lead to improved performance among low-achieving students. Researchers found that the majority of the low-achieving students responded positively to the policy. Students reported greater work effort and the value of learning increased, resulting in a positive impact on student motivation and performance. These findings were confirmed by teachers' reports. Approximately one third of the students, however, showed little work effort despite the desire not to be held back. Students with the lowest skills were least likely to respond positively to the policy, even with high levels of support from teachers. The authors concluded that policies relying on incentives to motivate students may be successful but may also place students with the lowest skills in a very difficult position. Some students did not translate their desire to be promoted into substantial work effort.

Other incentives, such as monetary incentives, were examined as potential motivators for students. O'Neil et al. (2005) paid 393 Grade 12 students $10 per correct answer on an otherwise low-stakes math test in order to examine the hypothesis that the monetary incentive would increase the perceived value of the assessment, student motivation, and performance. Students who received the incentives self-reported significantly more effort than a control group, but their performance on the math assessment was not significantly different than that of the control group. The average performance in this study was 59%. The authors concluded that improving motivation for a test that is difficult for students will not necessarily lead to higher scores, since performance is affected by motivation only if one knows the content.

Identify Unmotivated Students

Researchers developed methods to identify unmotivated students in a large-scale dataset. Statistics were used to detect inconsistencies between student's response patterns and a theoretical measurement model (e.g., Emons, 2008; Glas & Meijer, 2003; Karabatsos, 2003; Meijer & Sijtsma, 2001; Zhang & Walker, 2008). When the response pattern is unlikely to fit the theoretical measurement model, the response pattern is flagged and can then be removed or treated in some way as to minimize its influence on the overall results.

The challenge with methods for identifying unmotivated students is that such methods may not accurately identify why the response pattern does not fit the theoretical measurement model; therefore we cannot with confidence attribute unusual response patterns to lack of motivation as opposed to other explanations, like running out of time. The use of statistics to identify unmotivated students should be used as *one* source of evidence in an argument about motivation and large-scale assessment, but other evidence should be collected to corroborate the interpretation that unusual response patterns are resulting from motivation.

Statistical Models of Motivation

Researchers developed statistical models that attempt to describe the factors that contribute to student scores on a large-scale assessment (e.g., Petridou & Williams, 2007; Van der Linden & Guo, 2008). Some models include measures of motivation (e.g., Wise, 1996, Wise & DeMars, 2006). For example, Wise and DeMars (2006) developed an effort-moderated item response model that incorporated item response time into the estimation of student abilities and item parameter estimation. They found that their effort-moderated model yielded more valid test scores than those obtained from a standard item response model.

Multiple Perspectives

This part of the chapter is dedicated to gaining insights into multiple perspectives on the issue of student motivation and large-scale assessment. Toward that end, the coauthors describe their personal perspectives—grounded in their own experiences—that highlight the complexity of motivation orientations and the commitment we have to using large-scale assessment as a tool for learning.

A Student Perspective: Daphne

How is it possible to motivate students to apply themselves fully to large-scale assessments? The answer is not clear-cut, since the factors that affect motivation are both diverse and unique to each individual. Perhaps insights can be found through examination of my personal experience with large-scale assessment.

EXPECTATIONS AND VALUES: THE ROLE OF FAMILY IN CREATING INCENTIVES FOR SUCCESS
My experience with large-scale assessments was fortunately a successful one. I participated in large-scale assessments in Grades 6, 9, and 10. I did not participate in the Grade 3 large-scale assessment because the assessment was new and my parents were uncertain of its value. As my parents gained understanding of the testing, they encouraged my participation and success on the tests. For the various large-scale assessments I completed, I fulfilled the requested task of the testing—to demonstrate my knowledge to the best of my ability. I did well.

The reason why I did well on large-scale assessments is my motivation. Motivation to succeed on a test stems from the underlying motivation to learn and be a good student. So why am I a motivated student? This trait has to do with many factors, the basis of which is "internal motivation"—factors within oneself. Internal motivation is unique to each individual. I am a motivated student because of who I am. I was brought up in a family that encourages personal success through hard work but enjoyment. Since kindergarten, I loved learning and school and I strive to do my best. These values were always present and are the foundation to my motivation. My motivation can also be attributed to my birth order—the eldest child. Eldest children tend to be high achievers, leaders, and organizational thinkers—wishing to please their parents and be models for younger siblings. It is my personality that puts these values into action. I am extroverted, logical, and driven. I avoid procrastinating. In my agenda I develop charts that direct the priority of accomplishing tasks. This need for organization is reinforced by my busy schedule. I am involved with numerous extracurricular activities. I am motivated to get my homework done in a timely manner so that participation in extracurricular activities—a privilege—is possible.

Expectations and Values: The Role of School in Identifying Incentives for Success

I am internally motivated by my interest in school. I love learning and gaining a full understanding of the concepts being taught. If I didn't enjoy school and wasn't motivated to learn, I wouldn't do nearly as well.

School-related awards that recognize student success show the evolution of the *model* student over the past few decades. In the past, awards or scholarships were mainly based on academic achievement. Now, scholarships are for people who have demonstrated a high level of academic achievement *and* participation in extracurricular *and* contributions to their communities. As universities' admission requirements become increasing competitive, so do the students. A desire to go to university will drive the motivation of students to do well within and outside of school.

Having a long-term vision and being able to see the consequences of one's decisions is a form of motivation. For example, some students may say that Grade 9 marks don't matter. Although they are correct in that some universities consider Grade 12 marks for admission, this is a flawed mentality. First, knowledge is cumulative over the years. Second, if good work habits aren't established early on, the likelihood of their implementation in the senior grades decreases. It is sometimes difficult for students to have a "long-term" vision, to see the consequences of their decisions down the road. I have developed a long-term vision. I can predict possible consequences of poor work habits such as not doing homework, not paying attention, or skipping class. The quality of understanding will suffer, the result on the unit test will be reduced, which will affect the overall subject mark. Since acceptance into a specific university program depends on marks, one's career could ultimately be at stake. Therefore, long-term vision acts as another form of motivation.

Expectations: In General

One's relationship with parents and educators acts as a form of motivation. It is a human desire to accomplish or surpass expectations. Teachers set out challenges and assignments which most students desire to accomplish. Parents want their children to succeed so that they may lead the lives that they desire. It is natural for students to want to fulfill their parents' expectations (not necessarily with their parent's goals in sight, but with the car keys, the curfew, and/or the financial support for extracurricular/school/leisure in sight). Students are rewarded in some way or another by fulfilling the expectations of their parents or educators, which acts as external motivation.

My high level of motivation is created by the coupling of my desire and belief in my personal success, as well as the value I hold for any outcome. Some students, though they possess the ability to be successful, do not achieve their potential on large-scale assessments. The lack of motivation may be derived from low expectations for success, low self-esteem, and/or a lack of perceived value for the outcome. If one's expectation to be successful on tests could be increased, along with the perceived value of the outcome, then motivation to apply oneself on large-scale assessments would increase.

Combining Expectations and Values

Upon reflection on the reasons why my experience with large-scale assessments was successful, I propose possible solutions to the problem of student motivation. Although it is difficult to influence a student's internal motivation, other aspects of a student's motivation can be affected by educators, parents, and peers, in order to increase motivation toward large-scale assessments. By influencing the students' expectations to be successful along with their perceived value of the outcome, motivation can be increased. Through effective teaching and specific preparation for testing, a sense of confidence in one's knowledge and a positive attitude toward a successful evaluation will result. Students are more likely to see purpose in the testing when the value of the assessment relates to the students' immediate realm. This may be accomplished by increasing the teachers' expectations, increasing the weighting that the test bears on student marks, or by discussing the consequences that are associated with various degrees of success. Since each individual possesses a unique internal motivation, a variation in the emphasis placed on external motivation will affect students differently.

It is important to realize that motivation for large-scale assessments is dependent upon many internal factors that are not necessarily able to be influenced. For this reason, students should be encouraged to simply do their personal best on such assessments so that a positive attitude toward learning in general can be encouraged. Also, in order to motivate student success, discretion should be used when placing emphasis on level of achievement on large-scale assessments. By considering the motivational factors involved, both internal and external, student motivation toward large-scale assessments may be positively influenced.

A Teacher Perspective: Lori

As a teacher, I hold a number of responsibilities related to student motivation and large-scale assessment. Among these responsibilities are motivating my students to complete the tasks related to a large-scale assessment to the best of their capabilities, and developing my own knowledge about large-scale assessments and their potential value to students and teachers. In the sections that follow, I highlight my perspective on motivating students as well as my own professional development as it relates to large-scale assessment.

Set Clear Expectations for Students and Provide Support

Part of a student's motivation to engage in activities related to large-scale assessment comes from the overall expectations of the teacher toward the students, and how students are supported in their learning. When it is clear that students are expected to produce a certain quality of work in the classroom and teachers work diligently with the students to help them attain these benchmarks, students are motivated. Setting clear expectations and providing support is accomplished by focusing the instruction on specific curriculum expectations, using specific feedback on student work, and giving students the opportunity to improve by responding to the feedback. Teachers can also provide students extra support by grouping students according to their needs and working with them in small groups (e.g., guided reading or guided writing groups, math groups). Students who are supported by feedback and small-group learning situations gain confidence in their abilities and see timely improvement. The teacher, by continuing this cycle learning throughout the year, helps the students develop the thinking and skills necessary to be successful in all their work, and more specifically, the assessment.

Prepare Students to Be Successful on the Large-scale Assessment

Another motivator for students is to review examples of questions from the assessment to ensure they are prepared and able to answer the variety of questions that the assessment poses. Using past questions, the teacher structures a number of activities that engage the students in evaluation of the answers, the thinking that went into the answers, and the organization of the answers. This use of exemplars helps the students realize that they can also produce quality answers. Practicing the different types of questions (short answer, multiple choice, etc.) also motivates students to know that there will not be any surprises on the assessment. This type of preparation helps the students feel confident about their abilities to be successful.

Do not Focus Solely on the Assessment
A nonmotivator for the students is to focus solely on the assessment. Knowing that the work they are doing throughout the year is about "thinking" and better understanding literacy and numeracy provides them with the important bigger picture in regards to their development as students. Putting unnecessary pressure on them about doing well on the assessment for the sole purpose of the assessment is less motivating. The older students know that the assessment does not figure into their report card assessment, therefore, any practice or learning that is done has to be in the broader sense or the student's motivation disappears.

From my perspective, the students need to be engaged and motivated in their *daily* learning and know that what they are learning is important to their success as lifelong learners. In this way, they feel at ease with the large-scale assessment. The students need to see progress on a daily basis. They need to be taught to think critically; voice their opinions; find the importance in the reading selections; express themselves in writing in a concise, clear, organized manner; and use their math knowledge. This focused learning is not about the assessment in my mind but about developing good thinkers. Giving students the opportunity to speak their opinions and share ideas orally is motivating and stimulating. They are more involved in their learning and help develop assessment criteria and anchor charts. They receive more specific and timely feedback and are given more opportunity to upgrade or improve their work. I see how they react every day, and as their literacy and numeracy skills grow, so does their self-confidence. There is no greater motivation than attainable success.

My Professional Development as It Relates to Large-scale Assessment
I am self-motivated to learn, study, ask, and try out new strategies to enable my students to learn to the best of their ability, but I was wary when the large-scale assessment was introduced. What was the political agenda behind this assessment? Couldn't the money spent on this assessment be better used in the classrooms? Was the assessment going to be used to evaluate me as a

---

The assessment was in its fourth year of implementation and teachers still regarded it with a certain amount of disdain. A colleague, as part of her Masters of Education project, took it upon herself to educate the staff on the assessment: its format, the types of questions, and the evaluation. It wasn't until she succinctly explained how this assessment assessed the students' thinking, how the questions were formatted to delve into their reading comprehension strategies, how the writing portion looked at their overall skills and did not focus just on spelling and grammar, and how the math was designed to assess their abilities to apply big ideas that I had an "Aha" moment. I realized that the assessment was assessing important things, things that we should be teaching, such as higher-order thinking skills and reasoning skills applied to reading, writing, and math.

Figure 4.1 Teacher Description of the Moment When Her Perceptions Regarding the Importance of Large-Scale Assessment Changed

> *During our first Professional Learning Community (PLC) meeting of the school year, we received our school's data from the assessment. We spent time looking at the overall results and quickly saw that our students were still having difficulty with inferential thinking and making connections to their reading. At this point, we decided as a staff to focus on "Making Connections" as the reading strategy, with a reading-to-writing connection as our school goal. We looked at the percentage of students meeting the benchmark and set a goal for the school year. Then, in divisions, we planned a six-week pathway. Our first big idea that we focused on is "Respect." We chose mentor texts for read-alouds and guided and shared reading. We developed an open question for the pre-assessment and the post-assessment and developed a rubric. We also chose a graphic organizer to help the students organize their thoughts from the reading as they prepare to write. We felt excited about getting started as we have a clear goal for our students.*

Figure 4.2 Teacher Description of the Process of Using Large-Scale Assessment Data for Educational Decision Making

teacher? These questions may still linger in the minds of some, but by gaining information and experience with the assessment it was evident that there was a higher purpose—to ensure that our students learn to read with higher understanding, develop critical thinking skills, write with clarity, and apply mathematical concepts in a variety of situations.

With a vast amount of support from upper levels of government, I embraced the assessment for the information it provides and for the emphasis it has put on real teaching and learning. We teach with a purpose, focus on strategies that are proven to be effective, and look at each student's individual needs. After more than two decades of teaching, I feel that there is a consistency in what is being taught in the classroom. There is a communal sense of purpose, and, apart from the resistors, there is a sense of camaraderie and teamwork. This excitement comes from within and from being able to see the validity of the assessment and how this is being embraced by not just the enthusiastic, like me, but by many teachers.

In the decade since the large-scale assessments were implemented, I have had innumerable opportunities to learn and grow, to be encouraged and trained in order to really understand the usefulness and goal of the assessment. Over time and with more governmental support and funneling of district dollars into useful training sessions for teachers around rich assessment tasks and moderated assessment, the attitudes toward large-scale assessment have changed.

A very effective motivator for exploring the usefulness of large-scale assessments is the establishment of a professional learning community (PLC) at the school level. During PLC meetings, teachers, under the administrator's direction, set school goals and work toward these goals in a systematic way. Teachers share, discuss, plan, and implement strategies, then meet again and look at the data and the students' work and restart the process. With the PLC, teachers have a positive opportunity to review large-scale assessment data for their school, learn from each other, try new strategies from reputable resources, and learn to focus their teaching. It has been the best learning and impetus for change in the classroom that I have experienced in all my years of teaching.

Teacher responsibilities as they relate to large-scale assessment are not without stress. Part of the stress comes in the form of school inspections that are followed by feedback sessions to the staff. To say that these inspections did not cause much stress at the school level would be untruthful. During its first year, this form of external inspection caused many teachers and administrators to spend hours preparing for the visit. After experiencing three of these school visits, I was calmed, impressed, and motivated during the process and especially during the feedback sessions. The feedback always started off with general positive observations that any teacher could grab on to and feel proud about. The second part of the feedback included one or two very specific goals to work toward as a staff and a school. It's not just the message that put the teachers at ease, but the manner in which the message was delivered. Our administrators have a talent in imparting their message in such a way as to make everyone feel capable and able to make the changes suggested. This enables the teachers to feel support for success and is probably the most effective approach that I have experienced.

Our large-scale assessments have brought about incredible change in how we teach, in the focus it puts on the students and their learning, and in how the teachers have been supported through training and PLC initiatives. The assessment may mark a culmination of years of learning, but the teaching remains the key to the long-lasting, higher-order thinking that the students develop.

An Administrator Perspective: Sherri-Lynne

The goal of education is to ensure that students maximize their potential and become active, productive contributors to society. Educators work diligently toward that goal, and those who enter the education profession do so with a desire to make a difference in the lives of their students.

Large-scale assessment is a key method of informing us about whether the teaching and learning that is currently happening in this class, school, or system is helping students to learn the intended curriculum. As an administrator, it is my role to support and motivate other leaders and teachers regarding the importance of large-scale assessment, and to highlight the value of data to inform our school improvement plans. My goal is to connect large-scale assessment to the reason that most teachers are in the profession—making a difference for students.

While working with educational leaders, especially those working at schools with challenging demographics, it is at times difficult to see large-scale assessment as a priority. More pressing needs of food, shelter, and safety for students can occupy priorities, and high achievement on large-scale assessment may seem out of reach. Attitudes sometimes reflect a belief that some children cannot do as well as others because they are dealing with so much at home, they come to school with significant gaps in learning, they don't always have enough of the basic necessities, and they may not do as well as other students on large-scale assessments. Changing attitudes is often the first step in changing achievement. In my work, I found that the following steps are effective at motivating positive attitudes toward large-scale assessment.

Engage Their Values

Provide time for each teacher to share why they entered the profession. While individuals have different journeys to teaching, there is a common thread: to make a difference for students.

Discuss and Share Beliefs

Through discussion, share your beliefs that all children can learn and that all children can achieve at a high level, given time and support. This belief is the foundation to achieving success. When there is resistance, search for common ground and build shared beliefs from there. Ask questions like, "When our students graduate, how important do you think that it will be for them to have a high school diploma?" Most staff share the belief that a high school diploma is an absolute necessity for future success.

Share Data and Information

I read a study that indicated that 44% of students who score below standard on a Grade 3 large-scale assessment of reading, writing, and mathematics will not pass their first attempt at a literacy assessment required to graduate high school. When sharing statistics like this with staff, I put a face on it. In preparing to discuss the above study, I took the school's Grade 3 assessment results, cut out paper students, and said, "These are the children who, if we do nothing differently, are at risk of failing the large-scale assessment necessary to graduate high school. Are we willing to say in Grade 3 that these children won't be able to have the future of their dreams, that doors are closed for them?" A collective "No" usually emerges from the room. What can we do? While we cannot control social and demographic factors, we can control what we do with students every day, for the 5 hours a day when they are in our care. We can ensure purposeful, focused, high-level instruction, and we can employ high-quality assessments, both teacher-generated and large-scale assessments, that inform us about what students need. We can work to ensure that all children have a chance for a successful tomorrow.

Tell Stories of Success

Stories of success motivate and help to change beliefs. My favorite story to share with staff is of a young boy who entered Junior Kindergarten at age 4, nonverbal, with fetal alcohol syndrome and significant behavior challenges. Staff worked collaboratively to meet his needs, planned together, assessed together, and discussed next steps. By Grade 2, this child was reading at a mid-Grade 1 level. What an accomplishment! Our shared belief that all children can achieve, given time and support, ensured his success.

Set a Clear and Consistent Direction

Once a positive attitude and motivation is established, it must be quickly followed with a concrete, achievable plan of action. This must be a plan where all stakeholders contribute to development and are working together to achieve the common vision. It must be sustainable and long-term.

One strategy we use to make plans and then turn plans into actions are professional learning communities (PLC). PLCs focus on student learning and needs, as opposed to what the teacher taught. In our district, professional learning communities have very tight parameters. They always begin with the data. Administration and teachers deconstruct the assessment data piece by piece to determine what students do well and what they struggle with, to identify possible reasons for their struggles and to review trends over time.

Once there is a common understanding of the data from the large-scale assessment and staff have gleaned all of the information possible, a key priority focus area is decided upon. Then one or two key strategies from the literature are selected. Teachers discuss and agree on what they will bring back to the next PLC and how they will assess student learning.

At each successive PLC, teachers bring samples of student work from their class based on the established plan, and collaboratively mark to ensure there is a common understanding of the standard and to monitor student learning. Teachers do not move from the expectation plan until student learning has met the student learning target. Then the process is repeated monthly throughout the year. It ensures a common understanding of the standard, a common language, a common approach from year to year, a focus on student learning and student success, and a commitment to do whatever it takes to have children learn.

> *In one high needs school, the first literacy night held had a dismal turnout with only five parents. Our staff was discouraged and did not want to go to the effort of another one. I spoke with them and suggested that we reached five parents, how can we reach more? I asked them "What do you think parents want?" This changed the entire plan for the second literacy night. Instead of the focus being what the school as educators wanted to tell the parents, we focused on what the parents wanted. Brainstorming brought about the following ideas: to see their children involved, to feel comfortable, to leave with simple ideas to help their children at home, to have a way to care for the other siblings while attending, and to have food.*
>
> *We planned a new night. Students prepared a choral reading for the literacy event and we began with that. Babysitting was provided—the local health centre helped by providing the babysitting course free for our older students who were interested in babysitting. The choral read was followed by three sessions for parents and their children to participate in together— one was an Aboriginal artist who lead participants through creating a tableau of a story read aloud, the second was a local Aboriginal author who shared her journey to becoming an author and encouraged students to follow their dreams since anything is possible, and the third and final session was a sing along. A short discussion at the end about how dramatizing a story builds understanding and how singing promotes oral language development rounded out the evening, leaving parents with two simple ideas to try at home. All of this was wrapped up with tea, coffee, juice, and bannock, some door prizes for grocery gift certificates, and one book for every child to take home. Forty parents came to this session. Word of mouth did the rest and now, this school of 200 students has approximately 65-70 parents attending their family nights.*

Figure 4.3 A Successful "Literacy Night" for Families

> *For six years, the students of one teacher at an inner city school had consistently high large-scale assessment results. When asked why he thought this was, the teacher described his strategies to encourage students to do well. When asked why it was so important to him that his students do well, he replied, "Because the children in this neighbourhood are constantly made to feel they are 'less than' from the time they are very young. They have less money than other families, they have less food than others, their parents have less education than others, they have less opportunities to participate in sports, extra curricular activities, or travel, and this is something I can do to ensure, in the case of education, they will not be 'less than' anyone. It is my goal to ensure they achieve higher than any other school in this city. To do that, I review material, stay after school for tutoring, and teach in a variety of ways so that on the assessment, these kids see themselves as successful." He achieved that goal and his school is a model for our educational system.*

Figure 4.4 An Example of Exceptional Teaching at an Inner-City School

Monitor Leading and Trailing Indicators
Once schools are motivated to change practice, a key to success is ongoing monitoring by the school itself. Schools must monitor their own progress toward their goal, based on data from the large-scale assessment. These leading indicators will help schools predict how well they are progressing toward their targets of improving learning. The trailing indicator of the next year's large-scale assessment will help them to measure the impact of their strategies for improvement.

Encourage and Support

It is critically important to celebrate success, celebrate it early, and celebrate it often. There are difficult times on the journey to school improvement. Leaders must be prepared to navigate the difficult times and move individuals from a "why we can't" to a "how we can" attitude.

Involve Everyone

Parents want their children to be happy and successful at school. They want to know what they can do to help. Once they know, they do. The perspective of parents is important. In many of our schools in Thunder Bay, Ontario, Canada, Aboriginal parents have a family member who experienced residential school, and there can be a resulting distrust of educational institutions. Bridges need to be built and healing needs to take place.

Motivate Students

Children must see themselves and their lived experiences reflected in the school. Teachers must work to ensure the diversity of their students is reflected in the books they read, the role models and presenters they bring into the classroom, the parents they engage, and the content they share. Find their strengths, celebrate them, and use their strengths to help them learn.

Framework for Improving Research, Policy, and Practices

The research literature and the perspectives of the coauthors point to a number of ideas for improving research, policy, and practices related to motivation and large-scale assessment. The ideas for improvement can be summarized into two general strategies: (a) prepare participants of large-scale assessment to experience success and (b) demonstrate the value associated with outcomes of the large-scale assessment to participants. These strategies are informed by theories of motivation and should be considered in relation to assessment contexts and formats, and in relation to the students.

More generally perhaps the best way to improve research, policy, and practices related to motivation and large-scale assessment is to focus on improving communication between researchers, policy makers, and practitioners. Strategies to improve communications can build on models presented by Levin (2004, 2008) on knowledge mobilization, and by Rogers, Anderson, Klinger, and Dawber (2006) on the pitfalls and potentials of secondary data analysis. One of the goals of this textbook, in fact, was to demonstrate how researchers, policy makers, and practitioners can work together to share knowledge on large-scale assessment. Improved communications leads to increased collaboration, better use of resources through cost sharing, strong relationships between people with diverse expertise, the establishment of trusted critical friends, and ultimately meaningful and useful outcomes of research, policy, and practice decisions that improve our educational system for the benefit of all people.

Agenda for Future Research

Many questions remain for a future research agenda. The answer to these questions will clarify the role of motivation in large-scale educational assessment.

Issues Related to Theories of Motivation

1. What theories of motivation inform models of behavior in specific large-scale assessment contexts?

2. If the expectancy-value theory of motivation was adapted to include other constructs related to motivation (e.g., metacognition), would that lead to a better understanding of student motivation to engage in large-scale assessment?
3. What is the relationship between extrinsic and intrinsic motivators for students to engage in a large-scale assessment? How does this relationship inform our approach to motivating students to engage in large-scale assessment?

Issues Related to Measuring Motivation

1. What emerging technologies may be used to observe behaviors that represent student motivation in a given large-scale assessment context?
2. What standards of evidence are necessary and sufficient to confidently claim we are measuring motivation and not another test-taking behavior?
3. What are the limits to measuring motivation? What models would enhance the quality of information we obtain? What is a reasonable standard of accountability, given the limits of measuring motivation?

Issues Related to Minimizing the Impact of Low Motivation on Large-Scale Assessment Results

1. What are the best strategies for increasing student motivation in various contexts? How do the success of the strategies relate to contextual factors?
2. What should we do with students for whom support and incentives are not effective in raising motivation to engage in large-scale assessment? Who are the stakeholders and what are their perspectives on the answer to this question?
3. For a given large-scale assessment context, what are the costs and benefits of filtering unmotivated students from the dataset or including motivation in the statistical item response models? How are these methods best integrated into an overall system of large-scale assessment?
4. What degree of low motivation among students is acceptable in a given large-scale assessment context?

Issues Related to Multiple Perspectives of Motivation and Large-Scale Assessment

1. Whose perspective matters most and why? How do perspectives relate to standards of evidence for valid uses of information from large-scale assessments?
2. What conflicts in perspectives on tasks related to large-scale assessment exist and how do these conflicts (if any) relate to theories and measures of motivation?
3. What models and mechanisms work to support communications and collaborations between researchers, policy makers, and practitioners?

Conclusion

Motivating students to engage in activities related to a large-scale assessment is a complex process. As professionals in the field of large-scale assessment, administrators, and teachers, we are responsible for preparing our students to be successful and preparing the context and condition in which student success will occur. Since educational decision making includes using large-scale assessment data for school improvement planning, we must be confident that the inferences that we make based on the results of large-scale assessment are valid. Toward that end, we must be aware of student motivation as it relates to large-scale assessments and continue to examine ways of motivating students, identifying unmotivated students, and critically assessing the statistical models we use to represent the complex relationships between students and test items.

References

Atkinson, J. W. (1964). *An introduction to motivation.* Princeton, NJ: Van Nostrand.

Badger, E. (1989). *On their own: Student response to open-ended tests in math.* Quincy, MA: Massachusetts State Department of Education, Bureau of Research, Planning, and Evaluation.

Bolt, D. M., & Gierl, M. J. (2006). Testing features of graphical DIF: Application of a regression correction to three nonparametric statistical tests. *Journal of Educational Measurement, 43*(4), 313–333.

Cole, J. S., Bergin, D. A., & Whittaker, T. A. (2008). Predicting student achievement for low stakes tests with effort and task value. *Contemporary Educational Psychology, 33*(4), 609–624.

De Ayala, R. J., Plake, B. S., & Impara, J. C. (2001). The impact of omitted responses on the accuracy of ability estimation in item response theory. *Journal of Educational Measurement, 38*(3), 213–234.

Deci, E. L., Koestner, R., & Ryan, R. M. (1999). A meta-analytic review of experiments examining the effects of extrinsic rewards on intrinsic motivation. *Psychological Bulletin, 125*(6), 627–668.

DeMars, C. E. (2000). Test stakes and item format interactions. *Applied Measurement in Education, 13*(1), 55–77.

DeMars, C. E. (2007). Changes in rapid-guessing behavior over a series of assessments. *Educational Assessment, 12*(1), 23–45.

Duncan, T. G., & McKeachie, W. J. (2005). The making of the motivated strategies for learning questionnaire. *Educational Psychologist, 40*(2), 117–128.

Eccles, J. S., & Wigfield, A. (2002). Motivational beliefs, values, and goals. *Annual Review of Psychology, 53,* 109–132.

Eklof, H. (2006). Development and validation of scores from an instrument measuring student test-taking motivation. *Educational and Psychological Measurement, 66*(4), 643–656.

Elliot, A. J., & McGregor, H. A. (2001). A 2 × 2 achievement goal framework. *Journal of Personality and Social Psychology, 80*(3), 501–519.

Elliot, A. J., McGregor, H. A., & Gable, S. (1999). Achievement goals, study strategies, and exam performance: A mediational analysis. *Journal of Educational Psychology, 91*(3), 549–563.

Emons, W. H. M. (2008). Nonparametric person-fit analysis of polytomous item scores. *Applied Psychological Measurement, 3*(3), 224–247.

Finch, H. (2008). Estimation of item response theory parameters in the presence of missing data. *Journal of Educational Measurement, 45*(3), 225–245.

Freund, D. S., & Rock, D. A. (1992, April). *A preliminary investigation of pattern-marking in 1990 NAEP data.* Paper presented at the annual meeting of the American Educational Research Association, San Francisco, CA.

Glas, C. A. W., & Meijer, R. R. (2003). A Bayesian approach to person fit analysis in item response theory models. *Applied Psychological Measurement, 27*(3), 217–233.

Hong, E., Sas, M., & Sas, J. C. (2006). Test-taking strategies of high and low mathematics achievers. *The Journal of Educational Research, 99*(3), 144–155.

Karabatsos, G. (2003). Comparing the aberrant response detection performance of thirty-six person-fit statistics. *Applied Measurement in Education, 16*(4), 277–298.

Kim, J., & McLean, J. E. (1995, April). *The influence of examinee test-taking motivation in computerized adaptive testing.* Paper presented at the annual meeting of the National Council on Measurement in Education, San Francisco, CA.

Kim, S. H., Cohen, A. S., Alagoz, C., & Kim, S. (2007). DIF detection and effect size measures for polytomously scored items. *Journal of Educational Measurement, 44*(2), 93–116.

Kong, X. J., Wise, S. L., & Bhola, D. S. (2007). Setting the response time threshold parameter to differentiate solution behavior from rapid-guessing behavior. *Educational and Psychological Measurement, 67*(4), 606–619.

Levin, B. (2004). Making research matter more. *Education Policy Analysis Archives, 12*(56), 1–20.

Levin, B. (2008, May). *Thinking about knowledge mobilization.* Paper prepared for a symposium sponsored by the Canadian Council on Learning and the Social Sciences and Humanities Research Council of Canada.

Meijer, R. R., & Sijtsma, K. (2001). Methodology review: Evaluating person fit. *Applied Psychological Measurement, 25*(2), 107–135.

Nering, M. L., Bay, L. G., & Meijer, R. R. (2002). Identifying pattern markers in a large-scale assessment program. *Measurement and Evaluation in Counseling and Development, 35*(3), 182–194.

O'Neil, H. F., Abedi, J., Miyoshi, J., & Mastergeorge, A. (2005). Monetary incentives for low-stakes tests. *Educational Assessment, 10*(3), 185–208.

O'Neil, H. F. Jr., Sugrue, B., & Baker, E. L. (1996). Effects of motivational interventions on the national assessment of educational progress mathematics performance. *Educational Assessment, 3*(2), 135–157.

O'Neil, H. F. Jr., Sugrue, B., Abedi, J., Baker, E. L., & Golan, S. (1997). *Final report of experimental studies on motivation and NAEP test performance (CSE Tech Rep. No. 427)*. Los Angeles: University of California, Center for Research on Evaluation, Standards, and Student Testing.

Penfield, R. D. (2007). An approach for categorizing DIF in polytomous items. *Applied Measurement in Education, 20*(3), 335–355.

Penfield, R. D., & Algina, J. (2006). A generalized DIF effect variance estimator for measuring unsigned differential test functioning in mixed format tests. *Journal of Educational Measurement, 43*(4), 295–312.

Petridou, A., & Williams, J. (2007). Accounting for aberrant test response patterns using multilevel models. *Journal of Educational Measurement, 44*(3), 227–247.

Pintrich, P. R. (2004). A conceptual framework for assessing motivation and self-regulated learning in college students. *Educational Psychology Review, 16*(4), 385–407.

Pintrich, P. R., Smith, D. A. F., Garcia, T., & McKeachie, W. J. (1991). *A manual for the use of the motivated strategies for learning questionnaire (MSLQ)*. (Technical report no. 91-B-004). Ann Arbor, MI: University of Michigan, School of Education, National Center for Research to Improve Postsecondary Teaching and Learning.

Reynolds, W. M., & Mazza, J. J. (1998). Reliability and validity of the Reynolds Adolescent Depression Scale with young adolescents. *Journal of School Psychology, 36*(3), 295–312.

Roderick, M., & Engel, M. (2001). The grasshopper and the ant: Motivational responses of low-achieving students to high-stakes testing. *Educational Evaluation and Policy Analysis, 23*(3), 197–227.

Rogers, W. T., Anderson, J. O., Klinger, D. A., & Dawber, T. (2006). Pitfalls and potential of secondary data analysis of the Council of Ministers of Education, Canada, National Assessment. *Canadian Journal of Education, 29*(3), 757–770.

Ryan, K. E., Ryan, A.M., Arbuthnot, K., & Samuels, M. (2007). Students' motivation for standardized math exams. *Educational Researcher, 36*(1), 5–13.

Stocking, M., Steffen, M., & Eignor, D. (2001). *A method for building a realistic model of test taker behavior for computerized adaptive testing* [Draft research report]. Princeton, NJ: Educational Testing Service.

Sundre, D. L., & Kitsantas, A. (2004). An exploration of the psychology of the examinee: Can examinee self-regulation and test-taking motivation predict consequential and non-consequential test performance? *Contemporary Educational Psychology, 29*(1), 6–26.

Sundre, D. L., & Moore, D. L. (2002). The Student Opinion Scale: A measure of examinee motivation. *Assessment Update, 14*(1), 8–9.

Van Barneveld, C. (2007). The effect of examinee motivation on test construction within an IRT framework. *Applied Psychological Measurement, 31*(1), 31–46.

Van der Linden, W. J., & Guo, F. M. (2008). Bayesian procedures for identifying aberrant response-time patterns in adaptive testing. *Psychometrika, 73*(3), 365–384.

Wainer, H. (1993). Measurement problems. *Journal of Educational Measurement, 30*(1), 1–21.

Wigfield, A., & Eccles, J. S. (2000). Expectancy-value theory of achievement motivation. *Contemporary Educational Psychology, 25*(1), 68–81.

Wise, L. L. (1996, April). *A persistence model of motivation and test performance*. Paper presented at the annual meeting of the American Educational Research Association, New York, NY.

Wise, S. L., & DeMars, C. E. (2006). An application of item response time: The effort-moderated IRT model. *Journal of Educational Measurement, 43*(1), 19–38.

Wise, S. L., & Kong, X. J. (2005). Response time effort: A new measure of examinee motivation in computer-based tests. *Applied Measurement in Education, 18*(2), 163–183.

Wolf, L. F., & Smith, J. F. (1995). The consequence of consequence—motivation, anxiety, and test-performance. *Applied Measurement in Education, 8*(3), 227–242.

Wolf, L. F., Smith, J. K., & Birnbaum, M. E. (1995). Consequence of performance, test motivation, and mentally taxing items. *Applied Measurement in Education, 8*(4), 341–351.

Wolf, L. F., & Smith, J. F., & DiPaulo, T. (1996, April). *The effects of test specific motivation and anxiety on test performance*. Paper presented at the annual meeting of the American Educational Research Association, New York, NY.

Yang, X. D. (2007). Methods of identifying individual guessers from item response data. *Educational and Psychological Measurement, 67*(5), 745–764.

Zhang, B., & Walker, C. M. (2008). Impact of missing data on person-model fit and person trait estimation. *Applied Psychological Measurement, 32*(6), 466–479.

5

Computer-Based and Computer-Adaptive Testing

Richard M. Luecht

Introduction
A Brief History of CBT
CBT Venues and Platforms
    Dedicated Commercial Test Centers
    Temporary Testing Sites
    Multiuse Computer Labs
    Test at Home, Bring Your Own
Item Types and Interfaces
    The CBT Dashboard
    CBT Item Types
Test Designs for Delivering CBT
    Computerized Adaptive Testing (CAT)
    Computerized Adaptive Multistage Tests
    Test-Form Quality Control
Conclusion
    Where Is CBT Headed in the Future?

Introduction

Computer-based testing (CBT)—sometimes referred to as *computer-based assessment*—encompasses a large variety of assessment types, purposes, test delivery designs, and item types administered by computer. CBT is now used in educational achievement testing, college and graduate admissions testing, professional certification and licensure testing, psychological testing, intelligence testing, language testing, employment testing, and in the military.

CBT can be administered on networked PC workstations, personal computers (PCs), laptops, netbooks, and even handheld devices such as smart phones and tablet computers. Venues can include dedicated CBT centers; classrooms or computer labs in schools; colleges and universities; temporary CBT facilities set up at auditoriums, hotels, or other large meeting sites; and even personalized testing in the privacy of one's home, using a PC with an Internet connection and an online proctoring service.

Test items may comprise relatively simple multiple-choice or selected-response formats, constructed- or extended-response items, essays, technology-enhanced items using novel response-capturing mechanisms involving a mouse or another input device, and complex, computerized performance exercises that may simulate real-life tasks using synthetic challenges made engaging through virtual realism. Test assembly and delivery formats also vary widely and may include preconstructed test forms, test forms constructed in real time, or many varieties of computer-adaptive tests (CATs) that tailor the difficulty of each test form to the proficiency of every examinee.

In short, CBT is not limited to particular technology platform, item type, or test design. Rather, CBT is a vast collection of technologies and systems that serve many different test purposes, constituencies, and test-taker populations (Drasgow, Luecht, & Bennett, 2006; Luecht, 2005a). Following a brief historical overview of CBT, this chapter explores some of those technologies and systems from three perspectives: (a) CBT platforms and venues, (b) item types and interfaces, and (c) test designs for delivering CBT.

A Brief History of CBT

Obviously modern computing has come a long way from Sperry Corporation's UNIVAC mainframes in the early 1950s; the development of the first supercomputers by the Control Data Corporation (CDC), the mouse, and ARPANET in the 1960s;[1] the appearance of an Apple computer in the mid-1970s; the arrival of the IBM PC in the early 1980s; and the emergence of Internet protocols and service providers in the 1980s and 1990s. One of the first computer-based testing applications was the PLATO system, a computer-assisted instruction (CAI) system that included online assessments. By the late 1970s, the PLATO system encompassed several thousand terminals worldwide on nearly a dozen different networked mainframe computers. The PLATO project was assumed by the CDC, which built the original mainframe computers at the University of Illinois for PLATO-related CAI.

Four testing programs can be credited with demonstrating the practical feasibility of large-scale CBT and CATs. First, Drake Prometric, a Minneapolis-based firm that has links back to the original CDC PLATO project, helped to develop and deploy a large-scale certified network engineer (CNE) examination for Novell Corporation, which became operational in 1990. The CNE program moved to online computerized adaptive test (CATs) in 1991 and proved to be one of the first large-scale CAT applications (Foster, personal communication, 2011). Second, in 1992, the Graduate Record Examination (GRE) made its debut at Educational Testing Services (ETS) and Sylvan testing centers across the United States as a CAT.[2] The scale of testing operations and high visibility of the GRE naturally provided a great deal of impetus for both CBT and CAT (Eignor, Stocking, Way, & Steffen, 1993; Mills & Stocking, 1996). Third, the NCLEX examinations for nurses, offered by the National Council on State Boards of Nursing, went live with a CAT examination in 1994 (Zara, 1994). Since then, 2.4 million nursing licensure candidates have taken the NCLEX-RN and NCLEX-PN examinations. Finally, during the 1996–1997 period, following almost 20 years of extensive research and development funded by the US military, a CAT version of the Armed Service Vocational Aptitude Battery (ASVAB), went operational with online testing at Military Entrance Processing Stations (Sands, Waters, & McBride, 1997).

Since the early- to mid-1990s, computer-based testing has experienced fairly steady growth in many different sectors and for many different populations. The College Board introduced the AccuPlacer postsecondary placement exams in an adaptive format in the mid-1990s. The Graduate Management Admissions Council implemented a CAT version of the Graduate Management Admission Test (GMAT) in 1997; currently, over 200,000 examinees take the GMAT on an annual basis. Another high-stakes test, the United States Medical Licensing Examination, moved to CBT in 1999, adding highly interactive computerized patient-management simulations to the examinations (Dillon, Clyman, Clauser, & Margolis, 2002; Melnick & Clauser, 2005). Similarly, interactive accounting simulations were added to the Uniform CPA Examination in 2004 (Devore, 2002; Luecht, 2002) and implemented one of the first computer-adaptive multistage testing frameworks for large-scale applications (Breithaupt, Ariel, & Hare, 2010; Luecht, Brumfield, & Briethaupt, 2006; Melican, Breithaupt, & Zhang, 2010). CBT is also used for many types of psychological and employment tests. Finally, many states are now offering CBT options for end-of-grade and end-of-course testing as well as for high school graduation, while an even more expansive use of CBT within schools is taking place under the U.S. government's Race to the Top (RTTT) initiatives (www2.ed.gov/programs/racetothetop).

CBT Venues and Platforms

Modern CBT is usually implemented in one of four ways: (a) in dedicated test centers, (b) at temporary test centers, (c) in multipurpose computer labs, or (d) using a PC connected to the Internet. At the heart of CBT is a need for connectivity with rapid transmission of potentially large amounts of data—the capability to link multiple computers to the test delivery software and item bank and to transmit test materials, results, scores, and other information where and when they are needed. The earliest CBT facilities consisted of testing terminals (i.e., workstations) that were physically connected to a mainframe computer. The mainframe computer did all of the processing; the workstations merely displayed the information on screen and collected responses via a keyboard. The advent of PCs and local area networks (LANs) made it possible to connect stand-alone microcomputers—that is, smart terminals capable of handling some or all of the processing—to centralized storage file servers and shared processing resources. Wide area networks expanded this connectivity principle to allow remote networks to be connected across multiple physical locations.

However, until the widespread adoption of the Internet TCP/IP (packet switching protocols) in the mid-1990s, most networks used proprietary closed architectures that limited how computers and peripheral devices could be interconnected and communicate. That is, the use of proprietary network architectures limited the possibilities for truly collaborative computing using shared resources. This problem was further exacerbated by a plethora of different operating systems (platforms). For example, some systems used a particular version of Microsoft's MS-DOS. Others migrated to Microsoft Windows, LINUX or Sun Systems UNIX, Apple's Mac OS, and newer versions of these operating systems. In some cases, hardware drivers for graphics and other features of the early CBT interfaces were so specific to the operating system and particular hardware or interface cards that only a relatively small class of carefully tested PCs could be used for testing. TCP/IP and Internet changed all of that by offering more open networking architectures that could rather seamlessly communicate and share resources and data with one another.

Since the late 1990s, the introduction of virtualization (i.e., virtual machines, or VMs), advances in Internet browser capabilities, dramatic improvements in routing and switching technologies, and high-speed wireless connectivity have removed most of the practical barriers to networking and cross-platform computing anywhere in the world. In fact, recent advancements in cloud computing have essentially created a virtual computing environment that allows data and applications to follow an individual across different computer systems anywhere in the world. However, that does not necessarily mean that CBT is now possible on demand anywhere in the world.

Dedicated Commercial Test Centers

Dedicated test centers are usually commercial properties owned or franchised by a large testing company. Most centers have 10 to 30 computer workstations and a small staff to handle the onsite test administration activities: registering the examinees, possibly collecting testing fees, logging the examinees into their authorized test(s), and proctoring the examination sessions. These centers rarely do anything except administer tests for clients. The examinees show up at their scheduled testing time, take the test, and leave. For some examination programs, walk-in testing is allowed, subject to the availability of testing workstations.

Although a thorough discussion of the business side of commercial testing is far beyond the scope of this chapter, it is important to understand that many dedicated testing centers follow a particular business model that creates multiple revenue points tied to each testing transaction (i.e., one test taker completing one test form). The more lucrative cost drivers include *per exam fees* for registration, testing seat time, and other processing costs. Since the total fees charged to the client (examinee and/or testing organization) are directly tied to the number of examinees taking the test, lowering the cost of seat time and other per-exam usage fees is certainly not beneficial to the CBT provider's profit margin. In fact, other fees such as item bank maintenance and even psychometric services can be layered on top of these per-exam costs, sometimes offered "free of charge" (i.e., not listed in the direct costs).

There are some downsides to dedicated commercial test centers beyond the increased testing fees charged to examinees to pay for the physical commercial testing space and staffing. One rather obvious disadvantage is access. Most commercial testing centers are opened only in large metropolitan areas, since only these provide sufficient opportunity to fill a center's CBT seats on an ongoing basis. Examinees located in rural settings and smaller towns may have to travel fairly large distances to the available testing centers and then compete with local examinees for available testing time/date slots. Although this model seems to work for professional certification and licensure, it is not necessarily practical for elementary, secondary, or postsecondary students.

In the past, arrangements have been made to open small commercial test centers on some of the large university campuses to serve the local student body and the surrounding community. However, ensuring dedicated space just for testing throughout the year and having adequate staff has proven to be somewhat ineffective from a cost perspective for both the educational institutions and the CBT companies. Another downside is the impact of limited seating capacity on item production costs. Unused seats mean lost revenue. Therefore dedicated commercial testing centers usually attempt to maximize testing using the smallest number of seats needed—not unlike the airline industry, which eliminates flights in order to increase the number of filled seats on the remaining flights. By some estimates, there may be no more than 10,000 seats available at dedicated testing sites throughout the United States. Whereas 10,000 CBT seats may seem to be a fairly large number, it is actually trivial when we consider that as many as 77 million students would need to be tested each year from K–12 and postsecondary education institutions, in addition to the psychological, employment, admissions, professional certification, and licensure CBT that currently occupies most of the available testing center seats.

As a direct result of the limited capacity at dedicated centers, high-stakes testing programs must spread their testing out over a longer period of time—often using defined testing "windows" to allow examinees ample time to schedule a test during certain times of the year. But increasing the number of testing dates and time slots creates other security-related complications, such as item overexposure and collaborated theft of item banks when the same items are available for extended periods of time. A possible solution is to increase the size of item banks; however, that simply adds to the bottom-line costs, since item production is the other major cost driver in testing (Luecht, 2005b).

Temporary Testing Sites

Temporary testing sites have been used for many years to supplement testing activities at dedicated commercial test centers. Examples include providing testing sites for high-volume clients in locales where a dedicated center does not exist or holding large field trials simultaneously in multiple locations. As the label implies, a temporary testing site is a temporary network configuration of PCs that can be set up in high school or college auditoriums, large classrooms, or even meeting rooms at large conference centers. The site can be set up as a stand-alone network or may use the Internet for connectivity. The computers are usually rented and set up strictly for the testing event. They are later removed. The advantage of temporary testing sites is that capacity can generally be increased as needed. There are many logistical issues to overcome, however. For example, the sites must have sufficient electrical power and amperage, possible Internet access with high-speed routing, good cooling to overcome the heat of 50 or more computers running in an enclosed space, sufficient testing stations and seats, and enough computers that work reliably and meet minimal hardware requirements (memory, hard disk space, graphics capabilities, monitor resolution, etc.). Onsite proctoring and technical assistance may also be needed.

Although there are obvious operational costs and risks associated with setting up temporary testing sites, their feasibility to create large-capacity testing events on a limited number of testing dates makes this an appealing option, especially when coupled with the reduced item production costs associated with fewer testing dates.

Multiuse Computer Labs

Multiuse computerized testing labs may be used in the same way as temporary testing sites—discussed above—but with some additional advantages. First, when testing is not under way, the lab can be repurposed for instructional uses. Dual use of classroom or laboratory space—especially when revenue is tied to the space—can be an important selling point with educational administrators who oversee the operating budgets at an institution. Second, an instructional computer lab already has the requisite infrastructure (computers and connectivity) needed for most types of CBT. In fact, some Internet-based testing implementations have been specifically designed to make use of existing computer labs in elementary and high schools, at community colleges, and at 4-year colleges and universities. With approximately 132,600 public and private elementary and secondary schools in the United States, this solution to the CBT capacity issue seems highly appealing. Nonetheless, there are several pragmatic stumbling blocks.

First, computer lab facilities are often variable in size and quality at different educational institutions. This can lead to incompatibilities between system hardware and software, which may be difficult to resolve in an efficient and cost-effective way (e.g., using outdated or incompatible versions of an operating system, having low-resolution or smaller monitors that adversely impact the display of certain types of items, having security policies and software in place that limit caching or other functional capabilities required by the test delivery software). Second, many schools—in an effort to avoid recurring repair, upgrade, and replacement costs for laptops and microcomputers every 12 to 24 months—are moving to wireless computing support, where the students bring their own laptops, netbooks, tablet PCs, smart phones, or other mobile computing device to the campus to connect and learn. The investment in wireless access points is usually far less than maintaining computer labs. Now, however instead of dealing with an established computer lab, known equipment, and technical support personnel who can facilitate the changeover from instructional lab to secure CBT environment, each student essentially brings his or her testing workstation to the center and leaves with it after completing the test. Allowing students, or any examinees, to use their own computers is a frightening proposition to most security-conscious, high-stakes testing programs, including K–12 end-of-course and end-of-year testing programs.[3]

Test at Home, Bring Your Own

The final approach to offering CBT might be termed the *test-at-home* (TAH) approach. The concept is rather straightforward. The examinee registers and logs into the test from his or her home computer or laptop. The Internet browser is "locked down" to prevent any other software from intervening and the examinee completes the entire test online. Once the examinee has submitted his or her final item or test section, the TAH application erases all trace of itself from the local computer. During the examination, proctoring is accomplished by using high-definition video feeds monitored by proctors, requisite interactivity on demand with a proctor, and video scans of the at-home testing environment. Obviously for high-stakes examinations, there is always some possibility of beating these types of remote security measures. However, this same model can also be moved to a temporary site where secure registration and direct human proctoring can be provided. Although few testing companies are currently considering the TAH approach for their high-stakes examinations, this approach, combined with temporary testing sites, may soon prove to be a viable solution for large-volume examination programs regardless of the stakes of testing.

Item Types and Interfaces

A computer *interface* is one of the most important aspects of a CBT design. The interface provides the *view* that the test taker sees of the test and controls all interactions, allowing movement or navigation between items, responding to the items, as well as providing other capabilities such as monitoring timing on the test. It may not matter if highly sophisticated and efficient psychometric technologies lie beneath the surface of the interface. If the interface is marginal, that is the rating that test takers are likely to provide of the test as a whole.

Today, most computers employ graphic user interfaces (GUIs) with keyboard or mouse-oriented point-and-click capabilities. The operating system usually provides all of the necessary features of the GUI through a programming interface. The inclusion of a GUI as part of the operating system represented a major step forward in computer interactivity. Some of the early operating systems used an embedded character set for text-related displays and inputs and relied on special features of a graphic card to handle everything else. Programmers essentially created their own interfaces, which led to highly variable features even across programs with the same basic capabilities and functions. Apple's Mac OS was one of the first to adopt a functional GUI approach as part of the operating system. Microsoft's Windows operating system capitalized on the popularity of Apple's GUI and released Windows 3.0 in 1990 as a replacement for the text/console-based MS-DOS. LINUX and other operating systems have followed suit. Many CBT facilities have taken the additional step of moving toward enterprise computing using an Internet browser such as Mozilla's Firefox, Apple's Safari, and Microsoft's Internet Explorer as the GUI.

There are really two different GUI views for CBT. One view is at the test level; the other is at the item level. From a systems design perspective, it is best to separate these two views, allowing changes in one view (e.g., how navigation works) to have no direct effect on how the other view operates (e.g., the look and functionality of a particular item or class of items). The test level view is called the dashboard; the item-level view is rendered within a window, tab page, or designated area of the dashboard.

The CBT Dashboard

The core elements of a CBT GUI include presentational controls, access to ancillary tools, timers, and navigation. Essentially, any necessary software controls that are not specific to a particular test item or assessment task can be migrated to the dashboard and shared for all items. Presentation controls include palettes and color choices, the appearance of components and controls (e.g., 3-D beveled panels and buttons), text font styles, tiling/cascading windows and sizing, use of tabs, and so on. Ancillary tools can include online help and test features such as calculators, highlighting/marking tools, or reference materials that can be accessed throughout the test. Timers include count-down clocks or other pacing aids. Navigation controls include forward and backward control buttons, pagination controls, or other controls that allow the examinee to move to any point within a test or test section.

A useful term for describing a CBT interface is *dashboard*. Like the dashboard on a vehicle, a CBT dashboard provides the examinee with a view into the test and further with some degree of control over the testing experience. A good dashboard provides an adequate amount of control. Too much control can lead to confusion; too little can lead to frustration and anxiety. A good dashboard should be intuitive and provide unencumbered access to each test item and its relevant data and features. Functional requirements such as timing controls, help/instructions, access to auxiliary tools such as calculators, glossaries, or formula sheets, and basic navigation between items are all controlled by the dashboard.

Some of the common mistakes in dashboard design (adapted from Few, 2006) are as follows:

1. Exceeding the boundaries of a single screen—fragmenting the display or requiring scrolling or pagination
2. Supplying an inadequate or nonintuitive context for controls or other design features presented on the screen (e.g., nonintuitive icons)
3. Cluttering the display with useless decoration; displaying too much detail or precision, leading to confusion
4. Introducing meaningless contrast or variety (colors, text styles, patterns, background graphics); misusing/overusing colors and contrasts
5. Distorting perceptions or comparisons by inappropriate sizing
6. Arranging the components or data poorly to obfuscate functions and purpose
7. Highlighting important components inappropriately or not at all
8. Designing an aesthetically unappealing dashboard

In short, a CBT dashboard is a type of executive control that allows examinees to intuitively proceed through a test with an appropriate sense of control over their own test-taking strategies. That executive control must be facilitative, not punitive, and certainly not cumbersome or difficult to use. When an item appears, it becomes the focus and may take on new functionality and even add software controls beyond those included as part of the dashboard (buttons, navigation controls, graphic interfaces, etc.). A discussion of what happens at the item level follows.

CBT Item Types

While the GUI and dashboard control what happens at the test level, each rendered item, item set, or simulation task should provide a unique knowledge or skill challenge to examinee, possibly comprising a customized interface. Although an estimated 99% of all CBT facilities use some variation of the multiple-choice item theme, an extensive array of more interactive assessment tasks can be employed. The phrase *innovative items* (also called *technology-enhanced items*) is often used by subject-matter experts and test developers, signaling a strong desire to break out of the multiple-choice testing mold common to paper-and-pencil tests. Of course that desire must be aligned with a solid understanding of the skill and knowledge constructs to be measured as well as an understanding of how a particular innovative item type enhances the measurement information extracted from each examinee's responses (Luecht & Clauser, 2002).

Innovative CBT items range from more traditional selected- and constructed-response items to highly interactive computerized performance exercises such as the National Board of Medical Examiners' computerized case simulations used on the USMLE (Dillon et al., 2002; Melnick & Clauser, 2005), the accounting simulations included on the Uniform CPA Examination (Devore, 2002; Devore, Brittingham, & Maslott, 2011), or the graphic simulations used on the Architect Registration Examination (Bejar, 1991; Braun, Bejar, & Williamson, 2006).

A number of item-type taxonomies have been proposed (e.g., Luecht & Clauser, 2002; Parshall, Harmes, Davey, & Pashley, 2010; Zenisky & Sireci, 2002). Offering one of the more complete taxonomies, Parshall and colleagues recommend using seven dimensions to characterize most computerized item types: (a) assessment structure (selected or constructed response); (b) complexity of conceptual and functional aspects of the assessment task; (c) fidelity—that is, realism and accuracy of the reproduction of task objects used; (d) interactivity of the item or interface to the examinees actions; (e) inclusion of media ranging from graphics to audio, video, and animations; (f) response actions supported by the interface; and (g) scoring methods. This type of taxonomy is useful to emphasize the many possible task variations that examinees are challenged to complete, the extent of resources (facilitative and restrictive) allowed, and the types of valid performance information that is saved and ultimately used in scoring.

A compatible way to categorize the properties of innovative items is by considering each item to be a combination of software components drawn from any of three classes (Luecht, 2002). *Semipassive components* display information (text, graphics, audio-video, animations) and allow scrolling or over movement within the context of the item. Most semipassive components are benign from a measurement perspective and generally are not intended to provide score-related measurement information—although it would be possible to track and use as part of the scoring time spent viewing/reading text, graphics, or animations or listening to a sound clip, and this might be stored and used in some fashion.

Response-capturing components typically record specific choices or provide evidence of intentional actions by the test taker. These components include selection controls such as radio boxes, check boxes and pull-down lists, text input boxes (including rich text input controls that have many word processing–like editing features), input controls that allow examinees to click on defined regions of the screen—so-called hot-spot items), drag-and-drop controls that allow the test taker to move items from one place to another on a screen, slider controls, object palettes that allow the test taker to select objects, list-ordering controls, interactive components that "respond" to something the examinee does, and formal performance simulations that present a realistic scenario and require the test taker to use functional software applications or tools to solve problems (e.g., using accounting software to determine the financial standing of a company, using computer-aided design software to design a room or building). However, without flexible user interfaces, we would not have much variety in CBT item types.

Auxiliary tools include calculators, search tools, spell checkers, formula sheets, measuring tools, and other software components that are usually optional from the test taker's perspective. That is, a given test taker may or may not use the auxiliary tools. A particular auxiliary tool may facilitate performing some task or could be detrimental to performance, especially if the examinee is not familiar with the tool or uses it in the wrong way. In general, auxiliary tools do not provide score-related information. However, the appropriate or efficient use of certain auxiliary tools can provide useful measurement information in certain instances—for example, the scoring protocol for a medical specialty exam could evaluate whether or not the examinee consulted the appropriate reference materials before completing a diagnostic task. Special accommodations such as large-print viewports or text-to-speech readers would also fall into this category of auxiliary tools.

By viewing specific item types as discrete mixtures of components drawn from these three classes (semipassive components, response-capturing components, and auxiliary tools), it is relatively easy to see how a very large number of potential item types can be created. Furthermore, human-factors and usability research can be conducted to better understand the most appropriate uses of these component classes from the perspectives of flexibility, design utility, costs, production efficiency, quality of measurement information produced, and the potential introduction of "method" variance that could challenge the validity of a test.

A *template* can be designed to render the components within the relevant window or section of the dashboard reserved for item content. For example, a multiple-choice (MC) item can be modeled using a template comprising a display panel or frame, a text box to store the item stem and response instructions (e.g., "click on the one best answer"), a possible exhibit window, and some number of mutually exclusive radio buttons, with text or graphic caption properties used to store and display each of the MC distractor options. Another example of a template might include a numerical grid control—similar to a spreadsheet—used by the examinees to enter one or more numbers for a mathematical, statistical, or accounting assessment task. The template would govern where and how the grid control appears and other basic mathematical or statistical calculation functions available to the test taker. Item-specific data may indicate the number of rows and columns in the spreadsheet, fixed content (numbers and text) that populate the cells of the grid control when the item is rendered, and any constraints on the types of data that can be entered into the desired response cells.

Templates can also include scripts to add functionality and interactivity. For example, interactive animations associated with an item template can run with different outcomes, given certain choices that an examinee makes. The template may also indicate the scoring components to be used. Scoring components, sometimes called *scoring evaluators* (Drasgow et al., 2006; Luecht, 2007a) handle how test-taker responses are converted to particular response scores. For example, a MC item uses a simple match of a selected response to a keyed option from the item bank, resolves to *true* or *false*, and assigns the designated points for that item.

Templates serve three important purposes for CBT. First, they provide a concrete way to design new item types. The layout, look, and feel of the components can be visualized. For example, Figure 5.1 presents a mock-up of a template for a selected-response item type, with a graphic image, requiring the examinee to choose the best two of four possible response options.

In this example, the check boxes (or optional radio buttons) serve as the response-capturing components. The semipassive components include the stem and instructions, the graphic, the (possible) scroll bar, and the submit button. There are no auxiliary tools specified for this

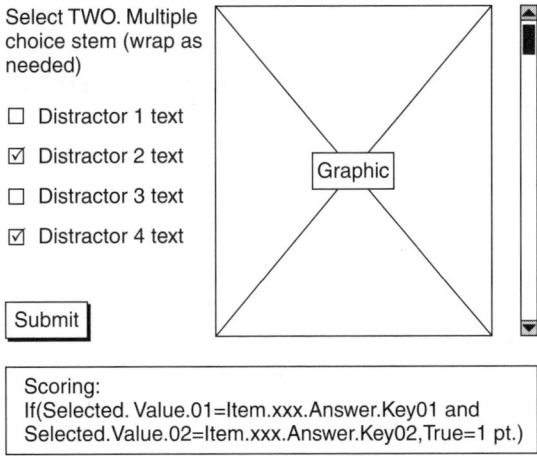

Figure 5.1 A Template Mock-Up for a Choose-Two Selected-Response Item

template. The scoring is also indicated as a simple pattern match of the two selected responses to two keyed answers. If the examinee gets both items correct, he or she gets the item right; otherwise the item will be scored as wrong.

The second advantage of using templates is that item writers can be constrained to generate only items that conform to desired specifications. Specifications, as a matter of standard test development policies and procedures for a particular testing agency, can range from exact to loose. Very precise controls can be included in the authoring templates, such as designated content topics, the length and readability of text strings, the required resolution and coloring of graphics, and even the cognitive complexity of elements (Lai, Gierl, & Alves, 2010; Luecht, Dallas, & Steed, 2010). Or item writers can be presented with a general rendering template and allowed to create their items largely constrained by the template with respect only to stylistic features.

The final advantage of using templates is that they naturally follow an object-oriented paradigm of being scalable and highly replicable (e.g., using the same template to render thousands of items). Templates also help guarantee that all items sharing the same template have a common appearance and functionality from the examinee's perspective (i.e., the same look and feel on different computer equipment, possibly deployed using different operating systems and browsers).

Test Designs for Delivering CBT

The test form that an examinee actually sees is an assigned list of items or assessment tasks attached to the dashboard for rendering and interaction with the examinee. The collection of items assigned to a test form—regardless of the item-to-list assignment mechanism used—can be called a test form list (TFL). Most popular CBT designs are really just different ways of preparing a TFL and tend to vary along three dimensions: (a) the nature of the item selection process—that is, the way that the TFL is generated; (b) the sizes of the test administration units assigned to the list; and (c) where the item selection, test assembly, and quality control of test forms take place (i.e., where the TFL is generated and checked). For example, as in paper-and-pencil test forms, items can be assigned to fixed positions on a CBT TFL, randomly assigned to the list, or adaptively selected for the list so that the final TFL of items is tailored to each examinee's proficiency. Any of these selection mechanisms can likewise be used to select individual items or larger units for the TFL (item sets, complex assessment tasks, or larger sets of items called *modules*). Finally, the TFLs can be generated in real time—while each examinee is taking the test—or preconstructed to provide the opportunity for stronger quality controls, including review by committees of experts on subject matter.

Computerized Adaptive Testing (CAT)

Computerized adaptive testing has a fairly long history of research (e.g., Chang & Ying, 1999; Green, Bock, Humpreys, Linn, & Reckase, 1983; Kingsbury & Zara, 1989; Lord, 1971, 1980; McBride & Martin, 1983; Segall, 1996; Stocking & Swanson, 1993; Vale, 1981; Van der Linden & Glas 2010; Wainer, 2000; Weiss, 1969, 1975, 1985; Weiss & Betz, 1973; Weiss & Kingsbury, 1984). Although a great deal of theoretical model-based psychometric research on CAT occurred in the late 1970s and throughout the 1980s, large-scale implementations did not begin to surface until the early 1990s.

CAT usually requires item response theory (IRT).[4] For generality, we can assume that all of the items in the item bank are calibrated using a three-parameter logistic (3PL) model that characterizes the probability of a correct response to item i as

$$P_i(\theta) = c_i + \frac{(1-c_i)}{1+\exp[-Da_i(\theta-b_i)]} \quad (1)$$

where θ is the latent ability or proficiency ranging from $-\infty$ to ∞, D is a scaling constant, a_i is an item parameter that indicates the relative sensitivity of each item to the underlying proficiency, b_i is a location parameter for the item denoting its difficulty, and c_i is a lower-asymptote parameter that may be related to random guessing and other sources of noise near the lower tail of the proficiency scale. Using calibrated estimates for the a_i, b_i, and c_i item parameters from the item bank, $i = 1,\ldots, I$, it is relatively straightforward to estimate θ, regardless of which items a particular examinee sees. The likelihood of two or more responses can be expressed as

$$L(\mathbf{u}_j|\theta) = \prod_{i=1}^{k} P_i(\theta)^{u_{ij}} [1-P_i(\theta)]^{1-u_{ij}} \quad (2)$$

where a best estimate of θ for examinee j occurs where $L(\mathbf{u}_j|\theta)$ is a maximum. This is called the *maximum likelihood (ML) estimate* and can be numerically estimated using an iterative algorithm that satisfies

$$\hat{\theta}_k^{ML} = \arg\max_{\theta} \{L(\theta|u_1,\ldots,u_k): \theta \in (-\infty, \infty)\} \quad (3)$$

(see, for example, Hambleton & Swaminathan, 1985; Lord, 1980).

Other estimators can be used to compute weighted ML, Bayes modal, and Bayes mean estimates of θ (Bock & Mislevy, 1982; Mislevy, 1986). A Bayes mean estimate can be computed by approximating the integral

$$\hat{\theta}_k^{EAP} = \int \theta \frac{L(\mathbf{u}_k|\theta)p(\theta|\mu,\sigma^2)}{\int L(\mathbf{u}_k|\theta)p(\theta|\mu,\sigma^2)d\theta} d\theta \quad (4)$$

where $p(\theta|\mu,\sigma^2)$ is an assumed prior density in the population of interest for θ. These different types of estimates are not necessarily exchangeable. Often, Bayes mean estimates—also referred to as *expected a posteriori* (EAP) estimates—are used for interim computations and item

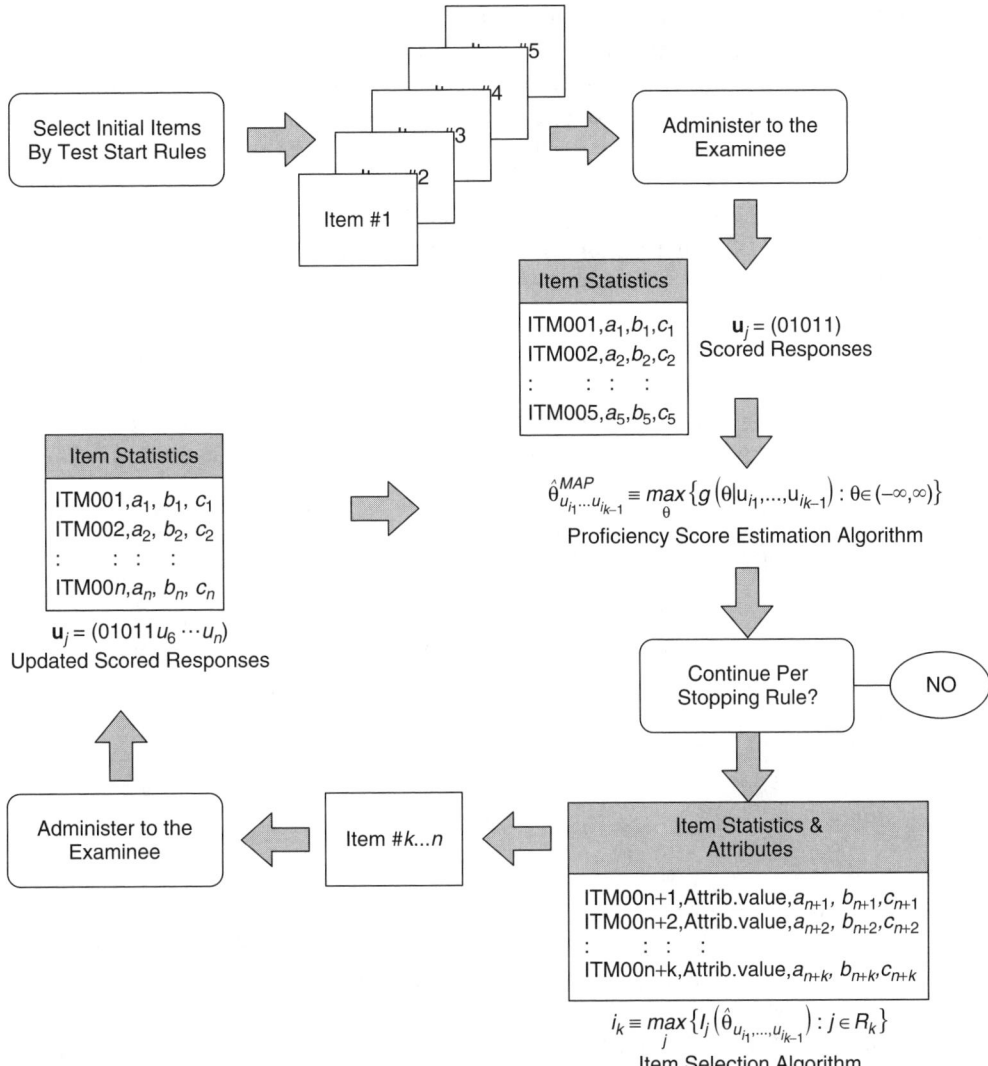

Figure 5.2 The Basic CAT Process

selections (Bock & Mislevy, 1982). ML or Bayes modal estimates can then be computed using the complete response string once the CAT terminates.

As noted earlier, a CAT algorithm involves an iterative process that sequentially builds a TFL of items tailored to an examinee's estimated proficiency—the provisional estimates of θ, computed following the administration of each item. The basic adaptive process is depicted in Figure 5.2. This figure outlines an item-level CAT. However, as described further on, multi-item testlets, item sets, computerized performance simulations, or preconfigured multiassessment task modules can also make up the adaptively selected test units.

As shown in Figure 5.2, the adaptive sequence needs a starting point. A small initial set of items may be randomly selected or an estimate of proficiency based prior performance can be used for selecting one or more items to start the adaptive sequence—that is, to start building the TFL. The test-delivery software scores all of the initially selected items. The IRT item statistics for the selected items are then used in conjunction with the response scores to compute the examinee's (provisional) proficiency estimate of θ (described below). A new item or test unit is then selected for the TFL—usually to maximize the precision of the current estimate of θ. The process continues until a particular stopping rule is satisfied. A stopping rule is merely a criterion for terminating the generation of the TFL. Two standard stopping rules for adaptive tests are (a) end the test when a fixed or minimum test length has been reached or (b) end the test when a minimum level of score precision has been satisfied.[5]

The most common CAT criterion for selecting items for the TFL is called the *maximum information* criterion (MIC). This criterion can be expressed as

$$i_k = \arg\max_r \left\{ I_{U_r}\left(\hat{\theta}_{u_{i_1},...,u_{i_{k-1}}}\right) : r \in R_k \right\} \tag{5}$$

(Van der Linden, 2005). The function inside the maximization search argument (*arg max*) is an IRT item information function (Birnbaum, 1968; Lord, 1980) and can be expressed for the 3PL model as

$$I_i(\hat{\theta}) = \frac{D^2 a_i^2 \left[1 - P_i(\theta)\right]\left[P_i(\theta) - c_i\right]^2}{P_i(\theta)(1 - c_i)^2}. \tag{6}$$

IRT item information is inversely proportional to measurement errors of estimate and is further additive across items (Birnbaum, 1968). That is, the conditional measurement error variance, $var(E|\theta)$, is inversely proportional to the test information function, $I(\theta)$:

$$\begin{aligned} var(E|\theta) &= \left[I(\theta)\right]^{-1} \\ &= \frac{1}{\sum_{i=1}^{n} I_i(\theta)} \end{aligned} \tag{7}$$

where $I_i(\theta)$ is the item information function in Equation 6 (Hambleton & Swaminathan, 1985; Lord, 1980). Every item therefore contributes some amount of measurement information to the reliability or score precision of the total test. Adding a *maximally* informative item to a test will *minimize* the error variance associated with the estimate of θ.

In addition to the statistical goal of maximizing the test information (and correspondingly minimizing the error variance of the estimated θ), many tests have content and other test specification requirements that must be met (e.g., cognitive skills coverage, response latencies, word counts or reading loads, topics, etc.). It is common to refer to these additional test specifications as *constraints* (Van der Linden, 2005).

Constraints effectively limit the solution space in which the algorithm must search for each new, optimal item. Severe constraints—that is, many different types of constraints placed on each item selection—can preclude the MIC from having much impact on the selection of items (Luecht, DeChamplain, & Nungester, 1997; Mills & Stocking, 1996; Stocking & Swanson, 1993; Van der Linden, 2000; Van der Linden & Reese, 1998). Mills and Stocking used the phrase "barely adaptive tests" to refer to this phenomenon. In addition to the constraints, a CAT usually needs to control the exposure of items to prevent the most informative items from always being chosen to satisfy the maximum information criterion. Conditional or unconditional item exposure mechanisms typically introduce a random, probabilistic elimination algorithm to attempt to buffer the likelihood of the most informative items from always being chosen (Hetter & Sympson, 1997; Revuela & Ponsoda, 1998; Stocking & Lewis, 1995, 1998, 2000; Sympson & Hetter, 1985).

The combination of continually seeking the most informative items, subject to possibly complex test assembly constraints and buffered by the exposure controls, can lead to a complicated item selection sequence for building each TFL. CAT is technically a heuristic by its very nature of depending on fallible estimates of θ as the basis for selecting each item (Bock & Mislevy, 1982). That means that it is not feasible to ever select a globally optimal test for any examinee because we never know his or her true ability, θ. Rather, after the test is completed, we might conclude that we would have selected a *different* sequence of items for the TFL, this time optimized more precisely at the final estimate of θ.

A CAT selection heuristic sequence is largely driven by two factors: (a) the demand for measurement information and various test-level specifications such as content and (b) the supply of items in the item bank relative to the demands. When the match between demands and supply is excellent or at least reasonable—something that occurs through good inventory controls and efficient planning of item writing assignments and item pretest scheduling—the CAT item-selection sequence is somewhat predictable, largely being driven by the MIC. When the demand is not directly achievable given the supply of items, various compromises occur, depending on the item-selection algorithm and criterion used.

More specifically, the construction of a CAT TFL is usually influenced by three dynamics: (a) the ratio of demand (content and other attribute constraints) to supply (item content and other attributes that satisfy constraints); (b) the relative ratio of the demand for information along the θ metric relative to the information density in the item pool; and (c) any exposure controls or "shut-off" mechanisms that may be employed.[6] Consider a simple example. If an item bank has only five items belonging to particular content area and the test specifications (content constraints) call for choosing two of those five items on every test form, the demand to supply ratio, $2(N_\theta):5$, will be higher than for another content area having the same demand but a greater number of items in the item pool.[7] The demand for information across the θ metric must also be considered. For a CAT using the MIC, the information demands will be proportional to the density of the θ distribution, especially if conditional exposure controls are used to limit the number of items exposed to examinees within various regions of the θ metric. In short, these three dynamics can interact in complex ways to influence the selection of items during the CAT.

Computerized Adaptive Multistage Tests

A type of preconstructed adaptive test that is gaining in popularity is called a computerized adaptive multistage test (ca-MST). A ca-MST has the same purpose as a CAT but uses larger units to build the TFL. The concept of multistage testing was introduced several decades ago (Lord, 1971). However, the operational complexities of building modules to optimize measurement precision, balance content, and control exposure—especially over extended periods of time—were not anticipated. Luecht and Nungester (1998) provided one of the first large-scale practical design specifications for implementing ca-MST.[8] Since that early design work, the ca-MST framework has been implemented for the Uniform CPA Examination (American Institutes of Certified Public Accountants) (see Melican et al., 2010) and several state examination programs. Ca-MST is also being seriously considered as replacement for item-level CAT for other high-stakes large-scale examinations (e.g., the 2011 GRE).

Under Luecht and Nungester's implementation of ca-MST, the primary test administration unit is called a *panel*. Each panel is a unique template for a configuration of multi-item units or assessment tasks called a *module*.[9] A panel template configuration is denoted by a series of integers, *ms*, representing the number of stages ($s = 1,\ldots, S$) in as well as the number of modules per stage (m_1-...-m_S). For example, a three-stage panel with one module at stage 1, three

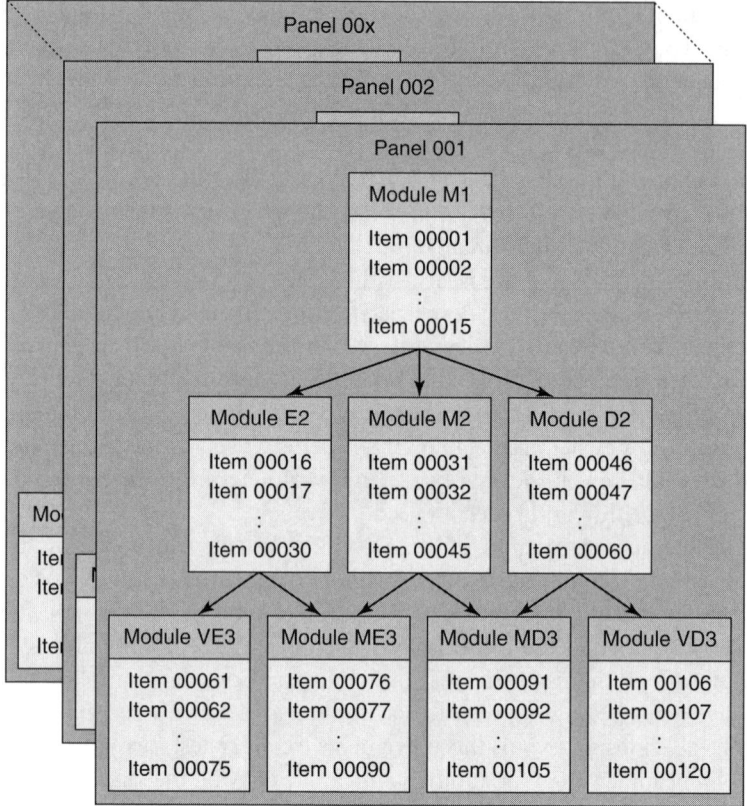

Figure 5.3 Panels With 15-Item MILs for a 1–3-4 ca-MST Template Configuration

modules at stage 2, and four modules at stage 3 would be denoted as a 1–3-4 panel. The first-stage module is typically of moderate difficulty or, for mastery tests, may be targeted near the cut score. The subsequent stages provide some degree of adaptation. The number of modules specified per stage, m_s, also provides a vague indication as to the amount of adaptation possible within the panel. For example, a 1–2-3 panel has less adaptation at stages 2 and 3 than the 1–3-4 panel configuration.

Figure 5.3 presents multiple panels (*Panel* 001, 002,..., 00*x*) for the 1–3-4 template configuration. Eight modules are shown as module item lists (MILs). Each list contains exactly 15 items for this example, implying that each panel requires a total of 120 items. The first-stage module (M1) is indicated by a 15-item MIL comprising items of moderate difficulty.[10] The second stage comprises three 15-item MILs: E2 contains easier items; M2 contains items of moderate difficulty; and D2 contains difficult items. The third stage has four 15-item MILs: VE3 is made up of very easy items; ME3 has moderately easy items; MD3 holds moderately difficult items; and VD3 has very difficult items.

Each module item list has a fixed size n_s, $s = 1,..., S$ stages. Within a particular stage, all MILs should be of equal length. However, there is no requirement that the sizes of the MILs be equal across the S stages. For example, the stage 1 MIL could have 15 items records, stage 2 might have 20 items, and stage 3 might have 25 items, producing 60-item test forms for any given examinee regardless of the route taken. Most implementations of ca-MST employ equal numbers of items per stage for convenience. Having smaller MILs in earlier stages and larger modules in later stages can be shown to increase the overall demand for items in the item bank (i.e., where $n_{s+1} > n_s$). There are inherent trade-offs between the size of the modules, the statistical targets used for assembling the modules and panels, the extent of adaptation possible given the item bank, item exposure, and the size of the error variances associated with the proficiency score estimates.

It is interesting to note the connection of panels and modules to the concept of test-form lists (TFLs) introduced earlier. Under ca-MST, a TFL is the union of the MILs that a particular examinee sees by following one of the prescribed routes through the panel. For example, a very high proficiency examinee assigned to Panel 001 (see Figure 5.3) would likely be administered the most difficult modules at each stage. His or her TFL might therefore be denoted "Examinee. TFL = P001.MIL.M1 + P001.MIL.D2 + P001.MIL.VD3." The number of items in the TFL is $n_{TFL} = \sum_s n_s$. Since each panel is preconstructed, it is actually possible to carry out reviews of the TFLs, at least for the primary (expected) routes through each panel. This capability to review full-length adaptive tests before they are administered to examinees provides an important quality-control benefit, which is discussed further on.

Increasing the number of available panels decreases the item exposure rates in a very predictable way. For example, having five nonoverlapping panels would create an expected exposure of 20% in the population of examinees eligible to test within a particular time frame (assuming simple random assignment of panels to examinees). Retest takers can also be prevented from seeing any panels sharing modules that those examinees previously saw. The routes between modules further subdivide the panel-level exposures.

The routes themselves can be turned on or off as a matter of testing policy. For example, given the 1–3-4 panels shown in Figure 5.3, it should be clear that examinees can only branch to an adjacent panel in stage 3. Restricting the possible routes reduces the potential benefit of examinees trying to game the adaptive mechanism and can be empirically informed by item exposure risk analysis.

The actual routing can be handled using the number-correct scores (Luecht, 2000; Luecht & Burgin, 2003; Luecht & Nungester, 1998). A cumulative number-correct score is computed after each stage in the panel. The number-correct score combined with the known route taken to that point is used to determine the next module to be assigned. Simple look-up tables with this type of routing information can be attached to each panel. The number-correct routing eliminates the need for IRT scoring and MIC-related module selection during the actual test. This simplified routing and scoring can provide some important system performance benefits, especially for Internet-based testing. IRT scoring can still be used at the end of the test if desired.

Although the adaptive routing can be handled with number-correct scores, it is feasible to use the maximum information criterion (MIC) as the basis for routing examinees to the modules after each stage of testing. In those cases, routing is based on interval boundary points computed at the intersections of module information functions. Those boundary points can readily be converted to expected-number-correct scores. Optionally, routing can be based on policy-determined item exposure requirements (e.g., routing 30% of the examinees to module E2, 40% to M2, and 30% to D2). Luecht and Burgin (2003) demonstrate how both the MIC and exposure requirements can be merged into a set of IRT target information functions for the modules that simultaneously achieve both goals.

Each panel can be preconstructed using automated test assembly (ATA) for item selection to match module-level target information functions (Luecht, 2000, 2007b; Luecht et al., 2006; Melican et al., 2010; Van der Linden, 2005; Zenisky, Hambleton, & Luecht, 2010). For example, Figure 5.4 shows eight target test information function (TIF) targets for the 1–3-4 panels shown earlier in Figure 5.3, with exactly 15 items per stage. The TIFs are inversely related to measurement error variance associated with the scores (see Equation 7). Higher TIF values can be targeted

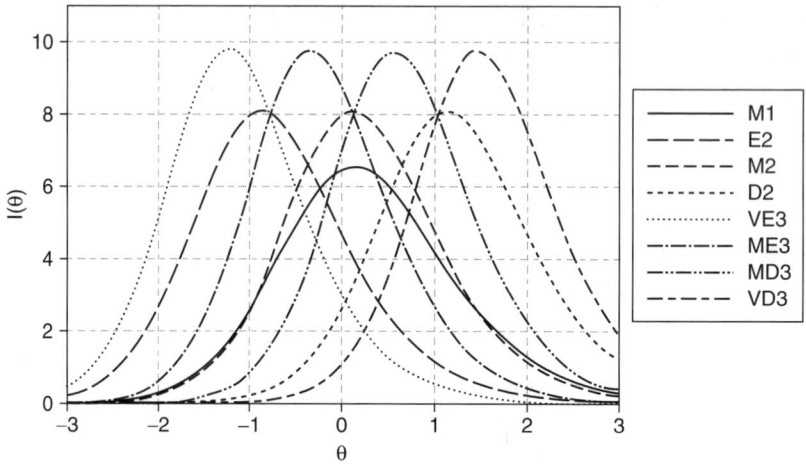

Figure 5.4 Eight TIF Targets for 15-Item MILs With Good Separation (1–3-4 ca-MST Panels)

to certain critical regions of the score scale (θ)—for example, having the TIF provide maximum information near the mean to provide reliable scores for most examinees or elsewhere along the scale for diagnostic scoring or other purposes. The module notations in Figure 5.4 (M, E, D, VE, ME, MD, and VD) were explained earlier in the context of Figure 5.3. When absolute TIF targets are used (Van der Linden, 2005), this type of ATA optimization problem can be characterized as a multiple-objective function/multiple-constraint set problem (Luecht, 2000, 2007b).

The M1 target is the stage 1 target (moderate difficulty). The peak of each TIF curve indicates where along the proficiency scale more information is desired. Subtle differences between the heights of the TIFs are noticeable. For example, the M1 TIF curve is the lowest in magnitude at its peak, and the stage 3 TIFs are all higher than the stage 1 and 2 curves. This is *intentional* and shows how less information can be allocated in the first stage of the ca-MST, reserving the more informative modules for later in the test (in this example, for stages 2 and 3). This incremental allocation of more information across the stages is conceptually identical to stratified-α or *b*-blocking CAT (Chang, Qian, & Ying, 2001; Chang & Ying, 1999) and demonstrates the high degree of flexibility that can be designed into the panel configurations. As long as the modules are constructed to match the targets, measurement precision can be allocated by location and amount exactly as needed for key decisions.

It is important to realize that the TIFs shown in Figure 5.4 are *targets* for test assembly—that is, idealized statistical specifications that *should be achievable for every panel*. If the item bank does not support this degree of separation of the modules or if rather severe content constraints create complex, competing demands for items across the modules, highly adaptive panels may simply not be possible. Figure 5.5 again shows eight plausible module TIF targets for $n_s = 15$ item MILs in a three-stage 1–3-4 panel. The contrast between Figures 5.4 and 5.5 is striking. The eight TIF target curves in Figure 5.5 are far less differentiated from one another along the θ metric and also have lower information peaks. Yet Figure 5.5 may represent a more realistic set of 1–3-4 TIF targets for panels built from an item bank originally designed to build fixed-length paper-and-pencil test forms—especially for a certification, licensure, or mastery test that might tend to have less discriminating items.

This problem of (lack of) separation of the items along the ability scale is not specific to ca-MST. In fact, it also occurs for CATs, but is often less apparent, due to the individualized selection of items and potential use of item exposure controls. Ca-MST makes it relatively easy

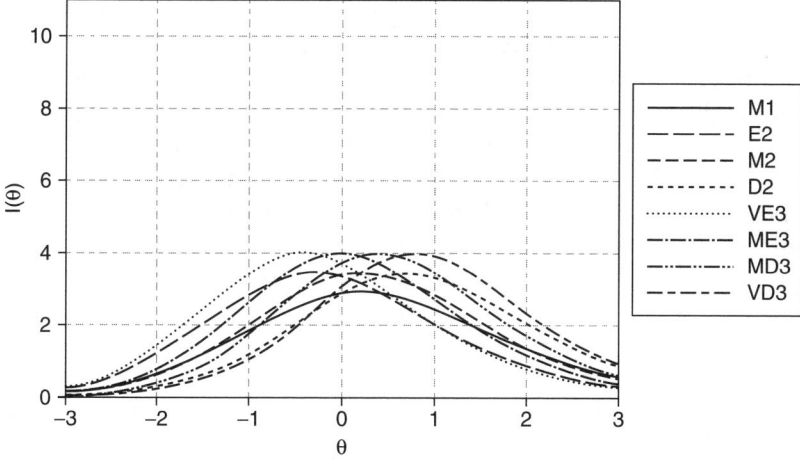

Figure 5.5 Eight TIF Targets for 15-Item MILs With Marginal Separation (1–3–4 ca-MST Panels)

to determine exactly how much separation of the modules is possible in terms of each module's distribution of item difficulty and discrimination. As illustrated by Figure 5.5, many item banks developed for fixed (paper-and-pencil) test forms do not have sufficient variability in item difficulty to support highly variable modules. *Relative targeting* and ATA solution strategies described by Van der Linden (2005; also see Melican et al., 2010) can be used in those cases to create as much separation as possible within a given item bank without explicitly targeting how much information is located at particular points of the scale.

Test-Form Quality Control

Test-form quality control (QC) implies that certain review or audit procedures are undertaken to ensure that each test form conforms to the requisite statistical and content-related specifications. High-stakes tests typically have stronger QC requirements than lower-stakes examinations. However, some amount of QC is certainly a good thing. With the advent of automated test assembly (ATA), many test forms can be simultaneously constructed by computer to adhere to the *formal* test specifications. Nonetheless, even with sophisticated ATA procedures in place, some amount of subject-matter expert (SME) committee review may still be used to at least audit the ATA outcomes (Luecht, 1998; Swanson & Stocking, 1993; Van der Linden, 2005). For example, the SMEs may look for overly redundant use of various themes within a test form or cuing of items. Those checks may not be easily specified in the formal constraints and objective functions employed with ATA.

Now suppose for a moment that we prohibit any SMEs from reviewing any of the test forms. What level of trust should we have in the ATA process? This question exemplifies the basic QC dilemma for CAT and for linear on-the-fly tests (LOFTs; Folk & Smith, 2002). It is not possible to carry out strong QC for CATs or LOFTs until after each test form is created and administered to the examinee. And even then the large number of unique test forms makes it infeasible to manually review every administered test form. Although preventive quality assurance (QA) procedures can be employed to evaluate *potential* test forms—often carried out using computer-generated simulations rather than real examinees—there is no guarantee that those potential test forms will be realized during the live test administration. QA affords some degree of trust, but it is fallible. Learning of problems on even a small number of test forms after their administration to real examinees degrades trust in the test assembly process.

Like preconstructed computerized fixed test forms (CFTs), ca-MST generates all of the active panels before they are released. This provides the opportunity for strong quality controls, including content reviews or audits by SMEs along the primary routes through each panel. The construction of a sufficient number of panels also provides the capability for strict exposure controls, as noted earlier, by using simple random assignment and tying exposure probabilities into the routing mechanism.

Another important aspect of QC is data integrity and data management. With preconstructed test units, each TFL (for CFTs)—or panel, module, and item (for ca-MST panels)—is a unique data *entity*. For ca-MST, MIL entities are hierarchically related to one another. As noted earlier, a test form list (TFL) is essentially an authorized route through the panel that can be denoted as the union of S module item lists (MILs) assigned to that panel. Items are likewise hierarchically assigned to MILs (modules). When a panel is assigned to a particular examinee, he or she can see only those modules and items assigned to that distinct panel. This aspect of data management—namely, strong *data identity controls* for panels, modules and items—is one of the reasons that ca-MST is often selected for large-scale, high-stakes applications that require adaptive testing. Since the TFLs for CFTs or ca-MST can also have data identities, every test form that any examinee sees can be checked for integrity against the known items assigned to that CFT form or route within a ca-MST panel. This capability makes it very easy to later reconcile and process the response data.

Conclusion

Operational CBT is usually far more complex than it is sometimes perceived to be by theoreticians and researchers. CBT implementation requires building a robust enterprise—a complex and fully integrated system or systems that handle end-to-end processing from item design, authoring, and banking through psychometric processing, scoring, and reporting (Drasgow et al., 2006; Luecht, 2005a). This system of systems must further be capable of handling both the well-behaved circumstances often assumed under theoretical models and computer-based simulations as well as the many exceptions that occur in real life. CBT is complicated.

This chapter has highlighted some of those complications, including CBT site considerations, with implications for security and potentially increasing the costs of testing seat time and item production, best practices for integrating new item types in an effective and efficient way, and deciding on a test delivery framework (CFT versus LOFT, or CAT versus ca-MST). There is no perfect CBT system. But careful design and proper use of modern, iterative systems design procedures and object-oriented design (OOD) can help ensure a vigorous, scalable, and extensible CBT enterprise.

Where Is CBT Headed in the Future?

There are many possibilities as to what CBT might look like in the future and how it will change the lives of test takers, test developers, and psychometricians. It would obviously be impossible to list all of those possibilities with any credibility; however, it seems reasonable to speculate as to what might materialize in the next decade or so.

One very likely change in the CBT landscape involves what we consider to be the *testing environment*. As suggested in this chapter, CBT must provide *full* capacity for on-demand testing—a capacity that, for K–16 education, is simply not feasible using fixed-site commercial testing centers or even temporary testing centers. The easiest and lowest-cost solution is obviously to test examinees on their own computers (laptops, netbooks, or tablets) or even on smartphones and related handheld devices. Securing these personal devices against theft of examination materials is not an insurmountable technical problem but will require ways to provide appropriate levels of security (e.g., full lockdowns of the browser and operating system with real-time proctoring) commensurate with the stakes and risks. What will also change is access, with new, robust assessment applications replacing the proprietary Internet browser–based test delivery software that is typically employed today. It is not a matter of *if* but rather, *when* these changes take place. The problem of test delivery capacity is very real—especially for K–16 education—and low-cost solutions are needed soon.

Another likely set of changes will occur insofar as what we test and how we devise assessments to test those constructs. Currently, most CBT setups rely heavily on multiple-choice/selected-response item variations, with some performance-based or technology-enhanced items thrown in to measure skills such as research, analysis, or a written synthesis of material. The actual test design and development process usually lets subject-matter experts determine what to measure and how to best measure it. Ultimately, following empirical tryouts of every item, we depend on psychometric calibration or equating models to help sort out the "signal" from the "noise," determine test-form difficulty differences, and devise a common score scale. This traditional approach to test design and development has to change. The demands for high-quality, cognitively oriented, skill-based items that dynamically inform learning and instruction are quickly outpacing our capabilities to write, pilot, and calibrate items. The reality is that teachers need multidimensional, formative assessments as an integral part of their lesson planning. Existing test design and development methods simply cannot address that need in a useful way.[11] Some of the most promising lines of measurement research and development involve new, more principled approaches to automated item generation, assessment engineering of task models and templates, and autoadaptive performance and simulation tasks. This research seeks to exploit the full capabilities of modern computing and approach test design as a scientifically based process aimed at articulating precise, cognitively based measurement claims of interest and then carefully designing assessment task templates that provide consistent measurement information about those claims. By applying manufacturing-engineering principles of replication and scalability to process, test design and template development have the potential to become enormously more efficient and truly capable of generating virtually unlimited numbers of precalibrated items and tests on demand.

The point is that measurement practices will change, ideally capitalizing on the enormous dynamic potential of high-speed, digital assessment. Hopefully measurement professionals will embrace the challenges and the technology and will let that potential emerge, as CBT advocates promised once upon a time.

Notes

1. ARPANET was the first packet-switching network; it consisted of four nodes in 1969: UC–Los Angeles, the Stanford Research Institute, the University of Utah, and UC–Santa Barbara. By 1981, it had grown to 213 hosts and would eventually become the Internet.

2. Per the ETS website (www.ets.org), the latest versions of the GRE are moving toward a multistage design rather than an item-level CAT.

3. There are ways to adequately secure a mobile PC or other device and mitigate many of the obvious risks of downloading a high-stakes test to an examinee's personal device. Theoretically all residual traces of a test can be deleted from an examinees hard disk, memory, and cache. However, the widespread use of this "bring your own assessment workstation" (BYOAW) option has not been extensively explored.

4. It is theoretically possible to use equated number-correct scores—especially for computer-adaptive multiple-stage tests—for both selection and scoring. However, most CAT implementations use IRT.

5. For the pass/fail mastery tests typically used in certification and licensure testing, a different stopping rule can be implemented related to the desired statistical confidence in the accuracy of the classification decision(s).

A simple ratio of the difference between the estimate of θ and the cut score to an appropriate standard error of estimate is usually used to carry out the hypothesis test.

6. A "shut-off" mechanism is a simple way to control exposure. When the count or proportion of examinees administered a particular item reaches a predetermined threshold, the item is shut off from further administration. The item may be turned on again at some future time.

7. The notation Nθ denotes the number of examinees in the population for whom this item would be chosen over all other items in the pool, based on the maximum information criterion.

8. Luecht and Nungester (1998) originally called ca-MST computer-adaptive sequential testing (CAST) to allow the design to flexibly apply in both adaptive and mastery settings. Other writers have referred to the basic design as multistage adaptive testing.

9. The concepts of panels and modules were borrowed from electrical engineering designs that employ modular, exchangeable components.

10. Module difficulty is usually controlled by using absolute or relative target IRT test information curve and automated test assembly (Luecht, 2000; Luecht & Nungester, 1998).

11. Reporting highly correlated domain-based subscores from a summative test is not formative assessment.

References

Bejar, I. I. (1991). A methodology for scoring open-ended architectural design problems. *Journal of Applied Psychology, 76*, 522–532.

Birnbaum, A. (1968). Estimation of an ability. In F. M. Lord & M. R. Novick (Eds.), *Statistical theories of mental test scores* (pp. 423–479). Reading, MA: Addison-Wesley.

Bock, B. D., & Mislevy, R. J. (1982). Adaptive EAP estimation of ability in a microcomputer environment. *Applied Psychological Measurement, 6*, 431–444.

Braun, H., Bejar, I. I., & Williamson, D. M. (2006). Rule-based methods for automated scoring: Application in a licensure context. In D. M. Williamson, I. I. Bejar, & R. J. Mislevy (Eds.), *Automated scoring of complex tasks in computer-based testing* (pp. 83–122). Mahwah, NJ: Erlbaum.

Chang, H. H., & Van der Linden, W. J. (2000, April). *A zero-one programming model for optimal stratification of item pools in a-stratified computerized adaptive testing*. Paper presented at the annual meeting of the National Council on Measurement in Education, New Orleans, LA.

Chang, H. H., & Ying, Z. (1999). A-stratified multi-stage computerized adaptive testing. *Applied Psychological Measurement, 23*, 211–222.

Chang, H. H., Qian, J., & Ying, Z. (2001). *a*-stratified multistage computerized adaptive testing item *b*-blocking. *Applied Psychological Measurement, 25*, 333–342.

Devore, R. (2002). *Considerations in the development of accounting simulations* [Technical Report]. Ewing, NJ: American Institute of Certified Public Accountants.

Devore, R., Brittingham, P., & Maslott, J. (2011, March). *Taking MCQ items to the next level–using simulations technology to enhance MCQ measurement and face validity*. Paper presented at the Association of Test Publishers Conference, Phoenix, AZ.

Dillon, G. F., Clyman, S. G., Clauser, B. E., & Margolis, M. J. (2002). The introduction of computer-based case simulations into the United States Medical Licensing Examination. *Academic Medicine, 77*(10), S94–S96.

Drasgow, F., Luecht, R. M., & Bennett, R. (2006). Technology and testing. In R. L. Brennan (Ed.), *Educational measurement* (4th ed., pp. 471–515). Washington, DC: American Council on Education/Praeger.

Eignor, D. R., Stocking, M. L., Way, W. D., & Steffen, M. (1993). *Case studies in computer adaptive test design through simulation* (RR-93-RR-56). Princeton, NJ: Educational Testing Service.

Few, S. (2006). *Information dashboard design: The effective visual communication of data*. O'Reilly Media.

Folk. V. G., & Smith, R. L. (2002). Models for delivery of CBTs. In C. Mills, M. Potenza, J. Fremer, & W. Ward (Eds.), *Computer-based testing: Building the foundation for future assessments* (pp. 41–66). Mahwah, NJ: Erlbaum.

Green, B. F., Bock, R. D., Humphreys, L. G., Linn, R. L., & Reckase, M. D. (1983). Technical guidelines for assessing computerized adaptive tests. *Journal of Educational Measurement, 21*, 347–360.

Hambleton, R. K., & Swaminathan, H. R. (1985). *Item response theory: Principles and applications*. Hingham, MA: Kluwer.

Hetter, R. D., & Sympson, J. B. (1997). Item exposure control in CAT-ASVAB. In W. A. Sands, B. K. Waters, & J. R. McBride (Eds.), *Computerized adaptive testing: From inquiry to operation* (pp. 141–144). Washington, DC: American Psychological Association.

Kingsbury, G. G., & Zara, A. R. (1989). Procedures for selecting items for computerized adaptive tests. *Applied Measurement in Education, 2*, 359–375.

Lai, H., Gierl, M., & Alves, C. (2010, April). *Generating items under the assessment engineering framework.* Invited symposium paper presented at the Annual Meeting of the National Council on Measurement in Education, Denver, CO.

Lord, F. M. (1971). The self-scoring flexilevel test. *Journal of Educational Measurement, 8,* 147–151.

Lord, F. M. (1980). *Applications of item response theory to practical testing problems.* Hillsdale, NJ: Erlbaum.

Luecht, R. M. (1998). Computer-assisted test assembly using optimization heuristics. *Applied Psychological Measurement, 22,* 222–236.

Luecht, R. M. (2000, April). *Implementing the computer-adaptive sequential testing (CAST) framework to mass produce high quality computer-adaptive and mastery tests.* Paper presented at the annual meeting of the National Council on Measurement in Education, New Orleans, LA.

Luecht, R. M. (2002, April). *From design to delivery: engineering the mass production of complex performance assessments.* [Technical Report]. Ewing, NJ: American Institute of Certified Public Accountants.

Luecht, R. M. (2005a). Operational Issues in Computer-Based Testing. In D. Bartrum and R. Hambleton (Eds.), *Computer-based testing and the Internet* (pp. 91–114). New York: John Wiley & Sons.

Luecht, R. M. (2005b). Some useful cost-benefit criteria for evaluating computer-based test delivery models and systems. *Association of Test Publishers Journal,* www.testpublishers.org/journal.htm

Luecht, R. M. (2007a). Using information from multiple-choice distractors to enhance cognitive-diagnostic score reporting. In Jacqueline P. Leighton & Mark J. Gierl (Eds.), *Cognitive diagnostic assessment for education: Theory and applications* (pp. 319–340). London: Cambridge University Press.

Luecht, R. M. (2007b, October). *Multiple objective function, multiple constraint set optimization models for automated test assembly.* Invited paper presented at the Annual Meeting of International Conference on Advances in Interdisciplinary Statistics and Combinatorics, Greensboro, NC.

Luecht, R. M., Brumfield, T., and Breithaupt, K. (2006). A testlet assembly design for the uniform CPA examination. *Applied Measurement in Education, 19,* 189–202.

Luecht, R. M., & Burgin, W. (2003, April). *Test information targeting strategies for adaptive multistage testing designs.* Paper presented at the Annual Meeting of the National Council on Measurement in Education, Chicago.

Luecht, R. M., & Clauser, B. (2002). Test models for complex computer-based testing. In C. Mills, M. Potenza, J. Fremer, and W. Ward (Eds.), *Computer-based testing: Building the foundation for future assessments* (pp. 67–88). Mahwah, NJ: Erlbaum.

Luecht, R. M., Dallas, A., & Steed, T. (2010, April). *Using item templates and automated item generation principles for assessment engineering.* Invited symposium paper presented at the Annual Meeting of the National Council on Measurement in Education, Denver.

Luecht, R. M., DeChamplain, A., Nungester, R. J. (1997). Maintaining content validity in computerized adaptive testing. *Advanced in Health Sciences Education, 3,* 29–41.

Luecht, R. M., & Nungester, R. J. (1998). Some practical examples of computer-adaptive sequential testing. *Journal of Educational Measurement, 35,* 229–249.

McBride, J. R., & Martin, J. T. (1983). Reliability and validity of adaptive tests in a military setting. In D. J. Weiss (Ed.), *New Horizons in Testing* (pp. 224–236). New York: Academic Press.

Melican, G. J., Breithaupt, K., & Zhang, Y. (2010). Designing and implementing a multistage adaptive test: the Uniform CPA Exam. In W. J. van der Linden & C. E. W. Glas (Eds.), *Elements of adaptive testing* (pp. 167–189). New York: Springer.

Melnick, D. E., & Clauser, B. E. (2005). Computer-based testing for professional licensure and certification of health professions. In D. Bartram and R. K. Hambleton (Eds.), *Computer-based testing and the Internet: Issues and advances* (pp. 163–166). West Sussex, England: Wiley.

Mills, C. N., & Stocking, M. L. (1996). Practical issues in large-scale computerized adaptive testing. *Applied Measurement in Education, 9,* 287–304.

Mislevy, R. J. (1986). Bayesian modal estimation in item response models. *Psychometrika, 86,* 177–195.

Parshall, C. G., Harmes, J. C., Davey, T., & Pashley, P. J. (2010). Innovative items for computerized testing. In W. J. van der Linden & C. E. W. Glas (Eds.), *Elements of Adaptive Testing* (pp. 215–230). New York: Springer.

Revuela, J., & Ponsoda V. (1998). A comparison of item exposure control methods in computerized adaptive testing. *Journal of Educational Measurement, 35,* 311–327.

Sands, W. A., Waters, B. K., & McBride, J. R. (Eds.). (1997). *Computerized adaptive testing: From inquiry to operation.* Washington, DC: American Psychological Association.

Segall, D. O. (1996). Multidimensional adaptive testing. *Psychometrika, 61,* 331–354.

Stocking, M. L., & Lewis, C. (1995*). A new method for controlling item exposure in computerized adaptive testing (Research Rep. No. 95–25).* Princeton, NJ: Educational Testing Service.

Stocking, M. L., & Lewis, C. (1998). Controlling item exposure conditional on ability in computerized adaptive testing. *Journal of Educational and Behavioral Statistics, 23,* 57–75.

Stocking, M. L., & Lewis, C. (2000). Methods of controlling the exposure of items in CAT. In W. J. van der Linden & C. A. W. Glas (Eds.), *Computerized adaptive testing: Theory and practice* (pp. 163–182). Boston: Kluwer.

Stocking, M. L., & Swanson, L. (1993). A method for severely constrained item selection in adaptive testing. *Applied Psychological Measurement, 17,* 277–292

Swanson, L., & Stocking, M. L. (1993). A model and heuristic for solving very large item selection problems. *Applied Psychological Measurement, 17,* 151–166.

Sympson, J. B., & Hetter, R. D. (1985, October). *Controlling item exposure rates in computerized adaptive tests.* Paper presented at the Annual Conference of the Military Testing Association. San Diego, CA.

Vale, D. (1981). Design and implementation of a microcomputer-based adaptive testing system. *Behavior Research Methods and Instrumentation, 14,* 399–406.

Van der Linden, W. J. (2000). Constrained adaptive testing with shadow tests. In W. J. van der Linden & C. A. W. Glas (Eds.), *Computer-adaptive testing: Theory and practice* (pp. 27–52). Boston: Kluwer.

Van der Linden, W. J. (2005). *Linear models for optimal test design.* New York: Springer.

Van der Linden, W. J., & Glas, C. A. W. (Eds.) (2010). *Elements of adaptive testing.* New York: Springer.

Van der Linden, W. J., & Reese, L. M. (1998). A model for optimal constrained adaptive testing. *Applied Psychological Measurement, 22,* 259–270.

Wainer, H. (2000) (Ed.). *Computerized adaptive testing: A primer* (2nd ed.). Hillsdale NJ: Erlbaum.

Weiss, D. J. (1969, August-September). *Individualized assessment of differential abilities.* Paper presented at the 77th annual meeting of the American Psychological Association.

Weiss, D. J. (1975). Computerized adaptive ability measurement. *Naval Research Reviews, 28,* 1–18

Weiss, D. J. (1985). Introduction. In D. J. Weiss (Ed.), *New horizons in testing: Latent trait test theory and computerized adaptive testing* (pp. 1–8). New York: Academic Press.

Weiss, D. J., & Betz, N. E. (1973, February). *Ability measurement: Conventional or adaptive?* (Research Report 73–1). Minneapolis: University of Minnesota, Department of Psychology, Psychometric Methods Program.

Weiss, D. J., & Kingsbury, G. G. (1984). Application of computerized adaptive testing to educational problems. *Journal of Educational Measurement, 21,* 361–375

Zara, A. R. (1994, March). *An overview of the NCLEX/CAT beta test.* Paper presented at the meeting of the American Educational Research Association, New Orleans.

Zenisky, A., Hambleton, R. J., & Luecht, R. M. (2010). Multistage testing: Issues, designs, and research. In W. J. van der Linden and C. E. W. Glas (Eds.), *Elements of adaptive testing* (pp. 355–372). New York: Springer.

Zenisky, A. L., & Sireci, S. G. (2002). Technological innovations in large-scale assessments. *Applied Measurement in Education, 15,* 337–362.

Part II
Assessing Diverse Populations

6

Academic Assessment of English Language Learners
A Critical, Probabilistic, Systemic View

Guillermo Solano-Flores and Martha Gustafson

Introduction
Population Misspecification and the Definition of English Language Learners
  Inaccurate Definitions of the ELL Individual
  ELL as a Population
Measurement Error, Sampling, and the Testing of English Language Learners
  English Proficiency Assessment
  Content Assessment
  Test Review
Measurement Error and Overgeneralization in Test Adaptation for English Language Learners
  Test Translation
  Testing Accommodations
Probabilistic Approaches for Improving Assessment Systems for English Language Learners
  Assessment System Evaluation
  Testing Modeling
Conclusion

Introduction

Serving linguistically diverse populations poses a double educational challenge to countries. On one hand, substantial—and, in many cases, rapidly growing—numbers of students whose native language is not the language of instruction make it necessary for educational systems to have indicators of academic achievement based on which appropriate strategies can be devised to better serve them. On the other hand, the validity of such indicators can be compromised owing to the inevitable fact that testing depends heavily on the use of language (American Educational Research Association, American Psychological Association, & National Council on Measurement in Education, 1999).

The assessment in English of students whose first language is not English is of special interest in an era of globalization. With about 470 million of native speakers, English is not only one of the most spoken and most rapidly spreading languages in the world but also probably the language used by most people in the world as a second language. It has been estimated that the number of nonnative English speakers in the world is three times the number of native English speakers (Crystal, 2003).

Given the global trends of accountability based on test scores, it is not difficult to infer that a substantial number of students who are not native speakers of English are being and will increasingly be tested in English. Only in the United States, more than 10.7 million students (approximately 20% of the entire student population) spoke a language other than English at home during the 2005–2006 school year (KewalRamani, Gilbertson, Fox, & Provasnik, 2007). According to data published in 2002, there were nearly 4.5 million students classified as English language learners (ELLs)—students with limited proficiency in English; this number constituted 9.3% of the total enrollment of students in Pre-K through Grade 12 public schools (Kindler, 2002). In 2005, the number of students enrolled as ELL students in public schools totaled over 5 million, an increase of 84% from 1993 (Gottlieb, 2006).

It is an unfortunate fact that the number of practitioners sufficiently qualified to serve linguistically and culturally diverse students does not match this dramatic increase in the number of ELLs. Many practitioners feel unprepared to meet the academic, social, emotional, and cultural needs of these students (Albers, Hoffman, and Lundahl, 2009; Darling-Hammond, 1994). Given this serious lack of training on issues of language and linguistic diversity among the teaching force, it is not a surprise that ELLs are alarmingly overrepresented in special education programs and underrepresented in talented and gifted education programs (Harry & Klingner, 2006; Klingner & Harry, 2006). The misuse of tests plays a key role in this set of unfortunate circumstances (see Shepard, 1992).

In spite of the threats to the validity of test scores that result from testing students in a language in which they are not proficient, ELLs are included in large-scale testing programs in the United States after being schooled in English for a relatively short time (Hakuta & Beatty, 2000). Sophisticated models of adequate yearly progress have been put in place to hold schools accountable for the progress of their students, as measured by large-scale content and English language development tests (see Abedi, 2004). For many ELLs, participation in large-scale testing programs may take place at a time when, although they may have developed basic communication and interpersonal skills in English (Cummins, 1981), they are still developing the academic language in English that they need to be validly tested in English (Echevarría & Short, 2002; Hakuta, 2001).

This chapter examines the limitations of current practices in the assessment of ELLs and discusses the actions that assessment systems should take if they are to ensure valid and fair testing for ELLs.[1] Although the chapter draws mostly on research generated in the United States, the experience discussed is relevant to other cultural and national contexts. The chapter contends that the mandatory inclusion of ELLs in large-scale testing programs should be matched by significant improvements in the ways in which language is treated as a source of measurement error. Testing practices concerning these students are essentially the same as the practices in use before their inclusion in large-scale testing became mandatory in the United States. Lack of defensibility of some practices and lack of fidelity in the implementation of defensible practices keep posing a limit to fair and valid assessment for ELLs.

Our discussion addresses the implications of testing in an era of accountability (see Linn, Baker, & Betebenner, 2002; Sloane & Kelly, 2003). We contend that, in order to properly implement standards for educational accountability systems (see Baker, Linn, Herman, & Koretz, 2002; Hamilton & Koretz, 2002) and basic principles of equity, evaluation, and monitoring in assessment systems (see Black & William, 2007; Wilson & Bertenthal, 2006), it is necessary to examine in detail the extent to which assessment systems address the complexity of language and ELL populations. We argue that the interpretation of the validity of measures of academic achievement for ELLs should take into consideration how effectively assessment systems deal with three sources of randomness in the assessment of ELLs: the misspecification of ELL populations, measurement error that results from the inappropriateness or the improper implementation of actions intended to address language issues, and the overgeneralization of findings from research on ELLs (Solano-Flores, 2009).

Our perspective can be described as critical, probabilistic, and systemic. *Critical* refers to the fact that we discuss how testing practices concerning language and ELLs are based on views of language that are not defensible according to knowledge from the language sciences—mainly, sociolinguistics and the disciplines that specialize in the study of language development and second language acquisition. *Probabilistic* refers to the notion that, rather than being static, languages are dynamic and linguistic groups are unstable, and the notion that language proficiency is shaped by multiple factors that cannot be properly described by categories such as *English proficient* or *limited English proficient*. *Systemic* refers to the fact that assessment systems take actions that are consistent with knowledge from the language sciences and with a probabilistic view of language and language groups.

This chapter is divided in four sections. The first discusses why current testing policies and practices cannot produce valid measures of student achievement if ELLs are not properly characterized. We discuss what an ELL is from the perspective of bilingualism as both an individual and a population—a distinction not clearly reflected in current approaches to ELL testing. Views of students as either proficient or limited proficient in English are not sensitive to the wide variety of patterns of language dominance among ELLs.

The second section examines how, in order to ensure valid and fair testing for ELLs, appropriate samples of these students should be included in the entire process of test development. Three aspects of assessment are considered: English proficiency assessment, content assessment, and test review.

The third section examines a common practice in ELL testing—adapting tests originally developed for a mainstream population. Although this practice is not necessarily wrong, its effectiveness greatly depends on the accuracy of the assumptions about the characteristics of ELL populations, the defensibility of the adaptations of tests, and the fidelity with which these adaptations are implemented.

The fourth section submits that the validity of measures of ELL academic achievement is linked to the capacity of assessment systems to address randomness and develop testing models consistent with basic principles about language and the nature of linguistic groups. We submit the notion that, as a step toward ensuring fair and valid testing for ELLs, assessment systems should be evaluated based on the extent to which their actions are consistent with these principles.

The chapter ends with a short summary and a reflection on the future use of our critical, probabilistic, systemic perspective in large-scale testing for ELLs.

Population Misspecification and the Definition of English Language Learners

An important challenge in ELL testing is population misspecification, which takes place when assessment systems fail to produce accurate, dependable information about ELLs that is relevant to obtaining valid measures of language proficiency (Solano-Flores, 2009). Two aspects need to be considered: how ELLs are defined and how they are viewed as a population.

Inaccurate Definitions of the ELL Individual

There is no simple definition of "English language learner." La Celle-Peterson and Rivera (1994) state that the term "refers to students whose first language is not English, and encompasses both students who are just beginning to learn English (often referred to as 'limited English proficient' or 'LEP') and those who have already developed considerable proficiency" (p. 75). The same authors point at the complex profile of ELL students and recognize that although all ELLs have in common the need to increase their proficiency in English, "they differ in language, cultural background, and family history" (p. 58).

Legal definitions reflect an attempt to capture this heterogeneity. Thus, the No Child Left Behind Act defines "limited English proficient" as a person whose "difficulties in speaking, reading, writing, or understanding the English language may be sufficient to deny the individual…the ability to successfully achieve in classrooms where the language of instruction is English" as part of the definition of ELL (No Child Left Behind Act of 2001).

The definition also has a strong operational component. It refers to the fact that those difficulties may deny the individual "the ability to meet the State's proficient level of achievement on State assessments" and to demographic factors that are associated but do not determine being an ELL (e.g., migratory status, first language). Moreover, the definition states that a LEP may be an individual "who comes from an environment where a language other than English has had a significant impact on the individual's level of English language proficiency"—which, against current knowledge on bilingual development (see Baker, 2006; Bialystok, 2001; Brown, 2007), wrongly implies that continuing developing their first language prevents bilingual individuals from developing a second language.

A definition like this is likely to render many false-negative and false-positive classifications of students as ELLs because it attempts to characterize each individual based on generalizations about populations, some of which are not necessarily relevant to language (Saunders & O'Brien, 2006). Missing in current approaches to defining ELLs is a view that recognizes the complexity of bilingualism and that allows the examination of ELLs as both individuals and populations.

ELL as a Population

Linguagrams come in handy to illustrate the complexity of bilingualism. They show that language variation is critical to understanding ELLs and properly addressing their needs (see Solano-Flores & Trumbull, 2008; Solano-Flores & Li, 2008). Linguagrams are back-to-back bar graphs that represent an individual's use of two languages for each of the four language modes: listening (L), speaking (S), reading (R), and writing (W) (Figure 6.1).

Representing language use in both the individual's first language (L1) and second language (L2) is consistent with the notion that, in bilingual individuals, L1 and L2 constitute one language system, not two separate language systems (Grosjean, 1989). The length of a bar to the left and to the right shows the level of proficiency, respectively, in the native language and in English

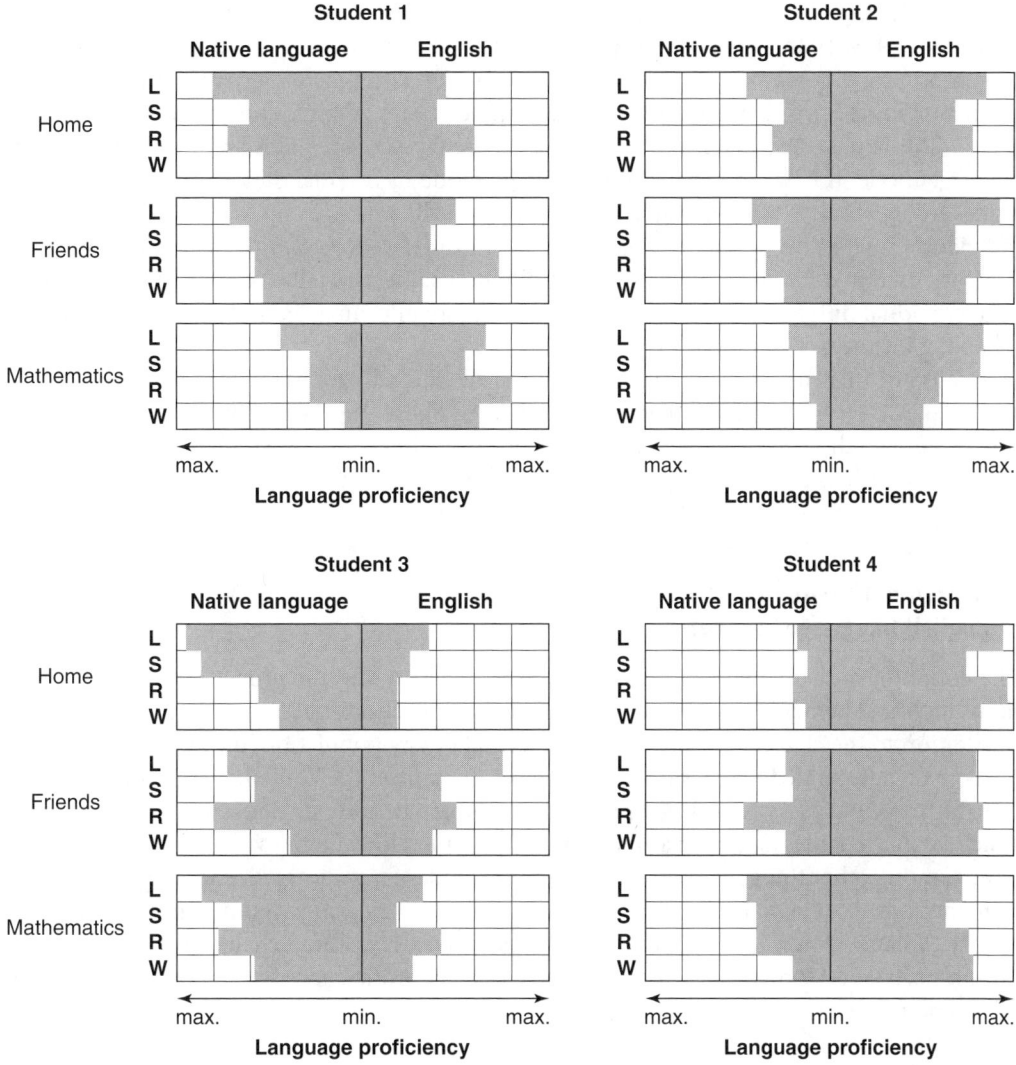

Figure 6.1 Linguagrams of Four Hypothetical ELL Students

for a given language mode. For the sake of simplicity, "proficiency" is used here broadly—it does not necessarily imply a measure from English proficiency tests.

The linguagrams shown in Figure 6.1 illustrate notions that have been well known in the field of bilingual development and sociolinguistics for a good number of years. First, bilingual individuals have different patterns of language dominance (Bialystok, 2002), as reflected by the fact that their linguagrams are different. Second, rarely are bilingual individuals equally proficient in their two languages (Mackey, 1962), as reflected by the fact that the lengths of the bars are asymmetrical across languages. Third, contrary to the image evoked by the terms *English language learner* and *limited English proficient*—an individual with a near to null proficiency in English—ELL individuals are not necessarily more proficient in their native language than in English for a given language mode. This is reflected by the fact that the bars on the left side of their linguagrams are not always longer than the bars on the right side. Fourth, within the same language, the level of proficiency of a given individual is not the same across language modes (Grosjean, 1985, 1989). This is reflected by the fact that the bars on the same side of the linguagrams have different lengths across language modes. Fifth, the pattern of proficiency of any given individual across language and language modes varies with the context in which language is used (Romaine, 1995; Wei, 2000). ELLs have different sets of strengths and weaknesses in each language mode in L1 as well as in each language mode in L2 (Bialystok, 2001; Genesee, 1994; Valdés & Figueroa, 1994). This variation results from differences in the ways in which bilingual individuals interact in different social contexts (Fishman, 1965) and the specialization of the language used in different contexts and with different subjects (Halliday, 1978, 1993). There are also individual differences in the development of academic language stemming from different schooling histories (Cummins, 1999, 2000, 2003).

Because of this variation, no single definition of ELL will apply to all individuals who are accessing ELL service in public schools in the United States. Yet the responsibility and expectation of public school systems is to meet the educational needs of all students, including those learning English as a second language. Meeting this responsibility is dependent upon a sound assessment system and testing practices for ELL students.

Measurement Error, Sampling, and the Testing of English Language Learners

The notion of measurement error is critical to test validity and the proper sample of observations that must be made in order to make valid generalizations of test scores (see Kane, 1982). In addition to the challenges inherent to the testing of any population, the assessment of ELLs poses challenges related to measurement error resulting from the limited capacity of assessment systems to address the vastness of language as a domain of competencies, the multiple ways in which language issues can be examined, and the tremendous linguistic diversity of ELLs that stems, among other things, from the fact that each student has a unique schooling history (e.g., in monolingual, bilingual, or second language education programs) and a unique migration history (Solano-Flores, 2009). In this section, we discuss how those challenges are reflected in three aspects of the process of ELL assessment: English proficiency assessment, content assessment, and test review.

English Proficiency Assessment

Tests of English proficiency have been used for a long time with ELLs. Also for a long time, concerns have been raised about the validity of the measures they produce. One of these concerns involves the multiplicity of conceptual frameworks used to construct such tests and the fact that they render very different classifications of students (see Del Vecchio & Guerrero, 1995). Another concern is that, in many cases, the process of test development is not well documented or has flaws in the procedures of student sampling and test review and validation that are used (General Accounting Office, 2006; Rabinowitz & Sato, 2006). Yet another concern is that many tests of English proficiency address isolated aspects of language (García, McKoon, & August, 2006).

Test developers have focused more on superficial aspects of English proficiency. For example, of the 213 commercially available and researcher-developed English proficiency tests examined by García and colleagues (2006), 36% focused on phonemics and phonemic awareness, 37% focused on reading comprehension, 24% focused on vocabulary, and less than 3% focused on pragmatics, morphology, or discourse.

As a result of the No Child Left Behind legislation in the United States, states are required to establish annual measurable achievement outcomes and use large-scale tests to assess English proficiency in ELLs. These tests are aligned with academic content standards, including English language arts, and are indexed to grade level, which allows examination of the growth in language proficiency for the purpose of school accountability (see Abedi, 2007).

In spite of the fact that they share multiple commonalities, developing a second language and learning a foreign language should not be seen as involving the same process (Brown, 2007; Shin, 2004). Failure to properly address this difference may lead to emphasizing formal aspects of language (e.g., spelling, pronunciation) over functional aspects of communication (see Trumbull & Farr, 2005) and a view of the English language as subject matter rather than a competency.

Because of the conceptual limitations of restricted categories of English proficiency, there is an urgent need for improved ways of classifying ELLs (Abedi, 2008). As mentioned before, many tests of English proficiency have been questioned because of poor documentation of the process of test development and validation. In addition, some English proficiency tests have been questioned for not reflecting currently accepted theories of second language development (MacSwan, Rolstad, & Glass, 2002; MacSwan & Rolstad, 2003). Also, in spite of the fact that English proficiency tests measure different aspects of language (García et al., 2006), rarely are they used in combination to make more informed ELL classifications.

Content Assessment

As test developers know, the development of tests is an iterative process in which items are reviewed, tried out with pilot students, and revised several times. Issues of language are of paramount importance in this process regardless of whether the target population of students is linguistically diverse or homogeneous. Many of the modifications made on items during this process have to do with refining the wording of the items in order to ensure that students interpret them as intended (Solano-Flores & Shavelson, 1997). How the language needs to be refined is determined by examining the students' written responses to the items, through cognitive interviews, or from inferring thinking processes based on students' think-aloud protocols (Linn, 2006).

Although *inclusion* is frequently used to describe the policy suggesting that ELLs be tested in English along with their native English-speaking counterparts (e.g., Thurlow, Thompson, & Lazarus, 2006), the use of the term has not been extended to promote practices that ensure the participation of ELLs in the process of test development. As discussed in the previous subsection, it is inappropriate to characterize ELLs as individuals who have null communication skills in English. Therefore it is inaccurate to assume that these students cannot provide valuable information for refining the wording of items (Solano-Flores & Trumbull, 2008). Although the current standards for educational and psychological testing (American Educational Research Association et al., 1999) state that procedures used to select the samples of test takers should be documented when tryouts and filed tests are conducted (p. 44), including appropriate samples of ELLs in the process of test development does not seem to be established as part of what counts as acceptable practice. Key documents such as assessment frameworks and item specifications for large-scale assessment do not provide detailed guidance or requirements on the types and sizes of samples of ELLs that should be included in this process.

First language and culture may be important influences shaping the ways in which students interpret test items (Lee, 2005; Luyks, Lee, Mahotiere, Lester, Hart, & Deaktor, 2007; Solano-Flores & Trumbull, 2003; Solano-Flores & Li, 2009; Trumbull, Greenfield, & Quiroz, 2004). Not

> José ate ½ of a pizza.
>
> Ella ate ½ of another pizza.
>
> José said that he ate more pizza than Ella, but Ella said they both ate the same amount. Use words and pictures to show that José could be right.

Figure 6.2 An Example of an Item Whose Linguistic Features May Be Biased Against ELL Students
Source: National Assessment of Educational Progress (1996). Mathematics items public release. Washington, DC: Author.

including ELLs in the samples of students who participate in the process of test development may result in biased linguistic features against these students. For example, the item shown in Figure 6.2 may not have been tried out with a sufficiently representative number of ELLs—native Spanish speakers—who constitute 79% of the ELL population in the United States (Payán & Nettles, 2008). Some native Spanish speakers might experience difficulty in making sense of the second sentence of the item, trying to figure out who "she" is in the second sentence, since in Spanish *ella* is the pronoun *she*, not a person's name.

Test Review

The wide variety of existing procedures and criteria for test review (Hambleton & Rodgers, 1995; Zieky, 2006) speaks to the complexity of language and the fact that, whereas nobody contests the notion that the linguistic features of items should be examined, no standard practice exists on the specific aspects of language that need to be considered, the depth with which language issues should be examined, the sources of information that need to be used to examine the linguistic properties of items, and what constitutes fairness. Evidence from both the context of testing across linguistic groups in international test comparisons and the testing of ELL students underscores the effect of item wording on differential item functioning (e.g., Allalouf, Hambleton, & Sireci, 1999; Ercikan, 1998; Gierl & Khaliq, 2001) and the value of using judgmental and empirical review methods in combination to assess the linguistic appropriateness of test items (Hambleton & Jones, 1994; Solano-Flores, Backhoff, & Contreras-Niño, 2009).

The Lunch Money item (National Assessment of Educational Progress, 1996) illustrates the notion that different sources of information need to be used in combination in order to properly examine the linguistic features of items. There is evidence that this item poses a wide variety of linguistic challenges to students from different linguistic backgrounds (Solano-Flores & Trumbull, 2003). Also, there is evidence that students from different cultural groups relate the content of this item to their personal experiences in different ways (Solano-Flores & Li, 2009). As Figure 6.3 and Table 6.1 show, judgmental review does not render information entirely consistent with empirical information on the linguistic challenges of test items. The table summarizes the results of an investigation on the effectiveness of teachers' judgments as an approach to detecting potential sources of language bias (Solano-Flores, Li, & Sexton, 2004). Thirty-four teachers from different cultural and linguistic backgrounds who taught linguistically and culturally diverse students were asked to identify features of the item that could prevent their students from interpreting it correctly. At the same time, those teachers' students were asked to read the item aloud and respond to it.

Table 6.1 Judgmental and Empirical Evidence of Language Bias in the Lunch Money Item

		Judgmental Review	Empirical Review	
Potential sources of bias identified in a previous investigation (Solano-Flores & Trumbull, 2003)		Anticipated by at least 20% of teachers	Observed in at least 20% of students' read aloud or written responses	Statistically significant differences between groups alpha=.05
Vocabulary	"purchase" is unfamiliar to students	No	Yes	Yes
	"least" is unfamiliar to students	Yes	Yes	No
Syntax	"$1.00 bills" in "His mother has only $1.00 bills" may be difficult to read	No	Yes[a]	Yes
	"$1.00 bills" in "What is the least number of $1.00 bills…" may be difficult to read	No	Yes[b]	Yes
Semantics	"only" may be difficult to interpret as restricting the number of dollar denominations	No	Yes[c]	Yes
Pragmatics	Sentence 4 may be interpreted as, "How much money does Sam need?"	Yes	Yes[d]	No

Source: Solano-Flores, Li, & Sexton (2004).
[a] As reflected by the analysis of errors made by students in sentence 3 while reading the item aloud.
[b] As reflected by the analysis of errors made by students in sentence 4 while reading the item aloud.
[c] Students misinterpreted *only* as restricting the number of dollar bills (*one dollar bill*), or as restricting the number of dollars (*one dollar*).
[d] As reflected by the strategies used by students to solve the problem in their written responses (e.g., giving up on lunch items, adding up to the total for one day; adding up to the total without rounding).

Errors made by the students in their read-alouds and written responses were examined to determine the extent to which they reflected the set of linguistic challenges identified in a previous investigation (Solano-Flores & Trumbull, 2003). As a criterion for gauging the effectiveness of the judgmental review, 20% was established as the minimal percentage of teachers that should be able to identify those linguistic challenges. Also, two criteria were used to gauge the weight of empirical evidence of the linguistic challenges: whether at least 20% of the students' read-alouds and written responses reflected those linguistic challenges and whether statistically significant differences between groups were observed in the frequencies of those errors.

As Table 6.1 shows, four of the six potential sources of bias were not detected by at least 20% of the teachers, and no statistically significant differences between groups were observed for the two issues identified by at least 20% of the teachers. These results are consistent with other evidence on the accuracy of teachers' judgments of test items. Culturally and linguistically diverse teachers (i.e., those who belong to nonmainstream cultural groups themselves, whose first language is not English, and/or who have experience teaching in culturally and linguistically diverse students) are more aware than mainstream teachers or teachers who teach only mainstream students of the importance of language and culture as factors shaping the performance of linguistic

> [1]Sam can purchase his lunch at school. [2]Each day he wants to have juice that costs 50¢, a sandwich that cost 90¢, and fruit that costs 35¢. [3]His mother has only $1.00 bills. [4]What is the least number of $1.00 bills that his mother should give him so he will have enough money to buy lunch for 5 days?

Figure 6.3 The Lunch Money Item
Superscripts indicate the four sentences of the item.
Source: National Assessment of Educational Progress (1996). Mathematics items public release. Washington, DC: Author.

or cultural minority students on tests or their learning in class. However, the two kinds of teachers do not differ significantly in the level of detail or accuracy with which they identify the specific aspects of test items or classroom situations that need to be improved in order to ensure cultural appropriateness (Nguyen-Le, 2010; Sexton & Solano-Flores, 2001). The use of teachers in the process of test review is necessary but not sufficient to ensure proper identification of the linguistic features of items that may pose serious challenges to ELLs. More sophisticated test review approaches need to be used that allow detailed examination of those linguistic features of items based on combining judgmental and empirical test review procedures.

Measurement Error and Overgeneralization in Test Adaptation for English Language Learners

As discussed above, a great deal of measurement error in ELL testing is closely related to how effectively assessment systems address the vastness of language as a domain of competencies, the tremendous linguistic diversity of ELL populations, and the multiple ways in which language issues can be examined. In this section, we discuss how multiple sources of measurement error can result from actions intended to address issues of language in the testing of ELLs when those actions are not properly implemented. We also discuss how failure to recognize the contextual factors that shape the effectiveness of those actions may lead to overgeneralization (Solano-Flores, 2009). We focus on translation and testing accommodations as forms of test adaptation that can constitute unintended sources of measurement error if they are not properly employed. Although test translations are usually considered as a special case of testing accommodations (e.g., National Center for Education Statistics, 2009), the two forms of test adaptation are discussed separately. This allows for a more detailed discussion of test translation.

Test Translation

Important improvements in the methods of test translation have been made in recent years that are oriented to ensuring that meaning and the constructs measured by test items are preserved in different languages (Cook & Schmitt-Cascallar, 2005; Grisay, 2003; Harkness, 2003; Sireci, Patsula, & Hambleton, 2005). However, these advances are the result of increased experience from testing students across languages in international comparisons, such as the Trends in Mathematics and Science Study (TIMSS), rather than improved approaches in ELL testing.

How effective these improved methods are in ensuring fair and valid testing for ELLs largely depends on the accuracy of the assumptions about the characteristics of the populations tested. Substantial differences between ELLs and students who participate in international test comparisons must be considered. Students who participate in international comparisons are given tests in their first language, which is also the language of their instruction. In contrast, the language in which ELLs are tested when they are given a translation is not necessarily the language in which they have been schooled. Unless ELLs are in bilingual programs or programs in which instruction is provided in their first language, the academic language of the subject of the tests may be unfamiliar to them.

Giving ELLs translated tests in L1 assumes that ELLs are more proficient in this language than in English. This assumption may be an erroneous assumption for many students because, as discussed above, every ELL has a unique pattern of language dominance. Indeed, there is evidence that, when ELLs are given the same set of items in both L1 and L2, a considerable percentage of the score variation observed is due to the interaction of student, item, and language (Solano-Flores & Li, 2006, 2008). In addition to varying on their knowledge of the subject tested, ELLs have different sets of strengths and weaknesses in both L1 and L2, and items pose different sets of linguistic challenges in each language.

Testing policies that allow the testing of students in their first language do not pay much attention to linguistic variation due to dialect. Against conventional wisdom, dialects are not corrupted forms of a language but different forms of the same language. Also against conventional wisdom, everybody uses dialects of their language, and no dialect is better or more logical than other dialects (Wolfram, Adger, & Christian, 1999). Translated tests used in ELL testing use the standard dialect of the students' first language, but that standard dialect is the most prestigious dialect, not the dialect that most students use or understand (Solano-Flores, 2006). As with testing across languages, there is evidence that, if students are given the same set of items in both the standard dialect version of their first language and the local dialect version of their first language, a considerable percentage of the score variation observed will be due to the interaction of student, item, and dialect (Solano-Flores & Li, 2006, 2008, 2009).

Effective approaches to addressing dialect variation may be developed in the future based on the notion of localization, or modification of the characteristics of the language used in the tests based on the characteristics of the local dialects used. However, these approaches may be difficult to accept because of the logistical challenges they pose to assessment systems, as they require the participation of educators who modify the wording of the items based on their knowledge of the language used in each school community (Solano-Flores, Li, Speroni, Rodriguez, Basterra, & Dovholuk, 2007).

Since translation tends to change the constructs measured by test items (Ercikan, Gierl, McCreith, Puhan, & Koh, 2004; Sireci & Allalouf, 2003), the complexity of translating tests and the time needed to do it properly should not be underestimated (see Stansfield, 2003). Test translation should be thought of as an endeavor that goes far beyond simply rewriting tests in another language (see Hambleton, Merenda, & Spielberger, 2005). It should include, as with the process of development of any test, several review-revision iterations in which the wording of items is refined based on trying them out with pilot students.

Tight time lines for test translation and limited or null opportunity for piloting and refining the wording of translated items affect fairness and validity in ELL testing. Yet some assessment systems may not have the expertise needed to properly translate tests for ELLs (General Accounting Office, 2006) or do not have clear translation procedures in place. For example, although the National Assessment of Educational Progress (NAEP) authorizes the use of bilingual versions of tests for ELLs (National Center for Education Statistics, 2009), it does not specify the characteristics of the process of translation that states should use or the qualifications that test translators should have.

Testing Accommodations

Testing accommodations have become critical as part of the actions intended to minimize the effect of language proficiency as a source of construct-irrelevant variance.

> Accommodations for ELLs involve changes to testing procedures, testing materials, or the testing situation in order to allow students meaningful participation in an assessment. Effective accommodations for ELLs address the unique linguistic and sociocultural needs of the student without altering the test construct. Accommodated scores should be sufficiently equivalent in scale that they can be pooled with unaccommodated scores. (Rivera, Acosta, & Shafer Willner, 2008, p. 2)

Practically every state assessment system uses a set of testing accommodations for ELLs (see Abedi, 2004; Rivera & Collum, 2006). In their analysis of testing accommodations used in the United States, Rivera and associates list dozens of accommodations used by state assessment systems with ELLs (Rivera, Collum, Willner, & Sia, 2006; see also Stansfield & Bowles, 2006). Some of these accommodations are questionable and could be described as bizarre (e.g., enhanced lighting conditions, large font size); others are vaguely stated and may be interpreted in multiple ways (e.g., preferential seating); others operate on factors that are only indirectly related to language (e.g., allowing additional time for completing the test) (see Abedi, Lord, & Hofstetter, 1998); and others are unlikely to be implemented with the same fidelity by different educators or to benefit all ELLs (e.g., providing directions in the students' native language) (see Solano-Flores, 2008). Not surprisingly, accommodations with little empirical or theoretical support or those borrowed from the field of special education are ineffective (see Abedi, Hofstetter, & Lord, 2004; Kopriva, Emick, Hipólito-Delgado, & Cameron, 2007).

In examining the effectiveness of testing accommodations, researchers need to ensure that they do not alter the construct that test items are intended to measure and that they do not give unfair advantage to students who receive accommodations over those who do not. The typical research design used in this field includes four groups of students: ELLs who receive and who do not receive the accommodation and non-ELLs who receive and who do not receive the accommodation. A powerful case for the effectiveness of an accommodation is that in which ELLs who receive the accommodation perform better than ELLs who do not receive the accommodation, but the performance of non-ELLs who receive the accommodation is comparable to the performance of non-ELLs who do not receive the accommodation (see the reviews by Abedi et al., 2004; and Sireci, Li, & Scarpati, 2003).

A growing body of research shows that extended time for completing the test and some forms of accommodation that provide direct linguistic support (including glossary and English dictionary, side-by-side dual-language tests, and the linguistic simplification of items) have positive effects for ELLs (Abedi, Courtney, Mirocha, Leon, & Goldberg, 2001; Abedi & Hejri, 2004; Abedi, Lord, Hofstetter, & Baker, 2001; Pennock-Roman & Rivera, 2007). However, the effectiveness of these accommodations is shaped by the students' language backgrounds.

The versatility of computer technology makes it possible to effectively implement some forms of testing accommodations that have existed for a long time but are difficult to implement. A case in point is the use of English dictionaries. As with many forms of accommodation, the effectiveness of this accommodation greatly depends on the accuracy of the assumptions made about the linguistic skills of ELLs (Solano-Flores, 2008). In the case of dictionaries and glossaries, the assumption is that the students who receive this accommodation have the metacognitive skills needed to identify the terms whose meaning they do not know and the alphabetical searching abilities needed to effectively find those terms.

Computer testing allows the provision of this form of accommodation without the potential interference of alphabetical searching skills as a confounding factor. Abedi (2009) investigated the effectiveness of computer-administered tests with a pop-up glossary, "a feature that provided a simple gloss of a word with the touch of the (mouse) pointer" (p. 198). He found evidence that computer administration with a pop-up glossary was an effective form of accommodation for ELLs. However, the degree of effectiveness varied with the grade of the students and the linguistic complexity of the items—which is consistent with the notion, discussed above, that the effectiveness of testing accommodations is shaped by multiple linguistic factors.

Substantial improvements in the ways in which testing accommodations are designed and used will need to take place before they are substantially more effective in ensuring fair and valid testing for ELLs. Research in the field has focused on identifying those accommodations that are most effective by examining score differences between ELLs and non-ELLs who receive and do not receive a given form of accommodation. Whereas this research can generate valuable knowledge on the broad properties and possibilities of different forms of accommodations, the extent to which its findings can be generalized is limited by the tremendous heterogeneity of ELL populations. Concluding that a certain form of accommodation is effective with all ELLs just because it has been found to be effective with a certain group of ELLs is a form of overgeneralization that may limit the possibilities for more valid testing. The development of theoretical frameworks that allow proper interpretation and generalization of findings from research and a more systematic process of selection and use of accommodations are among the improvements that need to take place.

Research by Kopriva and associates (e.g., Kopriva, Wiley, Chen, Levy, Winter, & Corliss, 2004; Kopriva, Koran, & Hedgspeth, 2007) shows that, in order for testing accommodations to effectively abate the effect of limited proficiency in the language of testing, each ELL student needs to receive a set of accommodation that matches his or her specific linguistic needs (see also Sireci & Pitoniak, 2007). However, scores from English proficiency tests do not provide information with the level of detail needed to determine the specific needs of each ELL student that would make it possible to determine the best set of accommodation.

STELLA, a sophisticated computerized accommodation taxonomy analytical tool for gathering and processing information on the linguistic proficiency of ELL students, holds promise as a resource for meeting this need (Kopriva et al., 2007). However, costs and practical constraints may limit its use with large populations of ELLs in the near future. In addition, even if this tool were to provide educators with individual detailed information on English proficiency, schools and assessment systems may not have the resources to properly provide each student with the best set of testing accommodations.

New forms of accommodation may be developed in the future from approaches that pay attention to nontextual elements of test items. These new approaches are consistent with the notion that reading involves the interaction of image and text (see Eisner, 1994), that literacy is more than mere reading and writing, and that it involves the visual mode of representation (Cope & Kalantzis, 2000). Martiniello (2009) notes that work that examines the linguistic complexity of mathematics test items has overlooked the importance of nontextual elements, such as graphs, diagrams, equations, and other representations. She examined the impact of those elements on the relationship between differential item functioning and the linguistic complexity of mathematics items. She observed that, for certain grades and for certain levels of linguistic complexity, schematic representations had an attenuating effect on the difficulty parameter estimates favoring non-ELL students over ELL students.

Consistent with a view that examines the interaction of text and image, vignette illustrations have been proposed as a form of testing accommodation for ELLs (Solano-Flores, 2010). Unlike visual representations included in test items as part of the information provided for students to solve problems, vignette illustrations are pictorial supports added to test items in order to illustrate certain contextual information or certain noncontent lexicons that may be unfamiliar to ELLs. A procedure for designing vignette illustrations has been developed based on cognitive psychology, semiotics, and sociocultural theory. The procedure prescribes careful discussion among test developers of the potential linguistic challenges that a given test item may pose to ELLs; this allows them to identify the intended functions that the illustration should serve to make the item accessible to students and provides a grammar of visual constituents for specifying the properties of the illustration.

Adequate conceptual frameworks need to be developed to identify how nontextual representations must be designed in order to constitute effective accommodations. For example, there is evidence that different nontextual features of mathematical items have a different load on their academic language. We (Solano-Flores & Prosser, 2009) compared the linguistic features of test items developed to assess mathematical knowledge and the mathematical academic language in ELLs (see Clarke, 2007). We observed that different categories of academic language features appeared with significantly different frequencies in the two types of items. Proportionally, mathematical knowledge items had more symbolic and visual features than mathematical language items. In contrast, mathematical language items had more lexical and analytical features and features that had to do with the use of testing register and mathematical discourse.

Probabilistic Approaches for Improving Assessment Systems for English Language Learners

In this section, we discuss two aspects that, from a probabilistic perspective, are critical to ensuring fair and valid testing for ELLs. One aspect is the capacity of assessment systems to deal with randomness. The other aspect is the capacity of assessment systems to model testing in order to make appropriate decisions about the ways in which different groups of ELLs should be tested.

Assessment System Evaluation

Throughout this chapter we have discussed how the validity of test scores for ELLs is threatened by the misspecification of ELL populations, measurement error that results from the inappropriateness or the poor implementation of actions intended to address language issues, and the overgeneralization of findings from research on ELL testing. These threats to validity are illustrated in Table 6.2. They can be thought of as sources of randomness in the process of ELL testing (Solano-Flores, 2009). Measures of academic achievement for ELLs are valid to the extent to which these sources of randomness are minimized. Following these reasonings, we argue that proper interpretation of the validity of measures of academic achievement for ELLs cannot take place without taking into consideration how effectively assessment systems deal with these three sources of randomness. Accordingly, evaluating the capacity of assessment systems to deal with randomness in the process of ELL testing is critical to ensuring fair and valid testing for these students.

Conceptually, the effectiveness of an assessment system concerning ELL testing can be thought of as a coefficient, e, that ranges between 0 and 1 and is defined by the extent to which it minimizes randomness (r) due to population misspecification, measurement error, and overgeneralization:

$$e = 1 - r \tag{1}$$

Table 6.2 Examples of Sources of Randomness in the Testing of ELLs

Population misspecification
- Using inaccurate definitions of ELLs
- Identifying students as ELLs based on tests of English proficiency that measure isolated aspects of language
- Failing to examine ELLs as a bilingual population and to address the social and dynamic aspects of language

Measurement error
- Using inaccurate measures of English proficiency that render different classifications of students
- Failing to ensure the use of appropriate samples of ELLs in the process of test development
- Using questionable testing accommodations or improperly implementing certain testing accommodations
- Using test review procedures that examine superficial aspects of language and potential linguistic challenges for ELL students

Overgeneralization
- Concluding that evidence on the effectiveness of a form of testing accommodation (e.g., *allowing extra time for completing a test has a positive effect in the performance of ELLs*) applies to all ELLs students without proper consideration of language background, schooling history, and cultural and contextual factors that may shape its effectiveness.

Table 6.3 presents eight dimensions that can be used to examine the effectiveness with which assessment systems address randomness in the process of ELL testing. The table should be regarded as a list of examples rather than a complete system of evaluation dimensions. The sources of information for evaluating assessment systems are multiple; they may include surveys, documents, direct observation, cross-examination, and studies that probe the effectiveness of the actions taken by the assessment system.

As an example of studies that probe the effectiveness of assessment systems concerning ELL testing, suppose that we are interested in determining the accuracy of ELL classifications made by an assessment system to decide when students should be tested in English. To this end, we perform an external classification of a sample of students from the population served by the assessment system. Unlike the classification made by the assessment system, in this external classification, students are identified as ELLs or non-ELLs based on measures from multiple tests of English proficiency used in combination. Since the external classification uses many more measures of English proficiency than the assessment system's classification, we assume that the external classification is more accurate.

To evaluate the accuracy of the classifications produced by the assessment system, we construct a confusion matrix—a table that compares the frequencies of cases classified consistently and inconsistently by the two classification systems (see Kohavi & Provost, 1998). As Table 6.4 shows, in our confusion matrix, a and d are the numbers of accurate classifications and b and c are the numbers of false-negative and false-positive cases of ELL classifications produced by the assessment system.

A series of coefficients can be readily computed that express the level of accuracy or inaccuracy of the classifications rendered by the assessment system or the proportion of false-negative and false-positive classifications produced. For example, a coefficient of classification accuracy, u, can be computed as the proportion of correct classifications relative to the total number of classifications:

$$u = \frac{a + d}{a + b + c + d} \tag{2}$$

Pray's (2005) study of the classifications produced by three tests commonly used to measure oral English proficiency in ELLs also illustrates the kind of studies that can be performed to

Table 6.3 Dimensions for Evaluating ELL Large-Scale Assessment Systems

Defensibility. The assessment system uses information on ELLs that is relevant to the condition of being an ELL according to current knowledge in the language sciences (mainly, sociolinguistics and the disciplines that specialize in the study of language development and second language acquisition).
- *Does the information on the students' language proficiency minimize false-positive and false-negative ELL classifications?*
- *Does the information collected on students reflect a view of English proficiency as a difference rather than a deficiency?*

Sensitivity. The assessment system uses information on language proficiency that allows examination of differences between ELLs and non-ELLs, between subgroups within the ELL population tested, and between individuals within broad linguistic groups of ELLs.
- *Are local dialect differences considered in the process of ELL testing adaptation?*
- *Are the linguistic features of tests aligned with the register and language used in the enacted curriculum?*

Sufficiency. The assessment system uses information on language proficiency that is critical to the condition of being ELL.
- *Are categories of English proficiency based on comprehensive information on the listening, speaking, reading, and writing skills?*
- *Is language proficiency in both L1 and L2 used to make decisions about the ways in which ELLs are to be tested?*

Certainty. The assessment system uses appropriate information that substantiates assumptions about the characteristics of the individuals involved in the process of ELL testing and the conditions in which testing take place.
- *What evidence exists that the individuals who develop, adapt, and translate tests for ELLs have adequate linguistic competencies?*
- *What evidence exists that the individuals who administer tests and implement testing accommodations for ELLs have adequate linguistic competencies?*

Inclusiveness. The activities performed by the assessment system are designed and implemented in ways that ensure the participation of ELLs.
- *How properly are ELLs represented as pilot students in the process of test development?*
- *Is the format of tests designed in ways that allow future possible adaptation for ELLs?*

Relevance. The actions taken by the assessment system concerning the testing of ELLs address aspects that are relevant to the condition of being ELL.
- *Are the testing accommodations used sensitive to each ELL student's particular listening, speaking, reading, and writing proficiency in L1 or in L2?*
- *How strong is the evidence that supports the forms of testing accommodation used?*

Control. The assessment system has appropriate mechanisms in place to ensure proper implementation of procedures concerning ELL testing.
- *How effectively does the assessment system communicate with school administrators and educators regarding the testing of ELLs?*
- *Do educators in charge of administering tests receive the training needed to appropriately provide testing accommodations for ELLs?*

Consistency. The procedures used by the assessment system to test ELLs are implemented in the same way and with the same level of quality for all students across classrooms and schools.
- *Are the testing accommodations implemented properly by all schools?*
- *Do all educators in charge of administering tests receive the same kind of training to provide testing accommodations for ELLs?*

Table 6.4 Confusion Matrix for Assessing the Accuracy of Classifications of Students as ELLs or Non-ELLs

		Classification Performed by the Assessment System	
		ELL	English proficient
External classification: multiple measures of English proficiency	ELL	a	b
	English proficient	c	d

probe the accuracy of ELL student classifications. Pray gave these tests to native English speakers and found that not all of them scored at the advanced level in spite of the fact that native English proficiency was used as the standard to assess English proficiency in ELLs. Although the statistical power of Pray's study is limited by the small size of the samples of participants used, it underscores the value of using both confirming and disconfirming evidence on the students' language as a strategy for evaluating the accuracy of the ELL classifications used by assessment systems.

Testing Modeling

Testing modeling for ELLs can be defined as the estimation, based on a limited number of observations, of the quality of academic achievement measures that a test is likely to produce with various samples of the universe of possible observations (e.g., different numbers of test items, with and without certain testing accommodation, in English or in the ELL's L1).

To address the notion that the development of testing models for ELLs should be consistent with basic notions from the language sciences, we (Solano-Flores & Li, 2006, 2008, 2009) have used generalizability (G) theory—a psychometric theory of measurement error (Brennan, 1992; Cronbach, Gleser, Nanda, & Rajaratnam, 1972; Shavelson & Webb, 1991, 2009)—to assess language as a source of measurement error. In the basic design of our investigations, ELLs are given the same set of items in L1 and in L2. Rather than testing students in two languages, the intent is to determine the amount of score variation due to the language in which tests are administered.

Evidence from this research shows that the interaction of student, item, and language can be the main source of measurement error in ELL testing (Solano-Flores & Li, 2006, 2008, 2009). These findings indicate that, in addition to their knowledge on the content area assessed, ELLs vary considerably on their proficiency in L1 and in L2. These findings also indicate that each item poses a specific set of linguistic demands in English and a specific set of linguistic demands in the native language. Also, the findings are consistent with the notion from the field of sociolinguistics that the proficiency of bilingual individuals in their two languages varies across contexts and topics (Fishman, 1965). They are also consistent with the notion that, in bilingual individuals, the two languages operate as one language system, not two separate systems (Grosjean, 1989).

We also found that the minimum number of items needed to obtain dependable scores for ELLs tested in L1 or in L2 varied across communities within the same broad linguistic group of native speakers of the same language. An important implication of this finding is the realization that practices such as testing ELLs in their native language may be limited in their effectiveness to produce valid measures of academic achievement because they fail to consider variation due to language (Bialystok, 2001; Genesee, 1994; Valdés & Figueroa, 1994).

All together, these findings indicate that whether ELLs should be tested in L1 or in L2 greatly depends on the characteristics of groups of ELLs at the local (i.e., school or school district) level (see Solano-Flores & Trumbull, 2008). In order to be effective, testing models for ELLs must consider local language variation.

Another investigation, based on the use of G theory, illustrates how testing practices for ELLs can be informed based on data regarding measurement error. We (Kachchaf & Solano-Flores, 2012) investigated the extent to which the language background of raters (whether or not they were native speakers of the ELL's L1) affected the quality of scoring of students' responses to short, open-ended items administered in L1 and L2. The information from this investigation has allowed us to refine the desired linguistic profiles of individuals who participate as raters in assessment systems that include ELLs.

Conclusion

The lack of fair and valid assessment systems and testing practices for ELLs has far-reaching consequences and implications for students and public schools alike. This may be especially true in schools and school districts that have experienced a rapid influx of ELLs in recent years. Fair and valid assessment for ELLs is imperative if school effectiveness is to be measured as outlined by federal, state, and district guidelines. Accreditation of schools is in the balance, as are adequate yearly progress determinations for schools. Proper placement in programming within schools, such as advanced classes and talented and gifted classes, is in the balance for ELLs.

As schools and states are increasingly held accountable for the performance of their students on standardized tests, the need for effective assessment systems has become increasingly evident. For example, the Committee on Test Design for K-12 Science Achievement (National Research Council, 2006, p. 4) recommends "that states develop a system of science assessment that...provide education decision makers with assessment-based information that is appropriate for each specific purpose for which it will be used." Legislation also requires that each state provides evidence of "a single, statewide system of annual assessments that are of high technical quality, are aligned with academic content and achievement standards, are inclusive, and are effectively reported" (National Research Council, 2006, p. 146).

The attainment of these goals in order to properly serve ELLs in public schools is a daunting challenge unlikely to be met without a serious examination of assessment practices for these students (see Durán, 2008) and an analysis of the extent to which assessment systems' actions are consistent with current knowledge from the language sciences (Solano-Flores & Trumbull, 2003). As explained in related work (Solano-Flores, 2008, 2009), a first step towards more fair and valid assessment for ELLs consists of examining the soundness of testing practices for each of the six interrelated components described by the question *who* is given *tests* in what *language, by whom, when,* and *where*? These components are the accuracy with which ELLs and their linguistic competencies are examined (*who*); the process of development, adaptation, and administration of tests (*tests*); the language and dialect of testing (*language*); the linguistic competencies of the individuals involved in the testing of ELLs (*by whom*); the time in which ELLs are tested in relation to their development of English and the number of occasions in which they are tested (*when*); and the set of contexts and linguistic groups across which generalizations of ELL test results and research findings are made (*where*).

As shown in this chapter, the integrity of this process can be seriously compromised at each of these six components owing to inaccurate or insufficient information about ELLs, flawed assumptions about the nature of language and linguistic groups, and inappropriate or poorly implemented actions performed by assessment systems with the intent of addressing the linguistic needs of these students.

In this chapter, we have argued that, given the uncertainty resulting from this combination of factors, valid interpretations of ELL test scores cannot be made without examining the quality of the actions assessment systems take with regards to these students. As we have shown, to be effective, these actions must be taken throughout the entire assessment process, not only at the end. Fairness in assessment should not be thought of as an attribute that is reached for one segment of the population and not for others.

Also, we have argued that a first step toward improved testing practices for ELLs consists of using a probabilistic approach to evaluate how effectively assessment systems deal with randomness in the process of ELL testing. We have presented a probabilistic view of assessment system evaluation and illustrated how testing for ELLs can be modeled based on psychometric approaches that take into account the fact that language is dynamic and linguistic groups are instable.

Although a great deal of the knowledge needed to improve assessment practices for ELLs already exists (see Kopriva, 2008), a deep transformation in the ways in which we think about assessment systems must take place before this improvement becomes a reality. The main challenge stems from the fact that programs and systems are usually evaluated based on the actions they report having taken in order to meet certain goals. In contrast, a critical, probabilistic, systemic perspective focuses on the ability of systems to acknowledge their fallibility and on the effectiveness of the actions they take in anticipation of failure. We hope that in the near future, practitioners, decision makers, and those who implement assessment systems will appreciate this perspective as necessary to accomplishing fair and valid assessment for ELLs.

Notes

Some of the research reported here was funded by NSF Grants REC-0126344, REC-0336744, SGER-0450090, and DRL-0822362. The opinions expressed here are not necessarily those of the funding agency.

1. The terms *assessment* and *testing* are used interchangeably in this chapter.

References

Abedi, J. (2004). The No Child Left Behind Act and English language learners: Assessment and accountability issues. *Educational Researcher, 33*(1), 4–14.

Abedi, J. (2007). English language proficiency assessment and accountability under the NCLB Title III: An overview. In J. Abedi (Ed.), *English language proficiency in the nation: Current status and future practice.* Davis, CA: University of California, Davis.

Abedi, J. (2008). An overview. In J. Abedi (Ed.), *English language proficiency in the nation: Current status and future practice.* Davis, CA: University of California, Davis.

Abedi, J. (2009). Computer testing as a form of accommodation for English language learners. *Educational Assessment, 14,* 195–211.

Abedi, J., Courtney, M., Mirocha, J., Leon, S., & Goldberg. J. (2001). *Language accommodation for large-scale assessment in science.* Los Angeles: University of California, National Center for Research on Evaluation, Standards, and Student Testing.

Abedi, J., & Hejri, F. (2004). Accommodations for students with limited English proficiency in the National Assessment of Educational Progress. *Applied Measurement in Education, 17*(4), 371–392.

Abedi, J., Hofstetter, C. H., & Lord, C. (2004). Assessment accommodations for English language learners: Implications for policy-based empirical research. *Review of Educational Research, 74*(1), 1–28.

Abedi, J., Lord, C., & Hofstetter, C. (1998). *Impact of selected background variables on students; NAEP math performance.* University of California, Los Angeles: Center for the Study of Evaluation; National Center for Research on Evaluation, Standards, and Student Testing; Graduate School of Education & Information Studies.

Abedi, J., Lord, C., Hofstetter, C., & Baker, E. (2001). Impact of accommodation strategies on English language learners' test performance. *Educational Measurement: Issues and Practice, 19*(3), 16–26.

Albers, C. A., Hoffman, A. J., & Lundahl, A. A. (2009). Journal coverage of issues related to English language learners across student-service professions. *School Psychology Review, 381,* 121–134.

Allalouf, A., Hambleton, R., & Sireci, S. (1999). Identifying the causes of DIF on verbal items. *Journal of Educational Measurement, 36,* 18–198.

American Educational Research Association, American Psychological Association, & National Council on Measurement in Education (1999). *Standards for educational and psychological testing.* Washington, DC: Author.

Baker, C. (2006). *Foundations of bilingual education and bilingualism* (4th ed.). Clevedon, UK: Multilingual Matters.

Baker, E. L., Linn, R. L., Herman, J. L., & Koretz, D. (2002). *Standards for educational accountability systems* (Policy Brief No. 5). Los Angeles, CA: University of California, Center for the Study of Evaluation.

Bialystok, E. (2001). *Bilingualism in development: Language, literacy, and cognition.* Cambridge, UK: Cambridge University Press.

Bialystok, E. (2002). Cognitive processes of L2 users. In V. J. Cook (Ed.). *Portraits of the L2 user* (pp. 145–166). Buffalo, NY: Multilingual Matters.
Black, P., & William, D. (2007). Large-scale assessment systems: Design principles drawn from international comparisons. *Measurement: Interdisciplinary Research and Perspectives, 5*(1), 1–53.
Brennan, R. L. (1992). *Elements of generalizability theory.* Iowa City, IA: American College Testing Program.
Brown, H. D. (2007). *Principles of language learning and teaching* (5th ed.). Boston: Addison Wesley & Longman.
Clarke, C. (2007). Evaluating *Math Pathways & Pitfalls* Practical Lessons Learned. Math and Science Partnership Regional Conference Dallas, Texas February 6–8.
Cook, L. I., & Schmitt-Cascallar, A. P. (2005). Establishing score comparability for tests given in different languages. In R. K. Hambleton, P. F. Merenda, & C. D. Spielberger (Eds.), *Adapting educational and psychological tests for cross-cultural assessment* (pp. 139–170). Mahwah, NJ: Erlbaum.
Cope, B., & Kalantzis, M. (2000). *Multiliteracies. Literacy learning and the design of social futures.* London: Routledge.
Cronbach, L. J., Gleser, G. C., Nanda, H., & Rajaratnam, N. (1972). *The dependability of behavioral measurements.* Hoboken, NJ: Wiley.
Crystal, D. (2003). *English as a global language* (2nd ed.). Cambridge, UK: Cambridge University Press.
Cummins, J. (1981). The role of primary language development in promoting educational success for language minority students. In California State Department of Education Office of Bilingual Education, *Schooling and language minority students: A theoretical framework* (pp. 3–49). Sacramento, CA: California State Department of Education Office of Bilingual Education.
Cummins, J. (1999, March). *Research, ethics, and public discourse: The debate on bilingual education.* Presentation at the National Conference of the American Association of Higher Education, Washington, DC.
Cummins, J. (2000). *Language, power, and pedagogy: Bilingual children in the crossfire.* Clevedon, England: Multilingual Matters.
Cummins, J. (2003). BICS and CALP: Origins and rationale for the distinction. In C. B. Paulston & G. R. Tucker (Eds.), *Sociolinguistics: The essential readings* (pp. 322–328). Malden, MA: Blackwell.
Darling-Hammond, L. (1994). Developing professional development schools: Early lessons, challenge, and promise. In L. Darling-Hammond (Ed.), *Professional development schools: Schools for developing a profession* (pp. 1–27). New York: Teachers College Press.
Del Vecchio, A., & Guerrero, M. (1995). *Handbook of English language proficiency tests.* Albuquerque, NM: New Mexico Highlands University, Evaluation Assistance Center, Western Region.
Durán, R. P. (2008). Assessing English language learners' achievement. *Review of Research in Education, 32,* 292–327.
Echevarría, J., & Short, D. J. (2002). *Using multiple perspectives in observations of diverse classrooms: The sheltered instruction observation protocol (SIOP).* Center for Research on Education, Diversity, and Excellence. Retrieved from http://crede.berkeley.edu/tools/policy/siop/1.3doc2.shtml
Eisner, E. W. (1994). *Cognition and curriculum reconsidered.* New York: Teachers College Press.
Ercikan, K. (1998). Translation effects in international assessment. *International Journal of Educational Research, 29,* 543–553.
Ercikan, K. (2002). Disentangling sources of differential item functioning in multi-language assessments. *International Journal of Testing, 2,* 199–215.
Ercikan, K., Gierl, M. J., McCreith, T., Puhan, G., & Koh, K. (2004). Comparability of bilingual versions of assessments: Sources of incomparability of English and French versions of Canada's national achievement tests. *Applied Measurement in Education, 17,* 301–321.
Fishman, J. A. (1965). Who speaks what language to whom and when? *La Linguistique, 2,* 67–88.
García, G. E., McKoon, G., & August, D. (2006). Language and literacy assessment of language-minority students. In D. August & T. Shanahan (Eds.), *Developing literacy in second-language learners: Report of the National Literacy Panel on Language-Minority Children and Youth* (pp. 597–626). Mahwah, NJ: Erlbaum.
General Accounting Office. (2006). No Child Left Behind Act: Assistance from Education could help states better measure progress of students with limited English proficiency. GAO Report to Congressional Requesters, July, (GAO-06-815).
Genesee, F. (Ed.). (1994). Introduction. In F. Genesee (Ed.), *Educating second language children: The whole child, the whole curriculum, the whole community* (pp. 1–11). Cambridge, UK: Cambridge University Press.
Gierl, M. J., & Khaliq, S. N. (2001). Identifying sources of differential item and bundle functioning on translated achievement tests: A confirmatory analysis. *Journal of Educational Measurement, 38,* 16–187.
Gottlieb, M. (2006). *Assessing English language learners: Bridges from language proficiency to academic achievement.* Thousand Oaks, CA: Corwin Press/Sage.
Grisay, A. (2003). Translation procedures in OECD/PISA 2000 international assessment. *Language Testing, 20*(2), 225–240.

Grosjean, F. (1985). The bilingual as a competent but specific speaker-hearer. *Journal of Multilingual and Multicultural Development, 6,* 467–477.

Grosjean, F. (1989). Neurolinguists, beware! The bilingual is not two monolinguals in one person. *Brain and Language, 36,* 3–15.

Hakuta, K. (2001). *How long does it take English learners to attain proficiency?* University of California Linguistic Minority Research Institute. Policy Reports. Santa Barbara: Linguistic Minority Research Institute. Retrieved from http://repositories.cdlib.org/lmri/pr/hakuta

Hakuta, K., & Beatty, A. (Eds.). (2000). *Testing English-language learners in U.S. schools: Report and workshop summary.* Washington, DC: National Academy Press.

Halliday, M. A. K. (1978). *Language as social semiotic: The social interpretation of language and meaning.* London, UK: Edward Arnold.

Halliday, M. A. K. (1993). Some grammatical problems in scientific English. In M. A. K. Halliday & J. R. Martin (Eds.), *Writing science: Literacy and discursive power* (pp. 69–85). Pittsburgh, PA: University of Pittsburgh Press.

Hambleton, R. K., & Jones, R. W. (1994). Comparison of empirical and judgmental procedures for detecting differential item functioning. *Educational Research Quarterly, 1,* 21–36.

Hambleton, R. K., Merenda, P. F., & Spielberger, C. D. (Eds.). (2005). *Adapting educational and psychological tests for cross-cultural assessment.* Mahwah, NJ: Lawrence Erlbaum Associates.

Hambleton, R., & Rodgers, J. (1995). Item bias review. *Practical Assessment, Research & Evaluation,* 4(6). Retrieved November 26, 2011 from http://PAREonline.net/getvn.asp?v = 4&n = 6

Hamilton, L. S., & Koretz, D. M. (2002). Tests and their use in test-based accountability. In L. S. Hamilton, B. M. Stecher, & S. P. Klein (Eds.), *Making sense of test-based accountability in education* (pp. 13–49). Santa Monica, CA: RAND.

Harkness, J. (2003). Questionnaire translation. In J. Harkness, F. J. R. Van de Vijver, and P. Mohler (Eds.), *Cross-cultural survey methods.* Hoboken, NJ: Wiley.

Harry, B., & Klingner, J. K. (2006). *Why are so many minority students in special education? Understanding race and disability in schools.* New York: Teachers College Press.

Kachchaf, R., & Solano-Flores, G. (2012). Rater language background as a source of measurement error in the testing of English language learners. *Applied Measurement in Education, 25,* 167–172.

Kane, M. T. (1982). A sampling model of validity. *Applied Psychological Measurement, 6,* 125–160.

KewalRamani, A., Gilbertston, L., Fox, M., & Provasnik, K. (2007). *Status and trends in the education of racial and ethnic minorities* (NCES 2007–039). Washington DC: National Center for Education Statistics, Institute of Educational Sciences, US Department of Education.

Kindler, A. L. (2002). *Survey of the states, limited English proficient students and available educational programs and services: 1999–2000 summary report.* Washington, DC: The George Washington University and National Clearinghouse for English Language Acquisition and Language Instruction Educational Programs.

Klingner, J., & Harry, B. (2006). The special education referral and decision-making process for English language learners: Child study team meetings and placement conferences. *Teachers College Record, 108* (11), 2247–2281.

Kohavi, R., & Provost, F. (1998). Glossary of Terms. *Machine Learning,* 30(2/3), 271–274.

Kopriva, R. J. (Ed.). (2008). *Improving testing for English language learners.* New York: Routledge.

Kopriva, R. J., Emick, J. E., Hipólito-Delgado, C. P., & Cameron, C. A. (2007). Do proper accommodation assignments make a difference? Examining the impact of improved decision making on scores for English language learners. *Educational Measurement: Issues and Practice,* 26(3), 11–20.

Kopriva, R., Koran, J., & Hedgspeth, C. (2007). Addressing the importance of systematically addressing student needs and test accommodations. In C. Cahalan Laitusis & L. L. Cook (Eds.), *Large-scale assessment and accommodations: What works?* (pp. 145–165). Arlington, VA: Council for Exceptional Children.

Kopriva, R., Wiley, D. E., Chen, C., Levy, R., Winter, P. C., & Corliss, T. (2004). *Field test validity study results: English language development assessment: Final report submitted to the Council of Chief State School Officers LEP-SCASS.* Baltimore: University of Maryland Center for the Study of Assessment Validity and Evaluation (C-SAVE).

La Celle-Peterson, M. W., & Rivera, C. (1994). Is it real for all kids? A framework for equitable assessment policies for English language learners. *Harvard Educational Review, 641,* 55–75.

Lee, O. (2005). Science education with English language learners: Synthesis and research agenda. *Review of Educational Research,* 75(4), 491–530.

Linn, R. L. (2006). The standards for educational and psychological testing: Guidance in test development. In S. M. Downing & T. M. Haladyna (Eds.), *Handbook of test development* (pp. 27–38). Mahwah, NJ: Erlbaum.

Linn, R. L., Baker, E. L., & Betebenner, D. W. (2002). Accountability systems: Implications of requirements of the No Child Left Behind Act of 2001. *Educational Researcher, 31*(6), 3–16.

Luyks, A., Lee, O., Mahotiere, M., Lester, B., Hart, J., & Deaktor, R. (2007). Cultural and home language influence in elementary students' constructed responses on science assessments. *Teachers College Record, 109*(4), 897–926.

Mackey, W. F. (1962). The description of bilingualism. *Canadian Journal of Linguistics, 7*, 51–85.

MacSwan, J., & Rolstad, K. (2003). Linguistic diversity, schooling, and social class: Rethinking our conception of language proficiency in language minority education. In C. B. Paulston & G. R. Tucker (Eds.), *Sociolinguistics: The essential readings* (pp. 329–340). Malden, MA: Blackwell.

MacSwan, J., Rolstad, K., & Glass, G. V. (2002). Do some school-age children have no language? Some problems of construct validity in the pre-LAS Español. *Bilingual Research Journal, 26*(2), 213–238.

Martiniello, M. (2009). Linguistic complexity, schematic representations, and differential item functioning for English language learners in math tests. *Educational Assessment, 14*, 160–179.

National Assessment of Educational Progress. (1996). *Mathematics items public release*. Washington, DC: Author.

National Center for Education Statistics. (2009). *National inclusion policy: Inclusion of special-needs students*. Retrieved from http://nces.ed.gov/nationsreportcard/about/inclusion.asp

Nguyen-Le, K. (2010). *Personal and formal backgrounds as factors which influence linguistic and cultural competency in the teaching of mathematics* (Unpublished doctoral dissertation). Boulder, CO: University of Colorado at Boulder.

No Child Left Behind Act of 2001 (2001). Pub. L. No. 107–110, 115 stat. 1961 2002. Retrieved from http://www.ed.gov/policy/elsec/leg/esea02/107–110.pdf

Payán, R. M., & Nettles, M. T. (2008, June). *Current state of English-Language learners in the U.S. K-12 student population*. English Language Learner Symposium, Princeton, NJ. Retrieved from http://www.ets.org/Media/Conferences_and_Events/pdf/ELLsympium/ELL_factsheet.pdf

Pennock-Roman, M., & Rivera, C. (2007). *The differential effects of time on accommodated vs. unaccommodated content assessments for English language learners*. Center for Assessment, Reidy Interactive Lecture Series. Retrieved from www.nciea.org

Pray, L. (2005). How well do commonly used language instruments measure English oral-language proficiency? *Bilingual Research Journal, 29* (2), 387–409.

Rabinowitz, S., & Sato, E. (2006, April). *Technical adequacy of assessments from alternate student populations: Technical review of high-stakes assessment for English language learners*. Paper presented at the annual meeting of the National Council on Measurement in Education, San Francisco, CA.

Rivera, C., & Collum, E. (Eds.). (2006). *State assessment policy and practice for English language learners: A national perspective*. Mahwah, NJ: Erlbaum.

Rivera, C., Collum, E., Willner, L. N., & Sia, Jr. J. K. (2006). Study 1: An analysis of state assessment policies regarding the accommodation of English language learners. In C. Rivera & E. Collum (Eds.), *State assessment policy and practice for English language learners: A national perspective* (pp. 1–136). Mahwah, NJ: Erlbaum.

Rivera, C., Acosta, B. D., & Shafer Willner, L. (2008). *Guide for refining state assessment policies for accommodating English language learners*. Arlington, VA: The George Washington University, Center for Equity and Excellence in Education.

Romaine, S. (1995). *Bilingualism* (2nd ed.). Malden, MA: Blackwell.

Saunders, W. M., & O'Brien, G. (2006). Oral language. In F. Genesee, K. Lindholm-Leary, W. M. Saunders, & D. Christian (Eds.), *Educating English language learners: A synthesis of research evidence* (pp. 14–63). Cambridge, UK: Cambridge University Press.

Sexton, U., & Solano-Flores, G. (2001, April). *A Comparative study of teachers' cultural perspectives across different cultures*. Poster presented at the annual meeting of the American Educational Research Association. Seattle, WA.

Shavelson, R. J., & Webb, N. M. (1991). *Generalizability theory: A primer*. Newbury Park, CA: Sage.

Shavelson, R. J., & Webb, N. M. (2009). Generalizability theory and its contribution to the discussion of the generalizability of research findings. In K. Ercikan & W. M. Roth (Eds.), *Generalizing from educational research*. New York: Routledge.

Shepard, L.A. (1992). Uses and abuses of testing. In Marvin C. Alkin (Ed.), *Encyclopedia of educational research* (6th ed., pp. 1477–1485). New York: Macmillan.

Shin, F. H. (2004). English language development standards and benchmarks: Policy issues and a call for more focused research. *Bilingual Research Journal, 28*(2), 253–266.

Sireci, S. G., & Allalouf, A. (2003). Appraising item equivalence across multiple languages and cultures. *Language Testing, 20*, 148–166.

Sireci, S. G., Li, S., & Scarpati, S. (2003). *The effects of test accommodation on test performance: A review of the literature*. Center for Educational Assessment (Research Report No. 485). Amherst, MA: University of Massachusetts at Amherst.

Sireci, G., Patsula, L., & Hambleton, R. K. (2005). Statistical methods for identifying flaws in the test adaptation process. In R. K. Hambleton, P. F. Merenda, & C. D. Spielberger (Eds.), *Adapting educational and psychological tests for cross-cultural assessment*. Mahwah, NJ: Erlbaum.

Sireci, S. G., & Pitoniak, M. J. (2007). Assessment accommodations: What have we learned from research? In C. C. Laitusis and L. L. Cook (Eds.), *Large-scale assessment and accommodations: What works?* (pp. 53–65). Arlington, VA: Council for Exceptional Children.

Sloane, F., & Kelly, A. (2003). Issues in high stakes testing programs. *Theory into Practice, 42*(1), 12–18.

Solano-Flores, G. (2006). Language, dialect, and register: Sociolinguistics and the estimation of measurement error in the testing of English-language learners. *Teachers College Record. 108*(11), 2354–2379.

Solano-Flores, G. (2008). Who is given tests in what language by whom, when, and where? The need for probabilistic views of language in the testing of English language learners. *Educational Researcher, 37*(4), 189–199.

Solano-Flores, G. (2009). The testing of English language learners as a stochastic process: Population misspecification, measurement error, and overgeneralization. In K. Ercikan & W. M. Roth (Eds.), *Generalizing from Educational Research*. New York: Routledge.

Solano-Flores, G. (2010, April-May). *Vignette illustrations as a form of testing accommodation for English language learners: A design methodology for use in large-scale science assessment*. Paper presented at the Annual Conference of the National Council of Measurement in Education, Denver.

Solano-Flores, G., Backhoff, E., & Contreras-Niño, L.A. (2009). Theory of test translation error. *International Journal of Testing, 9*, 78–91.

Solano-Flores, G., & Li, M. (2006). The use of generalizability (G) theory in the testing of linguistic minorities. *Educational Measurement: Issues and Practice 25*(1), 13–22.

Solano-Flores, G., & Li, M. (2008). Examining the dependability of academic achievement measures for English-Language Learners. *Assessment for Effective Intervention, 333*, 135–144.

Solano-Flores, G., & Li, M. (2009). Language variation and score variation in the testing of English language learners, native Spanish Speakers. *Educational Assessment, 14*, 1–15.

Solano-Flores, G., Li, M., & Sexton, M. (2004). *On the accuracy of teacher judgments of the linguistic and cultural adequacy of test items*. Unpublished paper, Oakland, CA: WestEd.

Solano-Flores, G., Li, M., Speroni, C., Rodriguez, J., Basterra, M. R., & Dovholuk, G. (2007, April). *Comparing the properties of teacher-adapted and linguistically-simplified test items for English language learners*. Paper presented at the annual meeting of the American Educational Research Association., Chicago.

Solano-Flores, G., & Prosser, R. R. (2009). *Analysis of the linguistic features of Math Path and Pitfalls items and their effect on student performance* (Research Report). Boulder, CO: University of Colorado at Boulder.

Solano-Flores, G., & Shavelson, R. J. (1997). Development of performance assessments in science: Conceptual, practical and logistical issues. *Educational Measurement: Issues and Practice, 16*(3), 16–25.

Solano-Flores, G., & Trumbull, E. (2003). Examining language in context: The need for new research and practice paradigms in the testing of English-language learners. *Educational Researcher, 32*(2), 3–13.

Solano-Flores, G., & Trumbull, E. (2008). In what language should English language learners be tested? In R. J. Kopriva (Ed.), *Improving testing for English language learners*. New York: Routledge.

Stansfield, C. W. (2003). Test translation and adaptation in public education in the USA. *Language Testing, 20*, 188–206.

Stansfield, C. W., & Bowles, M. (2006). Study 2: Test translation and state assessment policies for English language learners. In Rivera, C., & Collum, E. (Eds.), *State assessment policy and practice for English language learners: A national perspective* (pp. 175–221). Mahwah, NJ: Erlbaum.

Trumbull, E., & Farr, B. (2005). Introduction to language. In E. Trumbull & B. Farr (Eds.), *Language and learning: What teachers need to know*. Norwood, MA: Christopher-Gordon.

Trumbull, E., Greenfield, P.M., & Quiroz, B. (2004). Cultural values in learning and education. In B. Williams (Ed.), *Closing the achievement gap* (2nd ed., pp. 67–98). Alexandria, VA: Association for Supervision and Curriculum Development.

Thurlow, M. L., Thompson, S., & Lazarus, S. S. (2006). Considerations for the administration of tests to special needs students: Accommodations, modifications, and more. In S. M. Downing & T. M. Haladyna (Eds.), *Handbook of test development*. (pp. 653–673). Mahwah, NJ: Erlbaum.

Valdés, G., & Figueroa, R. A. (1994). *Bilingualism and testing: A special case of bias*. Norwood, NJ: Ablex.

Wei, L. (2000). Dimensions of bilingualism. In L. Wei (Ed.), *The bilingualism reader*. London: Routledge.

Wilson, M., & Bertenthal, M. (Eds.). (2006). *Systems for state science assessment*. Report of the Committee on Test Design for K–12 Science Achievement. Washington, DC: National Academy Press.

Wolfram, W., Adger, C. T., & Christian, D. (1999). *Dialects in schools and communities*. Mahwah, NJ: Erlbaum.

Zieky, M. (2006). Fairness review in assessment. In S. M. Downing & T. M. Haladyna (Eds.), *Handbook of test development* (pp. 359–376). Mahwah, NJ: Erlbaum.

7

Score Comparability of Multiple Language Versions of Assessments Within Jurisdictions

Kadriye Ercikan, Marielle Simon, and María Elena Oliveri

> Introduction
> Review of Research on Comparability of Multiple Language
>   Versions of Tests
> Current Practices Within Canadian Jurisdictions
>   Survey of Practices in Canadian Provinces and Territories
> Challenges and Solutions to Ensuring Score Comparability Within
>   Jurisdictions
>   Adaptation Process
>   Expert Reviews
>   Psychometric Evidence
>   Identifying Sources of Differential Item Functioning
>   Analysis of Student Cognitive Processes
> Conclusion

Introduction

For the past 30 years, large-scale assessments (LSAs) have been used widely by education systems around the world to inform and monitor their education policies (Lafontaine & Simon, 2008). These include assessments administered nationally such as the National Assessment of Educational Progress (NAEP) in the United States or the Pan-Canadian Assessment Program (PCAP) in Canada, as well as international assessments such as the Trends in International Mathematics and Science Study (TIMSS) and the Program for International Student Assessment (PISA). The results from these assessments are used to inform decisions about education practices, resource allocations, and education effectiveness. The meaningful interpretation of scores from these assessments is critically tied to the comparability of scores for all comparison groups.

In this chapter, we focus on the comparability of scores from multiple language versions of assessments administered within a jurisdiction. Many educational jurisdictions have more than one official language and therefore assess achievement in more than one language. In this chapter, the term *jurisdiction* is used to refer to a variety of education systems, such as that of a country (e.g., France), province (e.g., Ontario, Canada), linguistic region (e.g., German-speaking Switzerland), or linguistic community (e.g., the Flemish in Belgium). In such jurisdictions, comparisons of achievement scores are often made among linguistic subpopulations of students. For example, in Belgium, LSA scores of French-speaking students are compared with those of students from the Flemish-speaking community. In Switzerland, PISA assessment scores are compared across its three linguistic regions: German, Italian, and French. In Spain, PISA and TIMSS scores of minority groups, such as that of the Basque region, are compared to those of the majority Spanish groups. In Finland, PISA scores from minority students attending Swedish-language schools (or schools whose language of instruction is principally Swedish) are compared with scores from the majority of students attending Finnish-language schools. However, such comparative interpretations of findings from multiple language versions of LSAs are meaningful only if scores are shown to be comparable across language groups. When differences in test performance are observed between linguistic groups, such differences may reflect real differences in knowledge and competencies, or they may be due to incomparability of the two language versions of a test introduced by the translation and adaptation process (Ercikan, 1998; Ercikan & Lyons-Thomas, in press; Hambleton, Merenda, & Spielberger, 2005; Sireci, 1997), which may invalidate the comparisons.

The widespread use of multiple language versions of assessments highlights the significance of effects of incomparability of scores across language groups. In 2006, the Progress in International Reading Literacy Study (PIRLS) assessments were adapted into 44 languages and 15 jurisdictions—including Luxembourg, Belgium, Spain, Switzerland, and Canada—which administered PIRLS in more than one language, with some education systems administering it in up to 11 different languages (Lafontaine & Simon, 2008). PISA 2006 produced 81 national versions covering 42 languages administered in 57 jurisdictions (Turner & Adams, 2007). In Europe alone, the Charter of Fundamental Rights recognizes 20 official languages and 30 minority languages (Elosua & López-Jauregui, 2007, p. 39). Often the scores of linguistic subgroups are publicly reported and compared. For example, a study on the PISA 2006 results across Switzerland's three linguistic regions systematically indicate better performance by students from the German region than those from the French or Italian regions in all three disciplines assessed: reading, mathematics, and science (Pagnossin & Matei, 2008, p. 36). In Israel, students from Jewish schools obtain significantly higher scores on international and national large-scale assessments of achievement such as the Meitzav than those from Arab schools (Kashti, 2007).

The increasing worldwide use of multiple language versions of examinations has led to the emergence of guidelines for developing and using such assessments. These guidelines are intended to guide adaptation processes and verification of test and score comparability across languages. For example, the guidelines developed by the International Testing Commission (ITC) (ITC, 2000) as well as the more established Standards for Educational and Psychological Testing (American Educational Research Association, American Psychological Association, & National Council on Measurement in Education, 1999; Joint Committee on Standards for Educational Evaluation, 2003) state that to make meaningful comparisons of scores across language groups, different language versions of tests administered to these groups should be demonstrated to be comparable. Typically these guidelines are not fully implemented in international and national large-scale assessments and less so within jurisdictions that have relatively limited resources.

This chapter examines issues, challenges, and potential solutions regarding the comparability of scores from multiple language versions of LSAs. It concentrates on particular contextual conditions of such assessments. First, it addresses the comparability of scores from multiple language versions of assessments that have low to medium stakes, which provide results at group levels only rather than at the individual student level. Second, the focus is on LSAs of educational achievement rather than assessment for other purposes—such as licensure, accreditation, or employment—which have a different number and nature of sources of incomparability (Ercikan, 2002). Third, the chapter concentrates on comparability issues within jurisdictions instead of across jurisdictions, as in the case of international assessments, for two key reasons. First, although previous research has demonstrated evidence of incomparability in international assessments such as TIMSS and PISA (Ercikan & Koh, 2005; Ercikan & McCreith, 2002), these assessments are developed with great levels of resources (Grisay, Gonzalez, & Monseur, 2009), such as country teams that examine curricular and linguistic properties of items in test development. Typically, such resources are not available for jurisdictions dealing with small numbers of students from different language backgrounds. At jurisdiction levels, ministries of education do not necessarily have personnel with both linguistic and curricular expertise in all of the assessment content areas. Second, within a jurisdiction, the population size of its various linguistic groups may not be symmetrical. Most often, linguistic minority groups have small sample sizes and present specific conditions that prohibit using the statistical and psychometric analyses (scaling and linking) recommended for establishing and examining comparability of score scales for the linguistic groups.

A specific student population is targeted in this chapter—that is, linguistic subgroups of students who attend schools in their respective native languages and are tested in those languages. This means that the chapter does not examine specific issues related to the testing of English language learners (ELLs) or second language learners (SLLs), who by definition are more or less proficient in the language of the test. It is also not concerned with examining the context of immersion programs. Such discussions extend beyond the scope of this chapter, given the different test and population language issues integral to those contexts.

The chapter opts for the use of the term *multiple language versions of assessments* instead of *multilingual assessments, dual-language assessments* (Solano-Flores, Trumbull, & Nelson-Barber, 2002), *bilingual assessments*, or *assessment in the native language* (Bowles & Stansfield, 2008) because of its clear reference to two or more distinct linguistic versions of assessments taken by separate linguistic subgroups of students. In this chapter, development of a second-language version of a test based on a source version is referred to as *test adaptation* instead of *translation*. Developing multiple language versions of tests is rarely restricted to linguistic translation of the test from one language to another. Therefore we believe that test adaptation, which involves creating multiple language versions of tests that have not only linguistic comparability but also educational and cultural appropriateness, more accurately reflects this development process. The chapter is divided into three main sections. In the first section, we summarize and discuss research on test adaptation procedures that are very important aspects of score comparability of multiple language versions of assessments. In the second section, we summarize the current practices within Canadian jurisdictions. The final part of the chapter discusses challenges and solutions to ensure score comparability within jurisdictions.

Review of Research on Comparability of Multiple Language Versions of Tests

Meaningful comparisons of scores across groups in LSAs require tests to be *equivalent* for the comparison groups. The determination of equivalence of multiple language versions of assessments is challenging if not impossible because of potential differences in constructs being measured and differences in the properties of test items and tests in different languages. Guidelines

(AERA et al.; ITC) have been developed specifically to address comparability of test scores across multiple language versions of assessments. These guidelines recommend different language versions of assessments to be assumed as *incomparable* unless evidence of comparability is obtained (AERA et al., 1999; Ercikan & Lyons-Thomas, in press; Hambleton et al., 2005; ITC, 2000). Among the 10 ITC guidelines for test development and adaptation, the seventh, eighth and ninth statements emphasize the need to use and document appropriate statistical techniques to establish the equivalence of the different assessment versions and provide evidence of this equivalence. Similarly, those specifically related to the interpretation of scores state that score differences and comparisons between groups should be supported by empirical evidence. These guidelines are supported by the standards of AERA et al. found in Chapter 9 (see, for example, standard 9.9 on the comparability of multiple language versions of a test). Although these documents recommend a variety of judgmental and psychometric approaches—such as confirmatory factor analysis and the use of multi-method multitrait matrices to determine construct equivalency—these recommendations remain broad, failing to offer specific options for particular assessment conditions such as those within jurisdictions dealing with small sample sizes.

An impressive number of researchers have previously investigated comparability issues in multiple language versions of assessments for various purposes and within a variety of contexts, such as (a) for admissions to universities (Allalouf, 2003; Sireci & Allalouf, 2003); (b) within business or adult education contexts (Casillas & Robbins, 2005; Hambleton & Patsula, 1998; Prieto, 1992; Sireci & Berberoglu, 2000); (c) for credential examinations (Robin, Sireci, & Hambleton, 2003; Wang, Wang, & Hoadley, 2007); (d) for ELLs (Duncan et al., 2005; Reyes, 2007; Sireci, 1997; Stansfield, 2003); and (e) for SLL in immersion programs (Gierl & Khaliq, 2001; Lin & Rogers, 2005; Solano-Flores, Trumbull, & Nelson-Barber, 2002). Others have looked at multiple language versions of achievement tests across jurisdictions (Elosua & López-Jauregui, 2007; Grisay, 2003; Grisay, de Jong, Gebbardt, Berezner, & Halleux-Monseur, 2007). A relatively smaller group of studies have been conducted on the score comparability in multiple language versions of assessments of learning within jurisdictions (Ercikan, 1998, 2002, 2003; Ercikan, Arim, Law, Lacroix, Gagnon, & Domene, 2010; Ercikan, Gierl, McCreith, Puhan, & Koh, 2004; Ercikan & Koh, 2005; Ercikan & McCreith, 2002).

The procedures used to examine construct and score comparability in these studies relied on relatively large sample sizes, thus providing limited guidance for the study of comparability within jurisdictions with relatively small sample sizes. The only exception was the study by Ercikan et al. (2010) in which a think-aloud protocol approach was applied for examining the comparability of English and French versions of test items using a total of 48 students across two language groups.

Current Practices Within Canadian Jurisdictions

In Canada, education is the responsibility of 13 jurisdictions (10 provinces and 3 territories), and English and French are the country's two official languages. Francophone students in many provinces form the minority but are schooled and tested in French. They represent less than 1% in six jurisdictions, between 2% and 4% in five jurisdictions, 8% in another, and 29% in the only officially bilingual province (Statistics Canada, 2010). Conversely, in the province of Quebec, Anglophone students representing roughly 9% of the provincial student population form the minority and are schooled and tested in English. The performance results of language minority students (Francophone students outside of Quebec and Anglophone students in Quebec) are typically published in reports of international or national large-scale assessments.

Often these results are subject to numerous comparisons from testing agencies, media, and lobby groups. For example, the most recent Canadian version of the PISA report states that on the combined science scale, students in the minority language group performed lower than those in the majority language group in the same province. In PISA 2000 and PISA 2003, students enrolled in the French-language school systems in Nova Scotia, New Brunswick, Ontario, and Manitoba performed significantly lower in reading than did students in the English language system in the same province (Government of Canada, 2008). Such findings have also been reported in many other assessment contexts (Simon, Turcotte, Ferne, & Forgette-Giroux, 2007) and as early as in 1981 (Second International Mathematics and Science Study, or SIMSS).

Relatively few Canadian studies have looked at possible reasons for the consistent gap for the minority Francophone students. Some studies examined contextual factors, such as those related to family and students (Simon & Berger, 1999), classrooms and schools (Anderson, Ryan, & Shapiro, 1989), and curricular issues (Berger & Simon, 1997; CMEC, 2004). Other specific studies have looked at the possibility that the instrument itself, particularly its adaptation, may lead to assessing different abilities and skills for the two linguistic populations (Ercikan & Koh, 2005; Ercikan et al., 2004; Ercikan et al., 2010; Ercikan, 2002, 2003; Ercikan & McCreith, 2002; Oliveri & Ercikan, 2011; Simon, 1997). These studies indicate a lack of empirical evidence supporting the assumption that the multiple language assessment versions are indeed comparable, and, as expected, point to the particular challenges associated with assessing minority language groups within multiple language jurisdictions, such as the relatively low numbers of Francophone students in each grade. In 2006, the authors of this chapter set out to investigate the current assessment practices used for assessing students in English and French in the Canadian provinces and territories. The survey procedures and findings are summarized in the next section.

Survey of Practices in Canadian Provinces and Territories

An online survey was administered by the authors during the spring of 2007 to Ministry of Education officials in each province and territory in Canada, followed by telephone or face-to-face interviews. The survey featured sections on respondent information, assessment information (e.g., content specifications, time allotment), assessment development procedures (e.g., adaptation, pilot testing), scoring procedures (e.g., cut scores and standard setting), and psychometric procedures (interrater reliability, differential item functioning [DIF] and scaling and linking). More specifically, participants were asked to select an assessment in language arts/literacy or mathematics/numeracy given to the same-grade students in English and French and that focused on the highest relevant grade for which the chosen assessment was available. Respondents were asked to describe their chosen education assessment and the importance their jurisdiction gave to developing assessments that were comparable as well as specific procedures they used for ensuring comparability of scoring and psychometric properties of the assessments.

The survey was completed by 10 of the 13 Canadian jurisdictions. Four jurisdictions reported that comparability between the results of the linguistic populations was very important, two reported that comparability was somewhat important, and three jurisdictions reported that comparability was not formally intended. Another jurisdiction reported developing, administering, and reporting tests and their results separately for the two language groups. All participants reported that assessment results were often compared by various groups, including the media, school boards, universities, ministry and department staff, and bilingual classroom teachers. To ensure comparability of assessment characteristics, the jurisdictions utilized approaches such as referring to a common content blueprint and using similar assessment instructions, number

Table 7.1 Verification of Comparability of Assessment and Development Procedures

Characteristics	Number of Jurisdictions
Assessment instructions	8
Content specifications	7
Item development procedures	8
Item selection procedures	9
Number of items and sections	7
Item format	9
Time allotment	10

Table 7.2 Procedures Conducted to Verify Comparability of Assessments

Comparability Verification Procedures	Number of Jurisdictions
Back translation	2
Review of language versions by reviewers	8
Review of language versions by independent groups	4
Pilot testing with students	6
Comparing item difficulties	4
Using cultural sensitivity panels	4
DIF analyses followed up with bias reviews	4

of sections and items, and employing similar item selection development procedures. These are summarized in Table 7.1.

Jurisdictions reported several differences in their adaptation processes. For example, six jurisdictions first developed assessments in the source language and subsequently adapted them into the target language with the assistance of certified translators and classroom teachers. One jurisdiction used simultaneous adaptation processes wherein items were developed in one of the two languages and were immediately adapted into the second language as part of the development process. Some items originated in English, others in French. Another jurisdiction developed two tests independent of each other in the two languages.

Table 7.2 summarizes the types of procedures jurisdictions used to verify the adequacy of adaptation as well as additional procedures to ensure that Anglophone or Francophone students had a similar understanding of items and that items had similar difficulty levels for the two language groups. Adaptation verification procedures included back translation, review of language versions by bilingual reviewers, and bilingual reviewer groups. Other comparability verification procedures involved (a) conducting pilot studies with groups of students to review items, (b) comparing item difficulties and item-test correlations from the two language versions, (c) using cultural sensitivity panels to review items, and (d) employing DIF studies and follow-up with bilingual expert reviews of item content to investigate cultural biases in the assessments.

Jurisdictions used one or more of the following procedures to verify and establish score comparability: (a) minority language panelists to focus on challenges of minority language students during standard setting practices, (b) the same cut score on scales that were linked using common anchor items across the two language versions, or (c) the same cut score on a single scale including both linguistic samples together for item calibration.

Challenges and Solutions to Ensuring Score Comparability Within Jurisdictions

The reality of producing multiple language versions of assessments and ensuring comparability of results is characteristic of many education jurisdictions. However, some of the official languages in jurisdictions such as Hungary, Spain, and Lithuania and most of the Canadian jurisdictions are spoken by minority groups that make up less than 5% of the total population. In such contexts, challenges in developing comparable tests across languages and establishing comparability include (a) small sample sizes that prohibit the use of certain statistical procedures for linking score scales, (b) costs related to applying expert reviews and statistical analyses that require special data collection, and (c) limitations in finding specialized minority language staff in a variety of curricular areas as well as in psychometrics and for adapting tests. For example, in jurisdictions where there are less than 500 examinees in the assessed grade, it might be difficult to utilize psychometric approaches such as item response theory (IRT), based approaches to scaling tests and conducting DIF analyses. There are costs associated with writing items in multiple languages, translation and adaptation, verification and development of equivalence in different language versions of tests, development of supporting materials for administration, and providing empirical evidence of comparability (Casillas & Robbins, 2005). Although various strategies exist to reduce the impact of sources of errors that affect comparability of multiple language versions, only a small number of those procedures can be applied in jurisdictions where the minority groups are small and there are not enough resources to cover the costs. The sections below discuss four key aspects of establishing comparability across different language versions of assessments with special attention to within-jurisdiction contexts with small numbers of linguistic groups and limited resources: adaptation process, expert reviews, psychometric evidence, and student cognitive processes.

Adaptation Process

Various adaptation methods for developing comparable multiple language versions of assessments include parallel, successive, concurrent, and simultaneous assessment development. Parallel development involves having the linguistic communities develop separate language versions of an assessment using a single content blueprint and having sections of each version adapted to other languages. Depending on the available resources, single forward translation, a forward and back translation, or a double blind translation with follow-up reconciliation may also be applied (Grisay et al., 2007; Organisation for Economic Co-operation and Development, 2005).

In successive adaptation, monolingual or monocultural test developers produce an assessment in the source language (of the majority group) to use with students in that same language or culture. Once the test is developed, one or more translators forward-translate the test to the target language (of the linguistic minority group), and panels of bilingual teachers or experts review the test to make modifications so as to better match the test in the source language (Rogers, Gierl, Tardif, Lin, & Rinaldi, 2003; Tanzer, 2005). The adapted version of the test is then back-translated into the source language to monitor retention of the original meaning of the test as intended in the source language. This approach, however, has the limitation that the final evaluation of the test is conducted only in the source language of the test (Rogers et al., 2003).

An alternative to test adaptation is the concurrent construction of multiple language versions of an assessment (Solano-Flores et al., 2002). This approach uses the concept of "shells" or "templates," which are enhanced blueprints wherein the item structure and complexities that best match the nature of the cognitive skills being assessed are also specified. In the concurrent development of these more or less complex items, bilingual test developers interact at all stages of the assessment construction process. This process implies that shells must be made available and that bilingual test developers interpret their intent and use them correctly. This approach is most applicable in the development of extended-response items.

A fourth option is the simultaneous adaptation approach to the development of achievement tests. In this option, as for the concurrent approach, the emphasis is placed on the use of a multifaceted committee of experts in the targeted languages, in psychometrics, and in the subject domain for developing test items (Lin & Rogers, 2005; Tanzer & Sim, 1999). Typically bilingual item writers are chosen to become members of the committee. Items are developed in one language and immediately adapted into the other language. Given that individuals are not necessarily equally fluent in both languages, it becomes important to consider bringing together bilingual individuals who are native speakers from each of the assessment languages.

Among the various test development adaptation approaches, the simultaneous approach has been recommended (Rogers et al., 2003; Tanzer, 2005) because it enables the formulation and conceptualization of the construct and its measurement in the targeted languages at early stages of test development and in a balanced way for the different language versions. For example, there may be particular features of a construct, often beyond linguistic features, that are neither translatable nor applicable from the source culture to the target culture or language to which the test is being adapted. A simultaneous test development approach enables the source language test to be adapted or modified during test development stages to reflect decentralized views that are more encompassing of the target culture(s) and language(s). In addition, which language version is considered as "source" and which one as "target" can be alternated so that some items originate in one language and others originate in the other. Within jurisdictions with limited resources, this approach to developing multiple language versions of tests is not necessarily more costly or demanding of greater resources. However, it does require close collaboration between the linguistic communities from the beginning of the assessment development process.

Expert Reviews

Two key types of expert reviews include content and linguistic reviews. Once the multiple language assessment versions are developed, content reviews are conducted to establish content and construct related validity evidence (Bowles & Stansfield, 2008). These reviews include appropriateness of test items for the language groups that may be exposed to different curricula and instruction, and they may also have had different opportunities to learn the content covered by the assessment. Linguistic reviews are conducted to examine equivalence of meaning, cognitive requirements, difficulty of vocabulary and expressions, and cues given to help students solve the problem. Specifically, at the item level, common elements under examination are word difficulty, semantic differences, item format, item content, idiomatic relationship (Ercikan 1998, 2002; Allalouf, 2003), grammatical form or syntactic differences, reading level, sentence structure, familiarity with vocabulary, omissions or additions that may affect meaning (Ercikan, 1998, 2002; Gierl & Khaliq, 2001; Oliveri & Ercikan, 2011), and overall format—that is, punctuation, capitalization, typeface, and structure (Gierl & Khaliq, 2001).

Within jurisdictions with limited resources, expert reviews may be the most basic aspect of establishing equivalence between different language versions of tests. In order to achieve maximum effectiveness, review panels should consist of between four to eight individuals that (a) have their first language in the targeted language, (b) have experience in teaching (Bowles & Stansfield, 2008, Ercikan et al., 2004), (c) are familiar with the curriculum content (Casillas & Robbins, 2005), (d) are familiar with student thinking processes (Ercikan et al., 2004), and (e) understand the basic principles of test construction (Hambleton & Patsula, 1998). The addition of experienced teachers who are actually teaching the curriculum targeted by the assessment can also be a great asset to the panel. Ercikan et al. (2004, p. 312) offer the following linguistic review steps for ensuring comparability of both overall assessment and individual items: (a) group review of sample of items to discuss review criteria, (b) independent review of each item by individual reviewers, and (c) group discussion and consensus for rating adaptation differences between two language versions.

Psychometric Evidence

Psychometric analyses to evaluate comparability are typically grouped into three categories: (a) classic test theory–based analyses, (b) dimensionality analyses, and (c) identification of DIF and its sources. These approaches are described and discussed in the following subsections.

CLASSIC TEST THEORY–BASED APPROACH

Such analyses of test data usually involve examining individual groups' raw or adjusted mean performance (Duncan et al., 2005), item difficulty values (or P values), conditional P values (Muñiz, Hambleton, & Xing, 2001), item discrimination indices such as point-biserial correlations, and internal consistency reliability indices (Bowles & Stansfield, 2008).

To ensure comparability of scores across relatively small linguistic groups within jurisdictions, alternative validity studies—which do not require large sample sizes—can be applied, particularly when the stakes are low to medium. First, item statistics from both linguistic groups, such as item difficulty and item discrimination indices, can be compared. Correlations of item difficulty and discrimination indices between the language groups provide evidence of the degree to which items are ordered similarly with respect to difficulty and discrimination for the comparison groups.

DIMENSIONALITY ANALYSES

Dimensionality analyses provide a measure of the equivalence of factor structures at the test level (Ercikan & Koh, 2005, p. 25) for the language groups. These analyses may be based on exploratory (Oliveri & Ercikan, 2011) or multigroup confirmatory factor analyses (Ercikan & Koh, 2005; Oliveri, Olson, Ercikan, & Zumbo, in press), nonlinear exploratory procedures such as weighted multidimensional scaling (Robin et al., 2003), or confirmatory factor analyses using structural equation modeling (Wang et al., 2007). However, these methods require large sample sizes, such as several hundred cases per group, which may not be feasible in many within-jurisdiction comparisons.

DIF

Some DIF methodologies have been identified to work better with small sample sizes, particularly those based on Bayesian estimation approaches (Zwick, Thayer, & Lewis, 1999, 2000). In the empirical Bayes (EB) DIF approach, which builds upon previous Mantel-Haenzel (MH) enhancement DIF analysis approaches, estimates of DIF are obtained by combining the observed values of the MH index of DIF and an estimated standard error with an assumed prior distribution for the DIF parameters. The EB approach leads to more stable estimates of DIF than the original MH statistic, particularly in using small sample sizes, including target samples as low as 25 (Zwick et al., 2000).

Previous research suggests as well that the structural equation model based on the multiple-causes, multiple-indicators (MIMIC) model may be used to identify DIF, with tests containing as few as 20 items with small sample sizes (i.e., as few as 100 examinees) (Finch, 2005). In the MIMIC model, DIF is signaled when there is a statistically significant direct relationship between the language groups and the items that are not influenced by the construct being measured (Finch, 2005). Testing for direct effects consists of an iterative process in which the analysis of DIF is repeated for every item under investigation (Mast & Lichtenberg, 2000). In the MIMIC model, various factors underlying student achievement (i.e., socioeconomic status, ethnic or language proficiency background) can be analyzed simultaneously even if such factors are correlated (Mast & Lichtenberg, 2000). Despite the advantages of using either Bayesian estimation approaches or the MIMIC models for estimating DIF with small sample sizes, these methods are more complex to implement compared with traditional DIF detection methods and require more sophisticated knowledge of psychometric procedures.

Alternative approaches that may be easier to apply and have been shown to work with small sample sizes include the delta plot and the standardization index methods (Muñiz et al., 2001). The delta plot method may be used with binary items and involves plotting the P values for one cultural group on one axis, and those for the other group on the other axis. If the difficulties of the items are consistent across the two groups, they will fall on a line with a 45-degree angle. It is assumed that the P values are obtained from examinees from normal ability distributions on a scale with a mean of 13 and standard deviation of 4. Differences of 1.5 between two groups are reviewed further (Sireci, Patsula, & Hambleton, 2005).

The standardization index proposed by Dorans and Kulick (1986) is a "conditional P value" method in which separate P values are computed for each item conditional on total test score. In this approach, equivalent groups of examinees are established by matching examinees on the total test score. Typically test score intervals are computed to match examinees, and the proportion of examinees who answered the item correctly at each interval is computed and compared for each group. For nonproblematic items, the two groups of examinees should perform about the same. The standardization index may be used to flag items for DIF, and although there is no statistical test associated with the statistic, an effect size can be calculated (Sireci et al., 2005).

Statistical approaches exist that allow for the checking of properties of test items and score distributions for groups of examinees from various language groups who are matched on ability levels based on an external criterion. For example, for the purposes of assigning examinees to particular groups in bilingual designs, examinees may be matched using scores examinees obtain on alternative tests or subtests. Such scores may be used to obtain a conditional probability that an examinee will be assigned to one group (e.g., a lower-performing bilingual group) versus another (i.e., a higher-performing bilingual group) (Rosenbaum & Rubin, 1983; Sireci, 1997).

The use of logistic regression has been recommended as an alternative means of simultaneously conditioning on multiple ability estimates (Mazor, Kanjee, & Clauser, 1995). Specifically, Mazor et al. (1995) analyzed responses to a chemistry achievement test with a reference group of "English best language" examinees and a focal group of "other best language" examinees. When examinees were matched on total test score, numerous items were identified as displaying DIF. When an estimate of verbal ability was added to the model (i.e., use of an external criterion), many of these items ceased to be identified as displaying DIF, providing insights about some of the sources of DIF between the comparison linguistic groups.

Identifying Sources of Differential Item Functioning

Identifying sources of DIF is an essential aspect of meaningful interpretations of DIF and examining the validity of comparability. The key method for identifying sources of DIF has involved the review of items by curricular, cultural, and linguistic experts (Ercikan, 2002; Gierl & Khaliq, 2001; Hambleton et al., 2005; O'Neil & McPeek, 1993; Wu & Ercikan, 2006; Zwick & Ercikan, 1989). These reviews include examination of item content, language, and format for indicators of sources of DIF. A major consideration that needs to be taken into account in calling on individuals to review items for sources of DIF due to adaptation is whether their first language is the same as that of the targeted group. This gives them the advantage of capturing the linguistic nuances inherent in the adapted versions of items. Unfortunately, in jurisdictions with small minority linguistic communities, the scarcity of expert translators primarily fluent in the language of the target group may limit the possibility of meeting this condition. Bilingual experts review items in the two comparison languages for potential linguistic differences; they also evaluate and rate the equivalence of test items with regard to equivalence of meaning, difficulty of vocabulary and sentence structure, nonlinguistic presentation differences, and key words that may guide student thinking.

Analysis of Student Cognitive Processes

Expert review is the most commonly used method for examining comparability of test item characteristics and for identifying properties of test items, such as language and context, that may be the sources of DIF. However, expert reviews are based on surface characteristics of items. Whether differences identified by experts lead to differential performance for examinees from different language groups or whether these characteristics do indeed lead to DIF is an empirical question. For example, if the review process identifies that the vocabulary used in the English test version has a different meaning when translated to French, the review process does not tell us whether these differences lead to differential performance. To examine whether differences in item characteristics lead to differential performance, it is necessary to understand the interaction between test items and the thought processes of examinees from different language groups.

Ercikan et al. (2010) recently proposed think-aloud protocols (TAPs) as a new approach for examining the comparability of test items in different languages. The TAP approach is used to gather data about how different aspects of test questions may be affecting students' thought processes and ultimately their performance on the test; therefore this approach naturally lends itself to comparing the thought processes of different groups of examinees. Ercikan and colleagues examined whether examinees' TAPs confirmed the linguistic differences identified by expert reviewers as sources of DIF. In this research, TAPs confirmed differences identified by expert reviews for only 10 of 20 DIF items. The low agreement between TAPs and expert reviews has two key implications for methods used in investigating comparability: (a) item features identified in expert reviews may not be the real sources of DIF and (b) decisions about item bias cannot be based solely on expert reviews.

TAP methods may be useful in examining comparability in assessments given in multiple languages within jurisdictions that have low sample sizes for minority groups. TAPs are now considered vital methods of data collection for empirically examining student cognitive processes, understanding the constructs being measured, and gathering validity evidence (Baxter & Glaser, 1998; Ferrara et al., 2003, 2004). Ercikan et al. (2010) have identified two strategies that were effective in optimizing the accuracy with which TAPs revealed information about examinee thought processes. The first was to combine student verbalizations, test administrator observations, and students' answers, including their incorrect responses, as sources of evidence about examinees' thought processes. The second was to combine both concurrent (while problem solving) and retrospective (after task completion) verbalizations.

Conclusion

This chapter reviewed and summarized research, practices, and challenges and recommended methodologies for examining the comparability of test items and tests given in multiple languages. These issues were discussed within the context of low- to medium-stake educational achievement assessments and for assessment contexts where examinees are expected to take tests in their first language. Special attention was given to contexts where the sample size of one of the linguistic groups may be small and resources allocated to test development and verification of equivalence of tests across languages may be limited. In the first section, we summarized and discussed research on test adaptation procedures that constitute very important aspects of comparability of multiple language versions of assessments. This section was followed up with a summary of current practices within Canadian jurisdictions. This section is important for understanding contexts in which multiple language versions of tests are developed and used. As reported by the Canadian jurisdictions, comparability of results from different language versions of tests may not always be intended by test developers. Therefore, in such contexts, steps to verify and establish comparability are not prioritized or implemented. However, once test results are published, the media, school boards, universities, ministry and department staff, different education groups, and the public who are not aware of problems with comparability may go ahead and make unintended and inappropriate comparisons. The Canadian jurisdiction context revealed a wide range of methods used in test adaptation and development of multiple language versions of tests, but the majority of the jurisdictions first developed assessments in the source language and adapted them into the target language. Verification procedures ranged from back translation, review of language versions by bilingual reviewers or reviewer groups, pilot studies with groups of students, comparisons of item difficulties and item-test correlations, the use of cultural sensitivity panels to review items, as well as DIF studies and follow-up with bilingual expert reviews. Methods used for verifying and establishing score comparability included the use of minority language experts in standard setting, common item linking in creating scales, and use of the same cut score on a single scale that includes both linguistic samples together for item calibration.

The final part of the chapter discussed challenges and solutions to ensure score comparability within jurisdictions. The challenges include small sample sizes that prohibit the use of certain statistical procedures, costs related to special linking and comparability studies, and limitations in finding specialized expertise in curricular areas, psychometrics, and for adapting tests. This section also discussed the adaptation process, expert reviews, psychometric evidence, and student cognitive processes for establishing comparability across different language versions of assessments. Among the various test development adaptation approaches, we recommended the simultaneous test adaptation development approach to enable the formulation and conceptualization of the construct and its measurement in the targeted languages at early stages of test development and in a balanced way for the different language versions. Expert reviews are recommended as an essential aspect of establishing equivalence between different language versions of tests. Psychometric evidence based on classic test theory based approaches, dimensionality, and DIF analyses are discussed. Identifying sources of DIF and analysis of student cognitive processes are presented as critical aspects of examining measurement and construct comparability of different language versions of tests.

References

Allalouf, A. (2003). Revising translated differential item functioning items as a tool for improving cross-lingual assessments. *Applied Measurement in Education, 16*, 55–73.

American Educational Research Association, American Psychological Association, & National Council on Measurement in Education. (1999). *Standards for educational and psychological testing*. Washington, DC: AERA.

Anderson, L. W., Ryan, D., & Shapiro, J. (Eds.). (1989). *The IEA classroom environment study*. Toronto: Pergamon Press.

Baxter, G., & Glaser, R. (1998). Investigating the cognitive complexity of science assessments. *Educational Measurement: Issues and Practices, 17*, 37–45.

Berger, M. J., & Simon, M. (1997). *Projet interprovincial en lecture et en écriture*. Rapport final soumis au ministère de l'Éducation et de la Formation de l'Ontario.

Bowles, M. S., & Stansfield, C. W. (2008). *A practical guide to standards-based assessment in the native language*. Retrieved from www.ncela.gwu.edu/spotlight/LEP/2008/bowles_stansfield.pdf

Casillas, A., & Robbins, S. B. (2005). Test adaptation and cross-cultural assessment from a business perspective: Issues and recommendations. *International Journal of Testing, 5*(21), 5–21.

CMEC. (2004). *Pan-Canadian results of francophone students in a minority-language setting in the School Achievement Indicators Program (SAIP). Analytical report. A report prepared for the pan-Canadian French as a first language project*. Toronto, Ontario.

Dorans, N. J., & Kulick, E. (1986). Demonstrating the utility of the standardization approach to assessing the unexpected differential item functioning on the Scholastic Aptitude Test. *Journal of Educational Measurement, 23*, 355–368.

Duncan, T. G., del Río Parent, L., Chen, W.-H., Ferrara, S., Johnson, E., Oppler, S., & Shieh, Y.-Y. (2005). Study of a dual-language test booklet in eighth-grade mathematics. *Applied Measurement in Mathematics, 18*, 129–161.

Elosua, P., & López-Jauregui, A. (2007). Potential sources of item functioning in the adaptation of tests. *International Journal of Testing, 7*(1), 39–52.

Ercikan, K. (1998). Translation effects in international assessments. *International Journal of Educational Research, 29*, 543–553.

Ercikan, K. (2002). Disentangling sources of differential item functioning in multilanguage assessments. *International Journal of Testing, 4*, 199–215.

Ercikan, K. (2003). Are the English and French versions of the Third International Mathematics and Science Study administered in Canada comparable? Effects of adaptations. *International Journal of Educational Policy, Research and Practice, 4*, 55–76.

Ercikan, K., Arim, R. G., Law, D. M., Lacroix, S., Gagnon, F., & Domene, J. F. (2010). Application of think-aloud protocols in examining sources of differential item functioning. *Educational Measurement: Issues and Practice, 29*, 24–35.

Ercikan, K., Gierl, M. J., McCreith, T., Puhan, G., & Koh, K. (2004). Comparability of bilingual versions of assessments: Sources of incomparability of English and French versions of Canada's National Achievement Tests. *Applied Measurement in Education, 17*, 301–321.

Ercikan, K., & Koh, K. (2005). Construct comparability of the English and French versions of TIMSS. *International Journal of Testing, 5*, 23–35.

Ercikan, K., & Lyons-Thomas, J. (in press). Adapting tests for use in other languages and cultures. In K. Geisinger, *APA Handbook Testing and Assessment in Psychology*. Washington, DC: American Psychological Association.

Ercikan, K, & McCreith, T. (2002). Effects of adaptations on comparability of test items and test scores. In D. Robitaille & A. Beaton (Eds.), *Secondary Analysis of the TIMSS results; A Synthesis of current research* (pp. 391–407). Dordrecht, the Netherlands: Kluwer.

Ferrara, S., Duncan, T., Perie, M., Freed, R., McGivern, J., & Chilukuri, R. (2003, April). *Item construct validity: Early results from a study of the relationship between intended and actual cognitive demands in a middle school science assessment*. Paper presented at the annual meeting of the American Educational Research Association, Chicago.

Ferrara, S., Garcia Duncan, T., Freed, R., Vélez-Paschke, A., McGivern, J., Mushlin, S., et al. (2004, April). *Examining test score validity by examining item construct validity*. Paper presented at the annual meeting of the American Educational Research Association, San Diego, CA.

Finch, H. (2005). The MIMIC model as a method for detecting DIF: Comparison with Mantel-Haenszel, SIBTEST, and the IRT likelihood ratio. *Applied Psychological Measurement, 29*, 278–295.

Gierl, M. J., & Khaliq, S. N. (2001). Identifying sources of differential item and bundle functioning on translated achievement tests. *Journal of Educational Measurement, 38*, 164–187.

Government of Canada. (2008). *Highlights: Measuring up: Canadian results of the OECD PISA study. The performance of Canada's youth in science, reading and mathematics. 2006 First results for Canadians aged 15*. Retrieved from www.pisa.gc.ca/highlights-eng.shtml

Grisay, A. (2003). Translator procedures in OECD/PISA 2000 international assessments. *Language Testing, 20*, 228–240.

Grisay, A., Gonzalez, E., & Monseur, C. (2009). Equivalence of item difficulties across national versions of the PRILS and PISA reading assessments. *IERI Monograph Series, 2*. Chapter 3. IEA-ETS Research Institute. Retrieved from http://www.ierinstitute.org/IERI_Monograph_Volume_02_Chapter_03.pdf

Grisay, A., de Jong, J. H. A. L., Gebhardt, E., Berezner, A., & Halleux-Monseur, B. (2007). Translation Equivalence across PISA Countries. *Journal of Applied Measurement 8*(3), 249–266.

Hambleton, R. K., Merenda, P. F., & Spielberger, C. D. (2005). *Adapting educational and psychological tests for cross-cultural assessment.* Mahwah, NJ: Erlbaum.

Hambleton, R. K., & Patsula, L. (1998). Adapting tests for use in multiple languages and cultures. *Social Indicators Research, 45*, 153–171.

ITC. (2000). *ITC Guidelines for adaptation.* Retrieved from http://www.intestcom.org/test_adaptation.htm

Joint Committee on Standards for Educational Evaluation. (2003). *The student evaluation standards.* Arlen Gullickson, Chair. Thousand Oaks, CA: Corwin.

Kashti, O. (2007). *Haaretz.com.* Retrived from http://www.haaretz.com/hasen/spages/929083.html

Lafontaine, D., & Simon, M. (2008). Évaluation des systèmes éducatifs. *Mesure et évaluation en éducation, 31*(3), 95–123.

Lin, J., & Rogers, W. T. (2005). *Validity of the simultaneous approach to the development of equivalent achievement tests in English and French (stage II).* Poster presentation at the annual conference of the National Council for Measurement in Education, Montreal, Canada.

Mast, B. T., & Lichtenberg, P. A. (2000). Assessment of functional abilities among geriatric patients: A MIMIC model of the functional independence measure. *Rehabilitation Psychology, 45*, 94–64.

Mazor, K. M., Kanjee, A., & Clauser, B. E. (1995). Using logistic regression and the Mantel-Haenszel with multiple ability estimates to detect differential item functioning. *Journal of Educational Measurement, 32*(2), 131–144.

Muñiz, J., Hambleton, R. K., & Xing, D. (2001). Small sample studies to detect flaws in item translations. *International Journal of Testing, 1*(2), 115–135.

O'Neil, K. A., & McPeek, W. M. (1993). Item and test characteristics that are associated with differential item functioning. In P. W. Holland & H. Wainer (Eds.), *Differential item functioning* (pp. 255–276). Hillsdale, NJ: Erlbaum.

Organisation for Economic Co-operation and Development. (2005). *PISA 2003 Technical Manual.* Retrieved from http://www.pisa.oecd.org/dataoecd/49/60/35188570.pdf

Oliveri, M. E., & Ercikan, K. (2011). Do different approaches to examining construct comparability lead to similar conclusions? *Applied Measurement in Education, 24*, 1–18.

Oliveri, M. E., Olson, B., Ercikan, K., & Zumbo, B. D. (in press). Methodologies for investigating item- and test-level measurement equivalence in international large-scale assessments. *International Journal of Testing,*

Pagnossin, E., & Matei, A. (2008). Résultats internationaux et suisses. Dans Christian Nidegger (Éd.). *Pisa 2006: compétences des jeunes romands: résultats de la troisième enquête PISA auprès des élèves de 9e année.* Neuchâtel: Institut de recherche et de documentation pédagogique.

Prieto, A. J. (1992). A method for translation of instruments to other languages. *Adult Education Quarterly, 43*(1), 1–14.

Reyes, J. M. (2007). *An investigation of the construct validity of the Spanish version of the Texas Assessment of Knowledge and Skills Exam* (Unpublished doctoral dissertation). Stephenville, TX: Tarleton State University.

Robin, F., Sireci, S. G., & Hambleton, R. K. (2003). Evaluating the equivalence of different language versions of a credentialing exam. *International Journal of Testing, 3*(1), 1–20.

Rogers, W. T., Gierl, M. J., Tardif, C., Lin, J., & Rinaldi, C. M. (2003). Differential validy and utility of successive and simultaneous approaches to the development of equivalent achievement tests in French and English. *Alberta Journal of Educational Research, 49*(3), 290–304.

Rosenbaum, P. R., & Rubin, D. B. (1983). The central role of the propensity score in observational studies for causal effects. *Biometrika 70*(1), 41–55.

Sireci, S.G. (1997). Problems and issues in linking tests across languages. *Educational Measurement: Issues and Practice, 16*(1), 12–19.

Sireci, S. G., & Allalouf, A. (2003). Appraisng item equivalence across multiple languages and cultures. *Language Testing, 20*(1), 148–166.

Sireci, S. G., & Berberoglu, G. (2000). Using bilingual respondents to evaluate translated-adapted items. *Applied Measurement in Education, 35*, 229–259.

Sireci, S.G., Patsula, L., & Hambleton, R. K. (2005). Statistical methods for identifying flawed items in the test adaptations process. In R. K. Hambleton, P. Merenda, & C. Spielberger (Eds.), *Adapting educational and psychological tests for cross-cultural assessment* (pp. 93–115). Hillsdale, NJ: Erlbaum.

Simon, M. (1997). *Statistical and subjective bias analyses of translated educational achievement items* (Unpublished doctoral dissertation). University of Toronto, Toronto.

Simon, M., & Berger, M. J. (1999). Liens entre les attitudes, le sexe et le rendement aux tests provinciaux des élèves de 3ᵉ année et de 6ᵉ année dans les écoles de langue française de l'Ontario. Education Quality and Responsibility Office Research Series, Volume 3. Toronto: Queen's Press

Simon, M., Turcotte, C., Ferne, T., & Forgette-Giroux, R. (2007). Pratiques pédagogiques dans les écoles de langue françaises de l'Ontario selon les données contextuelles du PIRLS 2001. *Mesure et évaluation en éducation 30*(3), p. 59–80.

Solano-Flores, G., Trumbull, E., & Nelson-Barber, S. (2002). Concurrent development of dual language assessments: An alternative to translating tests for linguistic minorities. *International Journal of Testing, 2*(2), 107–129.

Stansfield, C. W. (2003). Test translation and adaptation in public education in the USA. *Language Testing, 20*(2), 189–207.

Statistics Canada. (2010). *Summary public school indicators for Canada, the provinces and territories, 2002/2003 to 2008/2009,* Ministry of Industry. Cat no 81–595-M, No. 088.

Tanzer, N. K. (2005). Developing tests for use in multiple languages and cultures: A plea for simultaneous development. In R. K. Hambleton, P. F. Merenda, & C. D. Spielberger (Eds.), *Adapting educational and psychological tests for cross-cultural assessment.* Mahwah, NJ: Erlbaum.

Tanzer, N. K., & Sim, C. O. E. (1999). Adapting instruments for use in multiple languages and cultures: A review of the ITC guidelines for test adaptations. *European Journal of Psychological Assessment, 15,* 258–269.

Turner, R., & Adams, R. J. (2007). The programme for international student assessment: An overview. *Journal of Applied Measurement, 8*(3), 237–248.

Wang, S., Wang, N., & Hoadley, D. (2007). Construct equivalence of a national certification examination that uses dual languages and audio assistant. *International Journal of Testing, 7*(3), 255–268.

Wu, A. D., & Ercikan, K. (2006). Using multiple-variable matching to identify cultural sources of differential item functioning. *International Journal of Testing, 6,* 287–300.

Zwick, R., & Ercikan, K. (1989). Analysis of differential item functioning in the NAEP history assessment. *Journal of Educational Measurement, 2,* 55–66.

Zwick, R., Thayer, D. T., & Lewis, C. (1999). An empirical Bayes approach to Mantel-Haenszel DIF analysis. *Journal of Educational Measurement, 36,* 1–28.

Zwick, R., Thayer, D. T., & Lewis, C. (2000). Using loss functions for DIF detection: An empirical Bayes approach. *Journal of Educational and Behavioral Statistics, 25,* 225–247.

8
Accommodating Special Needs for Large-Scale Assessments

Leilani Sáez, Elisa Jamgochian, and Gerald Tindal

Introduction
Accommodation Appropriateness
   Validity of Measurement Inferences and Accommodations
   Construct-Irrelevant Variance (CIV)
   Accommodation Interactions
Research on the Effectiveness of Accommodations
   Extended Time
   Alternate Responding
   Alternate Test Presentation
Determining Accommodation Appropriateness to Examine Effectiveness
Practical Implications
   Upgrading Research on Accommodations
   Upgrading Test Development by Using Universal Design
Upgrading Practice
   Clarity in Policy
   Structured LSA (and Accommodation) Training
Conclusion

Introduction

Large-scale assessments (LSA) "provide information about the [educational] attainment of individual students, as well as comparative information about how one individual performs relative to others" (National Research Council, 2001, pp. 38–39). Increasingly in the United States, LSA comprise state or district tests used to measure student and school performance against established standards and also to hold schools accountable for ensuring student learning (Almond, Lehr, Thurlow, & Quenemoen, 2002). The comparative nature of LSA demands "sameness" of administration and score reporting. Because students are presumably given the same measurement opportunity (i.e., same conditions for testing, same test or equivalent version), the obtained scores and interpretations of their meaning are assumed to be comparable. When test-taking students are viewed as the same, the assumption of score comparability goes unquestioned.

However, this assumption becomes more doubtful when students with special needs take LSA because they require, by definition, something that "surpasses what is common or usual" (American Heritage dictionary meaning of *special*) (Morris, 1981). They need something different. Historically, testing adaptations have been used to "level the playing field" (Fuchs & Fuchs, 1999; Tindal & Fuchs, 2000) when special needs create an unfair disadvantage. Beyond concerns of equitable testing, the issue of how to adequately measure what students with special needs know is a challenge because movement away from *sameness* increases the likelihood of measuring something other than the intended test construct, which should be the primary focus (American Educational Research Association, American Psychological Association, & National Council on Measurement in Education, 1999, p. 101). Theoretically, adaptations that are implemented to support special needs enhance the degree to which scores among *all* students can be fairly compared.

Adaptations can take two main forms: accommodations and modifications. A critical distinction between the two entails the extent to which testing changes maintain the construct being measured (American Educational Research Association et al.,1999). Although accommodations uphold the measurement of the same construct across all students, modifications may alter the construct (or the extent to which it is measured) in response to a student's particular special needs. Modifications complicate comparisons among scores because the adaptations fundamentally change the meaning of scores. In contrast, when accommodations are used, inferences drawn from original and adapted test scores are presumed to be equivalent (because performance on the same construct was measured).

In the United States, the right to testing accommodations for students with special needs is protected under the law (e.g., the Individuals with Disabilities Act and the Civil Rights Act). Typically, for students with disabilities (SWDs), adaptations are made to test conditions (e.g., scheduling, environment, and/or timing), item responding, and/or test form presentation (Ysseldyke, Thurlow, McGrew, & Shriner, 1994). English language learners (ELLs) may receive these same accommodations but are also entitled to native- and second-language accommodations (e.g., bilingual dictionary use, simplified or translated text) (Wolf, Kao, Griffin, Herman, Bachman, Chang, et al., 2008). Although there is a growing consensus among policy makers that students with special needs should participate in LSA with the support of accommodations to more precisely measure what they know (Christensen, Lazarus, Crone, & Thurlow, 2008), accommodation defining features, selection, and use can vary widely depending upon documented needs, state policy, and local decision making.

Differences in practice have caused some researchers to conclude that "many educational agencies are uncertain about what constitutes an appropriate accommodation" (Bolt & Thurlow, 2004, p. 142). For example, a recent study of test accommodation validity across four states revealed that "the same" accommodation (i.e., oral presentation of test items) was implemented differently in each location: some states used computer delivery while others used human readers (Olson, 2010). Moreover, one state allowed enhanced oral directions to provide scaffolding, which the others did not. Diverse uses of accommodations are similarly apparent among researchers (see literature review below). Thus we agree with Bolt and Thurlow (2004) but would further argue that the field in general may be unclear about what constitutes an appropriate *and* effective accommodation.

We believe that ambiguity regarding accommodations has emerged from the failure to thoroughly examine what it means to assess students with special needs beyond issues of equity.

Particularly with the rising reliance on LSA for accountability purposes, a closer look at how special testing needs are being met is warranted. Therefore in this chapter we examine this predicament from a measurement perspective that emphasizes greater precision regarding accommodation use, which we argue is crucial for evaluating accommodation effectiveness. In particular, we focus on the interplay between three factors that impact accommodation appropriateness and effectiveness: individual student characteristics, test construct measurement, and skills necessary for testing. As part of our discussion, we selectively review empirical studies of accommodation use. In addition, we consider practical implications for how to improve accommodation research, LSA test design, and educational practice.

Accommodation Appropriateness

Accommodations are typically implemented based on judgments about student needs identified on an Individualized Education Plan (IEP). For example, in the majority of states, policy selection and expectations for use of accommodations among SWDs are based on the following: instructional goals relevance, current level of functioning, and the nature/category of disability (Christensen et al., 2008). The unit of analysis, then, is the student rather than the test skills measured (Fuchs, Fuchs, Eaton, Hamlett, & Karns, 2000). However, this limits the extent to which accommodation appropriateness can be evaluated because the judgment of suitability is based solely upon what a student cannot do (e.g., read, pay attention, or speak English fluently). In addition, this approach does not guarantee enhanced measurement, positive effects on performance, or even assurances that such accommodations are not beneficial to all students. For example, in one study of accommodation use based upon IEP recommendations, although accommodations had a positive effect for a large percentage of SWDs, this was not the case for all students; in some cases, accommodations were found to also have a positive effect on the performance of nondisabled test-taking peers (Elliott, Kratochwill, & McKevitt, 2001).

We believe that a clearer understanding of the test construct and corresponding item functioning is needed to define requisite testing skills, which would provide a better basis for selecting accommodations *relative to a particular test, in addition to skills of a particular student.* Without this specificity, the anticipated fit of an adaptation is questionable because a specific explanation cannot be ascertained to describe how an accommodation bridges the performance gap between test demands and student capabilities. The current approach justifies the use of accommodations based on particular student characteristics largely independent of specific testing features that may or may not impact student performance. This shallow linking of testing opportunity and accommodations implicitly neglects conditions under which special needs do not necessitate adaptations in order to level the playing field. More importantly, it blurs the focus of LSA measurement away from its intended purpose (i.e., to examine skill performance).

Appropriate accommodations entail a well-defined understanding of the test requirements and the capacity of an accommodation to support performance. This involves clearly identifying the construct, which determines the domain of knowledge and skills on the test, as well as the anticipated cognitive abilities involved in test performance (Haladyna & Downing, 2004). In addition, test items, rather than broad domains (e.g., math, reading comprehension), need to be analyzed to establish what students are expected to do in order to show what they know. Moreover, this process explains the impact of deviations in test conditions, presentation, or responses that define the testing demands and the extent to which the use of adaptations is appropriate.

Validity of Measurement Inferences and Accommodations

The selection of an accommodation is complex, requiring great care to address student needs by providing differential support (i.e., aid to specifically address a difficulty unrelated to test-measured skills) that still allows for the same type of inferences to be drawn from the performance among all test takers, which is possible only when the construct is unchanged (Hollenbeck, Rozek-Tedesco, & Finzel, 2000).

For example, although there may be little question that enlarged print or oral administration accommodations can support the testing needs of a student with a visual impairment, the extent to which either of these is appropriate becomes less clear when the measured test construct (or skills) is also considered. Both enlarged print and oral administration may be appropriate accommodations for supporting math test performance because improving visual access to test content and substituting reading requirements with oral listening demands do not weaken the measurement of math skill competency. In contrast, for a test of reading comprehension, while enlarged print may be an appropriate accommodation because it affords visual access to the test content to be read, oral administration of test passages would not be appropriate because of the change in the intended construct measured from reading comprehension to listening comprehension. The resulting test score would then reflect the student's ability to listen to a passage and answer corresponding questions rather than read a passage and answer corresponding questions. "Accommodations are intended to remove the sources of difficulty [associated with special needs] and allow for the intended construct to be meaningfully and accurately measured" (Bolt & Thurlow, 2004, p. 142); they are not intended to change the measured construct underlying the test.

The challenge in determining appropriate and effective accommodations for students with special needs becomes increasingly difficult when the identified need is cognitively based rather than sensory or motor, such as the difficulties associated with learning disabilities, attention deficit hyperactivity disorder, emotional disturbance (e.g., depression or anxiety), or second language acquisition. Unlike special needs that arise as a consequence of difficulty that can be directly documented (e.g., the student who cannot see printed text, hear audio instructions, or write with his or her hands), the evaluation of appropriateness for a special need that stems from cognitive challenges requires greater explication. Efforts to level the playing field become more complicated when the playing field is less documentable or direct (i.e., because it is cognitive). Thus, the justification for using an accommodation must rely first on precise reasoning of the conditions when use is most appropriate and second on empirical evidence of effectiveness under these prescribed conditions.

Construct-Irrelevant Variance (CIV)

From a psychometric perspective, test accommodations are beneficial because they reduce construct-irrelevant variance (CIV) (Messick, 1984; Haladyna & Downing, 2004) that threatens to weaken the validity of the decision based on a measurement outcome. CIV is a source of measurement error unrelated to the construct that leads to a distorted understanding of student performance. Test anxiety, motivation, high reading demands on a math test, and fatigue are likely sources of CIV for students (Haladyna & Downing, 2004), although these are particularly likely to impact students with special needs. In addition, unnecessarily complex language on test items is often a source of CIV for ELLs (Abedi, 2006). The presence of special needs introduces the potential for measuring something other than the intended test construct (e.g., limitations in performance due to the disability or limited English proficiency). Thus use of accommodations can reduce CIV "noise" and enhance the precision of obtained test scores.

Theoretically, the reduction of CIV associated with special needs should be evidenced by an interaction that selectively improves the performance of students with special needs without also significantly improving the performance of their peers (i.e., *the interaction hypothesis,* described in Sireci, Scarpati, & Li, 2005). Therefore when an accommodation is administered to both students with special needs and their peers, a differential positive "boost" should result for the performance of students with special needs, which is presumed to equalize the opportunity (Phillips, 1994). In contrast, if the accommodation improves performance among all students, it is not likely to specifically address special needs, thus diminishing the appropriateness of its use for only a selected few (however "effective" it may be).

Accommodation Interactions

In light of this hypothesis, current research indicates mixed results regarding the specific effectiveness, and therefore appropriateness, of particular accommodations used for SWDs and ELLs, which we describe below. Albeit selective, we focus on studies that include comparison students without special needs (however, for more extensive reviews, see Abedi, Hofstetter, & Lord, 2004; Kieffer, Lesaux, Rivera, & Francis, 2009; Sireci, et al., 2005; Tindal & Fuchs, 2000; Thompson, Blount, & Thurlow, 2002). In addition, given the scope of this chapter, we limit our review to studies in which the special needs of students were cognitive (as previously discussed). Although in practice accommodations are often "bundled" and therefore not always implemented individually (Elliott, et al., 2001), we emphasize the literature regarding individual accommodations because, as others have noted (Fuchs, Fuchs, & Capizzi, 2005), the effectiveness of individual accommodations that are likely to comprise these bundles is still unknown. In particular, we discuss studies pertaining to the allowance of extended testing time, alternate responding, and alternate test presentation.

Research on the Effectiveness of Accommodations

Although the research on various accommodations is quite extensive, only three areas are presented here to illustrate the kind of findings typical of this body of work: extended time, alternate responding, and test presentations. It is this research base that supports the ultimate validity of inferences for the use of accommodations. In our review, we note that considerable variance exists in how students are described and labeled as well as how accommodations are assigned and implemented. Few validation data are collected on specific student characteristics or their relation to test demands, let alone the prior use of accommodations in the learning environment. In the end, much of this research is not replicated and the findings are limited in their generalizability, as each study represents what was done only in that study and not reflective of practice more generally.

Extended Time

The underlying rationale for granting this accommodation is the presumption that students with special needs require additional time to demonstrate what they know on a test. This may be a tenuous assumption regarding students with cognitively based special needs. That is, although speed-of-processing difficulties are presumed to be the main factor underlying slow responding, this may not always be the case (e.g., perseveration and anxiety may play a larger role, in which case more time is useful only to the extent that the student also engages in coping behaviors to minimize the impact on performance).

Because at best we can only infer the reason for slow performance, allowing extended time makes more sense when used to counteract the negative effect of engaging in additional activities above and beyond what other students must do during testing (e.g., to look up unknown English words in a glossary). However, when extended time was allowed for ELLs using supplemental dictionaries and glossaries, their performance was not significantly improved (Abedi, Hofstetter, & Lord, 2004). Furthermore, the application of extended time for completing tests appears to enhance the performance of all student test takers (Elliott & Marquart, 2004; Fuchs, Fuchs, Eaton, Hamlett, Binkley, & Crouch, 2000; Lewandowski, Lovett, Parolin, Gordon, & Codding, 2007; for further discussion of these issues, see Lovett, 2010), although the effect of extended time on performance may be larger for SWDs than for their peers (Fuchs, Fuchs, Eaton, Hamlett, & Karns, 2000). Thus extended time accommodations may lack the specificity needed to justify the appropriateness of use among only students with special needs. Moreover, the need for additional time on a test may be more revealing about test design limitations than student ability constraints (i.e., if extending time benefits the measurement of all students).

Alternate Responding

Few studies have examined the effectiveness of alternate responding accommodations. Use of this accommodation is presumed to reduce the negative impact of test performance demands. Methods of allowing students to respond in ways different from the standard protocol may vary from having students provide an alternate written response to substituting written with oral responses. For example, in one study, students wrote directly on their math tests rather than transferring their responses to an answer sheet (Tindal, Heath, Hollenbeck, Almond, & Harniss, 1998). Tindal et al. (1998) found that this form of alternate responding did not improve test performance for SWDs.

In contrast, both use of speech recognition and dictation to a scribe, as writing test accommodations, resulted in higher performance for SWDs but not for their peers (Macarthur & Cavalier, 2004). Macarthur and Cavalier (2004) argued that allowing students with learning disabilities to use alternative methods for constructing essays (instead of requiring handwriting) enabled them to focus more on the content and organization (i.e., quality indicators) of their product than the unmeasured but influential mechanics of handwriting or spelling. More research is clearly needed to uncover the conditions under which alternate responding may be best utilized. For example, little is known about the appropriateness of this accommodation for ELLs and the potential effectiveness of incorporating technology to support alternate forms of responding (e.g., computerized bilingual translation). In general, alternate response accommodations appear to be most effective when they reinforce specific test skill weaknesses (e.g., Macarthur & Cavalier, 2004) rather than student ability performance weaknesses (e.g., Tindal et al., 1998).

Alternate Test Presentation

The alteration of how tests are presented has been used as an accommodation to augment access to test content. The rationale for using this adaptation is grounded in the view that students with special needs require a change in the way that the test content is presented in order to fully engage with items. For example, simplifying the language used on math tests to reduce vocabulary and syntax complexity has been found to be specifically effective for ELLs (Abedi, Lord, Hofstetter, & Baker, 2000) although potentially less beneficial for SWDs (Tindal, Anderson, Helwig, Miller, & Glasgow, 2000). However, in a meta-analysis of ELL accommodations across 11 studies (e.g., simplifying English, providing bilingual dictionaries or glossaries, use of dual language options, and extra time), the only significantly effective adaptation was use of a customized English (i.e., second language) dictionary or glossary (Kieffer et al., 2009). This finding suggests that enhanced rather than altered presentation may be the best way to adapt test presentations for students with special needs.

For example, oral administration is used when reading skills unrelated to the targeted test skills measured are weak. In general, elementary school students with disabilities tend to have higher math test scores when test items are read to them (Fuchs, Fuchs, Eaton, Hamlett, & Karns, 2000; Johnson, 2000). Although higher performance was also found among their peers, the effect in these studies was nonsignificant. There was some indication that the effectiveness of having the test read aloud depended upon the skill measured. As a consequence, this type of accommodation may better support the completion of math word problems than calculation items (Tindal et al., 1998). However, this effect may be less pronounced as students reach middle and high school (Elbaum, 2007; Helwig, Rozek-Tedesco, & Tindal, 2002), particularly if pacing (i.e., speed of oral administration) is a moderating factor (Hollenbeck, Rozek-Tedesco, Tindal, & Glasgow, 2000).

In contrast to the above findings, which suggest that oral administration is an appropriate and effective accommodation for math tests, the research regarding its use for literacy tests is less convincing. Not only may this practice be inappropriate (i.e., when reading is the targeted skill, as previously discussed) but insufficient evidence exists for differential student effectiveness. For example, both SWDs and their peers demonstrate higher performance when a read-aloud accommodation is used on measures of reading comprehension (Meloy, Deville, & Frisbie, 2002; McKevitt & Elliott, 2003). Other researchers report a "differential boost" for SWDs compared with their peers when curriculum-based measurement data are used to predetermine accommodation need (Fuchs, Fuchs, Eaton, Hamlett, Binkley, & Crouch, 2000). Unlike the other studies, in the Fuchs et al. (2000) study, students—not test proctors—read aloud the test content. Because information regarding error correction procedures was not discussed, the extent to which students' performance was based solely on their reading ability (and not their corrected reading ability) is unclear. Thus, whether the "boost" resulted from the data-driven method used to assign accommodations or the oral administration accommodation is not known.

In general, the literature pertaining to oral administration as an alternate way to present test information warrants further examination. Although it appears to remove CIV related to weak reading skills among SWDs, which hinder math test performance, this effect may be contingent upon a clear match between test skill demands and student skill capability. This may explain in part why customized dictionaries were the only accommodation to consistently enhance ELL test performance in a recent meta-analysis (Kieffer et al., 2009). Although simplifying test language may benefit some ELLs (Abedi et al., 2000), especially those with extremely weak second language skills, other ELLs may need less support during test taking. Instead, the use of a reference book to define unknown words (instead of altering the test language) may be sufficient for measurement and therefore most appropriate and effective for ELLs with stronger English proficiency (Albus, Bielinski, Thurlow, & Liu, 2001).

Determining Accommodation Appropriateness to Examine Effectiveness

Below we describe an empirical study by Fletcher et al. (2006) to further illustrate the relation between accommodation appropriateness and accommodation effectiveness. In particular, what distinguishes this study from those previously reviewed is the careful consideration of the interaction between anticipated test item–specific difficulty (e.g., decoding of particular types of words) and test-necessary student skills (word reading and comprehension skills) that were anticipated to negatively impact test performance but reveal little about student ability (i.e., how well the students could comprehend text). Based upon student reading performance data and analysis of test demands, Fletcher et al. (2006) examined the use of extended test time and oral administration of test item elements (proper nouns within passages, test item stems, and response choices) on a statewide reading comprehension measure, comparing third-grade students with word decoding difficulties and their peers.

The researchers' rationale for selecting these particular accommodations follows. Extended test time was used to "counteract effects of fatigue and loss of interest because of word decoding difficulties" (p. 141). Reading aloud proper nouns on the test was also used because these specific types of words were deemed "idiosyncratic, excessively frustrating to poor decoders, and minimally associated with understanding the meaning of a passage" (p. 141). Moreover, reading aloud test item stems and response choices was used because the authors argued that "the determination of comprehension is not dependent on the student's ability to read the comprehension questions" (Fletcher et al., 2006, p. 141). A strong validity argument supports the reasoning used to select these accommodations because a direct link was made between identified test performance expectations (i.e., reading comprehension of passages and answering corresponding questions) and nontarget subskill influences (i.e., CIV) that threatened to undermine students' ability to demonstrate how well they could comprehend connected text.

A significant effect of the accommodations was found among the poor decoders who received accommodations compared with those who did not (Fletcher et al., 2006). In addition, there was no significant difference in performance between average decoders who received the accommodations and those who did not. Although the effectiveness of individual accommodations was not studied (i.e., their effect was analyzed as part of a "bundle"), the results highlight the benefit of precisely deconstructing test item demands and student skills in order to assemble accommodations that maintain the construct measured while simultaneously adjusting (i.e., minimizing) non-construct-related test performance factors to reveal what students know.

Practical Implications

In the previous sections, we addressed appropriateness and effectiveness of accommodations, noting important dimensions such as specificity in fit between the test demands and student needs, the requirement to validate inferences from their use, consideration of construct irrelevant variance, the analysis of interactions (both by students and outcomes), and a summary of research on accommodations (and its various limitations). In this section, we note current LSA accommodation policies and the policy-related implications of allowing accommodations (as distinct from modifications). Although we acknowledge that the research on accommodations needs to be upgraded (better use of experimental designs and student specifications), we argue that test development also represents a useful beginning. Rather than simply continuing to develop tests in the traditional model with test specifications that focus on content blueprints with passing reference to item formats, the focus may be improved by incorporating universal design principles that reference access and measured constructs in a more explicit manner. In addition, practice can be improved by greater specificity in the implementation of accommodations, reference to policy, and teacher training on decision making. Without this specificity, the distinction between accommodations and modifications may become blurred and, unwittingly, the validity evidence supporting various accommodations may not be supportive. In the end, score reporting suffers and confusion exists in the entire accountability effort.

Upgrading Research on Accommodations

Clearly the use of accommodations is best done on the basis of what we know and what we do not know but need to know (Malouf, 2005). But even then it is critical that the field should move forward on this basis and also that it should create an agenda for practice to extend this knowledge. We therefore acknowledge the limitations from this research in order to strengthen future empirical research studies.

As previously explained, one direction for improving research on accommodations is to be clear on the construct being measured as well as the demands of the measurement process; likewise, the skills of students need to be documented beyond classification labels (e.g., SWD or ELL). Clarity in defining constructs necessarily requires consideration of test conditions, administration procedures, and response demands in implementing a testing program. How can and should items be developed and assembled into a test so that students with special needs can have access to performance? What kind of differentiated support is then needed to compensate for the lack of access, yet not interfere with the construct being measured?

Ideally this type of analytical process would build on research findings such as those summarized previously on extended time, response demands, and presentation. Research has definitely documented accommodations of this kind to be effective under certain conditions. However, as we note, the findings are not always clear and often must be qualified by the lack of differential effects.

As helpful as this research can be for guiding practice, a number of limitations prevent it from being sufficient. The first and most critical involves research design. For example, Chiu and Pearson (1999) noted the effectiveness of several different accommodations over a decade ago. They found positive effects from extended time, oral administration, and a variety of administration changes. Their findings, however, did not consider the quality of research designs or specific descriptions of students.

In general there is inadequate use of group designs and, in particular, nested (students assigned to different treatment groups) over crossed (students participating in all treatment groups) designs that control for threats to internal validity (i.e., cause-effect inferences) differently (Shadish, Cook, & Campbell, 2002). In nested designs, the most significant threat to internal validity is addressed by random assignment of students to either of two conditions: an experimental (receive accommodations) or control (do not receive accommodations). However, students participate in only one condition, making it impossible to directly compare the effect for individual students. In contrast, a crossed design uses comparisons of students' performance with and without the treatment (with the order usually counter balanced to control for threats to internal validity). Therefore the effect of treatment can be directly compared for individual students. However, as Sireci et al. (2005) report, most research studies use quasiexperimental designs in which threats to internal validity are uncontrolled. "Non-experimental studies typically involve analysis of already existing data, in contrast to experimental studies that require manipulating the accommodation condition, randomly assigning examinees to conditions, and testing examinees at least once" (p. 467). Therefore causal inferences are uncertain at best.

A second and recurring limitation is the failure of the field to move past categorical labels in sampling student populations. More often than not, students with special needs are selected as participants because they share a label rather than because they exhibit weak performance in a specific area that impacts testing. For example, in the Fletcher et al. (2006) study, through the use of data, the sample was selected to comprise students with "word decoding difficulties." This is preferred over less precise labels, such as "students with reading disabilities" or "struggling readers." Whereas the latter group characterizations may serve a purpose in many education settings, they offer limited explanatory support for why an accommodation is found to be effective in a research study. In contrast, by emphasizing the skill at risk for interfering with test performance rather than the student classification status at risk for weak test performance, a clearer depiction of the role for a selected accommodation is apparent. Thus the need for enhanced precision begins as much with the study designed to examine accommodation effectiveness as the LSA designed to measure student skills or the accommodation implemented to maintain score comparability.

Upgrading Test Development by Using Universal Design

As previously mentioned, accommodations are typically post hoc testing adaptations (Bremer, Clapper, Hitchcock, Hall, & Kachgal, 2002). Although "accommodations can be an effective means for providing students with [special needs] access to a test, they can only go so far in correcting assessments that test extraneous knowledge and abilities, such as reading abilities in a science test" (Dolan & Hall, 2001, p. 5). What is warranted, then, is a different perspective about how special needs can be met in testing students in LSA programs. An alternative complement to accommodations includes the incorporation of universal design principles during test development.

A concept rooted in architecture and product development, universal design is intended to benefit people of all ages and abilities by "making products, communications, and the built environment more usable by as many people as possible" (Center for Universal Design, 2008, p. 2). In education contexts, the concept of universal design is applicable to both assessment and instruction.

In contrast to the *sameness* assumption that typically defines LSA, as noted by Rose and Meyer (2002), "Universal design does not imply 'one size fits all' but rather acknowledges the need for alternatives to suit many different people's needs" (p. 5). Thus, Universal Design for Assessments (UDA) extends the concept of universality to address issues of accessibility within assessment systems by promoting the widest possible participation of students and affording more valid interpretation of assessment results (Thompson, Johnstone, & Thurlow, 2002).

UDA has the potential to address some of the issues and limitations of accommodations by reducing the need for test adaptations to alter the testing opportunity based on individual student needs (Ketterlin-Geller, 2005). When accommodations and support are embedded into assessments rather than assigned as add-ons to the test, students are better able to access test content and demonstrate their knowledge and understanding, teachers (and other stakeholders) are able to more accurately compare student performance, and the validity of education decisions improves (Ketterlin-Geller, 2005). Often technology can be used to effectively support and standardize accommodations to reduce variability, promote independent access to test adaptations, and present an effective tool for creating tests with embedded accommodations and elements of UDA (Dolan & Hall, 2001; Dolan, Rose, Burling, Harms, & Way, 2007; Johnstone, 2003).

The National Center on Educational Outcomes (NCEO) (Thompson et al., 2002) identified seven elements of universally designed assessments through a review of assessment, universal design, and instructional design literature (see Table 8.1). Together, these elements help to guide test developers in designing and improving assessments to meet requirements for accessibility and to effectively measure the knowledge and skills of the widest range of students possible. However, universal design does not necessarily eliminate the need for accommodations. Some students may require additional changes to participate in testing and demonstrate their knowledge and skills.

For example, LSA can be intentionally designed to contain simple and clear instructions to reduce the cognitive load demands that can impair test taking performance (Elliott, Kurz, Beddow, & Frey, 2009). This difficulty can be particularly relevant for SWDs who demonstrate weak reading and/or language skills as well as for ELLs. Furthermore, tests developed with

Table 8.1 Universal Design for Assessment (UDA) and Test Development

UDA Element	Test Development Considerations
Inclusive assessment population	Responsiveness to diversity, the inclusion of all students, and the demands of accountability, including the range of abilities and skills within the population is reflected in assessment design.
Precisely defined constructs	Items reflect content standards and minimize unrelated skills. When the construct and purpose for assessment are clearly defined, construct-irrelevant barriers (i.e., cognitive, sensory, emotional, and physical obstacles) are reduced.
Accessible, nonbiased items	Bias may result from the language of an item, such as words or phrases that are place or culture-specific, or may contain language that is insensitive to a particular gender or culture. Content that might disadvantage any student subgroup is avoided.
Amenable to accommodations	Additional changes to test presentation, format, timing, or setting that don't change the intended construct may be necessary and are facilitated.
Simple, clear, and intuitive instructions and procedures	Directions and tasks should be understandable and consistent across sections of a test. Students should be able to work independently through the assessment (Tindal & Fuchs, 2000).
Maximal readability and comprehensibility	Conciseness and use of plain language do not alter the content, but instead improve comprehensibility and make content accessible to test takers. Text and definitions should be simple and clear; content and important ideas should be presented in logical sequence.
Maximal legibility	Text characteristics include appropriate contrast, type size, font, and spacing (between lines and letters). Illustrations, graphs and tables should support the content of the text and be clearly labeled; unrelated illustrations are unnecessary and often distracting (Johnstone, 2003). Black-and-white line drawings are the most clear. Generally, larger circles (for bubbles response tests) and allowing students to mark in their test booklet, rather than on a separate answer sheet, are recommended (Johnstone, 2003). Other response formats may need to be considered.

UDA principles assume the presence of variability—that abilities will vary along a number of dimensions. Meeting diverse special needs during test construction, rather than after, is a primary goal. Thus, the *sameness* that characterizes LSA is broadened to be more inclusive of all students.

To develop a test that incorporates the elements of UDA, a number of considerations are necessary. At all stages of test development, Thompson, Johnstone, Anderson, and Miller (2005) recommend the following eight considerations:

1. Incorporate elements of universal design in the early stages of test development.
2. Include disability, technology, and language acquisition experts in item reviews.
3. Provide professional development for item developers and reviewers on use of the considerations for universal design.
4. Present the items being reviewed in the format in which they will appear on the test.
5. Include standards being tested with the items being reviewed.
6. Pilot test items with students.
7. Field test items in accommodated formats.
8. Review computer-based items on computers.

In addition, content expert and stakeholder reviews of the assessment and item functioning can confirm or refine test content, analyze the test for potential bias, examine readability and legibility, and judge the suitability of materials and instructions (Hanna, 2005). Feedback from various stakeholders (e.g., students, parents, and teachers) can reveal issues regarding the appropriateness and uses of the test in terms of the target population (Ketterlin-Geller, 2005). Statistical procedures, such as differential item functioning (DIF) or item response theory (IRT), can ensure that the items accurately reflect the intended construct, thereby strengthening skill inferences made for decision making (Ketterlin-Geller, 2005). These considerations, in conjunction with the UDA principles, provide a process by which appropriate and accessible tests can be developed.

However, a test is only as good as the conditions under which it is administered. Effective measurement requires not only a solid test for sampling what students with special needs know but also well-defined policies for accommodation implementation and informed decision making. In many cases, teacher knowledge underlies the extent to which these factors can improve the use of LSA for students with special needs in practice.

Upgrading Practice

Change in the decision-making process is achievable only with specificity in implementation, clarity in policy, and structured teacher training and data use. Without all three conditions, the recommendations for and use of accommodations is unlikely to be appropriate and impossible to evaluate for effectiveness.

Clarity in Policy

For over a decade, the use of accommodations has been documented by the NCEO (Thurlow, Lazarus, Thompson, & Morse, 2005; see http://www.cehd.umn.edu/NCEO/). Over this time, states have become far more explicit on what is allowed and what is not allowed. Also, additional rationale has appeared in policies on why accommodations are allowed (or not allowed). Finally, policies have also become more detailed on how accommodations should be implemented, providing guidance in subtle issues that would otherwise contribute to CIV. The take-home message for practitioners is to analyze state policy for breadth (robust attention to a variety of accommodations) and depth (detailed explanations why accommodations are on each side of the list for allowance). Finally, specific descriptions should be provided on how to implement accommodations.

This clarity of implementation, however, needs to consider teacher perceptions and their accuracy (Crawford, Almond, Tindal, & Hollenbeck, 2002). Tracking perceptions needs to be both documentary (Gibson, Haeberli, Glover, & Witter, 2005) and evaluative (Hollenbeck, Tindal, & Almond, 1998). Of course the minimal documentation needs to be the IEP, which often provides unclear specification of accommodations. However, documentation also can be as simple as the systematic collection of information in a student's record or portfolio so that, over time, teachers in successive grade levels have access to it. Clarity must consider prevalence (Bolt & Thurlow, 2004) in order to provide systemic covariance with large-scale accountability regulations. The documentation cannot simply note an accommodation but must also include the conditions of use (when, how, and where an accommodation is needed). Finally, clarity needs to consider use as well as need (Shriner & Ganguly, 2007) to be certain that both sides of the equation are present (the demands of the test and the needs of the students). This kind of clarity reveals the rationale behind the use of accommodations, as it is not sufficient to simply describe their various conditions of use. Rather, an explicit connection must be made between test demands and student needs so as to provide both practice and principles.

Structured LSA (and Accommodation) Training

Any improvement in the LSA for students with special needs simply must be based on implementation by design not accident, requiring systemic training and use of data. A number of procedures can be used in gaining traction on implementation. At the state or district level, Thompson, Morse, Sharpe, and Hall (2005) developed a training manual that can serve as a good model for meeting special needs. This manual provides extensive coverage of issues in the use of accommodations, the rationale for them, examples and nonexamples in their use, and self-checks of understanding. Other approaches to implementation of accommodations are more model-based (Cahalan-Laitusis, 2007). In this view, a number of approaches to studying accommodations can be considered in which state educational agencies (SEAs) identify various data sources and designs (much like our recommendation to upgrade the nonexperimental research designs).

Another more explicit strategy is to guide teachers in selecting accommodations (Elliott, 2007). Precise assessments of student skills and needs should form the basis for making recommendations to provide specific accommodations (Tindal, 2006). Teachers need to be more skilled in the use of data for identifying appropriate accommodations (Fuchs et al., 2005). When use of objective data for accommodation decision making was compared with teacher judgments, positive effects (i.e., evidence of differential specific support to SWDs) were found for both math and reading performance (Fuchs, Fuchs, Eaton, Hamlett, Binkley, & Crouch, 2000; Fuchs, Fuchs, Eaton, Hamlett, & Karns, 2000). Teacher judgments are undoubtedly important for understanding the nuances related to students' special needs, especially when they are rooted in needs that extend into less formal assessments in the classroom. However, these judgments should be reinforced with data collected that specifically address student skills relevant to LSA use.

Ongoing professional development among teams of teachers with knowledge of various content areas and grade-level skill expectations can be marshaled to review LSA-measured skills, school-level data, and, when possible, test items. This group of professionals can cultivate expertise in educational measurement as it pertains to ensuring that testing opportunities at their school provide useful information for teachers and parents about what all test-taking students know.

For example, similar to the Fletcher et al. (2006) study, a large-scale test can be task-analyzed for the types of items, categorizing them into various response demands. Then, students can be assessed using curriculum-based measures to document their skills (e.g., oral reading fluency or math computation; for an example, see Fuchs et al., 2000). Consideration of other needs can be documented by using surveys of teachers' perception of student need and experience in other nonacademic areas such as time management, persistence, capacity to stay on task, and so on. This information can be used to deliver accommodations that are appropriate and therefore eligible for conducting research on their effectiveness, considering the interaction of items on students.

Conclusion

Adapted from Abedi, Hofstetter, and Lord (2004), we offer some final questions that we hope remain at the forefront in considering how to best address special needs pertaining to large-scale assessments:

- Who are ELLs? Who are SWDs?
- What is the relationship between proficiency and test performance?
- What does empirical research on accommodations tell us?

As we have discussed, the answers to these questions have important implications for research, practice, and policy. In general, "many accommodations have positive effects for certain groups of students. The remaining challenge is to implement these accommodations appropriately and identify which accommodations are best for specific students" (Sireci, Scarpati, & Li, 2005, p. 486). A shift toward more critically considering the role of skills (both measured and unmeasured) in LSA is central to delineating which accommodations for special needs are appropriate and effective, allowing for score comparability among *all* student test takers.

References

Abedi, J. (2006). Language issues in item development. In S. M. Downing & T. M. Haladyna (Eds.), *Handbook of Test Development* (pp. 377–398). Mahwah, NJ: Erlbaum.

Abedi, J., Hofstetter, C., & Lord, C. (2004). Assessment accommodations for English language learners: Implications for policy-based empirical research. *Review of Educational Research, 74*(1), 1–28.

Abedi, J., Lord, C., Hofstetter, C., & Baker, E. (2000). Impact of accommodation strategies on English language learners' test performance. *Educational Measurement: Issues and Practice, 19*(3), 16–26.

Albus, D., Bielinski, J., Thurlow, M., & Liu, K. (2001). *The effect of a simplified English language dictionary on a reading test* (LEP Projects Report 1). Minneapolis, MN: University of Minnesota, National Center on Educational Outcomes. Retrieved from http://education.cehd.umn.edu/nceo/

Almond, P. J., Lehr, C., Thurlow, M. L., & Quenemoen, R. (2002). Participation in large-scale state assessment and accountability systems. In G. Tindal & T. M. Haladyna (Eds.), *Large-scale assessment programs for all students: Validity, technical adequacy, and implementation* (pp. 341–370). Mahwah, NJ: Erlbaum.

American Educational Research Association, American Psychological Association, & National Council on Measurement in Education. (1999). *Standards for educational and psychological testing.* Washington, DC: American Psychological Association.

Bolt, S. E., & Thurlow, M. L. (2004). Five of the most frequently allowed testing accommodations in state policy: Synthesis of research. *Remedial and Special Education, 25*(3), 141–152.

Bremer, C. D., Clapper, A. T., Hitchcock, C., Hall, T., & Kachgal, M. (2002). Universal design: A strategy to support students' access to the general education curriculum. *Information Brief, 1*(3), 1–5.

Cahalan-Laitusis, C. (2007). A variety of approaches for studying accommodations on assessments. In C. Cahalan Laitusis, L. L. Cook, & C. Cahalan (Eds.), *Large-scale assessment and accommodations: What works?* (pp. 71–83). Arlington, VA: Council for Exceptional Children.

Center for Universal Design. (2008). *Universal design principles.* Retrieved from http://www.ncsu.edu/project/design-projects/udi/publications/

Chiu, C. W. T., & Pearson, P. D. (1999, June). *Synthesizing the effects of test accommodations for special education and limited English proficiency students.* Paper presented at the Annual Large-scale Assessment Conference of the Council of Chief State School Officers, Snowbird, UT.

Christensen, L. L., Lazarus, S. S., Crone, M., & Thurlow, M. L. (2008). *2007 state policies on assessment and accommodations for students with disabilities (Synthesis Report 69).* Minneapolis, MN: University of Minnesota, National Center for Educational Outcomes. Retrieved from http://www.cehd.umn.edu/nceo/

Crawford, L., Almond, P., Tindal, G., & Hollenbeck, K. (2002). Teacher perspectives on inclusion of students with disabilities in high-stakes assessments. *Special Services in the Schools, 18*(1/2), 95–118.

Dolan, R. P., & Hall, T. E. (2001). Universal design for learning: Implications for large-scale assessment. *IDA Perspectives, 27,* 22–25.

Dolan, R. P., Rose, D. H., Burling, K., Harms, M., & Way, D. (2007, April). *The universal design for computer-based testing framework: A structure for developing guidelines for constructing innovative computer-administered tests.* Paper presented at the National Council on Measurement in Education Annual Meeting, Chicago, IL.

Elbaum, B. (2007). Effects of an oral testing accommodation on the mathematics performance of secondary students with and without learning disabilities. *Journal of Special Education, 40*(4), 218–229.

Elliott, S. N. (2007). Selecting and using testing accommodations to facilitate meaningful participation of all students in state and district assessments. In C. Cahalan-Laitusis, L. L. Cook, & C. Cahalan (Eds.), *Large-scale assessment and accommodations: What works?* (pp. 1–9). Arlington, VA: Council for Exceptional Children.

Elliott, S. N., Kratochwill, T. R., & McKevitt, B. C. (2001). Experimental analysis of the effects of testing accommodations on the scores of students with and without disabilities. *Journal of School Psychology, 39,* 1, 3–24.

Elliott, S. N., Kurz, A., Beddow, P., & Frey, J. (2009, February). *Cognitive load theory: Instruction-based research with application for designing tests.* Paper presented at the National Association of School Psychologists' Annual Convention, Boston, MA.

Elliott, S. N., & Marquart, A. M. (2004). Extended time as a testing accommodation: Its effects and perceived consequences. *Exceptional Children, 70*(3), 349–367.

Fletcher, J. M., Francis, D. J., Boudousquie, A., Copeland, K., Young, V., Kalinowski, S., et al. (2006). Effects of accommodations on high-stakes testing for students with reading disabilities. *Exceptional Children, 72*(2), 136–150.

Fuchs, L. S., & Fuchs, D. (1999). Fair and unfair testing accommodations. *School Administrator,* 24–29.

Fuchs, L. S., Fuchs, D., & Capizzi, A. M. (2005). Identifying appropriate test accommodations for students with learning disabilities. *Focus on Exceptional Children, 37,* 6, 1–8.

Fuchs, L. S., Fuchs, D., Eaton, S. B., Hamlett, C. L., Binkley, E., & Crouch, R. (2000). Using objective data sources to enhance teacher judgments about test accommodations. *Exceptional Children, 67*(1), 67–81.

Fuchs, L. S., Fuchs, D., Eaton, S. B., Hamlett, C. L., & Karns, K. M. (2000). Supplementing teacher judgments of mathematics test accommodations with objective data sources. *School Psychology Review, 29*(1), 65–85.

Gibson, D., Haeberli, F. B., Glover, T. A., & Witter, E. A. (2005). Use of recommended and provided testing accommodations. *Assessment for Effective Intervention, 31*(1), 19–36.

Haladyna, T. M., & Downing, S. M. (2004). Construct-irrelevant variance in high-stakes testing. *Educational Measurement: Issues and Practice, 23*(1), 17–27.

Hanna, E. I. (2005). *Inclusive design for maximum accessibility: A practical approach to universal design* (PEM Research Report 05–04). Iowa City, IA: Pearson Educational Measurement.

Helwig, R., Rozek-Tedesco, M. A., & Tindal, G. (2002). An oral versus a standard administration of a large-scale mathematics test. *Journal of Special Education, 36*(1), 39–47.

Hollenbeck, K., Rozek-Tedesco, M., & Finzel, A., (2000, April). *Defining valid accommodations as a function of setting, task, and response.* Presentation at the meeting of the Council for Exceptional Children, Vancouver, Canada.

Hollenbeck, K., Rozek-Tedesco, M., Tindal, G., & Glasgow, A. (2000). An exploratory study of student-paced versus teacher-paced accommodations for large-scale math tests. *Journal of Special Education Technology, 15*(2), 29–38.

Hollenbeck, K., Tindal, G., & Almond, P. (1998). Teachers' knowledge of accommodations as a validity issue in high-stakes testing. *Journal of Special Education, 32*(3), 175–183.

Johnson, E. (2000). The effects of accommodations on performance assessments. *Remedial and Special Education, 21*(5), 261–267.

Johnstone, C. J. (2003). *Improving the validity of large-scale tests: Universal design and student performance* (Tech. Rep. No. 37). Minneapolis, MN: National Center on Educational Outcomes. Retrieved from http://www.cehd.umn.edu/nceo/

Ketterlin-Geller, L. R. (2005). Knowing what all students know: Procedures for developing universal design for assessment. *Journal of Technology, Learning, and Assessment, 4*(2), 4–21.

Kieffer, M. J., Lesaux, N. K., Rivera, M., & Francis, D. J., (2009). Accommodations for English language learners taking large-scale assessments: A meta-analysis on effectiveness and validity. *Review of Educational Research, 79*(3), 1168–1201.

Lewandowski, L. J., Lovett, B. J., Parolin, R., Gordon, M., & Codding, R. S. (2007). Extended time accommodations and the mathematics performance of students with and without ADHD. *Journal of Psychoeducational Assessment, 25*(1), 17–28.

Lovett, B. J., (2010). Extended time testing accommodations for students with disabilities: Answers to five fundamental questions. *Review of Educational Research, 80*(4), 611–638.

Macarthur, C. A., & Cavalier, A. R. (2004). Dictations and speech recognition technology as test accommodations. *Exceptional Children, 71*(1), 43–58.

Malouf, D. B. (2005). Accommodation research to guide practice: Comments on what we know and what we need to know. *Assessment for Effective Intervention, 31*(1), 79–84.

McKevitt, B. C., & Elliott, S. N. (2003). Effects and perceived consequences of using read-aloud and teacher-recommended testing accommodations on a reading achievement test. *School Psychology Review, 32*(4), 583–600.

Meloy, L. L., Deville, C., & Frisbie, D. A. (2002). The effect of a read aloud accommodation on test scores of students with and without a learning disability in reading. *Remedial and Special Education, 23*(4), 248–255.

Messick, S. (1984). The psychology of educational measurement. *Journal of Educational Measurement, 21*(3), 215–237.

Morris, W. (Ed.). (1981). *New college edition: The American heritage dictionary of the English language.* Boston, MA: Houghton Mifflin.

National Research Council. (2001). The nature of assessment and reasoning from evidence. *Knowing what students know: The science and design of educational assessment* (pp. 38–39). Washington, DC: National Academy Press.

Olson, J. F. (2010). *Guidebook for studies of the validity of test results for test accommodations*. Washington, DC: Council of Chief State School Officers.

Phillips, S. E. (1994). High-stakes testing accommodations: Validity versus disabled rights. *Applied Measurement in Education, 7,* 93–120.

Rose, D. H., & Meyer, A. (2002). *Teaching every student in the digital age: Universal design for learning*. Alexandria, VA: Association for Supervision and Curriculum Development.

Shadish, W. R., Cook, T. D., & Campbell, D. T. (2002). *Experimental and quasi-experimental design for generalized causal inference*. Boston: Houghton Mifflin.

Shriner, J. G., & Ganguly, R. (2007). Assessment and accommodation issues under the No Child Left Behind Act and the Individuals With Disabilities Education Improvement Act. *Assessment for Effective Intervention, 32*(4), 231–243.

Sireci, S. G., Scarpati, S. E., & Li, S. (2005). Test accommodations for students with disabilities: An analysis of the interaction hypothesis. *Review of Educational Research, 75*(4), 457–490.

Thompson, S., Blount, A., & Thurlow, M. (2002). *A summary of research on the effects of test accommodations: 1999 through 2001* (Tech. Rep. No. 34). Minneapolis, MN: University of Minnesota, National Center on Educational Outcomes. Retrieved from http://education.cehd.umn.edu/nceo/

Thompson, S. J., Johnstone, C. J., Anderson, M. E., & Miller, N. A. (2005). *Considerations for the development and review of universally designed assessments* (Tech. Rep. No. 42). Minneapolis, MN: University of Minnesota, National Center on Educational Outcomes. Retrieved from http://education.cehd.umn.edu/nceo/

Thompson, S., Johnstone, C. J., & Thurlow, M. L. (2002). *Universal design applied to large scale assessments* (Synthesis Report 44). Minneapolis, MN: University of Minnesota, National Center on Educational Outcomes. Retrieved from http://education.cehd.umn.edu/nceo/

Thompson, S. J., Morse, A. B., Sharpe, M., & Hall, S. (2005). *Accommodations manual–How to select, administer, and evaluate use of accommodations for instruction and assessment of students with disabilities*. Washington, DC: Council of Chief State School Officers.

Thurlow, M. L., Lazarus, S., Thompson, S. J., & Morse, A. B. (2005). State policies on assessment participation and accommodations for students with disabilities. *Journal of Special Education, 38*(4), 232–240. doi: 10.1177/00224669050380040401.

Tindal, G., Anderson, L., Helwig, R., Miller, S., & Glasgow, A. (2000). *Accommodating students with learning disabilities on math tests using language simplification* (Technical Report). Eugene, OR: University of Oregon.

Tindal, G., & Fuchs, L. S. (2000). *A summary of research on test changes: An empirical basis for defining accommodations*. Lexington, KY: Mid-South Regional Resource Center Interdisciplinary Human Development Institute.

Tindal, G., Heath, B., Hollenbeck, K., Almond, P., and Harniss, M. (1998). Accommodating students with disabilities on large-scale tests: An experimental study. *Exceptional Children, 64*(4), 439–451.

Wolf, M. K., Kao, J. C., Griffin, N., Herman, J. L., Bachman, P. L., Chang, S. M., et al. (2008). *Issues in assessing English language learners: English language proficiency measures and accommodation uses* (Technical Report 732). Los Angeles: University of California, National Center for Research on Evaluation, Standards, and Student Testing. Retrieved from http://www.cse.ucla.edu/products/reports.asp

Ysseldyke, J., Thurlow, M. L., McGrew, K. S., & Shriner, J. (1994). *Recommendations for making decisions about the participation of students with disabilities in statewide assessment programs* (Synthesis Report 15). Minneapolis, MN: University of Minnesota, National Center on Educational Outcomes. Retrieved from http://www.education.umn.edu/NCEO/OnlinePubs/Technical15.htm

Part III
Scoring, Score Reporting, and Use of Scores

9
Scoring Issues in Large-Scale Assessments

María Elena Oliveri, Britta Gundersen-Bryden, and Kadriye Ercikan

> *Introduction*
> ***Overview of Provincial LSAs Administered in British Columbia***
> *The Foundation Skills Assessment Program*
> *Provincial Certification Examinations*
> ***Scoring in LSAs of Educational Achievement***
> ***Diverse Models Used to Score the Foundation Skills Assessment***
> ***Conclusion***

This chapter represents the individual views of the authors and does not necessarily reflect the opinions of the organizations or institutions with which the authors may be associated.

Introduction

Canadian provinces administer large-scale assessments (LSAs) of educational achievement in order to collect data for evaluating the efficacy of school systems, guiding policymaking, making decisions regarding improving student learning, and—in the case of provincial secondary end-of-course examinations—playing a role in the certification of graduating students (Crundwell, 2005; Earl, 1999; Ercikan & Barclay-McKeown, 2007; Taylor & Tubianosa, 2001). The majority of these LSAs contain both closed-response and extended open-response items. The usefulness of the data from these assessments requires that scores be accurate indicators of the targeted learning outcomes (Watermann & Klieme, 2002). At the core of such accuracy are the procedures used for scoring examinee responses and performances.

The purpose of this chapter is to describe and discuss scoring procedures used in LSAs of educational achievement and the impact that scoring processes have on inferences and interpretations made based on assessment data. To illustrate various issues related to scoring, this chapter makes reference to various provincial assessments in British Columbia, Canada. An overview of provincial LSAs administered in British Columbia in the 20th and 21st centuries is followed by a discussion of the key purposes and evolutionary changes associated with these

144 • María Elena Oliveri, Britta Gundersen-Bryden, and Kadriye Ercikan

assessments. Next, is an overview of various scoring processes and models used for scoring provincial LSAs (e.g., centralized versus decentralized models) and a discussion of the advantages and drawbacks of different models. Third, a case study is presented to highlight particular issues associated with switching scoring processes from using centralized to decentralized models. The chapter concludes with a summary of the lessons learned in British Columbia in order to offer recommendations for enhanced scoring practices.

Overview of Provincial LSAs Administered in British Columbia

In Canada, students participate in a range of provincial, national, and international assessments. Education falls under provincial or territorial jurisdiction, and there is neither a national or federal department of education nor federal funding for K–12 education (Klinger, DeLuca, & Miller, 2008). Each province and territory has its own curriculum and LSA system. At the pan-Canadian level, a national assessment is conducted by the Council of Ministers of Education Canada (CMEC), a consortium of ministries of education from all 13 jurisdictions in Canada. In addition, jurisdictions have the choice to participate in international assessments such as the Progress in International Reading Literacy Study (PIRLS) and the Programme for International Student Assessment (PISA). British Columbia and other Canadian provinces and territories participate in national (e.g., the Pan-Canadian Assessment Program) and international LSAs with large enough samples to obtain reliable estimates for specific student groups (e.g., boys and girls) at the provincial and territorial level.

Assessments at provincial, national, and international levels have different purposes, and all have the potential to inform efforts to improve learning. National and international assessments provide information about how students are doing nationally and internationally and help provinces answer questions such as: "Is performance improving over time? How are the gaps in performance changing between girls and boys, between students of different socioeconomic status, between students who live in rural and urban areas?" Assessments at the national and international levels also serve to compare how the performance of students in one province/territory measures against that of students in other provinces and countries and to judge how well students are prepared to participate in a global context (Cartwright, Lalancette, Mussio, & Xing, 2003).

The provincial assessment program in British Columbia has two components: (1) the Foundation Skills Assessment (FSA) administered to students in Grades 4 and 7 and (2) secondary school graduation program certification examinations administered to students in Grades 10 to 12. These two assessment programs are discussed below.

The Foundation Skills Assessment Program

The FSA traces its roots back to the province's Provincial Learning Assessment Program (PLAP) and PLAP's English Language Arts Assessment, which was first administered in 1976. Between 1976 and 1998, twenty different assessments were administered under the PLAP umbrella. These assessments covered a range of subjects, with literacy-related topics receiving the greatest attention. Several assessments covered more than one subject area and most subject areas were assessed more than once: reading and/or writing (nine times); mathematics (five); science (five); social studies (three); physical education, French immersion and a kindergarten needs assessment (one time each). Different grades were covered with different assessments and there were no assessments in 1983, 1992, or 1997. Given the different design of each PLAP assessment, there was little use of common or "anchor" items and hence virtually no trend data.

Scoring procedures also differed, but in general the ministry organized centralized scoring sessions under the direct supervision of ministry staff.

In 1999, the FSA became the only provincial assessment in the PLAP. It was designed as an annual census assessment of Grade 4, 7, and 10 students (the Grade 10 tests were eliminated in 2004 when Grade 10 became part of the new Graduation Program). The FSA administration in 2000 provided the baseline for comparing reading and numeracy results over the next 7 years; the 2001 administration provided the baseline for the writing results. The FSA is administered to provide various stakeholders with ongoing information related to students' academic performance. Specifically, data collected from the FSA have been used by school planning councils and by boards of education to collect trend data and measure progress over time, look at the performance of various groups of students, and compare performance across grades and domains. For example, most school districts use FSA Grade 4 and 7 reading results as one indicator of progress in their annual provincial Achievement Contracts (British Columbia Ministry of Education, n.d.). Data collection and subsequent analyses can help identify areas of relative strength and areas that need improvement.

Provincial Certification Examinations

British Columbia's provincial examinations date back to 1876, when they were designed to set provincial standards and provide equitable access to Victoria High School, the "sole institution of higher learning west of Winnipeg" (Fleming & Raptis, 2005). The current set of provincial examinations hearkens back to 1984, when Grade 12 examinations were administered across 13 subjects (English, English literature, algebra, geography, history, biology, chemistry, physics, geology, French, German, Spanish, and Latin). In 2004, new required examinations in English, science, and mathematics were added at Grade 10 and in social studies at Grade 11 as part of the Graduation Program. By 2008, the number of Grade 12 examinable subjects had increased to 19: exams for algebra and Latin had been dropped and exams for English 12-First Peoples, Français langue première, communications, principles of mathematics, applications of mathematics, French immersion, Japanese, Mandarin, and Punjabi had been added. In addition to the required Grade 10 and 11 examinations, students are also required to write a Grade 12 language arts examination. All other Grade 12 examinations are optional.

The primary purpose of provincial certification examinations is that of "gatekeeping" (Nagy, 2000) or certifying that individual students have met specific requirements to earn a secondary school diploma (referred to as the Dogwood Diploma, named after the provincial flower that appears as the background watermark on the actual diploma). These examinations are also administered for secondary purposes, including collecting data to provide evidence of student achievement and informing teaching and learning at the school, district, and ministry levels. Certification examinations impact students to varying degrees. In British Columbia's Graduation Program examinations, results from the classroom assessment and provincial examinations are blended; in all cases the teacher-assigned classroom portion of the final mark has a greater weighting than the (external) examination-based portion of the final mark. For example, Grade 10 and 11 examination results count for a lower percentage (i.e., 20%) of the student's final grade than the classroom mark (i.e., 80%). At the Grade 12 level, examination results count for 40% and classroom marks count for 60%. The concept of blending provincial and classroom marks serves to lower the stakes for individual students and is an explicit acknowledgment that there are limits to the types of learning outcomes that can be effectively assessed in a large-scale testing environment.

Scoring in LSAs of Educational Achievement

This section provides an overview of scoring processes and models. The term *scoring* refers to the process of coding, wherein numeric codes that differentiate among levels of completion and correctness of student responses are assigned to responses to restricted-choice or open-ended test questions. The codes for restricted-choice items simply indicate correct/incorrect, whereas the codes for scoring open-response items correspond to ranges of performance articulated in scoring rubrics.

Scoring of open-ended test questions involves interpretation of examinee responses and performances in relation to what is intended to be assessed by the test. This interpretation is guided by scoring rubrics that are targeted to capture evidence of different levels of the relevant competencies in each response. Three aspects of the scoring process are essential in considering accuracy and meaningfulness of scores as indicators of student competencies. These are the degree to which (1) the scoring rubrics appropriately and accurately identify relevant aspects of responses as evidence of student performance, (2) scoring rubrics are accurately implemented, and (3) the application of scoring rubrics is done consistently across examinees. All three aspects are essential for ascertaining that scores are meaningful and accurate indicators of performance and to ensure that differences in performance results are attributable to differences among examinees rather than inconsistencies introduced by the scoring procedures. The following discussion focuses on the latter two aspects of the scoring process, the appropriate application of the scoring rubrics and consistency across scorers.

Rating consistency or achieving uniformity in scoring is central to achieving comparability of students' responses in LSAs. Specifically, scoring an item in the same way across groups of students is necessary to ensure that differences in results obtained from these assessments are attributable to differences among examinees rather than due to biases introduced by the use of differing scoring procedures. For example, in most LSAs, electronic scanning processes are used to score closed-response items. To ensure uniformity in the machine-based scoring of closed-response items, it is important to verify that answer keys have been entered correctly, that answer sheets are scanned and scores are recorded accurately, and, if required, that answer sheets are matched properly with students' open-response scores. Moreover, computer programs and manual checks are used to ascertain that closed-response scores are accurate and consistent. The human element, with the potential for genuine and legitimate differences in judgment, is introduced to the scoring process for open-response items. In British Columbia's FSA and provincial examinations, open-response items generally go far beyond short constructed responses. At the Grade 10, 11, and 12 levels, students are expected to write essays, analyze historical documents, construct case studies, and solve complex science and mathematics problems (West, 2009). Even with Grade 4 and 7 FSAs, students are expected to provide extended responses. At the center of issues related to extended open-response scoring is that, in theory, two different scorers may assign a different score to the same response, thus inserting an element of inconsistency in the final results.

Scoring of open-response sections of large-scale provincial assessments is usually conducted using either a centralized or decentralized scoring model. In centralized scoring, scoring is under the direct control of a central office such as the province through its ministry or department of education; in decentralized scoring, even though a centralized office oversees the scoring process, the responsibility for various aspects of the scoring has been devolved to the school or school district level. Local scoring refers to scoring that is carried out at the school and district levels and is not done under the direct supervision of the ministry or department of education.

The designers of large-scale examinations and assessments and the organizations responsible for the administration of these examinations and assessments take a number of steps to eliminate or at least minimize inconsistent assignment of scores. Typically, a five-step process is used to ensure consistency in scoring; these steps may overlap with aspects of test design and development and even with each other. Therefore these steps are meant to be viewed as components of the scoring process rather than steps conducted in a linear fashion.

The *first step* to ensure consistent assignment of scores is at the test design stage, wherein a key tool called test specifications or "blueprint" is developed to match the learning outcomes or construct(s) being assessed with the test items. The test specifications guide the development of the test and of the scoring rubrics, the latter of which is key to obtaining consistent scoring. The specifications include the particular weights and number of items needed to assess each intended construct; the specific format and relative weighing of the questions or items in the specifications in relation to the entire test and specific items included therein will depend on how a specific outcome can best be assessed. For example, some learning outcomes, such as those related to laboratory experiments or other hands-on activities, are typically more difficult to assess (i.e., difficult to score consistently) in LSAs and are often avoided. Recent research has shed light on innovative item formats that have the potential to assess in more authentic ways how students are learning in the classroom; such items are designed to simulate performance tasks in the real world and examine how students interact with stimuli that resemble situations that they will encounter in real life (Huff & Sireci, 2001). The administration of such items is typically conducted—and scored—by computer rather than by paper-and-pencil tests.

The *second step* is to determine which model will be used to score open-response items. The choice of scoring model and the scoring process itself contribute greatly to the accuracy of scores and therefore to the utility of the data that are collected through LSAs and examinations and the decisions that may be taken as a result. There are a number of lenses through which scoring models could be viewed; a common approach is to think of a scoring model as "centralized" or "decentralized." There are also hybrid models that combine centralized and decentralized elements. Centralized scoring sessions are generally models of efficiency that are organized and run by teams of personnel with experience and expertise in conducting such sessions; as mentioned, such processes are directly supervised by provincial ministries or departments of education. In decentralized models, scoring may take place in different locations and may be performed by a considerably greater number of teachers. In selecting a scoring model, testing organizations (typically ministries or departments of education) need to consider the primary and secondary purposes of a specific examination or assessment. In British Columbia, scoring models have been aligned with the various purposes of each of the following: Grade 12 examinations, Grade 10 and 11 examinations, and the FSA, wherein an effort is made to maintain a fine balance between consistency in scoring and involvement level. Generally the greater the need for scoring consistency (for example, with higher-stakes certification examinations or with examinations and assessments that rely solely on open-response items), the more likely it is that a centralized model will be used. For example, when the Grade 12 examinations were reintroduced in 1984, Jack Heinrich, then minister of education, highlighted the importance of striving for excellence in British Columbia's education system by introducing centrally marked provincial examinations as a way of improving student achievement and ensuring consistent standards of education throughout the province (Fleming & Raptis, 2005).

If one purpose of a low-stakes LSA is to develop a broader understanding of provincial expectations among teachers and principals and to inform classroom practice, it is more likely that a decentralized model will be used. In both centralized and decentralized models, attention is paid to the "human element." To help them assign a score, scorers are provided with a centrally prepared scoring guide (usually called a scoring rubric) as well as examples (exemplars) of student responses along each point in the performance scale.

British Columbia has traditionally used a centralized scoring model to score open-response items for Grade 12 examinations, with all scorers of a particular subject gathered together at the same site. An exception is the scoring of English 12 examinations, where scorers gather in two or three different venues across the province. For example, in June 2009, there were 74 English 12 scorers at the Greater Vancouver site, 40 at the Okanagan site, and 32 at the Vancouver Island site. Collectively they scored more than 27,175 examinations, each of which had three open-response items. Team leaders for each English 12 site communicate closely with each other during scoring sessions and use identical scorer training and recalibration materials and procedures to maintain consistency. All Grade 12 English examination scorers must successfully complete a "credentialing" or pretraining process prior to being contracted to score. Given the degree of ministry oversight and control, this multisite scoring is closer to a centralized model than a decentralized model. In British Columbia, approximately 85,000 students take the closed-response portions of the FSA online. These multiple-choice responses are immediately scored by computer. A number of Grade 12 examinations with both closed-response and extended open-response items may also be taken online. Approximately 25,000 Grade 12 students chose to take online versions in 2009. As a result, British Columbia has developed an online marking process for provincial Grade 12 online exams. This process replicates the centralized model, with small groups of trained teacher-markers scoring together in a computer lab at various locations but with a high degree of ministry oversight.

A decentralized scoring model has been used for scoring open-response items for Grade 10 and 11 language arts and social studies examinations as well as the open-response items for the FSA. This model has been implemented by devolving scoring responsibilities to the school or district level, following ministry guidelines and using ministry-prepared training materials as well as guidelines established by the *Principles for Fair Student Assessment Practices for Education in Canada* (Joint Advisory Committee, 1993). This type of scoring may introduce a higher degree of site-specific variance than a centralized scoring model; hence, it is typically used for tests that have lower stakes. To minimize this potential drawback, the ministry rescores a sample of these examinations and assessments during centralized summer "monitoring" sessions (see step 5).

The *third step* in the scoring process is to provide common tools (e.g., exemplars of students' work demonstrating various stages of performance) that will be used during a scoring session. It is important not only to determine the nature of the rubric but also to select exemplars at all of the scale points and to determine how the scorers will be trained to use these tools. Guidelines for scoring itself are also developed to answer questions such as, "How long should it take to score a response?" "Is double-scoring needed?" "How do scorers handle responses with disturbing content?"

The *fourth step* is the actual training of scorers; whether using a centralized or decentralized scoring model, training must take place before scoring, and monitoring must occur afterwards. Training and monitoring are the "bookends" that serve to reinforce common standards and consistency in the assignment of scores in either centralized or decentralized scoring models; they lead to a fair and accurate scoring. In centralized models, emphasis is placed on having a consistent process that, in turn, should lead to consistent scores. Training occurs prior to scoring and can recur during the session itself, especially if the session spans more than a day. Periodically, scorers will score a common response that has been "prescored" by scoring leaders; the individual scores will be reviewed to see if the same score has been given by all or most scorers. Scorers will be given feedback to explain the rationale for the specific score. This type of activity serves to recalibrate scorers during a scoring session. Another potential way to minimize site-specific variance is through computer-delivered training. British Columbia is taking initial steps in training scorers online, especially for those who are scoring provincial examinations that students write online.

Training can happen in a variety of ways. Generally scorers are trained to score a single item at a time; more extensive periods of time are spent training prior to initial scoring of any responses than at later stages of the scoring process (e.g., during monitoring). Training or retraining occurs throughout the scoring process, especially if there are many items to be scored. A "train the trainer" approach is often used. A small cadre of more experienced trainers or team leaders are trained first (usually by the department or organization that developed the assessment or examination); they, in turn, are responsible for training the scorers who will actually score the responses and, if needed, to make final judgment calls on the assignment of scores to responses that may vary significantly from those used in exemplars or other training materials.

It is during scorer training that trainers need to address such issues as the potential for the introduction of "scorer bias." For example, some scorers attribute "neat" handwriting to either boys or girls or the use of specific sentence structures or vocabulary to mother tongue or second language learners and use this information to predetermine an expected level of performance. Differences in scoring may be introduced if particular scorers assume that a response that has been typed should be more polished than a handwritten response and therefore set higher expectations for such responses (Nichols & Williams, 2009; Powers, Fowles, Farnum, & Ramsey, 1994). Moreover, some scorers may expect higher or lower levels of performance based on the jurisdiction, region, or even school attended by a student (even when this information is not obvious on a response form or test paper, a student may provide such information in a specific open response). Trainers and training materials that raise these issues allow scorers to be aware of such biases and therefore contribute to fair and consistent scoring.

The *fifth and final step* is to monitor the assignment of scores. This can be done in a number of ways. Checks for intermarker reliability involve having different scorers assign scores to the same response (one that has already been assigned a score by team leaders) and then checking to see if all scorers assigned the same score or looking at the range of differences in scores. This is often done during a centralized scoring session itself and serves as a retraining or "recalibration" activity, with scorers discussing the scores and rationales prior to returning to the actual scoring task. In a decentralized model, a sample of responses may be "rescored" by the testing agency following the decentralized scoring sessions, with feedback given to the original scorers on how close they came to assigning the agency-determined score. In British Columbia, school districts that have conducted local scoring of open-response sections of the FSA and Grade 10 and 11 provincial examinations are invited to send participants to summer monitoring sessions. Participants not only rescore responses but also gain expertise in organizing scoring sessions in their own districts. In British Columbia, student scores are not changed as a result of monitoring.

The above-mentioned steps in the scoring process are all needed but may be handled differently in centralized and decentralized models. The goal is to have an explicit set of procedures that will lead to consistency in scoring, which is essential for fair, accurate, and consistent results. The next section is a case study that uses the FSA to exemplify and highlight the potential benefits of going from a centralized to a decentralized scoring model; it also identifies some of the challenges related to such a switch in practice. Moreover, this case study serves to shine light upon issues related to the reliability of the FSA and the validity of inferences based upon scores from this assessment.

Diverse Models Used to Score the Foundation Skills Assessment

In 2008, in response to stakeholders' demands to have LSAs that were more meaningful and useful in informing classroom practice, significant changes were made to the FSA. Changes included moving its administration window from May to February and administering the closed-response sections of the reading and numeracy components to approximately 85,000 Grade 4 and 7 students using computers with an online, web-based application (as opposed to paper-and-pencil based administration, as had been done in previous years). In addition, a school- or district-based scoring model was introduced, and by March 31, parents or guardians were provided with students' open-response portions as well as a summary statement of performance on each of the three components (i.e., reading, writing, and numeracy). Changes of this magnitude required setting a new baseline for reporting results and measuring progress. In other words, comparing results from FSA 2007 and prior administrations with the FSA 2008 administration could lead to unwarranted conclusions and should only be made with appropriate caveats and cautions regarding the comparability of the data.

Moreover, in 2008, a decentralized scoring model was used for scoring the FSA. In British Columbia prior to 2008, a centralized model was used for scoring the FSA; then, approximately 350 teachers scored the open-response items in reading, writing, and numeracy for approximately 85,000 student booklets over 4 or 5 days. In 2008, school districts and boards of education were given responsibility for scoring the open-response sections of the tests, following ministry guidelines and using ministry-provided scoring rubrics. This decentralized model was characterized by educators (teachers on call, teachers, and administrators) conducting the scoring. To this end, in the fall of 2007, the ministry held "train the trainer" workshops across the province designed to prepare school district personnel to organize and conduct local scoring sessions. The Ministry of Education (2007) also produced a guide for trainers called the *FSA Grades 4 & 7 Training/Scoring Guide 2007/2008*. Schools and districts were given a degree of discretion in conducting their scoring sessions. For example, they could decide to score individually, in pairs, or in groups. They could choose to double-score only a few, some, or all of the responses.

Possible benefits of such a switch in scoring models include providing increased opportunities for professional development for educators and giving parents and school personnel more immediate feedback regarding students' performance. To illustrate, the change from a centralized to a decentralized model led to the involvement of more teachers in the scoring process. For example, British Columbia school districts reported that approximately 1,500 educators were involved in scoring FSA 2008. "Local" scoring was actually school district based scoring in most instances, with large groups of teachers and principals coming together and scoring tests from other classes or even schools. Compared with the centralized model, more than four times as many teachers were able to work with scoring rubrics and exemplars and to assign scores reflecting provincial standards to student responses. Specifically, through this change in scoring models, educators were able to become more familiar with a broad range of samples of student performance and to develop a deeper understanding of provincial standards and expectations for student achievement. Thus, a key benefit of decentralized models is the potential to involve a significantly higher number of trained scorers than the number of educators involved in scoring within centralized models. If scorers are educators, they may later apply tools such as rubrics and exemplars in their classroom practice and school environments and consider the performance of their own students in a broader provincial context. Teachers may also want to use the rating criteria to help their students mark other students' assignments within their class or their own writing samples.

Administering the FSA in February rather than May enabled earlier provision of feedback to teachers, students, and the school. Findings from previous studies suggest that giving immediate feedback to students about their performance is central to improving learning and guiding teaching (Black & Wiliam, 1998). In the case of LSAs, score reports and information about how students performed in the assessment should be provided to teachers, students, and the school in a timely fashion in order to have an impact on their learning. If teachers obtain assessment results at the end of the year or in the following year, such results are of limited use because teachers will not be likely to use them; that is, they are receiving results that pertain to students whom they are no longer teaching (Aitkin & Longford, 1986; Coe & Fitz-Gibbon, 1998; Ercikan & Barclay-McKeown, 2007; Goldstein & Thomas, 1996).

Moreover, a prompt return of results to educators in the form of raw data that includes receipt of students' test booklets may be more informative for teachers, as they can then see students' actual responses and make sense of students' performance on the test. These data may inform teachers about students' strengths and areas that they need to review in relation to provincial standards. The data provided to teachers may be helpful in identifying what their students need to learn, how to identify when these skills have been learned, and what to do for students who have not yet learned the material to the minimal satisfactory level. These data may also be helpful in writing school plans and targeting the areas upon which particular schools may need to focus.

Further, when test results are reported by domain or by learning outcomes, they can provide relevant information regarding students' specific areas of strengths and weaknesses, which teachers can then use to tailor their teaching. Although the FSA does not report domain or learning outcome results at the individual student level, it does report this information at the provincial, district, and school level. For FSA 2008 and beyond, this added information has also been provided before the end of the school year for the reading and mathematics components administered online. As an additional planning and intervention tool, teachers have access to data on overall student performance in different aspects of what is being measured.

With any LSA, changes in the timing of test administration, mode of administration, scoring models, and timing and format of reports may all have an impact on the collection of trend data. The overall purposes of the FSA did not change between 2000 and 2008. However, the various changes made to the FSA in the 2008 administration—including changes in the design of the test, mode of delivery (e.g., paper-and-pencil versus computer-based administration), scoring (e.g., use of centralized versus decentralized models), and timing of reporting—affect the comparison of results over time and point to the need to establish new trend data. Although it would not be appropriate to base trend data on direct comparisons between the results from FSA 2000 2007 and FSA 2008, 2009, or 2010, and so on, information related to specific groups of students as well as relative and general comparisons may still be used with caution. Reviewing the quality of data obtained from the FSA is important in order to ensure that data are interpreted carefully and that meaningful interpretations based on systematic analyses of different sources of evidence are derived from FSA scores. To this end, the concluding section provides recommendations for making the inevitable change process associated with LSAs smoother. It also offers a synopsis of lessons learned in British Columbia.

Conclusion

As LSAs evolve, so do the scoring procedures and practices associated with those assessments. A number of changes have been introduced to provincial examinations and assessments across Canadian provinces and territories in the past several years, and more are likely to come in the future. In British Columbia, some key lessons were learned that directly relate to scoring; this chapter in general and the case study in particular raised several points that link scoring models to the overall validity, reliability, and utility of results from LSAs like British Columbia's FSA. Two key issues are highlighted in this section: (1) the benefits and drawbacks associated with the use of a decentralized model and (2) a closer alignment of test purpose and test scoring attained through collaboration between educators and ministries and departments of education and testing organizations.

In this chapter, the benefits associated with the use of a decentralized scoring model were described. Three of these benefits are (1) professional development related to scoring, which arises by having a greater number of educators score LSAs; (2) increased understanding of provincial standards of student achievement by working with exemplars of students' work and rating them according to provincial standards; and (3) having a more rapid turnaround of results, leading to more immediate feedback for educators regarding the performance of students while they are still being taught. An important drawback of this model is the increased difficulty associated with the implementation of cross-check procedures to establish cross-scorer reliability to ensure consistency of scores and uniformity of instructions given to scorers. The following three structures may be put in place to reduce this drawback. First, teachers should be given adequate training time (e.g., 1 to 2 days of training prior to scoring the assessments) to demonstrate the use of training papers or exemplars of students' work and to illustrate the level of performance associated with each point on the scale. Second, discussion among teachers should be encouraged during the training session; this may involve reviewing exemplars that fall between scale points in the rubric. Third, for quality assurance purposes, table leaders (e.g., teachers with prior scoring experience) can sit at tables with teachers who are new to the scoring process. In addition, teachers may be asked to regroup every so often to verify difficulties or uncertainties related to the scoring process.

Moreover, central to the use of LSAs is aligning test design, test development, administration, and scoring of the test with the purposes of the test; otherwise inaccurate claims regarding student learning may be made. Close collaboration between testing organizations, ministries and departments of education, and educators is key to this alignment. This collaboration may take different forms and may occur at different stages of the scoring process. For example, it may arise during the development of test blueprints to ensure there are close ties between the curriculum and the test (stage one of the scoring process). Alternatively, it may occur during the actual scoring of tests as a way of enhancing educators' understanding of provincial standards of student achievement.

References

Aitkin, M., & Longford, N. (1986). Statistical modelling issues in school effectiveness studies. *Journal of the Royal Statistical Society Series A (Statistics in Society), 149*(1) 1–43.

Black, P., & Wiliam, D. (1998). Assessment and classroom learning. *Assessment in education: Principles, policy, and practice, 5,* 1–57.

British Columbia Ministry of Education. (n.d.). *Achievement Contracts.* Retrieved from http://www.bced.gov.bc.ca/schools/sdinfo/acc_contracts/

British Columbia Ministry of Education. (2007). *FSA Grades 4 & 7 Training/Scoring Guide 2007/2008.* Retrieved from: http://www.bced.gov.bc.ca/assessment/fsa/training/grade_4_7_scoring_guide.pdf

Cartwright, F., Lalancette, D., Mussio, J., & Xing, D. (2003). *Linking provincial student assessments with national and international assessments.* Report no 81–595-MIE2003005. Ottawa: Statistics Canada.

Coe, R., & Fitz-Gibbon, C. T. (1998). School effectiveness research: Criticisms and recommendations. *Oxford Review of Education, 24,* 4, 421–438.

Crundwell, R. M. (2005). Alternative strategies for large scale student assessment in Canada: Is value-added assessment one possible answer. *Canadian Journal of Educational Administration and Policy, 41,* 1–21.

Earl, L. M. (1999). Assessment and accountability in education: Improvement or surveillance. *Education Canada, 39*(3), 4–47.

Ercikan, K., & Barclay-McKeown, S. (2007). Design and development issues in large-scale assessments: Designing assessments to provide useful information to guide policy and practice. *Canadian Journal of Program Evaluation, 22*(3), 53–71.

Fleming, T., & Raptis, H. (2005). Government's paper empire: Historical perspectives on measuring student achievement in British Columbia schools, 1872–1999, *Journal of Educational Administration and History, 37*(2), 173–202.

Goldstein, H., & Thomas, S. (1996). Using examination results as indicators of school and college performance. *Journal of the Royal Statistical Society Series A (Statistics in Society), 159*(1), 149–163.

Huff, K. L., & Sireci, S. G. (2001). Validity issues in computer-based testing. *Educational Measurement: Issues and Practice, 20*(3), 16–25.

Klinger, D. A., DeLuca, C., & Miller, T. (2008). The evolving culture of large-scale assessments in Canadian education. *Canadian Journal of Educational Administration and Policy, 76*(3), 1–34.

Joint Advisory Committee. (1993). *Principles for Fair Student Assessment Practices for Education in Canada*. Edmonton, AL: Author.

Nagy, P. (2000). The three roles of assessment: Gatekeeping, accountability, and instructional diagnosis. *Canadian Journal of Education / Revue Canadienne de l'Education, 25*(4), 262–279.

Nichols, P. D., & Williams, N. (2009). Consequences of test score use as validity evidence: Roles and responsibilities. *Educational Measurement: Issues and Practice, 28*(1), 3–9.

Powers, D. E., Fowles, M. E., Farnum, M., & Ramsey, P. (1994). Will they think less of my handwritten essay if others word process theirs? Effects on essay scores of intermingling handwritten and word-processed essays. *Journal of Educational Measurement, 31*, 220–233.

Taylor, A. R., & Tubianosa, T. (2001). *Student assessment in Canada: Improving the learning environment through effective evaluation*. Kelowna, BC: Society for the Advancement of Excellence in Education.

Watermann, R., & Klieme, E. (2002). Reporting results of large-scale assessment in psychologically and educationally meaningful terms. Construct validation and proficiency scaling in TIMSS. *European Journal of Psychological Assessment, 18*, 109–203.

West, M. (2009). High achieving countries don't narrow. *Why we're behind: What top nations teach their students but we don't*. Washington, DC: Common Core.

10
Standard Setting
Past, Present, and Perhaps Future

Robert W. Lissitz

> *Introduction*
> *Performance Level Descriptors*
> *Traditional Standard-Setting Methods*
>   *A Priori Judgment of the Examinees: Contrasting Groups Method*
>   *Judgment of the Test Items*
>   *Judgment of the Answers: Holistic Methods*
> *The Big Picture*
> *Expected Future of Standard Setting*
> *Issues of Reliability and Validity for Standard Setting*
> *Conclusion*

I would like to thank Dr. Craig Deville of Measurement Incorporated for his extensive comments and advice on this chapter. He has extensive experience and thoughtful opinions on the conduct of standard setting.

Introduction

This chapter presents the reader with a short summary of the history of standard setting, a sense of the current state of affairs, guidelines for conducting standard setting, and some indication of where the field seems to be going in the near future. While the focus of this book is on education, this chapter interprets that in a more expansive way. In other words, recognizing that education includes language arts and that mathematics is important, education is also related to plumbing, medicine, law, and cosmetology. It is the author's hope that this chapter will be of interest to broadly defined practitioners.

Standard setting is likely to become more technical as psychometric procedures—especially latent class analysis–based mixture models (Jiao, Lissitz, Macready, Wang, & Liang, 2010)—become more widely known, implemented, studied, and improved. There are also interesting conceptual issues associated with standard setting; this chapter is intended to help the readers become more aware of these so that they may form their own opinions regarding them. Hopefully the reader will not only become familiar with some of the issues but be able to defend his or her own conclusions and explore implications with some degree of confidence.

The science and practice of standard setting is an important area of work in large-scale testing for a variety of reasons. One is that it just seems natural and desirable to divide test takers, or any other collection of people for that matter, into groups. We are all used to dealing with such divisions and encounter them regularly in our daily lives. For example, a doctor tells us that we have high blood pressure or we do not, we have a cholesterol problem or we do not, a teacher tells us we got a B on the test in addition to our numerical scores. We also know that some people are licensed or certified whereas others are not. For example, we might want to hire a licensed plumber, electrician, lawyer, doctor, or some other professional, and the fact that this person has taken a test and exceeded the standards gives us confidence that he or she has the skills we seek to employ.

Another reason for such standards, in the United States at least, is that in many contexts of K–12 public education we are required to categorize students by federal law. The federal law known as the No Child Left Behind Act (2001) actually demands that state education authorities divide students into at least three categories of proficiency. These can be labeled using any terminology that the state wishes, although "Basic," "Proficient," and "Advanced" are in common usage. If the state wants to use four proficiency categories of students' academic achievement in a content area, "Below Basic" might be used to designate the lowest category in addition to the three formerly named categories. There really are no determinative criteria for the selection of a state's labels for performance levels, although ease of memory and clarity of meaning become considerations. A long time ago, teachers might have used *robins* and *bluebirds* to designate groupings of students for instructional purposes, and the terms were usually chosen with the hope (illusion) that the students would not know which group was more advanced. That is not true in the present case. Now we typically designate levels of success as groupings along a scale of test scores or performance levels, and accurate as well as honest communication is now considered a virtue.

Linn (1994) outlined four reasons for using standard setting. The first is to motivate learners and instructors. The second is to clarify expectations and accomplishments. The third is for use in accountability, which is the main use today, with the No Child Left Behind Act. Finally, the fourth is to certify, as mentioned above, with regard to achieving graduation requirements, licensure, and so on.

It is important to recognize that the standard-setting process is being utilized to determine cut points, and these must be done in a credible way that generates confidence in the outcomes. This process might be considered from an evidence-centered design standpoint (Kane, 1994; Mislevy, Steinberg, & Almond, 2003)—in other words, creating an argument that supports the conclusions obtained from the process. In certification and licensure contexts as well as in K–12 public education, where the testing is what we call "high stakes" (i.e., there are consequences for the test takers), there are even legal motivations for careful justification of the standards being set. This author always recommends that the responsible party proceed with standard setting in the expectation that he or she will be sued. This orientation has a tendency to focus the mind on the process and its defense and justification and to discourage arbitrary shortcuts. A paper trail should be created for every important step of the process, with the expectation that someone outside will examine the paperwork as a defense for what has been done to obtain the cut scores.

This field has enjoyed a great deal of work and there are books on this subject (e.g., Cizek, 2001; Cizek & Bunch, 2007; Hambleton & Pitoniak, 2006; Jaeger, 1989) as well as training materials (e.g., Cizek, 1996) available to the interested reader. These materials are designed for application, and there is also an extensive literature that has attempted to study standard setting as a research topic. Research in this area is difficult to conduct owing to the time and energy needed to simulate standard setting. Also, generalization from these results is debatable because of the context-dependent nature of standard setting.

Performance Level Descriptors

Prior to any standard-setting activity, everyone concerned needs to understand the purpose and context of the test for which the cut points are being set. There is always a broadly defined intent as well as important consequences that underlie every standard setting, and it is important to try to appreciate that in order to come to the right decisions. The first step in conducting the standard setting is to determine the nature of the categories into which one wants to classify the test takers. The categories are formally designated by performance level labels (PLLs), which are associated with performance level descriptors (PLDs). Examples of the labels, as provided above, include *proficient, advanced,* and so on. If done right, there is considerable work involved in developing the details of the PLDs. These are typically created by a team of experts in the subject matter in which the testing is to take place. In a high school education environment, for example, the team might include a mixture of teachers of that specific subject (English, mathematics, science, etc.), with perhaps a few business people and even supervisors as added members to accommodate the perspectives of professionals who not only teach the test takers but also work with them in other contexts. In certification exams for professional groups, the team typically consists of people who have considerable credibility in that particular profession. The team might consist of successful practitioners along with people who play an important instructional role in that profession. In the industrial field, these people might be called subject matter experts (SMEs).

In any case, the members of the team are usually identified publicly, and it is considered an honor to be included on such a team. There are usually somewhere between 10 and 20 members and they are all experts, but in addition they are chosen to represent quite different constituencies or what are sometimes called stakeholder groups. In a state context of education testing, the team is usually chosen to be diverse and representative of demographic, racial, and gender groups as well as the school's socioeconomic status (SES), at least to the extent possible. The team typically works at tables of four or five members, and each table is assigned so as to preserve diversity to the extent possible.

Good PLDs provide a sense of the skills that characterize different levels of performance along the dimension of proficiency captured by the test material used for the certification, licensure, end-of-course, high school graduation, or other proficiency exam. The test might consist of multiple-choice as well as performance items. For example, in a test for cosmetology, students seeking certification might be asked to color a person's hair, shave a neck, and demonstrate a command of cognitive skills assessed in a more formal manner. The PLDs must be written to capture the fundamental differences in skill level that the test is designed to assess.

Bloom's taxonomy (Bloom, Englehart, Furst, Hill, & Krathwohl, 1956) or some other system (e.g., Quellmalz, 1987) for characterizing levels of expertise may be used to help define the PLDs. The choices of descriptors are very important because they not only define the results of standard setting and their corresponding decisions but are also the source for communication to parents, teachers, test takers, and any other test stakeholders regarding the outcomes of the assessment. The PLDs should drive everything that happens in the standard setting itself. Table 10.1 gives an example of a set of PLDs from a state Grade 11 literacy examination.

Table 10.1 Performance Level Descriptors for Grade 11 Literacy

Performance Level	Descriptors
Advanced	In reading, students clearly demonstrate thorough, thoughtful, and comprehensive understanding of the text and reflect recognition of concrete and abstract ideas. They analyze and/or evaluate purpose, meaning, form, and literary techniques, supporting their ideas with accurate and relevant examples from the text. In writing, students respond appropriately to the task and audience, consistently employing an effective organizational strategy; relevant, illustrative, and varied supporting details; and sophisticated and purposeful sentence constructions and rich language to enhance meaning. The students demonstrate consistent, though not necessarily perfect, command of grammar, punctuation, capitalization, and spelling.
Proficient	In reading, students demonstrate an overall understanding of the text that includes inferential and literal information. They identify and/or analyze purpose, meaning, form, and literary techniques, supporting their ideas with relevant examples from the text. In writing, students respond appropriately to the task and audience and use a logical organization. They use relevant details, specific vocabulary, and varied sentence constructions. The students demonstrate reasonable command of grammar, punctuation, capitalization, and spelling despite some errors.
Basic	In reading, students demonstrate general understanding and make literal interpretations of the text. They identify and use some aspects of text, make simple inferences, and draw conclusions. In writing, students respond to the task and audience displaying a sense of organization. They use supporting details, but these may be minimal, and demonstrate an adequate command of grammar, punctuation, capitalization, and spelling.
Below Basic	Students do not show sufficient understanding of skills in reading and writing to attain the basic level.

No set of PLDs is ever perfect, but this set has clearly been designed to capture levels of cognitive complexity. Notice that the description of "Advanced" uses such key words as *thoughtful*, *consistent*, and *comprehensive*.

Those key words can be compared with the key words in "Proficient," which can in turn be compared with the words in "Basic" and finally "Below Basic." Table 10.2 represents an effort to summarize and organize the key words.

First, notice what these descriptors are *not*. At one time, some PLDs contained phrases such as "could read simple material" for "Basic" and "could read more complex material" for "Proficient." Those were not well-defined descriptions. The use of what are called "action verbs" from the literature on objectives (Quellmalz, 1987) makes the judgments comparing levels of PLD much easier. Notice that the action verbs should generally show a steady increase in the cognitive sophistication required of a test taker to meet the qualifications of each successively higher PLD. The selection of the action verbs, and determining the extent to which the successive PLDs show an increasing cognitive sophistication, are some of the challenges that the PLD committee will face in creating their own PLDs for the selected test. The summary of the PLDs presented in Table 10.2 is an illustration of what one team developed. We might call such a table a proficiency growth summary (PGS) since it allows us to see what the instructional expectations are for students at different levels of intellectual growth with respect to the subject matter being assessed.

It would be nice if the test were designed to facilitate the standard-setting process, but that is rarely the case. The design of the test usually follows a method that does not include any consideration of the eventual standards to be set for it. Looking at the attempt to summarize the action verbs in the PGS (Table 10.2) in successive levels of English Grade 11 literacy helps us see what the standard setting is trying to capture. In addition, though, it would be nice if the

Table 10.2 Proficiency Growth Summary Based on Action Verbs for 11th Grade Literacy

Level	Proficiency
Basic	General understanding
	Literal interpretations
	Identify some aspects
	Simple inferences
	Draw conclusions
	Display sense of organization
	Use supporting details
	Demonstrate adequate command
Proficient	Overall understanding
	Literal and inferential
	Identify and/or analyze
	Use logical organization
	Use relevant details
	Demonstrate reasonable command
Advanced	Demonstrate thorough understanding
	Concrete and abstract ideas
	Employ effective organization
	Sophisticated and purposeful
	Demonstrate consistent command

test itself were systematically developed to capture that same cognitive growth. In other words, items might be written at advancing cognitive levels to capture performance changes across each level. However, that would require communication among the assessment teams, which would be hard to ensure. Such activities are very difficult, time-consuming, and costly as is, and coordination would only increase the work associated with such an effort. Perhaps a very large item bank would make such an effort possible, even if pursued retrospectively.

The committee will need a day or two to create a set of PLDs. Sample tests and materials related to the design and creation of the test in question will need to be presented to the team charged with defining the PLDs. The leader of the PLD development activity (usually a contractor) may decide to present samples of previously well-done PLDs. Also, having experts from the school system in attendance to serve as consultants to the PLD team is a good idea, along with assessment experts. This is also true for certification and licensure applications, with SMEs on the team who are supported by psychometricians or other testing experts. The members of the team must demonstrate a tolerance for open discussion of the PLDs, since give and take is critical to the group process, engineered to reaching consensus.

In the standard-setting process, team opinions that might not suit everyone must be tolerated. Remember, the outcome is a product created by the team of practitioners. Engaging the team in an explicit discussion about all PLD-relevant matters is important. The author once attended a standard-setting session that seemed to be creating cut points for a Grade 5 assessment that were more demanding than those created for a comparable Grade 7 assessment. It took a while for the observers to recognize that this reversal in performance expectations was inevitable, given the PLDs that were created. A PGS table showed that there were greater demands upon the fifth graders than upon the seventh graders. It was not until we started to set standards that this problem revealed itself. In such cases, where tests are linked or progressive across years of school, the PLDs need to be considered in that context and adjusted or aligned accordingly.

Traditional Standard-Setting Methods

The following methodologies have been used on a regular basis to define categories of test takers. In each case, the aim is to locate the cut score along the continuum of scores possible from the assessment and doing this consistent with the PLDs. At one time this task was a great deal easier than it is now. It was not uncommon for organizations to simply say that anyone taking the assessment and achieving a score of greater than or equal to 70% of the items correct is passing. This works for dichotomous decisions, often referred to as mastery/nonmastery categorizations. If divisions into more than two categories were required, similar arbitrary decisions were made. Fortunately the threat of a lawsuit motivated a more thoughtful approach, which, in turn, resulted in defensible rules and practices for dividing test takers into categories of proficiency. In other words, we now employ a systematic, thoughtful, valid approach to categorizing test takers. This section of the chapter describes some of the approaches to standard setting that have been in existence for many years and can be considered to be traditional. A later section describes some of the newer approaches to standard setting.

The reader will discover that the traditional standard setting procedures depend primarily upon human judgment, with some statistics or psychometrics added into the process. The difference between these procedures revolves around the source of the information upon which the human judgment focuses. These approaches are grouped into three sections, depending upon the different source of information that yields the basis for the judgments that determine the cut points. The three sections are organized around the source and focus of the judgment phase. The first depends upon the careful identification of the examinees themselves, who are thought to be representative of each of the PLD categories. The standard-setting judgment focuses on these representative students. The second section starts with the test items themselves and examines their level of cognitive demand, so the judgment has to do with determining the cognitive demand and where one PLD ends and another starts in terms of this demand. The third section examines student responses to the test items. This third group of methods is usually focused on tests that consist of extended responses to items, often known as essay or constructed response exams. The judgment in this case is to determine which extended responses capture which levels of PLD. The traditional (i.e., widely used) approaches fall into one of these three types of standard setting. The core decision processes for four of the best-known methods are discussed in some detail. Although there are dozens of approaches to standard setting, these four approaches illustrate the traditional approaches in the context of fixed-form assessments (i.e., nonadaptive assessments or assessments that are not different for different examinees at a single administration). Such assessments are typically administered by paper and pencil, although computer administration of the equivalent of the paper-and-pencil version is considered a minor variant, and one of the traditional approaches will work in that context as well. Most of the other approaches to standard setting that have been suggested are variations on one of these four.

A Priori Judgment of the Examinees: Contrasting Groups Method

The contrasting groups approach (e.g., Livingston & Zieky, 1982; Zieky & Livingston, 1977) requires experts who are very familiar with the subject matter to identify students (or trainees in an industrial environment) who are representative of each of the PLD groups. For this reason, the approach is often characterized as person-centered. The selected experts make their determination using the PLDs obtained from an earlier exercise, as described above. For example, teachers would be given the four PLDs from Table 10.1 and told to identify students who perform in class consistent with each PLD group. In this way students are identified who demonstrate performance consistent with the classification characterized by the PLDs. This is a difficult task requiring carefully crafted instructions and, even in the best of circumstances, formal training. The goal is to create a long list of students (at least 200 per PLD) who are representative of each of the performance groups. Obviously part of the carefully crafted instructions for the selector consists of the PLDs. They serve as the basic information required for successful application of this procedure. Notice that the selection is not based on the test scores for which standards are being set but on cognitive functioning and achievement within the classroom.

Great care should be attached to the materials that are sent to the teachers, supervisors, or others who are charged with selecting the "students" for this method of standard setting. This is particularly true when there is no further communication with the selectors other than a set of directions. The materials should be piloted in some manner that permits systematically collecting reactions to determine if the participants are clear about the communication and are going to be consistent in their identification of students in each category. The more students who are identified as members of a PLD group, the better the eventual result from a reliability standpoint, but of course more students means more cost.

The accuracy of this approach can be increased by choosing more than one teacher to select representative students from the same master list. In this way, agreement between the two judges can be used to increase confidence that the selected students are really representative of the group with which they are identified. Some reasonable percent agreement index (perhaps using Cohen's kappa) would be selected as minimum necessary to have confidence in the selections. Perhaps only using students who are simultaneously selected by two or more teachers will also increase our confidence in this process. If the design requires more than one teacher to identify the same student as a member of the same PLD group, that increases cost, but it also increases the confidence that we have in the process.

In most cases, the standard-setting task uses a test that has already been administered so that test scores can be easily obtained once the list of students in each category is available. Using the list of students, the contractor goes to the files and finds the test score associated with each "typical" student classified within each PLD group. The rest of this standard-setting approach is essentially statistical in nature. These test scores and the PLD with which they are associated permit construction of frequency polygons, as illustrated in Figure 10.1.

It is customary to select the two points at which adjacent curves cross to become the cut points for the two standards that differentiate these three PLDs. These points minimize the errors made by misclassification. It is also common to calculate the proportion of the population in each category. These are often called the impacts of the cut points. If the percent number in one category or another looks too large or too small, the cut points may be questioned. The perception of too large or too small is usually a combination of policy concerns, historical test results, and undefined intuitions about what the correct values should be. Adjustments to the process or to the final results, followed by a second round of effort, are not unusual.

In summary, here is the process for the contrasting groups method:

1. Define PLDs and focus on each category.
2. Identify experts to pick representative students.
3. Create documentation to provide experts the instruction they need to select students.
4. Pilot the documentation and determine if it is clear.
5. Select the students that fall into each PLD.
6. Collect test data for those selected students.

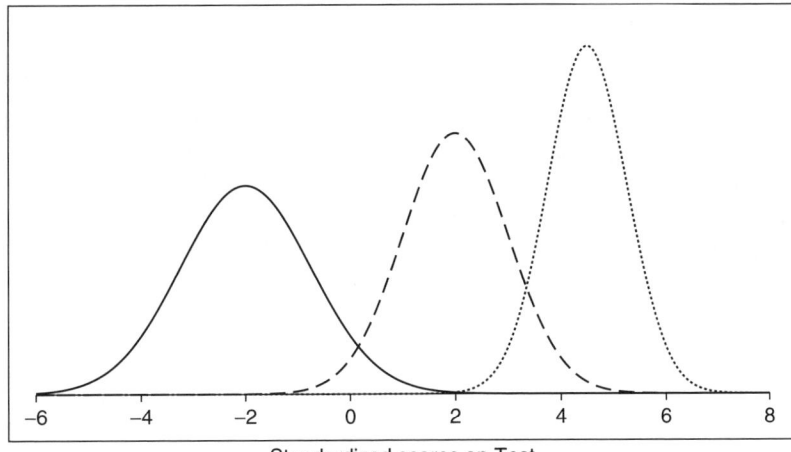

Figure 10.1 *From left to right*: Distribution for Basic, for Proficient, and for Advanced Y-Axis Is Frequency of Each Standard Score

7. Analyze for cut-point determination.
8. Examine and report the results.

Judgment of the Test Items

The judgments in the Angoff and bookmark approaches (Angoff, 1971; Lewis, Mitzel, & Green, 1996) focus on the test items. First, we consider the core decisions that a standard setter has to make and then outline and discuss the standard setting processes that surround this core judgment. So again, suppose we are concerned with setting cut points for a specific examination that has been administered and that has PLDs determined by a prior process. We would first obtain a copy of the test that was recently administered and is to have its standards set. In the case of large-scale testing, the associated test results would be analyzed to give us item response test (IRT) parameters as well as percentile ranks associated with each value of the latent ability parameter (see Hambleton & Swaminathan, 1984, for example, for an introduction to IRT). In a small sample testing situation, classic item statistics would be available.

In this approach to standard setting there is no consideration of actual students. Here the focus is on the test items and on a conceptually defined student known as the minimally competent student. This is a student who is just barely basic, or just barely proficient, or just barely advanced. The PLDs are used to help the standard-setting team understand what the "just barely" student is like. This discussion can take several hours and usually follows an examination of real test items and how the team believes the" just barely" student would perform on each item.

Before exploring the modified Angoff (1971) and bookmark (Mitzell, Lewis, Patz, & Green, 2001) methods in more detail, we want to talk briefly about the concept of a model that is, to my knowledge, never used anymore. Nedelsky (1954) introduced a procedure that tried to apply a simple probabilistic model to the problem of standard setting for multiple-choice items. In his model, Nedelsky asked each member of a team of standard setters to think about a student who was barely (minimally) competent and, with that concept firmly in mind, to look at one multiple-choice item at a time. The standard setter then considered whether any of the options in the first item could be eliminated by the minimally competent student as not possibly correct. The standard setter next assumes that the test taker would randomly select the correct answer from among the remaining options, where the probability of being correct is 1/m, where m is the number of options that remained. The sum of these probabilities across all items in the test is equal to the cut point for students who were at that barely competent level. Unfortunately, evidence suggests that this model is not particularly reliable (Melican, Mills, & Plake, 1989).

There is no contemporary interest in the Nedelsky model, but the two models we do want to focus upon are similar in many ways, and we owe Nedelsky thanks in terms of historical antecedence. Both the modified Angoff and bookmark procedures start by asking standard setters to use the PLDs and visualize (conceptualize) a barely competent student who is minimally basic, minimally proficient, or minimally advanced. The process thus shifted from an unrealistic statistical model to a model based on human judgment.

Core Process of Modified Angoff

The modified Angoff procedure actually takes several forms that differ by the nature of the judgment that a standard setter engages upon. Two of those are described below. The probability of getting the item correct is directly estimated in the first and probably most common modified Angoff approach. So the core task in this version is to conceptualize a minimally performing student in one of the categories summarized by the PLDs and, from that mental image of the student's cognitive skill level, estimate the probability of getting a given item correct. The sum of these probabilities across all the multiple-choice items in the test is the cut off for that category of performance. This approach is repeated for each category of student, resulting in a sum for the cut off for each category.

These sums should be in increasing order, with the lowest being for the minimally basic and then the minimally proficient and finally the minimally advanced. Some consultants prefer use of the term *just barely* in place of *minimally*. The term that is judged to communicate the concept best should be selected. The judgments will almost certainly increase for each member of the standard-setting team, but we will be working with 10 to 20 standard setters over a 2- or 3-day time period, and averages (medians or means) may not be so well behaved. The averages of the standard setters might contain a reversal of the cut offs. In that case, perhaps the cut score for "proficient" would be higher than the cut score for "advanced." How one deals with this becomes clear further on, but for now the author would like the reader to focus on the core decision process.

The other judgment that standard setters can be asked to make in a modified Angoff method is to guess whether the just barely competent student is most likely to get the item right or wrong. So, again, the rater looks at each item and conceptualizes the student as barely proficient (or barely at some other PLD). Next the rater is asked to look at each multiple-choice test item and to decide if the student with the specified minimal level of cognitive functioning is sufficiently likely to get that item correct. The cut point becomes the sum of the number of items judged likely to be answered correctly.

The modified Angoff approaches are most often applied to a test consisting of dichotomous items. If the test consists of items that are not just multiple-choice or true-or-false items or otherwise dichotomous, however, the standard setter can consider whether the minimally performing person taking a polytomous test item is most likely to get a certain number of points correct. It could be that the judge thinks that the minimally performing student is most likely to get no points on the polytomous item or perhaps is most likely to get one point, or two, and so on. In that case, again, the cut-off is determined by summing the points judged most likely to be obtained by that type of student over all the items.

The author actually uses this form of the modified Angoff to set grades in his courses. The author creates the test, which usually consists of short-answer problems in which calculations or comments are elicited, and they are graded from 0 to 5 points. Then he thinks about a minimally performing "A" student and goes through each item selecting the number of points most likely to be obtained on each item by such a student. The sum of the points is the cut-off for a grade of A minus. He next thinks about a minimally performing "B" student and estimates the number of points such a student would likely get right on each question. That sum is the cut-off for a grade of B minus. This approach can be used by multiple standard setters in a formal environment, as happens with state standard setting or with certification exams. The cut scores for a team of standard setters is the median or mean of the cut scores determined by each member of the team.

The following is a brief summary of the core steps to conduct a modified Angoff standard setting:

1. Define PLDs and focus on minimal performance levels.
2. Present the items to the standard setters.
3. Collect the judgments of the standard setters for each item for each minimal PLD.
4. Sum the judgments for each PLD for each standard setter.
5. Calculate the median judgment for each PLD.

Core Process of Bookmark

This approach to standard setting maintains the concept of the minimally competent student, but the context of the decision is greatly simplified. In this case, the test is not just presented to the rater in the form that it is taken. Instead, test items are ordered and presented according to difficulty. The concept of an ordered item booklet is critical to conducting a bookmark standard setting. This approach requires that the test has been administered and that item analysis data have been collected. Usually the consultant has access to the data for the full item bank along with the data for a specific test form. These data include two difficulty measures. One is the percent correct if analysis is done with classic test theory. The other and preferable one is the IRT difficulty parameter (or level of theta) from the same scale as the person ability parameter and associated with a specific response probability.

Representative test item page from an ordered item booklet

Item number	Order in the Booklet
XX	YY

Achievement level (theta) necessary to obtain a .67 probability of getting the answer right is: ZZ

NOTE: The classic difficulty level of the item (percent correct responses) might be substituted for the IRT correct difficulty level, if necessary.

Item stem goes here

Options go next (be sure to mark the correct answer)
(If this is a performance item—there is still an item stem, but now in place of the options is a representative test taker's response)

Figure 10.2 Item Information Summary Sheet

Having such parameterization of the items allows the organizer of the standard setting to prepare an ordered item booklet in which the easiest item appears first and the hardest item appears last and the items in between are ordered by difficulty. Note that ordering by difficulty is assumed to be the same as ordering by how much cognitive ability a person needs to get the item right, assuming that performance on the test is fully governed by a single dimension of latent ability. Now the most distinguishing element of the bookmark procedure is that the standard setters, using the concept of minimal capability or just barely, simply puts a bookmark between the last item that a person is likely to get right and the first item that they are likely to miss (and the next highest cognitive level person is likely to get right). This bookmarking process is repeated for each of the cut points differentiating each of the PLD groups. A sample of the recording form for such a set of judgments is included in Figure 10.3.

It is important to tell the standard setter to check beyond the place where he or she first encounters an item that appears to demand skills not specified in the PLD, because the difficulty is not a perfect indicator of needed ability. It may be that the standard setter will encounter an item that is too hard for the group in consideration but that the next item could be answered correctly and maybe even a few items after that. In that case, the marker could be placed a little later than the spot first encountered.

There are various ways to structure the ordered item booklet, but one of the most popular is to consider the conditional response probability. This is defined in terms of the probability that the student who is conditionally performing gets the item correct. In this case, Huynh (2000) suggests that if the student has a probability of a correct response equal to 0.67 or higher, the standard setter could consider the item response to be correct. In other words, the most common advice to standard setters is to place the marker where the probability of getting the item right has dropped not below 0.5 but below 0.67. The argument for this approach is that the probability of getting the item right should exceed the chance level by some reasonable amount above 0.5. This is usually presented to the standard setters as "Out of a hundred students with minimal ability, where would 67% of them achieve a correct answer?" The usual b parameter is no longer appropriate to use to order the test items. IRT will allow the items to be ordered in this slightly modified approach. The difficulty level of the item from the theta scale should be placed on each page and is the one associated with a response probability of getting the item correct equal to 0.67 (see Figure 10.2).

So far, the presentation of the core judgment of the bookmark method has been in terms of multiple-choice or another dichotomous item type, but that does not have to be the case. If the test has polytomous items, they can be separated by the number of score points possible and placed in the ordered item booklet, again according to how difficult it is to get that number of points. For example, a short-answer item that got the minimal number of points (this might be zero or one, depending upon the scoring rubric) correct would be at the beginning, but the same item with response difficulty associated with three points correct might be placed farther along the ordered item booklet. The order in the booklet is still dictated by the level of theta associated with the response probability of getting that number of points correct. In these cases an actual response associated with that number of points would be produced under the item itself, along with the item statistics at the top of each page. In other words, the ordered item booklet has all the items organized from easiest point(s) to hardest point(s), each on one page. The standard setter proceeds by turning pages until they come to a point where the ability needed to get the item correct exceeds the minimal level under consideration. Only in the case of polytomous items does the standard setter see an actual item response, and that is a single, typical response for illustrative purposes only. Selection of this typical response will require careful consideration.

This is the answer sheet to use to record your placement of your bookmark:

		Bookmark placed	
Round 1	Between page	_____ and	_____
Bookmark for Basic		_____	_____
Bookmark for Proficient		_____	_____
Bookmark for Advanced		_____	_____
Round 2			
Bookmark for Basic		_____	_____
Bookmark for Proficient		_____	_____
Bookmark for Advanced		_____	_____
Round 3			
Bookmark for Basic		_____	_____
Bookmark for Proficient		_____	_____
Bookmark for Advanced		_____	_____

Figure 10.3 Sample Answer Sheet for Standard Setting Bookmarks Using the Ordered Item Bookmark System

The following is a brief summary of the core steps in the bookmark standard setting:

1. Define PLDs and focus on minimal performance levels.
2. Create an ordered item booklet.
3. Present the ordered item booklet and elicit a bookmark for each cut-off.
4. Collect the judgments of each standard setter.
5. Calculate the median judgment for each PLD cut-off.

Judgment of the Answers: Holistic Methods

The core approach to the holistic judgment of performance items (e.g., Kingston, Kahl, Sweeney, & Bay, 2001) is quite different from the Angoff variants and the Bookmark approach. In this case, the focus is on the actual responses that test takers have provided to test items. A typical performance item using a holistic method is one where students provide an extended constructed response. The information confronting the consultant organizing the holistic standard setting might be a writing prompt and a series of page-long constructed responses from a number of students. If more than one writing prompt must be attempted in the test, data on each of the writing prompts will be available. These writing responses have already been scored according to a set of rules developed in the form of a rubric. Prior to the standard setting, a considerable amount of work has already taken place. Extensive training sessions for item scorers are needed to ensure that the responses are scored reliably and according to the rubric. One of the assumptions is that the team responsible for the holistic standard setting is being exposed to items that were scored accurately by trained raters. The contractor has selected a series of extended responses to the item prompt(s) that have ratings representing the range of student responses. The task of the standard setters is to decide in which PLD each item response best fits. They do this by classifying essays as, in their judgment, typical of a specific performance level. Although the focus of these approaches is upon performance items, a few multiple-choice items can be accommodated. If there are a large number of multiple-choice items, it is common to use the holistic approach for the performance items and then switch to one of the other approaches for the multiple-choice items. The overall cut score is then the sum of the two obtained cut scores.

The body of work approach (Kingston et al., 2001) may be the most involved of the holistic methods, but for purposes of this chapter, the basic approach to holistic standard setting as it is often implemented in practice is outlined below. The starting point is always the PLDs, and their determination must precede the holistic standard setting, just as for all other approaches. The next step in the process involves the contractor selecting a set of papers that have established scores from a prior scoring process. A polytomous IRT approach may have been applied to these ratings, but it is not critical that a sophisticated psychometric approach be utilized in the process. What is critical is that reliable scores be associated with each item response. These are needed for the analysis phase but are not shared with the standard setters.

The critical step is that papers be selected that define the full range of possible ability scores. These papers can be presented to the standard setters in ranked order, similar to the ordered item booklet; or to set a marker; or simply presented in random order for classification into one of the PLD classes. If a marker is placed, the items between cut points are selected and their scores identified. If a classification system is used, then again all the papers within a class are collected and their scores obtained. The statistical process is similar to that used by the contrasting groups approach, in which frequency polygons (see Figure 10.1) are created using the score values for each paper in the collection of papers in a PLD class and the cut point becomes the scale value where the adjacent curves cross.

A vocabulary exists from the "body of work" approach, which is helpful to facilitate communication. The set of papers that are selected as representing the scale are called "range finding" papers since they span the range of possible scores. These papers are selected from a set of papers sometimes called "pinpointing" papers, which are often double scored and, in the case where more than one paper represents a student's work (when multiple item prompts are presented in the tests), are judged to be similar in their measure of that student's performance ability. In other words, if the standard setting includes two or more performance papers for the same student and the standard-setting judgment is to be based on both, it is critical that each represent the same level of proficiency score for a single student. The idea is to get a clear picture of the competence of the student and then a classification into which category that level of performance falls.

The following is a summary of the steps for holistic standard setting:

1. Define and discuss PLDs.
2. Select papers to be used.
3. Have judges classify each paper into a PLD.
4. Create a frequency polygon for scale scores from each PLD.
5. Find the point where each pair of curves intersect.

The Big Picture

The core procedure of standard setting fits into an approximately 3-day process. As said above, it is assumed that a separate team of 10 to 20 people meet for at least a day and create credible

PLDs to define the PLLs that had been agreed upon by the state or other ruling body that determines such matters. In most standard-setting sessions it is assumed that the PLDs are inviolable. In other words, they can be discussed for meaning but no changes are to be made. Rarely there is a belief that the PLDs are not well defined; in such cases the team is permitted to make modest changes. The role of the standard-setting committee (the team) must be very explicitly defined. In most cases they are advisory to a higher body, such as a state legislature or a department of education. They recommend results and do not determine the standards. The next step is to do the standard setting itself. The outline of events in Figure 10.4 summarizes what is a reasonably typical process consisting of a series of three rounds of judgments to complete the determination of the recommendation of the cut scores for the Angoff, bookmark, and holistic approaches.

Notice that, with one exception, standard setting tends to be repeated for three rounds. The contrasting groups approach is generally done in one round and not redone, although that does not have to be the case. In other words, it is common for the modified Angoff, bookmark, and holistic approaches to be multistage processes with considerable group discussion interspersed between the judgments. The results of the judgments are collected and then discussed twice; then empirical test-taker performance information is typically brought to bear after the second round of judgments. This additional information is called impact data and represents the PLD percentages from past testing effort(s) that summarize the impact of the specific cut points from round two. In other words, if we use these cut scores, these are the percentages of students who will be categorized into each PLD. Choosing more demanding performance cut-offs for the advanced category, for example, will cause fewer students to be classified in that category. Notice that up to this point, the standard setting appears to be a criterion-referenced activity. The cut points are set without regard to student statistical results on the actual assessment. No direct normative information from the test affects the judgments until the impact data are presented. In contrast, the last round is based upon the same criterion-referenced comparisons (the PLDs), but now an additional factor comes into play, and that is the normative (the impact on the percent of students in each PLD) data.

Also notice that the participants are asked prior to each round if they are ready (Figure 10.5 contains a sample survey) to proceed, and they are asked at the end if they are confident about the overall process. As indicated above, approaching this problem as though it were to result in a court case leads one to be extra careful that all the participants support the activity as a fair and thoughtful approach to standard setting. Getting the team members to sign such a form is one way to ensure that they will testify formally or informally to that effect.

Figure 10.5 is a sample of the forms you will need to conduct a standard setting. This is the one to be signed after the training and just before the standard setters start making their judgments in round one, two, or three. The form administered prior to the third round should include a question about their understanding of the impact data. A final form after round three is usually given to ask if the panelist feels positive about the whole process.

Note that there is one more very important form. That is, it is important to have participants sign a nondisclosure agreement prior to their beginning any of the tasks and even before the opening orientation.

Expected Future of Standard Setting

There is a famous quote from Glass (1978, p. 237): "They cannot determine 'criterion levels' or standards other than arbitrarily." The procedures that have been presented are arbitrary, but they are not capricious, careless, or casual. They are in fact thoughtful, systematic, careful approaches to a difficult problem that has been historically approached as a matter of human judgment. There are and were procedures that are not arbitrary, though, and they are becoming

Day 1   Morning
        Get security signature – all materials are classified
        Seating to maximize diversity at each table
        Introductions and provide a general orientation to what will take place
        Self-administer an actual copy of the examination to have standards set
        Self score the test results by standard setting participants
        Discuss the results and gather general comments

Day 1   Afternoon
        Introduce and discuss the PLLs and PLDs
        Relate to exam and look for examples that illustrate each
        Teach the basics of the standard setting procedure to be used
        Practice with a short version of the test
        Sign in every piece of paper

Day 2   Morning
        Discuss the standard setting procedure again at table as a full room
        Present any general data regarding prior or related standards
        Fill out "ready to judge" form and look at results
        When ready, do the first round of the standard setting
        Score results of the first round and present them
        Discuss at tables and as a full room

Day 2   Afternoon
        Fill out "ready to judge" form for round two
        If ready, complete round two judgments
        Score results and present them
        Discuss round two and look at impact data
        Sign in every piece of paper

Day 3   Morning and maybe early afternoon
        Further discussion of round two results with impact data
        Fill out "ready to judge" form for round three
        When ready, do third round of standard setting
        Score and report on results
        Stress secrecy of test, and standards cut-points
        Stress that they can talk about process only
        Sign in every piece of paper
        Fill out "evaluation of overall process"
        Do paperwork needed for expenses and any payment to participants

Another Day
        Write report on overall process and results
        Discuss cut points, and impact expected with those who commission task
        Present executive summary to leadership

Figure 10.4 Time and Effort to Complete Standard Setting

Standard Setter Number _____

Please fill in your number, above, then respond to the following questions by circling the answer that best captures your feelings. SD means strongly disagree, D means disagree, A means agree, and SA means strongly agree.

1. The orientation to standard setting provided clear instructions.

    SD   D   A   SA

2. I understand what I am supposed to do to set standards for this test.

    SD   D   A   SA

3. I have reviewed the test content and it has helped me understand my task.

    SD   D   A   SA

4. Reviewing the Performance Level Descriptors has helped me understand my task.

    SD   D   A   SA

5. The training for the Bookmark Method was clear.

    SD   D   A   SA

6. I believe I am ready to apply what I have learned.

    SD   D   A   SA

Do you have any additional questions?

Do you have any further remarks?

Figure 10.5 Sample Ready to Judge Form

more popular, at least in the research literature. Even in 1978 there was a literature on latent class analysis (e.g., Goodman, 1974) that used statistical procedures to identify latent classes. These approaches define student categories by the patterns of responses to the various items of a test. They do not begin with a definition of the PLDs but instead begin with examinee item data and the assumption that different patterns of response depend upon the latent class in which a student resides.

Newer models are being developed that permit easier application to large-scale testing situations; one generalization is called a mixture Rasch model. This approach was developed in a series of papers by Kelderman and Macready (1990), Mislevy and Verhelst (1990), and Rost (1990). These models also make the assumption that examinees are members of latent classes, but within a class the test performance is expressed by a Rasch measurement model. There are many examples that have attempted to apply these models to the standard setting problem, including a paper by Jiao and colleagues (2010). This approach is statistical in nature and would usually replace the use of judgment-based procedures. Naturally they can also be used to supplement judgment-based procedures, but doing the standard setting twice (one using statistics and once for judgment) increases the time and expense.

The paper by Lissitz and Li (2010) presents yet another approach to standard setting. This involves looking at the domain of the test (the table of specifications) and considering if there are skills that should be demonstrated by persons in each PLD. In other words, an analysis of the domain specifications and their relation to the PLD, in a carefully designed test, leads one to identify sets of items that demand skills at different levels of cognitive development. In this concept, standard setting becomes a matter of clustering items into sets that measure different levels of performance implied by the PLDs. Scoring these clusters of items separately as a determiner of the PLD in which a student resides is another way to set standards. Other researchers (e.g., Sadesky & Gushta, 2004) have examined related but more statistical approaches, and these appear to be another promising way to set standards. These approaches trace back to the introduction of cognitive diagnostic models (Tatsuoka, 1983) that permit a formal solution to the standard-setting problem.

The reader might notice that the conceptualization of standards across a continuum of ability, indicated in several places including the proficiency growth summary (PGS) (Table 10.2), makes standard setting a special case of growth modeling. In other words, as a student gets more and more proficient, they move from one PLD to the next and these changes become an indication of the student's cognitive growth. The simple transition model used in Delaware growth modeling (2006) is an explicit example of such a conceptualization. Students are categorized in one year based upon their test scores and categorized again using test scores in the next year. Collection of this transition matrix showing student movement from one year to another is a generalization of the standard setting practice in the wider context of growth modeling. In some ways this generalization seems obvious, but redefining the standard setting process as a stepwise growth model brings a new set of considerations as well as a very different orientation and associated vocabulary to an old challenge.

Evaluating growth is one of the priorities of the new federal legislation known as Race to the Top (2010), or RTTT, so there are some advantages to thinking of standard setting and growth as closely related issues. This has to do with the work ready and the higher education readiness requirements of RTTT. In this model, education for K-12 has a special purpose, which is to prepare students for either a job or for more education. Again, the challenge sounds like a standard-setting problem in which we try to classify students as college-ready, work-ready, or not ready for either. Once the instructional system has specified a long-range criterion other than the immediate test outcome, the assessment levels (cut points) can be referenced to that ultimate criterion, and we now have access to another set of models for standard setting. For example, suppose a student is transitioning from high school to college. In this example, one can ask about a minimally qualified graduating high school student and how high the performance cut-off must be set in order to make the student's probability of success in college meet some predetermined level. Suppose we want the probability to be .75 that a student ending his or her freshman year in college will obtain a GPA of at least 2.5. Now, backing up from that ultimate criterion, we can ask how high a performance standard must be set in the senior year of high school to obtain a probability of that level of success in college. Notice that now the judgment has been shifted to the question of how confident you want to be that the student can demonstrate college or work readiness, and the problem is a relatively straightforward statistical one.

Another important consideration is the growing demand for more computer-based and even computer-adaptive (CAT) frameworks. Again, this demand is due in part to the anticipated requirements coming from RTTT implementation. RTTT seems to require formative, interim, and summative evaluations. It is nearly impossible to see how these requirements of RTTT can be met unless the efficiencies of CAT are utilized. Without using more efficient testing approaches such as CAT, there would be just too much testing. Fortunately, from a standard-setting viewpoint, CAT is typically an IRT-based approach, and the cut-offs from any of the traditional standard-setting procedures can be immediately translated into an IRT theta value, hence preserving the applicability of the cut-off to this newer testing environment. In other words, even though there is not a single test form in CAT, the use of IRT modeling allows cut scores to be translated from any standard-setting approach to that context. Approaches to standard setting that are designed especially for CAT do exist (Wainer, 2000; Lissitz & Kroopnick, 2007).

Issues of Reliability and Validity for Standard Setting

There is both research and practical interest in the reliability of standard-setting participants' judgments across rounds, in the comparability of the various approaches that are commonly utilized, as well as in the degree of alignment of standards set in different grades and on different subject matter assessments. If one thinks of this as a generalizability problem (Brennan, 2001), one can consider generalizing across judges, across methods, across grade levels, and even across subject matter areas. Consistency of ratings is usually not quantified; instead, graphs of judges' ratings are prepared and compared across the three rounds. Typically there is a considerable spread of judgments in the first round and a great deal of overlap across PLDs for the various judges. That usually disappears by round three, as the judges reach greater agreement around some median point on the scale for each PLD. Sometimes coefficient alpha is calculated, although a clear interpretation is not altogether obvious from such analyses and is rarely if ever helpful.

Unfortunately there is very little consistency across methods, as demonstrated by a series of studies (e.g., Jaeger, 1989). One state tried to do standard setting by using two independent sets of judges for the same test. In that example, the judges arrived at similar results, which added somewhat to the confidence of the state officials. Unfortunately what they did not seem to realize is that the consultants orchestrating the two "independent" standard setting activities were not independent. Even though two different consultants led activities in the two different rooms, they met periodically, compared results, and then encouraged discussion in their groups, which led to increasing agreement as the rounds progressed.

The comparability of ratings across grades and subject matter has generated some research interest. Moderated standard setting (Lissitz & Huynh, 2003) is a very judgmental approach to bringing some orderliness to the cut points across grades. This is an approach that involves judges looking at test designs and various test data across grades as aids to developing consistency in school expectations. It is often the result of having a committee, sometimes called an articulation committee, meet and consider a set of cut points, looking for a rule or concept that will lead to an orderly progression of the results (often involving impact data). This, like traditional standard setting, is a consensual effort leading to general agreement by persons who might be considered subject matter experts (teachers, for example). The approach that Lissitz and Wei (2008) explored was applied to what are called augmented testing environments, in which normative national data exist along with the local criterion-referenced test data. It is not unusual to see testing that combines a set of items from a nationally marketed test with items created for a specific locale, such as a county or state. The national data can be used as an anchoring mechanism to bring some consistency to the local testing application. This approach can be applied across grades as well as across subject matter. Answering a question such as whether a student is better at English than at mathematics has always been a challenge that is of interest to many practitioners who set standards or use the results of standard setting. Normative data is one approach to such questions.

Validity is especially hard to determine and, as is often the case, reliability is interpreted as a positive sign for the existence of validity (Lissitz & Samuelsen, 2007). For example, high interrater reliability is often interpreted as an indication that the raters' agreement about the material must indicate that their judgments are based on the correct elements of the process being judged. It does seem that interrater agreement indicates that the raters are attuned to similar elements, but whether they are rating the wrong things or the right things is much more difficult to determine. In the prediction model mentioned in the context of being school- or work-ready, the interpretation of validity may be more justified, since there seems to be an agreed upon criterion in this case. In most standard-setting situations, though, there really is no objectively "correct" result; hence a validity argument is hard to construct in such a situation.

Conclusion

The assumption in all standard setting is that test takers can be separated so that they fall naturally into relatively homogeneous groups. Grouping students becomes very arbitrary if the students are actually ordered along a dimension rather than existing as members of groups. This implies that some of the student differences are more qualitative than quantitative and that test takers fall into what are sometimes called latent classes. An example of a test that really makes sense within this conception of classes of people is a test of pregnancy. A woman who takes the test is either pregnant or she is not. There is no "barely pregnant" category. Many testing situations are not really like that. In fact, if there is a somewhat continuous group of students at each data point with seemingly no natural breaks, classification is more difficult to accomplish, less reliable, and harder to justify.

The traditional standard setting described above is, in fact, a social process of compromise among many different viewpoints (Hein & Skaggs, 2009). Hein and Skaggs's (2009) study suggests that standard setters do not always approach the problem as they are trained to do or as the participants claim to be doing when asked in public. The system works because of the faith that most people have in such consensual negotiations, the credibility of the participants, and the good faith with which most people claim to operate in social situations. The underlying reality may be quite different.

This problem area is challenging, interesting, and rewarding, making it a fun area in which to work. At its simplest level, setting standards is time-consuming (even when using the Bookmark method), but at least there is considerable agreement about the necessary steps once the consultant has selected a method. Related issues are harder to resolve, such as whether these approaches are providing cut points that are truly indicative of the PLDs, as claimed. There is a fundamental belief that standard setting is implemented for one of several reasons, as mentioned at the beginning of this chapter (Linn, 1994). That may be true, but whether standard setting is even the best way to accomplish any of these goals is an important question and one that is hard to determine. Other approaches are being developed as better ways to report student success. Growth modeling is one such competitor that is gaining some increased interest at the federal and state levels. If growth is defined as change in proficiency level, then it is a simple extension of standard setting. Other growth models can be much different. It remains to be seen which of the various models for meeting the goals enumerated by Linn will emerge as most favored.

References

Angoff, W. H. (1971). Scales, norms, and equivalent scores. In R. L. Thorndike (Ed.), *Educational measurement* (2nd ed., pp. 508–600). Washington, DC: American Council on Education.

Bloom, B., Englehart, M., Furst, E., Hill, W., & Krathwohl, D. (1956). *Taxonomy of educational objectives: The classification of educational goals. Handbook I: Cognitive domain.* New York and Toronto: Longmans, Green.

Brennan, R. L. (2001). *Generalizability theory.* New York: Springer-Verlag.

Cizek, G. J. (1996). Standard-setting guidelines. *Educational Measurement: Issues and Practice, 15*(1), 12–21.

Cizek, G. J. (Ed.). (2001). *Setting performance standards: Concepts, methods and perspectives.* Mahwah, NJ: Erlbaum.

Cizek, G. J., & Bunch, M. B. (2007). *Standard setting: A guide to establishing and evaluating performance standards on tests.* Thousand Oaks, CA: Sage.

Delaware Growth Model. (2006). Retrieved from http://www2.ed.gov/admins/lead/account/growthmodel/de/index.html

Glass, G. (1978). Standards and criteria. *Journal of Educational Measurement, 15*, 237–261.

Goodman, L. A. (1974). Exploratory latent structure analysis using both identifiable and unidentifiable models, *Biometrika, 61*, 215–231.

Hambleton, R. K., & Pitoniak, M. J. (2006). Setting performance standards. In R. L. Brennan (Ed.), *Educational measurement* (4th ed., pp. 433–470). Westport, CT: Praeger.

Hambleton, R. K., & Swaminathan, H. (1984). *Item response theory: Principles and applications.* Hingham, MA: Kluwer, Nijhoff.

Hein, S., & Skaggs, G. (2009). A qualitative investigation of bookmark standard setting: Participant deviations from the bookmark procedure and difficulties with item ordering. *Applied Measurement in Education, 22*, 207–228.

Huynh, H. (2000, April). *On item mappings and statistical rules for selecting binary items for criterion-referenced interpretation and bookmark standard settings.* Paper presented at the annual meeting of the National Council on Measurement in Education, New Orleans.

Jaeger, R. (1989). Certification of student competence. In R. L. Linn (Ed.), *Educational measurement* (3rd ed., pp. 485–514). New York: Macmillan.

Jiao, H., Lissitz, B., Macready, G., Wang, S., & Liang, S. (2010, April). *Exploring using the Mixture Rasch Model for standard setting.* Paper presented at the annual meeting of the National Council on Measurement in Education, Denver.

Kane, M. T. (1994). Validating the performance standards associated with passing scores. *Review of Educational Research, 64*, 425–461.

Kelderman, H., & Macready, G. B. (1990). The use of loglinear models for assessing differential item functioning across manifest and latent examinee groups. *Journal of Educational Measurement, 27*, 307–327.

Kingston, N. M., Kahl, S. R., Sweeney, K. P., & Bay, L. (2001). Setting performance standards using the body of work method. In G. J. Cizek (Ed.), *Setting performance standards: Concepts, methods and perspectives.* Mahwah, NJ: Erlbaum.

Lewis, D. M., Mitzel, H. C., & Green, D. R. (1996, June). Standard setting: A bookmark approach. In D. R. Green (Chair), *IRT-based standard-setting procedures utilizing behavioral anchoring.* Symposium conducted at the Council of Chief State School Officers National Conference on Large-Scale Assessment, Phoenix AZ.

Linn, R. L. (1994, October). *The likely impact of performance standards as a function of uses: From rhetoric to sanctions.* Paper presented at the National Center for Education Statistics and National Assessment Governing Board Joint Conference on Standard-Setting for Large-Scale Assessments, Washington, DC.

Lissitz, R. W., & Huynh, H. (2003). Vertical equating for state assessments: issues and solutions in determination of adequate yearly progress and school accountability. *Practical Assessment Research and Evaluation, 8*(10). Retrieved from http://PAREonline.net/getvn.asp?v=8&n=10

Lissitz, R. W., & Kroopnick, M. (2007, April). *An adaptive procedure for standard setting and a comparison with traditional approaches.* Paper presented at the national meeting of the National Council of Measurement in Education, Chicago.

Lissitz, R. W., & Li, F. (2010, April). *Standard setting in complex performance assessments: An approach aligned with cognitive diagnostic models.* Paper presented at the annual meetings of the National Council on Measurement in Education, Denver.

Lissitz, R. W., & Samuelsen, K. (2007). A suggested change in terminology and emphasis regarding validity and education. *Educational Researcher, 36*, 437–448.

Lissitz, R. W., & Wei, H. (2008). Consistency of standard setting in an augmented state testing system. *Educational Measurement: Issues and Practice, 27*(2), 46–56.

Livingston, S. A., & Zieky, M. J. (1982). *Passing scores: A manual for setting standards of performance on educational and occupational tests.* Princeton, NJ: Educational Testing Service.

Melican, G. J., Mills, C., & Plake, B. (1989). Accuracy of item performance predictions based on the Nedelsky standard setting method. *Educational and Psychological Measurement, 49*(2), 467–478.

Mislevy, R. J., Steinberg, L. S., & Almond, R. G. (2003). On the structure of educational assessments. *Measurement: Interdisciplinary Research and Perspectives, 1*(1), 3–62.

Mislevy, R. J., & Verhelst, N. D. (1990). Modeling item responses when different subjects employ different solution strategies. *Psychometrika, 55*(2), 195–215.

Mitzel, H. C., Lewis, D. M., Patz, R. J., & Green, D. R. (2001). The Bookmark procedure: cognitive perspectives on standard setting. In G. J. Cizek (Ed.), *Setting performance standards: Concepts, methods, and perspectives* (pp. 249–282). Mahwah, NJ: Erlbaum.

Nedelsky, L. (1954). Absolute grading for objective tests. *Educational and Psychological Measurement, 14,* 3–19.

No Child Left Behind Act. (2001). Retrieved from http://www2.ed.gov/nclb/landing.jhtml

Quellmalz, E. S. (1987). Developing reasoning skills. In J. Baron & R. Sternberg (Eds.), *Teaching thinking skills: Theory and practice* (pp. 86–105). New York: Freeman.

Race to the Top. (2010). Retrieved from http://www2.ed.gov/programs/racetothetop/index.html

Rost, J. (1990). Rasch models in latent classes: An integration of two approaches to item analysis. *Applied Psychological Measurement, 14,* 271–282.

Sadesky, G. S., & Gushta, M. M. (April, 2004). *Applying rule-space methodology to the problem of standard setting.* Paper presented at the annual meeting of the National Council on Measurement in Education, San Diego, CA.

Tatsuoka, K. (1983). Rule space: An approach for dealing with misconceptions based on item response theory. *Journal of Educational Measurement, 20*(4), 345–354.

Wainer, H. (2000). *Computerized adaptive testing: A primer.* Hillsdale, NJ: Erlbaum.

Zieky, M. J., & Livingston, S. A. (1977). *Manual for setting standards on the basic skills assessment tests.* Princeton, NJ: Educational Testing Service.

11

From "Here's the Story" to "You're in Charge"
Developing and Maintaining Large-Scale Online Test- and Score-Reporting Resources

April L. Zenisky and Ronald K. Hambleton

> *Introduction*
> *A Brief Overview of Online Reporting Resources*
> *Guidelines for Static, Results-Oriented Online Documents*
> *Guidelines for Interactive Results-Oriented Tools*
> *Guidelines for Programmatic/Informational Web Pages*
> *Guidelines for Test- and Score-Reporting Website Home Pages*
> *Developing Score-Reporting Resources: The Hambleton and Zenisky Model*
> *Conclusion*

Introduction

Score reporting is among the most challenging aspects of test development facing testing agencies today. In many ways it is no longer enough to have a psychometrically sound instrument that provides a valid and reliable measure of student proficiency, nor is summarily labeling test performance with a single scale score satisfactory. Stakeholders, including the examinees themselves, want context for the scores test takers receive and increasingly seek information that connects the scores back to the purpose of the test and what it purports to measure (Ryan, 2006). Context can mean many things, depending on the purpose of the test and the intended uses of the data, but it includes (and is not limited to) comparison to/between reference groups, diagnostic performance data at the subdomain or perhaps even item level, narrative descriptions of strengths and weaknesses, and/or performance-level descriptions that elaborate on what examinees at different proficiency levels know and can do.

In addition, how people access information about tests is changing, and the direction of change is very definitely toward online reporting. Whereas the web is not the only means by which testing programs are disseminating results and other information, the increasingly key role of websites as sources for quick access to information about tests is unsurprising in today's world. To be certain, score reports that provide information about individual test-taker performance are in many cases sent by mail; but more and more testing agencies are offering examinees the option of seeing scores immediately after completion of a test (for computer-administered exams) and/or online access to scores at a later date via a website with a secure login process. At the group level, agencies commonly share results that focus on aggregate scores and other materials with the broadcast and printed media, and many testing programs are also developing and maintaining increasingly extensive websites to report on test performance that users can access at their convenience (Knupp & Ansley, 2008).

Websites for large-scale educational assessments generally include content that is results-oriented as well as other information about a testing program (technical documentation, policies, released test items, etc.). For example, much information about the U.S. National Assessment of Educational Progress (NAEP) testing program, including multiple years' worth of results for a number of content areas including core subjects such as mathematics and reading, is currently available on the NAEP website (http://nces.ed.gov/nationsreportcard/). Via this website, users have the opportunity to access a considerable amount of information on the entire NAEP testing program, from executive summaries of results and interactive tools to more general policy information about the NAEP program and the content of the assessments. Although it is common for results to be presented as static displays (text, charts, and graphs), the communication of test data over the Internet has also given testing agencies the opportunity to fundamentally change how score reporting occurs by developing interactive web-based tools that give intended users of test score data the flexibility to explore results corresponding to their own interests.

The purpose of this chapter is to first describe some of the score-reporting resources typically being made available online by testing programs. Then we provide a set of guidelines for agencies tasked with developing online score reporting resources, drawing on examples from NAEP but also other high-profile large-scale testing programs—such as the Programme for International Student Assessment (PISA), the Trends in Mathematics and Science Study (TIMSS), and the Progress in International Reading Literacy Study (PIRLS)—as well as various state testing agencies and credentialing groups. For persons involved in reporting the results of high-stakes assessments, the online reporting efforts presently in place in different testing contexts can be instructive as to the kinds of materials that testing programs can make available to consumers and the ways in which test data and information can be shared in an online setting. Topic areas of particular interest are static, results-oriented online documents, interactive results-oriented tools, programmatic/informational web pages, and testing program home pages. For each of these topic areas we offer guidance and examples of reporting content and strategies.

It should be noted that although many of the examples here are drawn from educational testing contexts, the guidelines described have application in any testing context in which aggregate results will be communicated to stakeholders via the Internet. In terms of what is meant by "aggregate" results, it is common for educational data to be grouped by school, district, region, state or province, and/or country, but it is also quite common for groupings by other demographic variables such as gender and race/ethnicity to be used. These are all analysis levels applicable to a wide range of testing contexts that report descriptive results for groups of examinees, including admissions, professional certification and licensure, and psychological testing.

A Brief Overview of Online Reporting Resources

Online score-reporting resources generally fall into three categories: (1) static, data-oriented Web pages or PDFs of results; (2) interactive Web-based tools; and (3) programmatic/informational

Web pages. A fourth consideration included in this chapter concerns testing program home pages, as these are a metaphorical "front door" for sharing reporting results and can be structured to serve as a way for agencies to highlight information and results in an accessible and positive way.

The first type of score reporting resources that are the focus of this chapter are those that are structured and posted online as a static document rather than an on-demand compilation of specific results. These report-style types of materials may be in the format of an executive summary or may be considerably more in depth to provide a full accounting of test performance. An example of a full-length report is the *TIMSS 2007 International Mathematics Report: Findings from IEA's Trends in International Mathematics and Science Study at the Fourth and Eighth Grades* (Mullis, Martin, & Foy, 2008), which is a 488-page compilation of fourth- and eighth-grade students' mathematics achievement in each of the 59 participating countries and 8 benchmarking participants, including trends in mathematics achievement over time as well as performance at the TIMSS International Benchmarks. In recent years, NAEP has taken to publishing longer results-oriented documents as subject-specific "report cards" as well as smaller pieces such as "state snapshots" and "highlights." These reports are typically crafted to provide results in tables and graphs accompanied by interpretive text to facilitate understanding of test performance.

In terms of interactive Web-based tools, this category actually refers to tools that can vary along a continuum of analysis, from those that provide results that are purely descriptive in nature to those that function as a statistical package to carry out original analyses. The more straightforward of these uses a menu-driven approach to allow users to select a population and content and thus to obtain descriptive results as need or interest dictates. For example, someone might be interested in middle-school results in mathematics for a particular school within a particular district, so that person would go to the state's testing website, find the reporting tool, and then choose the district, school, grade level, and content area; increasingly, administration year is often an option as well. Given those search parameters, the tool would then provide results and might include data such as average scale scores, percentages of students scoring in various performance levels, and normative comparisons of the school to the average for the district and the state. Often these data are displayed as tables, but on occasion graphs are generated as well. Some implementations of these tools will also allow for the further selection of demographic groupings based on gender, race/ethnicity, socioeconomic status, and/or individual education plan (IEP) status. Examples of US states with these kinds of publicly accessible tools include Maryland (http://www.mdreportcard.org/) and Massachusetts (http://profiles.doe.mass.edu/).

Another example of a descriptive but interactive Web-based score reporting tool is the NAEP state comparison tool (http://nces.ed.gov/nationsreportcard/statecomparisons/), in which users can choose a grade, subject, and student group (gender, race/ethnicity, school lunch eligibility, and administration year); the tool then generates a table with the accompanying data. Another click brings up a color-coded map of the United States, where individual states are shaded to reflect performance that is either significantly lower, higher, or not different than a chosen reference group. For example, consider the 2009 Grade 8 mathematics results and a display of the performance of female examinees. When the reference group is national public schools, the average scale score for female students in Grade 8 in 28 states/jurisdictions was significantly higher than the average scale score for female Grade 8 students in the national public sample (these states are shaded green). Seven yellow-shaded states/jurisdictions exhibited no significant difference from the average scale score for the national public sample, and 17 states/jurisdictions coded to display in a soft orange color were significantly lower on the outcome variable of average scale score among female Grade 8 math examinees. The visual display of these results can be quite striking and can change quite easily as a user clicks on different points on the map;

thus this tool is noteworthy in its effectiveness for communicating comparison data in a very clear and easy-to-understand fashion.

A third NAEP data tool of interest is the NAEP question tool (http://nces.ed.gov/nationsreportcard/about/naeptools.asp), where site visitors can access not only the text of hundreds of released NAEP items but also item-level performance data. These questions are coded by type (typically multiple-choice, short constructed response, and extended constructed response) and difficulty (with the range of difficulty collapsed to easy, medium, and hard). It is possible to seek out certain content classifications and complexity levels as well. By electing to view "question details," people can view the actual question, the key (or scoring guide for polytomous items), and performance data on the question for either the national sample or individual states.

The counterpoint to the tools typically found on websites for state testing programs that generate descriptive results is the analysis tool implemented for NAEP, the publicly available NAEP Data Explorer (NDE; http://nces.ed.gov/nationsreportcard/about/naeptools.asp). The NDE gives site visitors the opportunity to carry out actual statistical analyses with NAEP datasets and create tables, charts, and maps. Users begin by selecting a subject and grade, and the sample for analysis can be national, regional, or restricted to a certain state or states. Users can choose to look at public and/or private schools. Variables for analysis can be selected from a range of categories, such as student factors, school factors, community factors, and so on. Results can be expressed in terms of either scale scores or NAEP achievement levels (cumulative or discrete). Typical analyses here include obtaining average scores for various groups of test takers, creating maps to illustrate significant differences between jurisdictions, running cross-tabulations, comparing jurisdictions, evaluating trends over time, and conducting gap analyses. Ultimately the NDE is a highly flexible data analysis tool that puts score reporting in the hands of intended audiences.

A tool similar to the NDE is available for the Trends in International Math and Science Study (TIMSS) and Progress in International Reading Literacy Study (PIRLS) assessments from the International Association for the Evaluation of Educational Achievement (IEA) (http://www.ieadata.org/webview/index.jsp). The IEA Online Data Analyzer is online software, much like the NDE, and allows users to actively carry out a range of analyses with IEA data, such as univariate statistics as well as breakdowns, correlations, and regressions. The IEA has also made available a downloadable plug-in for the Statistical Package for the Social Sciences (SPSS), called the IEA International Database Analyzer, which provides researchers with a mechanism for combining and analyzing data from IEA assessments (which is available on the IEA website).

Along with the previously discussed "score report" materials and tools, testing agencies typically include a variety of other materials to further assist in score interpretation. These programmatic and/or informational details can encompass web pages that provide score interpretation guides for different audiences (such as parents, teachers, and test takers themselves), an overview of the testing program, the assessment frameworks for content and cognitive skills, as well as test specifications, test policies such as participation requirements, and technical documentation. The notion of "audiences" is an important consideration here, as it must be noted that for many testing programs the results needs for different groups of stakeholders vary accordingly, as does the familiarity that groups will have with testing, test scores, and interpreting results (Jaeger, 2003).

Some programs have implemented a few particularly interesting mechanisms to provide context for scores, such as the use of item maps in NAEP (http://nces.ed.gov/nationsreportcard/itemmaps/) and benchmarking (the SAT Skills Insight, http://sat.collegeboard.org/practice/). A common criticism of testing generally is that since every test has its own scale (be it 1 to 10, 200 to 800 in increments of 10, 100 to 700, or something else), it can be hard to know what a particular score on a particular test represents in terms of proficiency. NAEP uses an approach to adding context to its scores called item mapping (Beaton & Allen, 1992; Hambleton, Sireci, & Huff, 2008). In an item map, the difficulty level of the item is used to figure out a point on the NAEP scale where students are more likely to answer it correctly. By repeating this process for a number of items and a range of points on the NAEP scale, people who are interested in NAEP score reporting can see that in 2007, Grade 4 students who scored around a 255 on the NAEP scale in mathematics were generally able to answer a multiple-choice question involving using place value to determine the amount of increase correctly. Benchmarking is a criterion-referenced approach to reporting that similarly maps performance on educational tests to standards, thereby facilitating comparisons on an absolute scale. The SAT Skills Insight application invites test takers to develop an understanding of their test performance by looking at skills and items within different score ranges (see, for example, Hambleton, Sireci, & Huff, 2008).

The last area for communicating results online that is a consideration at present is a testing program home page. As the jumping-off point for many people looking for information about test performance online, a clear and accessible home page can provide stakeholders a foothold into the world of assessment and facilitate communication of not only technical, statistical results but also practical, real-world understanding of what examinees know and can do as measured by a test. In this regard, principles of good Web design and site usability are critical, as (again) is an awareness of the varying audiences for test results and information.

Guidelines for Static, Results-Oriented Online Documents

We begin our Web reporting guidelines for static, results-oriented online documents by noting that not all online reporting is interactive, nor does it have to be. In many cases, agencies put results on the Internet in structured tables, charts, and/or text formats that website users cannot manipulate, or post links to downloadable PDFs that package information in easy-to-print formats for user review, often in traditional technical report-style layouts with tables of contents. A summary of the guidelines in this area is provided in Table 11.1.

In some ways, the reporting of static results online need not be very different from the way in which such results are reported in traditional paper-based reports. At the same time, score reporting in general has too often been an afterthought to the larger process of test development and maintenance. Therefore, Document-Based Online Reporting Guideline A concerns *ensuring that static results available on the web follow best practices for report development* (see Goodman & Hambleton, 2004, and Hambleton & Zenisky, in press, for an overview of principles for report design).

Second, the issue of variation among audiences has been covered here, but it bears repeating that in preparing score reports, the end user should be a critical consideration throughout the process,

Table 11.1 Summary of Guidelines for Static, Results-Oriented Online Documents

Document-based online reporting guideline A	Refer to the guidelines for developing reports in the assessment literature (Goodman and Hambleton, 2004; Hambleton and Zenisky, in press; Ryan, 2006; Wainer, 1997; Wainer, Hambleton, & Meara, 1999).
Document-based online reporting guideline B	Pay attention to the reporting interests and needs of users, as presenting results in static format means users see only what is shown to them.
Document-based online reporting guideline C	Try out different report formats (summary, highlights, full-length reports) and data displays (text, graph, and tables) with intended audiences to ensure that materials are understood and the conclusions being drawn are appropriate.

and *reporting needs and interests of stakeholders can guide decisions to improve the understanding, use, and accessibility of report materials* (Document-Based Online Reporting Guideline B). This can be ascertained through due diligence at the outset of report development, with the use of activities such as surveys and focus groups.

Document-Based Online Reporting Guideline C also addresses understanding, use, and accessibility of results by suggesting that persons involved in report development *engage in research with prototype or draft reports as materials are produced*. Involving intended users in the evaluation of the utility of materials prior to full public release assists in quality control of reports and promotes validity in terms of helping users to understand what kinds of inferences are appropriate in given testing contexts.

Guidelines for Interactive Results-Oriented Tools

Reporting test scores and information on the web allows users to access data on demand, but that is just one benefit of online reporting. In *administering* tests by computer, one true advantage of computerized delivery is harnessing the power of the computer to assess knowledge and skills in ways that cannot be done well in other test formats; so too with online *reporting*, the opportunity is there to disseminate results with creative and innovative tools. Interactive/media tools are defined by a high degree of user choice in generating what results and/or analyses are called up to be displayed on a page. This includes the use of multimedia and clickable data resources that, for example, might allow users to manipulate the format (tables or graphs), information (scale scores, proficiency levels, percentiles), and type of results displayed (national, state, subgroups, gaps, etc.).

Of course making such resources available comes with some caveats. Score reporting has traditionally been a passive exercise for the intended users of test data, where a testing program determined not only what information to share but created a report that in large part (if not entirely) directed how the stakeholders would understand and interpret the results, within fairly proscribed parameters. However, increasing the level of interactivity in accessing test results means that testing programs lose progressively more of that control over what information is seen and what the statistics are computed. This is an important consideration for testing programs to understand and anticipate in creating such tools since motivated users might well explore data in unanticipated ways, and there should be a process in place for responding to inquiries. In addition, ensuring anonymity and the security of data should be paramount. For example, some programs may have rules in places that do not allow data to be displayed in certain drill-down cells if the count of examinees in that cell drops below a certain frequency threshold, perhaps 10 or 20 examinees.

Increasingly, the interactive features of testing program websites are ushering in a new era in large-scale score reporting where the shift is from prepackaged reports to the onus being placed on users to pose and answer their own questions. These tools are absolutely the result of a significant investment of time and resources, and testing agencies can and should consider ways to engage site visitors in terms of data analysis and presentation while at the same time fostering appropriate interpretations and use of data consistent with the test purpose.

Interactive Reporting Guideline A (Table 11.2) is intended to help guide the development of such online tools and again invokes consideration of intended users: *identify what user interests and needs are, and build reporting tools accordingly*. That is, developers should take into account the kinds of questions users have about test performance in a particular context and the analyses that users might want to do in order to answer those questions.

The development of interactive reporting resources need not always be an exercise in reinventing the wheel and can be advanced by consideration of the kinds of tools that other groups

Table 11.2 Summary of Guidelines for Interactive Web-Based Reporting

Interactive reporting guideline A	As with the home page, have users articulate their data analysis needs. Is rank-ordering performance key information? Or do users who are educators want item-level data to help inform their instructional practices?
Interactive reporting guideline B	Look into what others have done. Many states and publishers are being very creative in developing online interactive tools.
Interactive reporting guideline C	Start with things that are manageable, and look into developing comparatively simple web interfaces supported by databases that let users select results for a content area, unit of analysis (school, city/town, region/county, state), and perhaps limited demographic characteristics.
Interactive reporting guideline D	Different users have different capabilities for understanding quantitative data, so look into presenting data in multiple formats when possible (tables, graphs, narrative, etc.).
Interactive reporting guideline E	Online reporting doesn't always mean that an online tool carries out the full analysis, as sometimes testing programs make available menu-driven tools that provide site visitors with downloads of data stripped of names for import into external data analysis programs such as SAS, SPSS, or Excel.

have developed. Interactive Reporting Guideline B (Table 11.2) notes that *a range of tools exist from a range of testing entities*. Different tools accomplish different goals, and these tools should be developed in ways that are mindful of varied (appropriate) test purposes.

Similarly, agencies interested in developing interactive reporting need not go straight to the NAEP or TIMSS/PIRLS approach of developing online statistical modeling software. *A simple web interface that allows users to make some choices about the results they see is a great start* (Interactive Reporting Guideline C, Table 11.2) and can encourage site visitors to explore data on their own time and according to their own data needs/interests.

In building analysis tools, the structure and format of the output matters. Interactive Reporting Guideline D (Table 11.2) recommends that *output should be presented in multiple ways (as tables and graphs, when possible) to give users flexibility and options for reviewing results.*

The final guideline for interactive Web-based reporting notes that score reporting need not mean developing tools but in some cases has *involved creating large datasets and making them available to users for the purpose of carrying out their own studies of test performance* (Interactive Reporting Guidelines E, Table 11.2). It is possible to envision a menu-driven tool where users can make certain selections and a text file of data is generated, although in this regard agencies have a responsibility to maintain the anonymity of specific data records, particularly in the presence of potentially identifying demographic characteristics.

Guidelines for Programmatic/Informational Web Pages

Programmatic/informational web pages are typically text-based resources accessible by branching off the home page. Most other test information not described to this point can be considered to exemplify auxiliary information about a test that intended users of the results might want to have available. In the case of NAEP and many US states, the range of materials that fall under this heading is vast and includes such things as the links to technical documentation cited earlier as well as information about sampling and participation in a large-scale test like NAEP. Other relevant pieces of information may include a section on frequently asked questions (FAQ), an introductory document formatted as a PDF, and the policy for inclusion of students with disabilities. Also in the "About NAEP" menu are links for some of NAEP's special programs and studies, including long-term trends and the transcript study. Prominently featured here too is a link to a series of pages with technical documentation of the assessment program. Per the *Standards*

Table 11.3 Summary of Guidelines for Programmatic/Informational Web Pages

Informational resources guideline A	Ask stakeholders what information about the testing program would be helpful for them to know.
Informational resources guideline B	Review other testing programs' websites to find out the kind of programmatic documentation they make available.
Informational resources guideline C	Post the technical manual and updates online as available.

for Educational and Psychological Testing (American Educational Research Association, American Psychological Association, & National Council on Measurement in Education, 1999) test developers have a responsibility to make this information available to prospective test users, and this area of the NAEP website illustrates the kinds of things that other publishers might consider as ways to make these often complex psychometric details public. We summarized guidelines for the programmatic and informational Web pages in Table 11.3.

In determining the content to include on programmatic/information Web pages, Informational Guideline A in Table 10.3 suggests that agencies contact stakeholders and identify resources of interest.

Informational Guideline B promotes the idea *of identifying the most common resources made available by other, comparable testing programs.* These documents might include (but are not limited to) the following:

- Program overview
- Participation requirements
- Testing schedule
- Test administration resources
- Information on test design and development, including technical manuals and reports
- Released test questions
- Performance samples and scoring guides (constructed-response questions)
- Curriculum frameworks/test specifications
- Sample annotated score reports
- Performance-level descriptors
- FAQ document

The final guideline for programmatic/informational Web pages detailed in Table 11.3 is concerned with the *dissemination of the technical manual.* Testing programs too often let documentation fall by the wayside; the shift toward online reporting and test information is a way to prioritize such materials.

Guidelines for Test- and Score-Reporting Website Home Pages

In most cases, stakeholders for tests and test data will begin their online experience with a testing program at the program's Internet home page. However, depending on the test's purpose and population, the generic term *stakeholders* may unhelpfully lump together a widely heterogeneous grouping of interested audiences. Such audiences may include the test takers themselves, parents, educators, policy makers, researchers, and other groups who in truth often bring very diverse interest levels, reporting needs, and quantitative literacy skills to the score reporting materials being disseminated. For this reason, Home Page Guideline A (Table 11.4) recommends that *testing agencies cultivate familiarity with their stakeholders' reporting needs and interests and build that knowledge into the design of the home page.* One example of how this is

Table 11.4 Summary of Guidelines for Test and Score Reporting Homepages

Homepage Guideline A	Be aware of your stakeholders and their interests, and build that into the design of the homepage.
Homepage Guideline B	Provide users with clear and direct access to results or information that is in high demand/commonly accessed.
Homepage Guideline C	Be timely about what is important to site visitors and when, and maintain the homepage accordingly.
Homepage Guideline D	Research with stakeholders can help to inform site design and content to maximize usability: don't be afraid to talk with them and show them mockups!

done successfully is on the NAEP home page, where prospective audiences for NAEP are listed separately, and the groups listed (parents, researchers, media, and educators) can access information tailored for each group (which is informed by NAEP-specific research studies of reporting needs: e.g., Hambleton & Slater, 1997; Jaeger, 2003; Levine, Rathbun, Selden, & Davis, 1998; Simmons & Mwalimu, 2000).

The organization of a test- and score-reporting website is the next critical consideration. The use of vertically or horizontally arranged menus and other organizing structures allows different visitors to identify how to find the information they want quickly without getting bogged down in dead ends and irrelevant links.

The next important point for test- and score-reporting home pages also relates to content, but specifically the timeliness and relevance of the materials being made available. A site that leaves outdated or incorrect information out there for site visitors is likely to be a source of considerable frustration for stakeholders with specific questions about the testing program. Home Page Guideline C (Table 11.4) states that testing programs must *be timely about what is important to site visitors and when, and maintain the home page accordingly.* By *timely,* the recommendation suggests that programs rotate information on a regular basis; if (for example) there is a release of results for a mathematics test, it might also be advisable to include a link to the mathematics test framework or sample mathematics questions. The test results can thereby be reviewed in the appropriate context by site visitors, who will not need to search around to find relevant information. The home page for the Uniform CPA Examination (http://www.cpa-exam.org/) prominently locates a dedicated section on its home page to highlight news about the testing program, whether it is a release of results or to announce the opening of a testing window. Similarly, the PIRLS 2011 website (http://timss.bc.edu/pirls2011/index.html) details information about a test that will not be administered for a year or two but is used as a way to disseminate information to participating countries (and prospective participants).

In terms of developing online reporting resources, some take-home guidelines for testing programs regarding the home page of a test and score reporting site are given in Table 11.4.

Developing Score-Reporting Resources: The Hambleton and Zenisky Model

It is critical that reports of educational data be developed with clearly articulated ideas about their purposes and intended users in mind and with a procedure in place to obtain feedback from stakeholders about report quality (and, perhaps more importantly, to ensure that a strategy exists to integrate any substantive comments received into revisions). As with the typical process of developing score reports, developing reports for online dissemination can be guided by a formal series of steps suggested by Hambleton and Zenisky (in press). This model can be expressed in terms of a sequence of seven steps.

Before any data report is drafted, there are three activities that should take place that inform report development. These three steps (which can occur concurrently) involve (1) defining report purpose, (2) identifying the intended audience, and (3) reviewing existing reports and the psychometric reporting literature for examples and ideas. In terms of Web-based reporting, defining the purpose of the reporting website and the pages that the site encompasses is a necessary step. Related to this is the idea of who the website is intended for (it could be one or more than one stakeholder group (such as examinees themselves, their parents [for minors], educators, etc.). Third, viewing report examples provides report developers with the background and perspective necessary to be familiar with what other relevant agencies are doing and to consider what additional/different features might be necessary in their own reporting context. Armed with information and decisions as to what is needed, who will use it, and, some ideas as to structure and format, (4) online report development is the next step. Development here is thought of as a process, with draft reports designed by collaboration among individuals in a wide range of roles, such as psychometricians, information-technology specialists, Web designers, marketing or public relations personnel, and content specialists. From there, the next step is to (5) obtain feedback on the draft report sites from potential site visitors. This can happen in several ways, where visitors are observed in either directed or undirected site visits. The feedback data should be both attitudinal (what was liked/not liked) and empirical (whether users could find and report back on specific information) and should touch on both contents and usability/navigability. Report developers should then (6) incorporate user feedback and, if necessary, conduct additional field tests to gather information about the success of the revisions. At that point, materials can be made live, but it is likewise key for testing agencies to (7) monitor the use of reporting resources over time.

Conclusion

By making vast quantities of data and information available to be accessed at the convenience of users who are online, increasingly more testing agencies are responding to the processing needs of their stakeholders and being proactive to ensure their continued significance and the utility of their reports. Online reporting offers testing programs the opportunity to connect with stakeholders and communicate information in ways that more and more consumers of data have come to expect. Rather than a prefabricated "story" about test results, online reporting is often implemented in such a way as to put website visitors in charge of deciding on what information is important to them as well as on the means for communicating those findings (graphs versus tables). Relinquishing that control is a significant departure for score reporting, but with research and best practices it can increase the relevance of large-scale assessments and engage intended audiences as never before.

In review, the first area of guidelines discussed involved static, results-oriented online documents. These materials are most akin to traditional score reports, made available online. It is critical that these reports be developed in a thoughtful, purposeful way, incorporating best practices for report development by involving stakeholders and designing the reports in such a way that they are clear and useful for stakeholders. The second area of guidelines is interactive web-based reporting. This is the area that is at once the source of a great deal of reporting innovation but likewise challenge. Developing a database and a graphic user interface does not alone promote good reporting, so testing programs must take into account not only data considerations such as security but also test purpose and the intended audience.

The third set of guidelines promotes materials that are slightly peripheral to reporting but important for testing programs to share (programmatic/informational web pages). Materials such as program overviews, test content, testing schedules, and participation rules provide necessary background for users and assist in creating a sense of public openness within testing programs. Similarly, the final set of guidelines is aimed at testing program home pages. Often results get accessed by "click-throughs" from a home page, and some attention to details at the outside can enhance users' site experiences.

Our goal in this chapter has been to offer a description of some of the most common types of web-based reporting strategies and information and to provide some guidelines for the content, format, and structure of these resources. We also advocate for a systematic approach for the development of web-based reporting that is consistent with what we believe is necessary for paper-based reporting (Hambleton & Zenisky, in press). We believe that Web-based reporting is an important direction for the communication of test results (for individuals and in the aggregate), but as with many aspects of test development, these efforts need to be critically evaluated for their information value and ease of use. Connecting with stakeholders at multiple points to identify site content and modes of dissemination has the potential to have great value, and enlisting expertise in website development likewise helps to ensure that a score-reporting website is truly as functional and informative as intended.

References

American Educational Research Association, American Psychological Association, & National Council on Measurement in Education. (1999). *Standards for educational and psychological testing.* Washington, DC: American Educational Research Association.

Beaton, A. E., & Allen, N. L. (1992). Interpreting scales through scale anchoring. *Journal of Educational Statistics, 17*(2), 191–204.

Goodman, D. P., & Hambleton, R. K. (2004). Student test score reports and interpretive guides: Review of current practices and suggestions for future research. *Applied Measurement in Education, 17* (2), 145–220.

Hambleton, R. K., Sireci, S., & Huff, K. (2008). *Development and validation of enhanced SAT score scales using item mapping and performance category descriptions* (Final Report). Amherst, MA: University of Massachusetts, Center for Educational Assessment.

Hambleton, R. K., & Slater, S. (1997). *Are NAEP executive summary reports understandable to policy makers and educators?* (CSE Technical Report 430). Los Angeles, CA: National Center for Research on Evaluation, Standards, and Student Teaching.

Hambleton, R. K., & Zenisky, A. L. (in press). Reporting test scores in more meaningful ways: A research-based approach to score report design. In K. F. Geisinger (Ed.), *APA handbook of testing and assessment in psychology.* Washington, DC: American Psychological Association.

Jaeger, R. M. (2003). *NAEP validity studies: Reporting the results of the National Assessment of Educational Progress* (Working Paper 2003–11). Washington, DC: US Department of Education, Institute of Education Sciences.

Knupp, T., & Ansley, T. (2008, April). *Online, state-specific assessment score reports and interpretive guides.* Paper presented at the meeting of the National Council on Measurement in Education, New York.

Levine, R., Rathbun, A., Selden, R., & Davis, A. (1998). *NAEP's constituents: What do they want? Report of the National Assessment of Educational Progress Constituents Survey and Focus Groups* (NCES- 98–521). Washington, DC: US Department of Education, Office of Educational Research and Improvement.

Mullis, I. V. S., Martin, M. O., & Foy, P. (with Olson, J.F., Preuschoff, C., Erberber, E., Arora, A., & Galia, J.). (2008). *TIMSS 2007 International Mathematics Report: Findings from IEA's Trends in International Mathematics and Science Study at the Fourth and Eighth Grades.* Chestnut Hill, MA: TIMSS & PIRLS International Study Center, Boston College. Retrieved from http://timss.bc.edu/TIMSS2007/mathreport.html.

Ryan, J. M. (2006). Practices, issues, and trends in student test score reporting. In S. W. Downing & T. M. Haladyna (Eds.), *Handbook of test development* (pp. 677–710). Mahwah, NJ: Erlbaum.

Simmons, C., & Mwalimu, M. (2000). What NAEP's publics have to say. In M. L. Bourque & S. Byrd (Eds.), *Student performance standards on the National Assessment of Educational Progress: Affirmation and improvements. A study initiated to examine a decade of achievement level setting on NAEP* (pp. 184–219). Washington, DC: National Assessment Governing Board.

Zenisky, A. L., & Hambleton, R. K. (2007). *Navigating "The Nation's Report Card" on the World Wide Web: Site user behavior and impressions.* Technical report for the Comprehensive Evaluation of NAEP. (Also Center for Educational Assessment Report No. 625. Amherst, MA: University of Massachusetts, School of Education.)

12

Making Value-Added Inferences From Large-Scale Assessments

Derek C. Briggs

Introduction
Value-Added Models
  The Production Function Approach
  The EVAAS Approach
How Well Do VAMs Estimate the Effects of Teachers or Schools on Student Achievement?
Value-Added Inferences and Shoe Leather
  The Role of Shoe Leather
The Stability of Value-Added Indicators
  Measurement Error at the Classroom or School Level
  Measurement Error at the Student Level
Implicit Assumptions About Large-Scale Assessments
  Test Validity
  Test Scaling
  Vertical Linking
  Unidimensionality
  Measurement Error
Conclusion

Introduction

As longitudinal data from large-scale assessments of academic achievement have become more readily available in the United States, educational policies at the state and federal levels have increasingly required that such data be used as a basis for holding schools and teachers accountable for student learning. If the test scores of students are to be used, at least in part, to evaluate teachers and/or schools, a key question to be addressed is how? To compare them with respect to the average test score levels of their students would surely be unfair, because we know that student test performance is strongly associated with variables that are beyond the control of teachers and schools—prior learning, the social capital of a child's family, and so on. The premise of value-added modeling is to level the playing field in such comparisons by holding teachers and schools accountable for only that part of the student learning that it would be possible for them to influence. For example, imagine the availability of test scores in mathematics for some population of students across two grades, 4 and 5. For each student, performance on the math test in Grade 5 is predicted as a function of other variables known to be associated with academic achievement. These variables would include, at a minimum, performance on the Grade 4 math test, but they might also include test performance in earlier grades and on other test subjects, and information such as whether or not students were eligible for free and reduced lunch services, were English language learners, and so forth. Finally, the Grade 5 test score that is actually obtained for any given student can be subtracted from the score that was predicted. These values can be aggregated at the classroom or school level. If the resulting number is positive, it could be considered evidence that a teacher or school has, on average, produced a positive effect on student learning. If negative, a negative effect could be presumed. This approach, known as value-added analysis, is increasingly being promoted as a fair and objective way of making judgments about teacher (and/or school) effectiveness (Gordon, Kane, & Staiger, 2006; Harris, 2009).

The purpose of the present chapter is to provide the reader with a survey of key issues that need to be grappled with before one engages in the process of making value-added inferences from large-scale assessments. The use of value-added modeling to evaluate the quality of teachers and schools in the United States is controversial. Many have expressed alarm at what they perceive to be an unbridled enthusiasm for the approach, given the technical limitations that are inherent to it (Baker et al., 2010; Braun, Chudowsky, & Koenig, 2010). Others, while acknowledging the concerns, argue that even with its deficiencies, value-added analyses represent a marked improvement relative to preexisting approaches to educational accountability (Glazerman, Loeb, Goldhaber, Raudenbush, Whitehurst, & Policy, 2010). Although I have my own opinions on these matters (Briggs, 2008; Briggs & Domingue, 2011) and these will probably become evident to the reader, I attempt to maintain an objective perspective in the five sections that follow. I begin by defining the distinguishing features of value-added models and go into some detail to present the functional form of two widely used approaches. (For those readers uninterested in the esoteric details of these models, these subsections can be skipped without losing the narrative thread.) The second section addresses the question of whether, in a statistical sense, value-added models can be used to make direct causal inferences about the effects of teachers and schools on student achievement. There has been some heated academic debate on this topic, and I summarize key points of contention. In the third section, I present the perspective that value-added estimates are best interpreted as descriptive indicators rather than causal effects. In doing so I draw an analogy between the approach taken by John Snow, the father of epidemiology, to attribute the cause of a cholera outbreak to contaminated drinking water, and the approach that would be required to attribute a value-added indicator to a teacher or school. The fourth section addresses the issue of the stability of value-added estimates. To the extent that these estimates are clouded by measurement error, the value-added signal may be overwhelmed by noise. I describe a number of approaches commonly taken to adjust for measurement error. In the fifth section, I briefly take note of five implicit assumptions typically made about large-scale assessments that serve as the key inputs before a value-added output can be computed: alignment with standards, curriculum, and instruction; interval scale properties; vertical links across grades; unidimensionality; and constant measurement error. I conclude the chapter with a summary of the major points that have been raised.

Value-Added Models

For other more comprehensive reviews of value-added modeling, the interested reader may consult any of a number of monographs and published articles (Braun et al., 2010; Hanushek & Rivkin, 2010; Harris, 2009; McCaffrey, Lockwood, Koretz, Louis, & Hamilton, 2003; McCaffrey, Han, & Lockwood, 2009). In this section I begin by focusing attention on the distinguishing features that separate value-added models from other psychometric or statistical models sometimes used in the assessment and evaluation of student learning (see for example, Zumbo, Wu, & Liu, Chapter 16, this volume). In the National Research Council report *Getting Value out of Value-Added*, Braun et al. (2010) define value-added models (VAMs) as "a variety of sophisticated statistical techniques that use one or more years of prior student test scores, as well as other data, to adjust for preexisting differences among students when calculating contributions to student test performance." According to Harris (2009), "the term is used to describe analyses using longitudinal student-level test score data to study the educational input-output relationship, including especially the effects of individual teachers (and schools) on student achievement." From these definitions, two key features of VAMs are implicit. First, all VAMs use, as inputs, longitudinal data for 2 or more years of student test performance. Second, VAMs are motivated by a desire to isolate the impact of specific teachers or schools from other factors that contribute to a student's test performance. It follows from this that the output from a VAM is a numeric quantity that can be used to facilitate causal inferences about teachers or schools. In what follows I will refer to these numeric quantities as value-added *estimates* or, alternatively, as value-added *indicators*.

The Production Function Approach

Let Y_{igts} represent an end-of-year test score on a standardized assessment for student (i) in grade (g), in a classroom with teacher (t) in school (s). The VAM is specified as

$$Y_{igts} = \alpha_g + \beta' X_{ig} + \gamma' Z_{ig}^{(ts)} + \sum_t \theta_t D_{ig} + \varepsilon_{igts} \tag{1}$$

The covariates in this model are captured by X_i, which represents test scores from prior grades,[1] and $Z_{ig}^{(ts)}$, which could represent any number of student-, classroom-, or school-specific variables thought to be associated with both student achievement and classroom assignment. In this particular specification of the model, the key parameter of interest is the fixed effect Θ_t, which represents the effect of the current year's teacher on student achievement (i.e., the model above includes a dummy variable indicator for each teacher in the dataset). The model could also be written such that fixed effects for schools were the key parameters of interest.

The validity of the model hinges upon the assumed relationship between the unobserved error term ε_{igts} and Θ_t. If, conditional upon X and Z, ε_{igts} and Θ_t are independent, in theory it is possible to obtain an unbiased estimate of Θ_t. In other words, if one can control for the variables that govern the selection process whereby higher- or lower-achieving students land in certain kinds of classrooms, then one can approximate the result that would be obtained if students and teachers had been randomly assigned to one another from the outset. This is a controversial proposition, and much of the debate over the use of VAM for teacher accountability has focused on (1) the nature and number of covariates that need to be included in X and Z, and (2) evaluating the extent to which adding more variables or student cohorts serves to reduce bias in $\check{\Theta}_t$.

The production function model has a long history in the economics literature (Hanushek & Rivkin, 2010; Todd & Wolpin, 2003) and helps to explain why this has been the preferred specification approach among economists who have contributed to the VAM literature.[2]

The EVAAS Approach

The Educational Value-Added Assessment System (EVAAS) (Sanders, Saxton, & Horn, 1997) has the longest history as a VAM used for the purpose of educational accountability. Although a detailed presentation is outside the scope of this chapter, a key point of differentiation between it and the approach presented above can be seen by writing out the equation for a single test subject in parallel to Equation 1.

$$Y_{ig} = \alpha_g + \sum_{g^* \leq g} \theta_{g^*} + \varepsilon_{ig} \qquad (2)$$

In contrast to the fixed effects specification from the production function approach, the EVAAS represents a multivariate longitudinal mixed-effects model. As such, teacher effects for a given grade are cast as random variables with a multivariate normal distribution, such that $\theta_{g^*} \sim N(0, \tau)$. Only the main diagonal of the covariance matrix is estimated (i.e., teacher effects are assumed to be independent across grades). The student-level error term is also cast as a draw from a multivariate normal distribution with a mean of 0, but the covariance matrix is left unstructured. The EVAAS is often referred to as the "layered model" because a student's current grade achievement is expressed as a cumulative function of the teachers to whom a student has been exposed during the current and previous year. For example, applying the model above to longitudinal data that span Grades 3 through 5 results in the following system of equations:

$$Y_{i3} = \alpha_3 + \theta_3 + \varepsilon_{i3}$$
$$Y_{i4} = \alpha_4 + \theta_3 + \theta_4 + \varepsilon_{i4}$$
$$Y_{i5} = \alpha_4 + \theta_3 + \theta_4 + \theta_5 + \varepsilon_{i5}$$

In the model above, no teacher effects can be computed for Grade 3 because they are confounded with variability in student achievement backgrounds. In contrast, when certain assumptions hold, it is possible to get an unconfounded effect for the Grade 4 teacher. This can be seen by substituting the first equation into the second equation in the system, such that $Y_{i4} - Y_{i3} = \alpha_4 - \alpha_3 + \theta_4 + \varepsilon_{i4} - \varepsilon_{i3}$. This shows that the sufficient statistic for estimates of teacher effects under the EVAAS are test score gains from one grade to the next. It is for this reason that the EVAAS (and other mixed-effect modeling approaches related to it) has long been presumed to require test scores that had been vertically scaled (Ballou, Sanders, & Wright, 2004; McCaffrey, Lockwood, Koretz, Louis, & Hamilton, 2004).[3]

This simplified presentation may obscure two significant aspects of the EVAAS that contribute to its purported ability to validly and reliably "disentangle" the influence of teachers from other sources that influence student achievement. In particular, the EVAAS

- Makes use of panel data for up to 5 years of longitudinal cohorts per teacher simultaneously
- Models multiple test subject outcomes jointly as a multivariate outcome.

Although it has been criticized because it does not control for additional covariates beyond a student's test score history (Kupermintz, 2003), teacher value-added estimated by the EVAAS with and without student-level covariates have been shown to be strongly correlated (Ballou et al., 2004). A more equivocal issue is whether or not one should control for classroom- or school-level characteristics (McCaffrey et al., 2004). Controlling for classroom characteristics can lead to overadjustments of teacher effect estimates; controlling for school characteristics will restrict teacher comparisons to a within-school reference population. Finally, note that the

EVAAS assumes that the effects of students' teachers in the past persist undiminished into the future. McCaffrey et al. (2004) and Lockwood, McCaffrey, Mariano, and Setodji (2007) have demonstrated empirically that this may not be a viable assumption in the context of teachers; Briggs & Weeks (2011) show that it is probably not viable in the context of schools.

How Well Do VAMs Estimate the Effects of Teachers or Schools on Student Achievement?

Historically most educational research has focused on interventions that are "manipulable" from a policy perspective. By manipulable it is meant that it would be relatively easy (though not necessarily cheap) to expose students to more or less of the intervention. Examples would include reductions in class size, the introduction of web-based learning technologies to a curriculum, and test-based grade retention. What has made the value-added approach simultaneously intriguing and controversial has been a shift in focus since the late 1990s to define teachers and schools themselves as the principal educational interventions of interest.

When a VAM is used to estimate the effect for a more traditionally manipulable educational intervention, the intended interpretation is relatively straightforward. Indeed, the average causal effect of a manipulable intervention has a natural "value-added" interpretation: it is the amount by which a student's test score outcome differs from what it would have been in the absence of the intervention (i.e., the counterfactual outcome). In contrast, Rubin, Stuart, and Zanutto (2004) and Raudenbush (2004) have pointed out that the value-added estimates associated with teachers and schools are very difficult to conceptualize in a similar, counterfactually meaningful way. This is largely because as an educational intervention, the amalgamated characteristics of the teachers and/or schools to which a student is assigned are difficult to change—that is, to manipulate—over a finite period of time. The more technical objection to the causal interpretation of a value-added estimate is that such estimates are likely to be biased because students and teachers are sorted—or sort themselves—into classrooms and schools on the basis of many different variables that are plausibly related to how students perform on achievement tests. For some variables that are observable—such as a student's prior academic achievement, free or reduced lunch status, parents' education level, or English language proficiency—it may be possible to control for confounding statistically as part of a regression modeling approach. However, to the extent that much of this sorting occurs because of unobserved variables that might be known to a school's principal but not to a value-added modeler (e.g., student motivation, parental involvement, teacher rapport with students, etc.), there is usually good reason to suspect that estimates of a teacher or school effect will be biased.

In a sequence of papers, Rothstein, (2009, 2010) demonstrated, using data from North Carolina, that teacher effects from three commonly specified VAMs were significantly biased owing to student and teacher sorting. Rothstein (2010) accomplished this by implementing a simple yet ingenious "falsification" check. Logically, it would be impossible for a teacher in the future to have an effect on student achievement gains in the past. If this were found to be the case, a plausible explanation would be that the model was capturing the impact of one or more omitted variables from the model that is correlated with teacher assignments. As a result, the effect of these omitted variables would have been erroneously attributed to a future teacher. Therefore, the argument goes, the omission of these variables will also lead to the erroneous attribution of effects to current-year teachers. By showing that commonly used VAM specifications (e.g., subsets of Equation 1 above) failed his falsification check, Rothstein was able to call into question the premise that VAMs are capable of disentangling the effects of teachers from the effects of other factors on student achievement. Rothstein (2009) also found that under certain simulated scenarios in which students are assigned to teachers by principals on the basis of variables that would not be available to the value-added modeler, the magnitude of bias in estimates of teacher effectiveness could be substantial.

Where Rothstein's falsification check has been applied to test the validity of similar VAM specifications with data from the Los Angeles and San Diego Unified School Districts, others have found similar evidence of bias in the value-added estimates (Briggs & Domingue, 2011; Koedel & Betts, 2011). However, some researchers appear to have reached more optimistic conclusions about the validity of value-added inferences in using more complex VAM specifications to evaluate the effectiveness of teachers and schools. For example, although Koedel and Betts (2011) corroborated Rothstein's principal finding, they also found that evidence of bias could be greatly mitigated by averaging teacher value-added estimates across multiple cohorts of students while also restricting the comparison to those teachers who had shared the same students over time. This argument hinged upon the notion that sorting is transitory from year to year—a teacher may get a favorable class one year but not necessarily the next. In the San Diego schools examined by Koedel and Betts, this seems to have been the case to some extent. Whether this assumption would hold in other contexts is less clear.

The most optimistic case for the validity of teacher effects estimated using value-added models comes from a randomized experiment conducted by Kane and Staiger (2008) using a sample of 78 pairs of classrooms from Los Angeles schools. In their study, Kane and Staiger were able to estimate value-added effects for teachers before they were randomly assigned to classrooms in a subsequent year. Kane and Staiger argued that if value added can be used to accurately distinguish effective from ineffective teachers, then a significant proportion of the variability in classroom-to-classroom achievement levels at the end of the experiment should be attributable to differences in prior-year estimates of teacher value added. Their results were supportive of this hypothesis. By the end of the school year in which teachers had been randomly assigned, within-school differences in classroom student achievement could be accurately predicted from prior differences in the estimates of value added for the respective teachers in each classroom. On the basis of these results, Kane and Staiger argued that "conditioning on prior year achievement appears to be sufficient to remove bias due to non-random assignment of teachers to classroom (p. 3)"—a finding that would seem to directly contradict the more pessimistic conclusions reached by Rothstein.

There are, however, several relevant criticisms of Kane and Staiger's study and the implication that even a very simple VAM could be used to support direct causal inferences about teacher effectiveness. First, because elementary schools self-selected to participate in the original experiment, it would be plausible that the principals at those schools agreed to participate because teachers were already assigned to classrooms in a manner that was very close to random before the experiment began. To the extent that this is true, the weight placed upon a VAM to adjust statistically for biases due to the purposeful sorting of teachers and students is lessened considerably. Second, Rothstein (2010) has argued that because the experiment involved a relatively small number of classrooms and teachers, it did not have sufficient statistical power to detect significant discrepancies between the observed effect attributed to teachers and that predicted by the VAM. Third, in no case did Kane and Staiger show evidence that a VAM specification that *only* conditioned on prior achievement was an accurate predictor of "true" differences in teacher effectiveness. Rather, all VAM specifications in Kane and Staiger's study controlled for both prior achievement and a number of other demographic characteristics at both the student and classroom levels. It follows, then, that even if one were to agree that Kane and Staiger had successfully isolated the effects of teachers from other possible factors, the VAMs used to accomplish this were, in fact, quite complex.

This issue seems particularly relevant when the results from a VAM are to be used to classify teachers directly into categories of effectiveness; in some cases differences in the variables included in the model can lead to significant differences in teacher classifications. As a case in point, on August 14, 2010, just prior to the start of the 2010–2011 academic school year, the *Los Angeles Times* published results from a value-added analysis of elementary schools and teachers in the Los Angeles Unified School District (Felch, Song, & Smith, 2010). The data for this analysis came from multiple cohorts of students taking the reading and math portions of the California Standardized Test between 2003 and 2009. The VAM used to estimate teacher effects consisted of a regression model that controlled for five student-specific variables: prior year test performance, gender, English language learner (ELL) status, enrollment in a school receiving Title 1 funding, and whether or not the student had been enrolled in the district as of kindergarten (Buddin, 2010). Based directly on the estimates from this model, teachers were placed into normative quintiles of "effectiveness," and these ratings were made publicly available at a dedicated website. Yet in a reanalysis of the same data, Briggs and Domingue (2011) showed that the VAM being used by the *Times* not only failed the Rothstein falsification test but that, if additional control variables had been included in the model, 54% and 39% of Grade 5 teachers would have received different effectiveness classifications in reading and math respectively.

A major driver of these differences in classifications was the decision by Briggs and Domingue to include average classroom achievement (intended as a proxy for peer influence) and additional prior test-score information as control variables for each student in the data. Hence it could be argued that the biggest problem with the *Times's* decision to publish value-added ratings of teachers was that the VAM they had applied was not sufficiently complex to adequately support a valid causal inference. But even this position can be problematic. For example, as noted previously, the decision to include classroom- or school-level control variables for achievement and/or poverty in a VAM can lead to overadjustment if, for example, more effective teachers tend to seek jobs in higher-achieving and affluent schools (McCaffrey et al., 2004; Ballou et al., 2004). And though it has been established that the inclusion of multiple years of prior test scores can reduce the bias in estimated teacher effect (Rothstein, 2010), such specifications would typically preclude the use of a VAM for teachers in the early years of elementary school.

In summary, the question of whether VAMs can be used to make direct causal inferences about teacher effectiveness is still a matter of ongoing debate. For more optimistic perspectives, see Goldhaber and Hansen (2010), Sanders and Horn (1998), and Sanders et al. (1997). For more tempered perspectives, see Ishii and Rivkin (2009), McCaffrey et al., (2003), Newton, Darling-Hammond, Haertel, and Thomas (2010), and Reardon and Raudenbush (2009). Although there are probably few researchers who would argue that VAMs can fully disentangle the influence of the teacher from all other factors contributing to student achievement,[4] there are many who are convinced that certain VAMs can at least validly distinguish between those teachers who are at the low and high extremes of a hypothetical effectiveness distribution. At the time this chapter was being written, a large-scale replication of Kane and Staiger's value-added experiment in Los Angeles was being conducted in five urban school districts across the country (the Measures of Effective Teaching project funded by the Gates Foundation). To the extent that the results of this replication corroborate the initial findings from Kane and Staiger's original study, it would lend support to the use of VAMs as a central element of high-stakes evaluations. However, although the results from this study will be eagerly anticipated, it seems unlikely that they will settle the issue unequivocally.

Value-Added Inferences and Shoe Leather

Should the numeric outcomes from a value-added analysis be interpreted as direct estimates of teacher or school effectiveness? Or, alternatively, should they be seen as descriptive indicators that lead only indirectly to inferences about effectiveness? This subtle distinction may explain why there continues to be confusion over the distinction between a growth model and a VAM. Like VAMs, growth models depend upon the availability of longitudinal data on student test performance. Unlike VAMs, many growth models (see Zumbo, Wu, & Liu, Chapter 16, this volume) are used first and foremost to support descriptive and exploratory analyses in which inferences about students, rather than classrooms or schools, are of primary interest. The key distinction between growth and value added—inferential intent—is easy to blur, because the moment that student-level growth statistics are summarized at the classroom or school level, high or low values attributed to teachers or schools in a causal manner will often be unavoidable. Yet while all growth models applied to students in educational settings may well encourage direct causal inferences about teacher effectiveness, in the absence of additional evidence, there may be no compelling theoretical reason to believe that these inferences are valid. At the same time, the fact that value-added models are intended to support direct inferences about teacher and school effects does not necessarily make them any more valid than growth models when both are used for the same purpose.

Because of the difficulties inherent in claiming that a statistical model can be used to estimate the effect of a teacher or school on student achievement, some have argued that the outputs from a value-added analysis are best interpreted as descriptive indicators (Briggs, 2008; Hill, Kapitula, & Umland, 2010). The interpretation of a classroom- or school-level statistic as a descriptive indicator rather than a causal effect shifts the technical conversation from a consideration of *internal validity* to a consideration of *construct validity*. That is, if a numeric quantity associated with a teacher is to be interpreted as a causal effect, the fundamental validity issue from a statistical point of view is whether we can obtain parameter estimates that are unbiased and precise. In contrast, if that same number is to be interpreted as a descriptive indicator, the fundamental validity issue is the extent to which empirical evidence can be provided that collectively supports the intended interpretation and use of the indicator (see Kane, 2006). The latter task is just as challenging as the former and is decidedly messier and much less proscriptive as a process. Nor does it mean that issues of causal inference can or should be avoided. If a descriptive measure is a significant source of evidence being used to reward or sanction teachers, the implied inference that, for example, higher-quality teaching is associated with higher values of the descriptive indicator would need to be defended empirically. Nonetheless, the labeling of teacher or school growth statistics as fundamentally descriptive communicates the message that more evidence must be gathered before any high-stakes decisions on the basis of these indicators are warranted.

To illustrate this, we now look more closely at the educational accountability context in the state of Colorado. (In this example, we focus on schools rather than teachers as the principal units of analysis.) The student growth percentile model (Betebenner, 2009) and its accompanying graphic interface (www.Schoolview.org) have become the backbone of Colorado's approach to educational accountability. In short, the student growth percentile model computes for each student a conditional test score percentile. This conditional score percentile is found, in essence, by comparing the test score performance of a student in a given grade with the performance

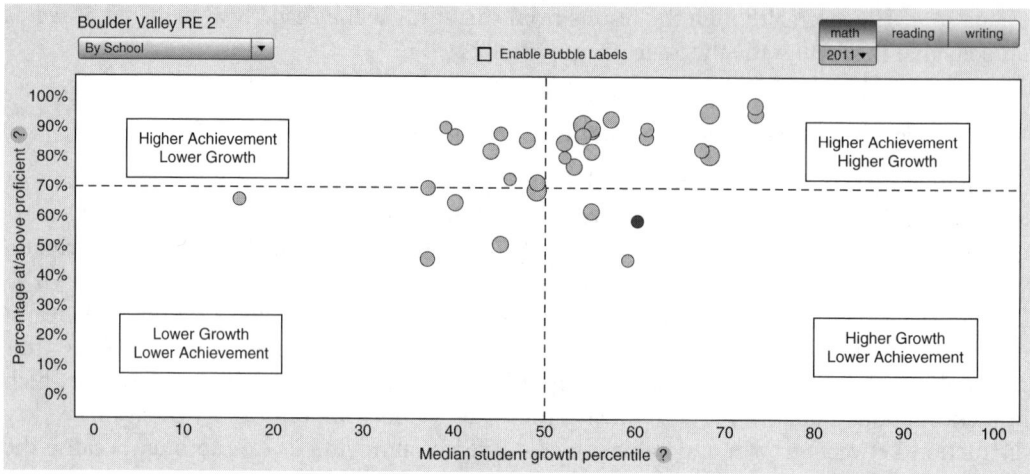

Figure 12.1 Plots of School-Level Achievement and Growth, Boulder Valley School District, 2011

of all students in the state having the same test score history in all prior grades. A student who scores at the 50th percentile of this conditional distribution is one that is inferred to have shown "growth" representing "one year of learning." An estimate of classroom- or school-level growth can then be computed by taking the median over all student growth percentiles for students with test scores in at least two adjacent grades. Note that in this approach the concept of growth is an inference—we infer that if a student has a performance rating that is higher than predicted relative to similar students, the reason is that he or she has learned more (i.e., shown more growth) than these similar students. This stands in contrast to the growth models described by Zumbo, Wu, and Liu (Chapter 16, this volume), all of which are focused on making growth inferences in terms of changes in absolute magnitudes.

The bubble plot in Figure 12.1 shows how the student growth percentile model is likely to promote value-added inferences about school quality. Each "bubble" in the plot represents a unique elementary school in the Boulder Valley school district. The size of each bubble is proportional to the number of students attending a given school. The vertical axis represents the percentage of students in a given school that have been classified as proficient or advanced on Colorado's large-scale assessment in mathematics. In contrast, the horizontal axis represents a school's median student growth percentile. In this example, the horizontal line at 50 (the median) represents the demarcation between schools that are performing better or worse than would be expected given the prior test performance of their students. The vertical line at 70 represents the threshold set by Colorado for a school to be considered "high achieving." Figure 12.1 makes it possible to distinguish among four "types" of schools:

1. Quadrant I: Higher achievement, higher growth
2. Quadrant II: Higher achievement, lower growth
3. Quadrant III: Lower achievement, lower growth
4. Quadrant IV: Lower achievement, higher growth

The frames of reference for the descriptors *higher* and *lower* are the vertical and horizontal thresholds established by the Colorado Department of Education. The further a school departs from these thresholds, the clearer the designation of a school within each quadrant. The school in the plot with the bubble shaded in blue is an example of a school that greatly benefits from taking a two-dimensional perspective on academic success. From the perspective of achievement status, the students at this school are not on pace with what is expected of them academically. Yet relative to their prior achievement, they appear to be learning a significant amount of mathematics.

The student growth percentile model is a great example of why the terms *growth model* and *value-added model* are sometimes used interchangeably: because student growth percentiles can be easily aggregated to the classroom and school levels, they are often given a de facto attribution as value added. In the example above, it would be difficult to sidestep the inference that "effective" and "ineffective" schools are those with median growth percentiles above and below 50, respectively. Are such inferences problematic? This will depend on the process through which such inferences lead to direct sanctions or rewards as part of an overarching system of educational accountability. At one extreme, we could imagine a scenario in which value-added estimates are combined across available subject domains (i.e., math and reading) and then used to classify schools into categories of effectiveness. Schools found to be ineffective would be sanctioned and schools found to be effective rewarded. At another extreme, value-added estimates would be combined with scores from holistic rubrics used to assess (for example) school climate through direct observation. A composite index might be formed, and this, along with purely qualitative information (e.g., a principal's narrative account, parent interviews, student work products) would be used in the attempt to root out the causes of any positive or negative trends being observed. (These same two extremes could just as easily be envisioned when teachers rather than schools are being evaluated. See Hill et al., 2010, for a thorough illustration.) In the first scenario, one would probably be hard pressed to defend the use of something like the student growth percentile model to make an immediate and direct causal attribution. In contrast, for the second scenario, a value-added estimate is no longer being directly attributed as the effect of a school on student achievement. Instead, it is one of multiple sources of information being used in what will ultimately require a subjective judgment about school quality by personnel at the district or state level. In this second scenario, the question of whether or not the value-added estimate is biased in a statistical sense may no longer be the salient issue as long as it is used as part of a larger pool of evidence leading to desirable and defensible outcomes.

The Role of Shoe Leather

The eminent statistician David Freedman (1987, 1991, 2004, 2006) was notoriously pessimistic about the notion that statistical modeling, in and of itself, could lead to direct causal attributions (Freedman, 1991, p. 292):

> I do not think that regression can carry much of the burden of a causal argument. Nor do regression equations, by themselves, give much help in controlling for confounding variables.... I see many illustrations of technique but few real examples with validation of the modeling assumptions.

Freedman would often argue that it was not statistical modeling in isolation but the use of statistical reasoning supported primarily by old-fashioned detective work that led to important breakthroughs in causal inference. The most famous example Freedman was known for relaying was that of John Snow, the father of epidemiology, credited for establishing the causal link between polluted drinking water and death by cholera.

During a devastating outbreak of cholera in London's Soho neighborhood in the summer of 1854, Snow was able to trace the root cause of the outbreak to the contaminated water from the nearby Broad Street pump in Soho's Golden Square. At the time of the outbreak, Snow was in the process of tabulating the results from a natural experiment in which a subset of London residents had been exposed—for all intents and purposes at random—to the drinking water from two companies, one of which (Lambeth) had moved its site for water acquisition to an unpolluted section of the Thames River and another of which (Southark & Vauxhall) had not. Sometime after the cholera outbreak that devastated the Soho neighborhood, Snow was able to establish, through the quantitative results of his "grand experiment," that the drinking of polluted drinking water was the principal cause of cholera. However, at the time of the 1854 outbreak, Snow did not yet have this evidence at his disposal. He was able to build a strong correlational case nonetheless by creating a street map of the area surrounding the Broad Street pump and showing that there was a strong association between mortality rates and distance from the pump. The force of his argument convinced the Board of Governors of St. James Parish to remove the handle from the pump, and this almost surely averted a subsequent outbreak (Johnson, 2006).

Snow's success in making a convincing causal attribution in this instance did not come from using a statistical model that could disentangle the effect of drinking well water from other possible causes (e.g., miasma, unsanitary living conditions, etc.). Rather, it was possible because he had spent years developing the hypothesis that cholera was a waterborne agent contracted not by breathing polluted air (the predominant hypothesis at the time) but by eating or drinking contaminated food or water. Over the course of a decade, Snow had developed increasingly convincing tests of his hypothesis while simultaneously ruling out alternate hypotheses. By the time of the cholera outbreak at Golden Square, Snow already had a good idea of where to look for the root cause. Snow gathered evidence to support his theory by knocking on doors and interviewing the remaining residents (even as most of them were fleeing the scene). What Snow learned in the process was not gleaned from the ingenious specification of a regression model but from wearing down his shoe leather as he made the rounds in the streets of London.

Of course, one can only go so far in drawing the analogy between the process of attributing death by cholera to the drinking of contaminated water and the process of attributing variability in student achievement to the quality of schools or teachers. In the value-added context, the outcome of interest, student learning, is a latent construct that is decidedly more difficult to measure than death! And although it was ultimately possible to validate Snow's theory at the microscopic level,[5] it will never be possible to establish definitively that a given school or teacher was responsible for what a group of students have or have not learned.

But certain parallels are relevant. What can be established through a value-added analysis is suggestive evidence that certain schools and teachers are associated with greater gains in student achievement than others. This is not that much different from Snow showing that proximity to the Broad Street pump was strongly associated with mortality rates. To go from association to a convincing argument for causation, Snow had to track down and explain away all the instances that worked against his theory (e.g., residents who had died without drinking from the Broad Street pump, residents who had drunk from the Broad Street pump and not died). One would expect the same approach to unfold when value added is used to evaluate schools or teachers. If a teacher's students have, on average, performed worse than expected, this can be cast as a hypothesis as to the quality of the teaching students have received. To ignore this evidence altogether would be irresponsible. On the other hand, there may be competing hypotheses from other sources of evidence that lead to different inferences. Some of this evidence may be entirely qualitative (e.g., obtained through interviews with parents, peer observations of teaching practice), or it may come from quantitative scrutiny (e.g., finding that the statistical model used to generate the value-added estimate failed to account for a critical variable). The key point is that almost irrespective of the particular statistical approach taken to generate a value-added indicator, the validity of high-stakes decisions about teachers and schools will depend upon the way that these indicators are understood by stakeholders and the extent to which they facilitate the kind of detective work needed to make a causal attribution.

The Stability of Value-Added Indicators

Measurement error can pose problems for the stability of value-added indicators in two different ways at two different levels. First, to the extent that the student-level regression equations at the foundation of a value-added analysis include prior-year test scores as "control" variables, measurement error in these observed scores will lead to an attenuation of *all* regression coefficients in the model (Fuller, 1987; Buonaccorsi, 2010). Second, regardless of the quality of instruction to which they are exposed, it may be the case that some cohorts of students are simply "better" or "worse" than others.[6] Given this, when teachers or schools are the units of analysis regarding which inferences are being made, it has been argued that some portion of the observed variability in estimates of value added can be explained by chance (Kane & Staiger, 2002; McCaffrey, Sass, Lockwood, & Mihaly, 2009). The key distinction here is that measurement error at the student level is assumed to have a functional relationship with the number of test items that students have been administered; at the teacher or school level, measurement error is assumed to have a functional relationship with the number of students. The analogy here is essentially that students are to schools what items are to students. Taken together, both of these sources of measurement error could explain the phenomenon in which value-added estimates appear to "bounce" up and down in a volatile manner from year to year—even if the true value is actually constant over time.

Measurement Error at the Classroom or School Level

The year-to-year correlation of teacher value added has been found to be weak to moderate, ranging from about 0.2 to 0.6 (Goldhaber & Hansen, 2008; McCaffrey et al., 2009). Kane and Staiger (2002, 2008) have argued that such intertemporal correlations can be interpreted as an estimate of reliability, in which case any intertemporal correlation less than .5 would imply that more than half of the variability in value added can be explained by chance unrelated to characteristics of teacher or school quality that persist over time. After conducting a simulation study, Schochet and Chiang (2010) conclude that 35% of teachers are likely to be misclassified as either effective or ineffective when classifications are based on a single year of data.

Three adjustments are typically made, sometimes in tandem, to account for the instability of value-added indicators. One adjustment is to increase the number of years of data over which value added is being computed. Schochet and Chiang (2010) find that going from 1 to 3 years of data reduced the error rate for teacher effectiveness classifications in their simulation from 35% to 25%. Using empirical data from Florida, McCaffrey et al. (2009) find that going from 1 to 3 years of data increases, on average, the reliability of value-added estimates for elementary and middle school teachers from .45 to .55 and .56 to .66 respectively. Two related adjustments are to use these estimates of reliability to "shrink" value-added estimates back to the grand mean (i.e., the average value added of all teachers in the system) and/or to compute a confidence interval around each value-added estimate.

When the reliability of value added is low, it will typically be a mistake to attempt to classify teachers or schools into more than three categories (e.g., significantly below average, average, significantly above average). In such instances, if teachers are instead classified into quintiles of the value-added distribution (five equally spaced categories instead of three unequally spaced categories), misclassification rates are likely to increase dramatically (Aaronson, Barrow, & Sander, 2007; Ballou, 2005; Briggs & Domingue, 2011; Koedel & Betts, 2007).

Measurement Error at the Student Level

Considerably less research has been done to evaluate the impact of student-level measurement error on value-added analyses. The problem appears to be relevant only to regression models in which prior-year test scores are included as independent variables. Such cases lead to the classic "errors in variables" problem that is well understood in the econometrics literature. Although there are many possible adjustments that could be used to correct this problem (see Fuller, 1987; Buonaccorsi, 2010), the adjustments that have been applied in the literature to date (see Buddin & Zamarro, 2009; Rothstein, 2009) have been based on the assumption of constant measurement error across the test score distribution, an assumption that is clearly unrealistic given the way that large-scale assessments are designed (see next section). Whereas it is clear that failure to adjust for the error in the variables problem can have a significant impact on value-added inferences, the practical impact of imposing linear instead of nonlinear adjustments is unclear. This is likely to be an active area for research studies in the coming years.

Implicit Assumptions About Large-Scale Assessments

Test Validity

Value-added analyses tend to be agnostic about the quality of the underlying assessments used to generate test score outcomes. But if the underlying assessments are judged to be invalid because of either construct underrepresentation or construct-irrelevant variance, it makes little difference whether a value-added estimate can be used to reliably isolate the direct effect of teachers or schools on student achievement. Much of this will hinge upon the alignment between the standards and expectations of what students should know and be able to do from grade to grade, the curriculum and instruction to which students are exposed, and the questions they are asked when they take a summative assessment at the end of the school year. Along these lines, teachers and schools can be expected to have discernible effects on student achievement only when test items are sensitive to relatively short-term instruction. Yet not all tests are designed with this intent. As just one example, the items on the SAT are designed to measure quantitative and verbal critical reasoning, which is developed gradually over the course of many years of schooling (Messick, 1980). In contrast, the sorts of tests used within systems of educational accountability are presumed to be sensitive to high-quality instruction. This constitutes a fundamental assumption that has seldom been formally investigated.

Test Scaling

With the exception of the student growth percentile model, the models used to conduct value-added analyses implicitly assume that test score outcomes exist on an interval scale. This means that score differences should have the same meaning in an absolute sense whether the initial score came from, for example, the low or high ends of the scale. Ballou (2009) argues that this assumption is both implausible and impossible to evaluate empirically. He suggests that value-added analyses would be on a surer footing if they were to statistical methods that required only data with ordinal properties. Briggs (2010) has argued that good empirical methods do exist for psychometricians to evaluate whether test scores have interval properties but that such methods and their importance are not well understood or appreciated by most psychometricians. For more on this issue, see Michell (1997, 1999, 2000, 2008).

Vertical Linking

Value-added analyses can be conducted whether or not test scores have been placed on a vertically linked score scale. For models in which prior-year test scores are used as control variables, this is readily apparent. But even for models that use repeated measures as the outcome of interest, the presence or absence of a linking step after scores have been scaled within a grade has been shown to have a negligible impact on normative value-added rankings (Briggs & Weeks, 2009; Briggs & Betebenner, 2009). It can be shown that the presence or absence of a vertical link between the test scores from adjacent grades will have an impact on value-added ranking only when there is a substantial change (e.g., increase or decrease of more than 20%) to the variability of test scores from grade to grade. This is not to argue that vertical scales are not valuable for other reasons—if carefully designed, they offer great promise for more meaningful criterion-referenced interpretations about growth magnitudes (Stenner, Burdick, Sanford, & Burdick, 2006; Stenner & Stone, 2010). But for the purpose of making value-added inferences, a vertically linked scale is not necessary.

Unidimensionality

Test scores from large-scale assessments are ultimately composites of the different components of the knowledge, skill, and ability that constitute a measurement construct. In some cases it may be reasonable to treat this composite as a single coherent dimension; in other cases this may lead to a loss of important information about what students know and can do. Lockwood, McCaffrey, Hamilton, et al. (2007) examined 4 years of longitudinal data for a cohort of 3,387 students in Grades 5 through 8 attending public schools in the state of Pennsylvania from 1999 to 2002. Of interest was the sensitivity of teacher effect estimates to the complexity of the VAM being specified. The authors chose four different VAMs in order of the complexity of their modeling assumptions. They also chose five different sets of control variables to include in the VAMs: none, demographics, base year test score, demographics plus base year test score, and teacher-level variables. Finally they considered one novel factor seldom explored in prior VAM sensitivity analyses: the dimensionality of the outcome measure. Students in the available sample had been tested with the Stanford 9 assessment across Grades 5 through 8. Upon examining the items contained in the Stanford 9, Lockwood et al. disaggregated the test into two different subscores as a function of items that emphasized problem solving (40% of the test) and items that emphasized procedures (60% of the test). Having established three factors for their sensitivity analysis (type of VAM, choice of covariates, choice of test dimension), the authors estimated teacher effects for each three-way factor combination and asked the question: Which factor has the greatest impact on inferences about a given teacher's effect on student achievement? What they found was that, by far, the choice of test dimension had the biggest impact on teacher effect estimates. Regardless of the choice of VAM or covariates, estimates of teacher effects tended to be strongly correlated (.8 or higher). On the other hand, the correlations of teacher effects estimates by outcome were never greater than .4 regardless of the underlying VAM or choice of covariates. This suggests that violations of the assumption of unidimensionality can have a significant impact of value-added inferences.

Measurement Error

The most commonly applied adjustments for measurement error in VAMs assume (1) that observed test scores are a linear function of two independent components, the "true" value of interest and chance error, and (2) that the variance of the chance error is a constant. This assumption does not mesh well with the way in which modern assessments are designed and maintained using item response theory (IRT). Specifically, a major distinction between IRT and classical test theory is that measurement error can be expressed as a function of a student's location on the score scale. Because students and test items can be placed on the same scale in IRT, it is easy enough to see that measurement error is always lowest at locations of the scale where there are the most items. A usual consequence of this is that measurement error curves for large-scale assessments will tend to follow a U shape, in which the magnitude of error is minimized in the middle of the scale, where the bulk of the test items and respondents tend to be located. At the extremes of the scale, where there are both fewer respondents and fewer items, measurement error will tend to be larger. Put in more general terms, if a large-scale assessment features relatively few items that would be considered very easy or very difficult for test takers, it will be hard to measure the lowest- and highest-performing students with the same precision as those students who are closer to the center of the score scale (e.g., within two standard deviations).[7] All this implies that traditional adjustments for measurement error in value-added contexts are likely to be wrong when the adjustment relies solely upon a transformation of a summary statistic for score reliability, such as Cronbach's alpha. Just how far off the adjustment will be is less clear and will depend upon two factors, the shape of the measurement error curve (i.e., the test information function), and the proportion of students located at the tails of the distribution where measurement error is the largest.

Conclusion

Value-added inferences are unavoidable when large-scale assessments are used for summative purposes. In this chapter, different perspectives have been presented with respect to the way that estimates of value added can be used to evaluate the quality of instruction that students receive from year to year. One perspective focuses primary attention on how we can isolate the effect of teachers and schools through statistical modeling and adjustment. In taking this perspective, the key issue that must be grappled with is whether statistical adjustments adequately account for the nonrandom manner in which teachers and students find themselves in different schools and classrooms. A second perspective—not necessarily incompatible with the first—is that the direct attribution of value added to teachers or schools will always by equivocal, no matter how complex the underlying model. Given this, value added should be viewed primarily as a descriptive indicator, and inferences based on these indicators can be validated only by referencing other sources of information, many of which may be qualitative in nature. In short, the observation that a teacher has a low or high value-added "score" in a given year raises the hypothesis that the teacher was ineffective or effective. Whereas it would be irresponsible to ignore this evidence, it would also be irresponsible to avoid the subsequent detective work that would be necessary to reject or fail to reject the initial hypothesis. In taking this perspective, a case can be made that even less sophisticated growth models would be sufficient as the initial basis for a value-added inference as long as the model takes the prior achievement of students into account and is transparent to stakeholders.

The stability and persistence of value-added estimates is important to consider irrespective of the underlying model used to compute them. Measurement error at the student level and at the classroom or school level can pose problems and may explain why value-added estimates appear to bounce up and down from year to year. Although statistical adjustments for measurement error at both levels are possible, they are not straightforward; when scrutinized, they may well turn out to be inadequate. Given our limited understanding of how chance processes interact to create noise that clouds the value-added signal, it will usually be advisable to be conservative initially in classifying teachers or schools as "effective" or "ineffective" on the basis of their value-added estimates.

Finally, although large-scale assessments are not—and should not be—designed according to the criterion of supporting value-added inferences, if the validity of the underlying tests is suspect, so too will be the validity of the value-added inferences that derive from them. Much is often implicitly assumed about the psychometric properties of test scores before they become the fundamental ingredients of a VAM: alignment with standards, curriculum, and instruction; interval scale properties; vertical links across grades; unidimensionality; and constant measurement error. Violating one or more of these assumptions will not necessarily render value-added inferences meaningless (in fact, as was pointed out, the assumption of a vertical link is not needed), but it is a mistake to ignore assumptions being made about the underlying test scores altogether.

Notes

1. Depending on the current year grade of the student, the number of available prior test scores in the same subject could range anywhere from 1 (if current year grade of student is 4), to 8 (if current year grade of student is 12).

2. For example, this is the specification that underlies the VAM used by the University of Wisconsin's Value-Added Research Center, which has taken an active role marketing its services to urban school districts across the country (e.g., New York City, Milwaukee, Los Angeles).

3. As it turns out, although it can matter how a test has been scaled, it will generally make little difference to value-added rankings of teachers or schools whether the tests have or have not been vertically linked.

4. William Sanders and colleagues who have developed the EVAAS may be a notable exception. For example, SAS makes the following explicit claim in marketing its Educational Value Added Assessment System: "It is much more than teacher or classroom level analyses; it assesses the effectiveness of districts, schools and teachers, as well as provides individual student projections to future performance. SAS EVAAS for K–12 provides precise, reliable and unbiased results that other simplistic models found in the market today cannot provide." Retrieved from http://www.sas.com/govedu/edu/k12/evaas/index.html

5. The Italian scientist Filippo Pacini is credited with the discovery of *Vibrio cholerae* in 1854, but his discovery appears to have been ignored by the scientific community at the time. It was the German physician Robert Koch who later won more widespread acceptance for the etiology of cholera after his (independent) discovery of the bacterium in 1884.

6. This is sometimes described as "sampling error" rather than measurement error, but the concept is the same.

7. An alternative way of casting this issue is with respect to floor or ceiling effects. Koedel and Betts (2011) have argued that ceiling effects will tend to bias the observed variability in teacher effects from a VAM downward.

References

Aaronson, D., Barrow, L., & Sander, W. (2007). Teachers and student achievement in the Chicago public high schools. *Journal of Labor Economics, 25*(1), 95–135.

Baker, E., Barton, P. E., Darling-Hammond, L., Haertel, E., Ladd, H. F., Linn, R. L., et al. (2010). *Problems with the use of student test scores to evaluate teachers. Economic Policy Institute* (EPI Briefing Paper #278). Washington, DC: Economic Policy Institute.

Ballou, D. (2005). Value-added assessment: Lessons from Tennessee. In R. Lissitz (Ed.), *Value added models in education: Theory and applications* (pp. 272–303). Maple Grove, MN: JAM Press.

Ballou, D. (2009). Test scaling and value-added measurement. *Education Finance and Policy, 4*(4), 351–383.

Ballou, D., Sanders, W., & Wright, P. (2004). Controlling for student background in value-added assessment of teachers. *Journal of Educational and Behavioral Statistics, 29*(1), 37–65.

Betebenner, D. (2009). Norm- and criterion-referenced student growth. *Educational Measurement: Issues and Practice, 28*(4), 42–51.

Braun, H., Chudowsky, N., & Koenig, J. (2010). *Getting value out of value-added.* Washington, DC: National Academies Press.

Briggs, D. C. (2008). *The goals and uses of value-added models.* Paper prepared for a workshop held by the Committee on Value-Added Methodology for Instructional Improvement, Program Evaluation and Educational Accountability sponsored by the National Research Council and the National Academy of Education, Washington DC: November 13–14, 2008.

Briggs, D. C. (2010). *The problem with vertical scales.* Paper presented at the 2010 Annual Meeting of the American Educational Research Association, Denver, May 3, 2010.

Briggs, D. C., & Betebenner, D. (2009). *Is growth in student achievement scale dependent?* Paper presented at the invited symposium "Measuring and Evaluating Changes in Student Achievement: A Conversation about Technical and Conceptual Issues" at the annual meeting of the National Council for Measurement in Education, San Diego, CA, April 14, 2009.

Briggs, D. C., & Domingue, B. D. (2011). *Due diligence and the evaluation of teachers: A review of the value-added analysis underlying the effectiveness rankings of Los Angeles Unified School District Teachers by the Los Angeles Times.* National Education Policy Center. Retrieved from http://nepc.colorado.edu/publication/due-diligence

Briggs, D. C., & Weeks, J. P. (2009). The sensitivity of value-added modeling to the creation of a vertical score scale. *Education Finance and Policy, 4*(4), 384–414.

Briggs, D. C., & Weeks, J. P. (2011). The persistence of school-level value-added. *Journal of Educational and Behavioral Statistics, 36*(5), 616–637.

Buddin, R. (2010). *How effective are Los Angeles elementary teachers and schools?* Unpublished manuscript. Retrieved from http://documents.latimes.com/buddin-white-paper-20100908/

Buddin, R., & Zamarro, G. (2009). Teacher qualifications and student achievement in urban elementary schools. *Journal of Urban Economics, 66*(2), 103–115.

Buonaccorsi, J. P. (2010). Measurement error: Models, methods, and applications. New York: Chapman and Hall/CRC.

Felch, J., Song, J., & Smith, D. (2010, August 14). Who's teaching L.A.'s kids? *Los Angeles Times.* Retrieved from http://www.latimes.com/news/local/la-me-teachers-value-20100815,0,2695044.story

Freedman, D. A. (1987). As others see us: A case study in path analysis. *Journal of Educational and Behavioral Statistics, 12*(2), 101–128.

Freedman, D. A. (1991). Statistical models and shoe leather. *Sociological methodology, 21,* 291–313.

Freedman, D. A. (2004). Graphical models for causation, and the identification problem. *Evaluation Review, 28*(4), 267–293.

Freedman, D. A. (2006). Statistical models for causation: what inferential leverage do they provide? *Evaluation Review, 30*(6), 691–713.

Fuller, W. A. (1987). *Measurement error models.* Hoboken, NJ: Wiley.

Glazerman, S., Loeb, S., Goldhaber, D. D., Raudenbush, S., Whitehurst, G. J., & Policy, B. I. B.C. E. (2010). *Evaluating teachers: The important role of value-added.* New York: Brown Center on Education Policy at Brookings.

Goldhaber, D., & Hansen, M. (2008). Is it just a bad class? Assessing the stability of measured teacher performance. CRPE Working Paper 2008_5. Seattle: Center on Reinventing Public Education.

Goldhaber, D., & Hansen, M. (2010). Using performance on the job to inform teacher tenure decisions. *American Economic Review, 100*(2), 250–255.

Gordon, R., Kane, T., & Staiger, D. O. (2006). *Identifying effective teachers using performance on the job* (Policy Brief No. 2006-01). Washington, DC: The Brookings Institution.

Hanushek, E. A., & Rivkin, S. G. (2010). Generalizations about using value-added measures of teacher quality. *American Economic Review, 100*(2), 267–271.

Harris, D. N. (2009). Would accountability based on teacher value added be smart policy? An examination of the statistical properties and policy alternatives. *Education Finance and Policy, 4*(4), 319–350.

Hill, H. C., Kapitula, L., & Umland, K. (2010). A validity argument approach to evaluating teacher value-added scores. *American Educational Research Journal, 48*(3), 794–831.

Ishii, J., & Rivkin, S. G. (2009). Impediments to the estimation of teacher value added. *Education Finance and Policy, 4*(4), 520–536.

Johnson, S. (2006). *The ghost map: The story of London's most terrifying epidemic—and how it changed science, cities, and the modern world.* New York: Riverhead Books.

Kane, M. (2006). Validation. In R. L. Brennan (Ed.), *Educational measurement* (4th ed., pp. 17–64). Westport, CT: American Council on Education/Praeger.

Kane, T. J., & Staiger, D. O. (2002). The promise and pitfalls of using imprecise school accountability measures. *Journal of Economic Perspectives, 16*(4), 91–114.

Kane, T., & Staiger, D. (2008). Estimating teacher impacts on student achievement: An experimental evaluation. *NBER working paper.* Retrieved from http://www.nber.org/papers/w14607

Koedel, C., & Betts, J. R. (2007). Re-examining the role of teacher quality in the educational production function. Working Paper. Columbia, MO: University of Missouri.

Koedel, C., & Betts, J. R. (2011). Does student sorting invalidate value-added models of teacher effectiveness? An extended analysis of the Rothstein critique. *Education Finance and Policy, 6*(1), 18–42.

Kupermintz, H. (2003). Teacher effects and teacher effectiveness: A validity investigation of the Tennessee Value Added Assessment System. *Educational Evaluation and Policy Analysis, 25*(3), 287.

Lockwood, J. R., McCaffrey, D. F., Hamilton, L. S., Stecher, B., Le, V., & Martinez, J. F. (2007). The sensitivity of value-added teacher effect estimates to different mathematics achievement measures. *Journal of Educational Measurement. 44*(1), 47–68.

Lockwood, J. R., McCaffrey, D. F., Mariano, L. T., & Setodji, C. (2007). Bayesian Methods for Scalable Multivariate Value-Added Assessment. *Journal of Educational and Behavioral Statistics, 32*(2), 125–150.

McCaffrey, D. F., Lockwood, J. R., Koretz, D., Louis, T. A., & Hamilton, L. S. (2003). *Evaluating value-added models for teacher accountability* (Vol. 158). RAND Research Report prepared for the Carnegie Corporation.

McCaffrey, D. F., Lockwood, J. R., Koretz, D., Louis, T. A., & Hamilton, L. (2004). Models for value-added modeling of teacher effects. *Journal of Educational and Behavioral Statistics, 29*(1), 67.

McCaffrey, D. F, Sass, T. R., Lockwood, J. R., & Mihaly, K. (2009). The intertemporal variability of teacher effect estimates. *Education Finance and Policy, 4*(4), 572–606.

McCaffrey, D.F., Han, B., & Lockwood, J. (2009). Turning student test scores into teacher compensation systems. In M. Springer (Ed.), *Performance incentives: Their growing impact on American K-12 education* (pp. 113–147). Washington, DC: Brookings Institution Press, 2009.

Messick, S. (1980). *The Effectiveness of coaching for the SAT: Review and reanalysis of research from the fifties to the FTC.* Princeton, NJ: Educational Testing Service:.

Michell, J. (1997). Quantitative science and the definition of measurement in psychology. *British Journal of Psychology, 88*(3), 355–384.

Michell, J. (1999). *Measurement in psychology: Critical history of a methodological concept.* Cambridge, UK: Cambridge University Press.

Michell, J. (2000). Normal science, pathological science and psychometrics. *Theory & Psychology, 10*(5), 639.

Michell, J. (2008). Is psychometrics pathological science? *Measurement: Interdisciplinary Research & Perspective, 6*(1), 7–24.

Newton, X. A., Darling-Hammond, L., Haertel, E., & Thomas, E. (2010). Value-added modeling of teacher effectiveness: An exploration of stability across models and contexts. *Education Policy Analysis Archives, 18,* 23.

Raudenbush, S. W. (2004). What are value-added models estimating and what does this imply for statistical practice? *Journal of Educational and Behavioral Statistics, 29*(1), 121–129.

Reardon, S. F., & Raudenbush, S. W. (2009). Assumptions of value-added models for estimating school effects. *Education Finance and Policy, 4*(4), 492–519.

Rothstein, J. (2009). Student sorting and bias in value-added estimation: Selection on observables and unobservables. *Education Finance and Policy, 4*(4), 537–571.

Rothstein, J. (2010). Teacher quality in educational production: Tracking, decay, and student achievement. *Quarterly Journal of Economics, 125*(1), 175–214.

Rubin, D. B., Stuart, E. A., & Zanutto, E. L. (2004). A potential outcomes view of value-added assessment in education. *Journal of Educational and Behavioral Statistics, 29*(1), 103–116.

Sanders, W. L., & Horn, S. P. (1998). Research findings from the Tennessee Value-Added Assessment System (TVAAS) database: Implications for educational evaluation and research. *Journal of Personnel Evaluation in Education, 12*(3), 247–256.

Sanders, W. L., Saxton, A.M., & Horn, S. P. (1997). The Tennessee value-added assessment system, a quantitative, outcomes-based approach to educational measurement. In J. Millman (Ed.), *Grading teachers, grading schools: Is student achievement a valid evaluation measure?* (pp. 137–162). Thousand Oaks, CA: Corwin Press.

Schochet, P. Z., & Chiang, H. S. (2010). *Error rates in measuring teacher and school performance based on student test score gains.* Washington, DC: National Center for Education Evaluation and Regional Assistance,

Institute of Education Sciences, U.S. Department of Education. Retrieved from http://ies.ed.gov/ncee/pubs/20104004/pdf/20104004.pdf

Stenner, J., Burdick, H., Sanford, E., & Burdick, D. (2006). How accurate are lexile text measures? *Journal of Applied Measurement, 7*(3), 307–322.

Stenner, J., & Stone, M. (2010). Generally objective measurement of human temperature and reading ability: Some corollaries. *Journal of Applied Measurement, 11*(3), 244–252.

Todd, P. E., & Wolpin, K. I. (2003). On the specification and estimation of the production function for cognitive achievement. *Economic Journal, 113*, 3–33.

Part IV

Psychometric Modeling and Statistical Analysis

13
Complex Person and Item Sampling
Implications for Analysis and Inference

Jessica L. Mislevy, Laura M. Stapleton, and André A. Rupp

Introduction
Sampling and Statistical Inference
Types of Sampling Designs for Students and Items
  Simple Versus Complex Sampling
  Complex Sampling of Students
  Complex Sampling of Items
  Section Summary
Motivating Example
Impact of Sampling Design on Estimation and Inference
  Implications of Complex Sampling Design for Students
  Implications of Complex Sampling Design for Items
Accommodating Complex Sampling Designs of Students in Analyses
  Design-Based Approaches for Correcting Bias in Parameter Estimates
  Model-Based Alternatives for Correcting Bias in Parameter Estimates
  Design-Based Approaches for Correcting Bias in Standard Error Estimates
  Model-Based Alternative for Correcting Bias in Standard Error Estimates
Accommodating Complex Sampling Designs of Items in Analyses
  Analysis of Example Data
  Limitations of Plausible Values Methodology
Conclusion

Introduction

Studies that use large-scale assessments of student achievement, also known simply as educational surveys, are a ubiquitous component of systems monitoring in education. Internationally, some of the best-known studies include the Programme for International Student Assessment (PISA), the Trends in International Mathematics and Science Study (TIMSS), and the Progress in International Reading Literacy Study (PIRLS). Nationally, the School Achievement Indicators Program (SAIP) as well as its successor, the Pan-Canadian Assessment Program (PCAP) in Canada and the National Assessment of Educational Progress (NAEP) in the United States, supplement such international studies. Moreover, many provinces or states within a given country conduct independent educational surveys, which are administered to a representative sample or the entire population of students at regular intervals. American examples include the New Jersey Assessment of Skills and Knowledge (NJ ASK) and the Oregon Assessment of Knowledge and Skills (OAKS).

The primary objective of large-scale assessments of achievement is to obtain reliable information about student achievement in one or more content domains of interest. A secondary objective is to obtain reliable information about the item properties in development stages of the assessments. This chapter discusses how the selection (i.e., sampling) process for students and items in these assessments affects the subsequent estimation process of the statistical models that are applied to the student response data. We designed the chapter so that researchers and practitioners can understand the critical steps during sampling and estimation that ensure coherence between the empirical information and the interpretations that are made about students and items.

This chapter is divided into four primary sections. In the first section, we discuss basic principles of sampling and statistical inference; the following three sections discuss means to statistically accommodate the complex sampling processes of students and items common to educational surveys. Throughout the chapter we provide examples of how the concepts discussed are realized in these assessment contexts.

Sampling and Statistical Inference

To understand some of the more subtle considerations about sampling addressed in this chapter, we briefly review a few basic concepts. A *population parameter* is simply a number whose value is computed across all elements of the population. It can be a mean or a proportion, a difference between two means or a correlation coefficient, as well as a regression coefficient or an error variance. Because population parameters depend on all elements in the population and information typically is not available on all of these elements, they are generally unknown. Only a subset of elements, known as a *sample,* is selected from the population and measurements are taken on the sample elements. An estimate of the population parameter, known as the *sample statistic* for that parameter, can then be calculated from the sample data, and inferences about the population parameter can then be made based on the sample statistic.

Oversimplifying somewhat, *inferential statistics* is concerned with bounding the uncertainty that exists about the population parameter based on the limited information available in the sample statistics. Key techniques in inferential statistics include hypothesis tests and confidence interval estimation, which rely on utilizing the *sampling distributions* of the sample statistics to make these inferences. Sampling distributions describe the general behavior of sample statistics and can be used to gauge the amount of uncertainty that a particular statistic carries about the population parameter that it is estimating. They are either theoretically postulated based on a certain set of model assumptions or empirically estimated based on simulation techniques.

Sample statistics need to be created so that they are unbiased and as efficient as possible within the constraints of the sampling design of the students and the items. A statistic is *unbiased* if, on average over hypothetical replications of the sample selection and analysis, it provides the correct value for the population parameter. A procedure for estimating a statistic is *efficient* if the statistic is estimated with the least amount of sampling error possible given the design constraints of the survey.

Although the discipline of statistics is predominantly concerned with modeling data from variables that are measured without error, the discipline of *psychometrics* is concerned with making inferences about *latent characteristics* of individuals using unobservable *latent variables* that are measured with error. Latent characteristics (e.g., ability, depression) are measured with error because they cannot be measured directly under any circumstance, unlike manifest characteristics of individuals (e.g., age, income). To estimate the latent variable scores of the students in an educational survey accurately and comprehensively, they are given *items* on a *survey instrument* (e.g., a test, questionnaire, or survey) that is designed to measure the latent characteristic(s) of interest.

Establishing an appropriate link between the observed item responses and the latent profiles of the students in educational surveys requires the use of specialized statistical models with *latent variables,* also called *psychometric models*. In educational surveys, latent variable scores for particular dimensions in a statistical model are used to characterize differences in student achievement, especially for groups of students. Thus the use of latent variable models helps to quantify the *measurement error* that is inherent in the measurement procedure over and above the *sampling error* that exists due to the random sampling of students from the population. Inferences about mean achievement differences for particular subpopulations from the target population (e.g., students from different sexes, ethnic groups, or school types) will be made based on sample statistics such as mean difference scores on latent variables.

The focus of this chapter is to discuss the implications that more complex random sampling techniques for students and items in educational surveys have on the structure of the statistical inferences about population parameters. In order to make these inferences as unbiased and efficient as possible, it is critical to incorporate the information from the complex sampling of both students and items into the psychometric models that are used for the analysis of the response data.

Types of Sampling Designs for Students and Items

Simple Versus Complex Sampling

The sample arising from the most basic sampling design upon which traditional sampling theory and statistical inference are built is known as a *simple random sample* (SRS). Statistically, a SRS assigns equal probabilities of selection to each element in the population (Groves, Fowler, Couper, Lepkowski, Singer, & Tourangeau, 2004). Each population element is selected into the sample in one step, independent of previous and subsequent selections of elements and without any additional selection constraints. Sampling designs other than SRSs, broadly known as *complex sampling designs,* are typically multistep processes where different selection constraints are put in place to select elements from a population. As stated above, educational surveys typically involve samples that are complex with respect to students and items.

Complex Sampling of Students

The complex sampling of students can involve various combinations of stratification, multistage sampling, and the use of disproportionate sampling rates. *Stratification* is a technique that is used to ensure that the sample contains specific proportions of elements of the population. Stratification implies that the population is heterogeneous with respect to the latent characteristic of interest and can be divided into relatively homogenous, mutually exclusive subgroups known as the *strata*. For example, a population of students could be divided into strata based on whether they attend a public school or private school, whether they are boys or girls, whether they come from urban or rural settings, or whether they are an ethnic minority or not.

Once elements in the population are divided into strata, independent selections are made from each stratum. These selections can be made with equal probabilities across all strata or with unequal probabilities across strata. *Disproportionate sampling* using unequal sampling probabilities can be used to *oversample* students from small segments of the population so that subgroup estimates can be calculated with a targeted level of precision. For example, let us assume that the number of students in private schools is much smaller than the number in public schools. In this case, private school students can be oversampled to obtain sufficiently precise estimates of the average performance of private school students. If a SRS of students were drawn without stratification and the use of unequal sampling rates, it could happen by chance that the sample would not include any private school students or at least too few to draw reliable inferences about their average proficiency.

Multistage sampling is a technique that can be used when elements in the population belong to naturally occurring groups. Instead of selecting students directly from the population, groups of students, known as *clusters,* are selected into the sample. The sampling of clusters typically reduces the cost and burden associated with data collection, particularly when the population is spread out geographically. In educational surveys, students are always naturally grouped within schools. Thus one could sample schools instead of individual students and administer the survey to a number of students in each selected school. This method is much more efficient and cost-effective than selecting students randomly without any constraints. In that case, more schools might need to be visited with only a few students selected in each of them.

With multistage sampling, the researcher might assess all students in a cluster, which is referred to as *cluster sampling*. In practice, however, multistage samples for educational surveys typically involve various combinations of stratification using disproportionate sampling across multiple stages of sampling. For example, school districts might be sampled in a first stage; the districts are called the *primary sampling units* (PSUs) in this case. Certain schools within those districts are then sampled in a second stage; these schools would be *secondary sampling units* (SSUs). Finally, subsets of students are sampled in a third stage; these students are called the *ultimate sampling units* (USUs) in this case. Additionally, stratification is typically used at most or all stages of sampling. Districts could be stratified by geographic region and sampled at equal rates in the first stage, schools may be stratified by type with private schools oversampled in the second stage, and students may be stratified by race/ethnicity with minority students oversampled in the third stage.

Complex Sampling of Items

The complex sampling of items in educational surveys is the conceptual counterpart to creating fixed-form assessments. A *fixed-form assessment* consists of one form that presents all students with the same items in the same order; in essence, such forms can be considered a SRS of items from a hypothetical population of items in an item pool. Increasing the number of highly discriminating items across the response scale for each latent variable provides more precise estimates of the latent variable scores. However, practical constraints limit the number of items a student can be expected to answer, much as they make it infeasible to obtain measurements from every student in the population. Additionally, presenting all students with the same set of items limits the breath of the content domain that can be covered by the assessment.

In contrast, a complex sampling design for items selects several sets of items from the item bank to construct multiple forms, typically known as *booklets* in the context of educational surveys. Assignment of items to booklets is typically done by grouping items first into *blocks* of common length (e.g., 20 minutes of testing time) and then assigning the blocks to the different booklets within a specific booklet design structure. Such complex sampling designs of items are often referred to as *incomplete block* or *matrix sampling designs* (e.g., Childs & Andrew, 2003; Frey, Hartig, & Rupp, 2009; Thomas & Gan, 1997). Students respond only to particular subsets of items from the bank because they only respond to one particular test form that is assigned to them.

The different booklets are *linked* to one another via a single common block of items across all booklets or common blocks of items across pairs or sets of booklets. The items in the common item blocks are known as *anchor items* and ensure that one can statistically link all students' latent variable scores across the different booklets onto one or multiple common scales. To form a strong link between booklets, it is advantageous to include a large number of anchor items into the common blocks. Research suggests that the anchor items are a miniversion or "market basket" of the entire survey, both in terms of statistical item properties and in terms of the design characteristics regarding the content domain (e.g., Mislevy, Johnson, & Muraki, 1992; von Davier, Carstensen, & von Davier, 2006).

Complex sampling designs for items are desirable in the context of educational surveys because they allow the assessment designers to cover a relatively broad number of content areas or curricular units. Such broad coverage is typically desired because the surveys are supposed to report population estimates of proficiency, or a relatively coarse-grained snapshot of student proficiencies, rather than a detailed fine-grained picture of high-dimensional skill profiles. Such sampling designs for items also make the administration of the educational survey feasible, thus lessening the time demand on each individual student.

Section Summary

Table 13.1 summarizes the various characteristics of samples that may arise from the intersection of simple and complex sampling designs for students and items.

Quadrant A on the upper left represents a simple scenario wherein all students are randomly sampled without design constraints and are presented with a single test form. In contrast, quadrant D on the lower right represents the most complex case, where both students and items are selected with a complex sampling design. Because most large-scale assessments are designed to cover several broad content areas and need to provide reasonably precise parameter estimates for multiple student groups while remaining cost-efficient, they typically employ complex sampling designs for both students and items. Whereas the complex sampling of students and items can be efficient and cost-effective from an administrative standpoint, it has implications for the estimation of the population parameters of interest as well as their standard errors; these issues are discussed in more detail in the following three sections.

Motivating Example

To make the concepts associated with complex sampling designs more concrete and to illustrate the effect the sampling design can have on parameter estimation and associated

Table 13.1 Summary of Sampling Designs

		Sampling Design for Items	
		Simple	Complex
Sampling design for students	Simple	Students are selected into the sample independently and at equal rates with no other constraints; all students are administered the same items on a single fixed form. (A)	Students are selected into the sample independently and at equal rates with no other constraints; students are administered some common and some unique items across forms. (B)
	Complex	Students are selected into the sample jointly, at different rates, and/or with other constraints; all students are administered the same items on a single fixed form. (C)	Students are selected into the sample jointly, at different rates, and/or with other constraints; students are administered some common and some unique items across forms. (D)

statistical inference, a small data set is used as an example. It will also be used to demonstrate the different statistical approaches that can be employed to obtain unbiased and efficient estimates of model parameters and their standard errors. In the simple example here, we assume that the data come from a statewide educational survey measuring sixth graders' English reading proficiency, among other skills and abilities. In the state, there are 100 schools, 70 public and 30 private. Each public school has 150 sixth-grade students and each private school has 50 sixth-grade students. Within both public and private schools, 80% of the students are native English speakers and 20% are nonnative English speakers. Thus our target population of interest consists of the 12,000 sixth-grade students in the state, as depicted in Table 13.2.

We assume that the state uses a multistage sampling design for students, with schools as the PSUs and students within schools as the USUs. At the first stage, the schools are grouped into strata based on whether they are public or private, and 5 schools are randomly selected in each stratum for a total of 10 selected schools. At the second stage, school records are used to group students into strata based on whether they are native or nonnative English speakers. Within each selected school, 5 native English speakers and 5 nonnative English speakers are randomly selected, for a total of 100 students across the 10 selected schools. As shown in Table 13.2, relative to their representation in the population, private schools are oversampled in the first stage and nonnative English speakers are oversampled in the second stage. The full sample dataset for the 100 students is included in Appendix 13.A.

Also displayed in Table 13.2 are the average English reading proficiencies for the population overall and for each population subgroup. Although researchers would not have these population parameter values in reality, knowing the true values in our example will help demonstrate the impact of using appropriate and inappropriate statistical models on population inference, given the complex sampling design. Based on the population values displayed in Table 13.2, we see that the stratification variables are related to English reading proficiency. On average in the population, students in private schools have a higher proficiency level in reading whereas nonnative English speakers have a lower proficiency level in reading, which is true across both public and private schools.

Table 13.2 Population and Sample Considered in Example

Stratum		Number of Schools in Population	Number of Students in Population	Average True English Reading Proficiency	Number of Schools in Sample	Number of Students in Sample
Public school	Native English speaker	70	8,400	101	5	25
	Nonnative English speaker		2,100	94		25
Private school	Native English speaker	30	1,200	107	5	25
	Nonnative English speaker		300	97		25
Total		100	12,000	100	10	100

In order to cover a broad content area in the statewide assessment, a complex sampling design for items is utilized also, and each student is assigned a booklet of items designed to measure English reading proficiency with common anchor items. To keep the illustrations in this chapter at a manageable level of complexity, we do not discuss the particular structure of the booklet design. Students are also asked to complete a background questionnaire, which collects information on students' demographic characteristics (e.g., race/ethnicity, socioeconomic status, gender, and disability), classroom experiences, and educational support. One item on the background questionnaire asks students to self-report the amount of time (minutes) they spend reading outside the classroom each week.

Let us now assume that a secondary analyst is interested in determining the relation between English reading proficiency and the number of minutes spent reading each week. In other words, the analyst is interested in building a simple linear regression model with the amount of reading in minutes measured as a ratio-scaled independent variable (X) and English reading proficiency measured by a latent variable score as the interval-scaled dependent variable (Y).[1] Thus the model takes the form

$$Y_i = \alpha + \beta X_i + \varepsilon_i$$

where Y_i is the English proficiency score for student i, X_i is the minutes of reading for student i, α is the population intercept of the regression line, β is the population slope of the regression line, or *regression coefficient*, and ε_i is *error term* for student i (i.e., population difference between the observed and model-predicted proficiency score for student i). Although researchers will not know the true population values that they are estimating, we can calculate them here for the full population of 12,000 students using their true English reading proficiency scores and their minutes of reading, which yields $\alpha = 75.260$ and $\beta = 0.205$. This means that an individual who spends no time reading outside the classroom each week (i.e., zero minutes) has a predicted proficiency score of about 75. Also, on average, the predicted proficiency score increases by 0.205 for each additional minute spent reading outside the classroom.

The sample, however, offers only estimates of English reading proficiency ($\hat{Y}_i$) for $n = 100$ students. Hence, α and β are the unknown population parameters that the researcher is interested in estimating from the sample data. The equation for the simple linear regression model in the sample can thus be written as

$$\hat{Y}_i = a + bX_i$$

where the sample intercept a is an estimate of α and the sample slope b is an estimate of β. The researcher in our example is primarily interested in the slope estimate b, because the regression coefficient measures the amount of change produced in the dependent variable that is induced by a one-unit change in the independent variable. We now shift our focus to the impact that the complex sampling design for both students and items has on the estimation of model parameters of interest, in this case β. In this chapter the statistical program SAS 9.1 (SAS Institute, Cary, NC) is used to perform analyses and provide sample code when appropriate.

Impact of Sampling Design on Estimation and Inference

The literature on inferential statistics provides formulas for estimating population parameters via sample statistics (Kish & Frankel, 1974). As discussed in the first section, statistical inference requires computing the standard errors associated with the sample statistics and using suitable sampling distributions for the statistics to draw proper inferences about likely population parameter values. The accurate estimation of standard errors is particularly important for developing confidence intervals around estimates of population parameters and conducting hypothesis tests. For instance, the standard error associated with the slope estimate b in our example is used to determine whether or not we can conclude that the population slope is different from zero (i.e., whether X is a worthwhile predictor of Y). Whereas the estimation process is trivial in SRS contexts, this process can be rather complicated when the sampling design of students and items is complex.

If the educational survey had been using a simple design as in quadrant A of Table 13.1, traditional estimates from a standard simple linear regression routine with the typical standard error formulation would be appropriate. However, since our example educational survey is found in quadrant D, parameter estimates and standard error estimates using traditional formulas may be biased because the design structure is not appropriately accommodated in the statistical model.

Implications of Complex Sampling Design for Students

The violation of the SRS assumption in complex sampling designs has two key effects. First, if disproportionate sampling across strata is used, the parameter estimates computed under traditional techniques may be biased, leading to distorted or inaccurate estimates of the magnitude and directionality of effects. Second, with both stratification and multistage sampling, the estimates of the standard error of the parameter estimates computed under traditional techniques may be biased. This leads to a systematic *underestimation* (i.e., an overly optimistic estimation of precision) or *overestimation* (i.e., an overly pessimistic estimation of precision) of the uncertainty associated with the parameter estimate.

IMPACT OF COMPLEX SAMPLING OF STUDENTS ON ESTIMATES OF POPULATION PARAMETERS
The accuracy of traditional estimates of population values can be affected when a disproportionate sampling design is applied after the population is stratified on key variables. A stratified sample with unequal selection probabilities, in its raw form, is a severe distortion of the population from which it was drawn (Thomas & Heck, 2001). Different subgroups of students are not represented to the same degree in the sample as they are in the population. If such a sampling design is ignored during analyses, population estimates are disproportionately swayed by students who make up a small proportion of the population but a relatively large portion of the sample, and vice versa. This disproportionate influence on parameter estimates is particularly

problematic when the characteristics of interest are correlated with the probability of selection. As the strength of the relation between the variables used in selection and the characteristic of interest increases, so will the bias in traditional estimates of population values.

Let us return to our motivating example to make this idea concrete. Assume we are interested in determining the average English reading proficiency in the population using sample data. We know from our population data that both of our stratification variables (i.e., school type and language status) are indeed related to the characteristic of interest because average English reading proficiency varies across these groups. In a particular sample, we may find that nonnative speakers across public and private schools have a mean proficiency of 91 while native speakers have a mean proficiency of 101. Thus the heavily overrepresented nonnative speakers with lower proficiency scores will unduly sway the sample mean downward, closer to 96 instead of the true population average of 100 (assuming equal numbers of native and nonnative speakers in the sample).

IMPACT OF COMPLEX SAMPLING OF STUDENTS ON SAMPLING VARIANCE OF PARAMETER ESTIMATES
The complex sampling of students also violates the assumptions underlying traditional formulas that are used to calculate standard errors. The bias in standard error estimates may be either positive or negative, depending on the sampling design and the data themselves. Stratification often leads to sampling variance estimates that are too large (i.e., *positively biased*) if traditional formulas are used. This happens because stratification ensures that the sample is representative of the population in terms of relevant characteristics reflected by the stratification variables. The reduction in sampling variance that can be obtained via stratification is greatest when elements across the strata are very different from one another but internally homogeneous within strata. However, if students are not sampled at the same rate across strata, some of this additional estimation precision is lost and traditional variance estimates may be too small (i.e., *negatively biased*). This occurs because disproportionate sampling across strata yields a nonoptimal sample in the sense that estimates for some subgroups will be fairly precise while the estimates for other subgroups will be less precise.

A more difficult problem with complex sampling designs is that multistage sampling explicitly violates the assumption of independent observations because groups of students that share a common context—such as students within schools and schools within districts—are selected into the sample jointly. Students from the same cluster bring less unique information to the sample than students independently selected from the population. These within-cluster dependencies can be quantified via the *intraclass correlation coefficient* (ICC), which measures the ratio of the between-cluster variation to the total variation on an outcome variable of interest. In other words, the ICC indicates the amount of variability in the outcome variable that can be accounted for by the clustering.

The ICC for a given cluster sample can be approximated using variance components from an *analysis of variance* (ANOVA) on the variable of interest, using the cluster identifier as the between-subjects factor,

$$ICC \approx \frac{MS_B - MS_W}{MS_B + (n-1)MS_W} \quad (1)$$

where MS_B is the mean square for the between-subjects factor, MS_W is the mean square for the within-subjects factor or error, and n is either the sample size per cluster if the design is balanced in this regard or the average sample size per cluster if the design is unbalanced in this regard. In the most extreme case, an ICC value close to 1 indicates all the elements in the cluster are nearly

Table 13.3 Sampling Design Characteristics and their Prototypical Design Effects and Impact on Estimates

Characteristic of Sampling Design	Bias Due to Use of Traditional Formulas		Design Effect
	In Parameter Estimate	In Standard Error Estimate	
Simple random sample	None	None	1
Stratification			
Equal selection probabilities	None	Overestimated	<1
Unequal selection probabilities	Over- or underestimated	Underestimated	>1
Clustering	None	Underestimated	>1
Multi-stage			
Equal selection probabilities	None	Underestimated[a]	>1
Unequal selection probabilities	Over- or underestimated	Underestimated	>1

[a] Typically the sampling of clusters outweighs the efficiency of the stratification.

identical with respect to the outcome variable and that most of the variance is found between clusters as opposed to within clusters. Such an extreme ICC value is not often found for individual-level variables in educational contexts; however, even small ICCs can have implications for an analysis. Whenever the ICC is greater than 0, then traditional formulas will yield negatively biased estimates of sampling variances.

The degree to which traditional estimates of sampling variance for a model parameter are biased can be quantified through a measure known as the *design effect* (deff). This is defined as the ratio of the sampling variance of a statistic $\hat{Q}$ given the complex sampling design over the sampling variance that would have been obtained from an SRS of the same size (Kish, 1965):

$$deff(\hat{Q}) = \frac{Var(\hat{Q}_{complex})}{Var(\hat{Q}_{srs})} \qquad (2)$$

Design features of a complex sampling design that improve the precision of parameter estimates relative to a SRS result in design effects less than 1, whereas features that decrease the precision result in design effects greater than 1. Table 13.3 shows how the different combinations of stratification, clustering, and multistage sampling prototypically relate to the directionality of the design effect and the bias in traditional estimates of population parameters and their standard errors.

Thus a necessary preliminary step when data are collected via a multistage sample is to compute the *ICC* and *deff*. For our example data, the results of an ANOVA with school as the between-subjects factor is shown in Figure 13.1.

Using Equation 1, the estimate of the ICC is 0.215, indicating that just over 20% of the variability in English reading proficiency is accounted for by the school grouping, while roughly 80% is accounted for by individual variability within the schools.

To translate this ICC into an estimate of the design effect, we use the following approximation for deff using the intraclass correlation (ICC) and the sample size per cluster (n)

$$deff \approx 1 + ICC(n-1) \qquad (3)$$

and obtain a deff estimate of 2.935. A deff approaching 3 indicates a relative inefficiency of the design. The sampling variance under our multistage sampling design is nearly three times that

The ANOVA Procedure					

Dependent Variable: Reading Proficiency (Y_1)

Source	DF	Sum of Squares	Mean Square	F Value	Pr > F
Model	9	8133.35318	903.70591	3.74	0.0005
Error	90	21762.61837	241.80687		
Corrected Total	99	29895.97154			

Figure 13.1 SAS Analysis of Variance Output from Example Dataset with School as Between-Subjects Factor

of a simple random sample of the same size. Thus it seems imperative to adjust the estimates of sampling variance to account for the complex sampling of students. Note that the estimated deff only reflects the dependency due to the multistage aspect of the sampling design and not the precision resulting from the use of stratification. Determining the design effect from more complex sampling designs that incorporate several different sampling characteristics is not as straightforward as that provided in Equation 3 and will generally require analysts to undertake the appropriate sampling variance estimation for their data, as defined later in this chapter (Lee, Forthoffer, & Lorimor, 1989).

Implications of Complex Sampling Design for Items

For educational surveys found in quadrants A and C in Table 13.1, a single-form assessment simplifies estimation and inference because all students are administered the same set of items and observations are available on each item for every student (except for data that are missing at random as a result of student nonresponse). Designs based on complex samples of items, however, lead to a large amount of item nonresponse, or data that are missing by design.

These missing data complicate the estimation of population scores on the theoretical "complete" assessment that consists of all items (Hombo, 2003). Responses to items that are not administered to a student cannot be used to help estimate his or her latent characteristics. Thus, proficiency estimates for individual students are typically accompanied by relatively large amounts of measurement error because they are based on relatively few pieces of information. This is why most educational surveys implemented for accountability purposes can be used only to provide reasonably reliable group-level inferences based on mean scores or mean score differences. Importantly, this is also why the reliability of mean scores is more relevant for such assessments than the reliability of individual scores, which is typically relatively poor.

At a general level, compared with accommodating the complex sampling design of students, accommodating the complex sampling design of items is much simpler once the data have been collected. Modern psychometric models can handle the estimation process with relative ease. The most important effect of a complex sampling of items is a large amount of data missing by design in the overall data matrix and the relative sparseness of information about latent characteristics for individual students.

Accommodating Complex Sampling Designs of Students in Analyses

Corrective strategies used to address the statistical issues associated with complex sampling designs of students can be classified into two types of approaches: design-based and model-based approaches (e.g., Muthén & Satorra, 1995; Thomas & Heck, 2001). In *design-based* approaches, corrective adjustments are made outside of the model to account for aspects of the sampling design such as unequal selection probabilities and clustering. In *model-based* approaches, characteristics of the sampling design are directly incorporated in the model, automatically adjusting parameter estimates and their standard errors. The choice to correct for aspects of the sampling design via a design-based approach versus a model-based approach usually depends on the nature of the research question. If the design features are part of the causal structure posited by the researcher, it would be appropriate to model them directly using a model-based approach; if they are essentially nuisance features, a design-based approach would be preferred.

To illustrate this point, consider again our motivating example, which contains as the primary dependent variable reading proficiency scores obtained under a stratified multistage sampling design with unequal selection probabilities. In our simple linear regression example, we are interested in globally predicting reading proficiency using the number of minutes of reading. The design features, such as the clustering of students and the stratification by school type and language background, are not explicit features of this analytical objective because we are interested in the global relationship, not the relation within specific subgroups or differences in the relation across subgroups. Since the design characteristics are essentially a nuisance, a design-based approach is appropriate.

In contrast, let us assume that the researcher is interested in examining how average reading proficiency varies across public and private schools and students with different language backgrounds. In this case, the clustering of students within schools and the stratification by school type and language status are explicit parts of the analytical objective. Thus a model-based approach would be appropriate because structural characteristics of the sample can be directly incorporated into the model and no additional corrections for the sampling design outside the model are necessary. Because a design-based approach is appropriate for the research question considered in our simple example, the following sections focus on design-based approaches to accommodate aspects of a complex sampling design. Alternative model-based approaches are mentioned, though not addressed in detail, and interested readers are referred to additional resources to learn more about these approaches.

Design-Based Approaches for Correcting Bias in Parameter Estimates

The design-based approach for controlling bias in parameter estimates is to include sampling weights within analyses. A *sampling weight* for a student is equal to the inverse of the selection probability for a student in stratum h, denoted (p_h), and can be expressed as follows:

$$w_h = \frac{1}{p_h} = \frac{N_h}{n_h} \tag{4}$$

where N_h is the stratum population size and n_h is the stratum sample size. This inverse relation means that students selected into the sample with high probabilities will have smaller weights than students selected into the sample with low probabilities. In turn, the influence

Table 13.4 Steps for Calculating Sampling Weights

Stratum (h)	Population Size (N_h)	Sample Size (n_h)	Probability of Selection (p)	Raw Sampling Weight (w_{raw})	Relative Sampling Weight (w_{rel})
Public school					
Native English speaker	8,400	25	0.003	336	2.8
Nonnative English speaker	2,100	25	0.012	84	0.7
Private school					
Native English speaker	1,200	25	0.021	48	0.4
Nonnative English speaker	300	25	0.083	12	0.1
Total	12,000	100			

of oversampled students in the estimation of parameters will be decreased during a weighted analysis and vice versa.

Table 13.4 displays the sampling weights for students in our example dataset and the numbers utilized in their calculation.

Relative to their representation in the population, students in private schools and nonnative English speakers have been oversampled. Looking across public and private schools, the raw weight for native English speakers in private schools is smaller than the weight for native English speakers in public schools because private schools were oversampled. Looking just within private schools, the raw sampling weight for nonnative English speakers is smaller than the raw sampling weight for native English speakers because they too were oversampled. The same is true for public schools. When weights are applied during the analysis, the composition of the sample will be adjusted to match the composition of the population in terms of both public and private schools and native and nonnative English speakers.

In the case of multistage sampling, the selection probabilities for an individual student at each stage of the analysis can be multiplied together to obtain his or her actual selection probability across all stages, which are displayed in Table 13.4. For example, for native English speakers in public schools, the final selection probability is equal to the chance of the public school being selected in the first stage (5/70) multiplied by the chance of the native English speaker being sampled in the second stage (5/120), conditional on the school being sampled.

$$p = p_{school} \cdot p_{student} = \left(\frac{5}{70}\right)\left(\frac{5}{120}\right) = \left(\frac{25}{8400}\right) = 0.003 \tag{5}$$

In other words, across all stages of the design, a native English speaker in a public school has approximately a 0.3% chance of being selected into the sample. The final weight for native English speakers in public schools is equal to the inverse of their overall sampling fraction, or 336 in this case, meaning each such student in the sample represents 336 students of that type in the population.

For the sake of simplicity, all native English speakers in public schools have the same sampling weight in our example, and the same is true for the other three subgroups. This happens because we fixed the size of all public schools in the state to be the same and the number of students to be the same within each selected schools. Had the schools in our population differed in size and/ or had we sampled a different number of students within selected schools, the weights for all native English speakers in public schools would not be equal. However, the same computational approach could still be utilized to determine the final selection probability and sampling weight for each individual student.

Despite the intuitive appeal of the raw sampling weight, there is a statistical problem with it. Depending on the equations used to calculate standard errors, the raw weights can imply that the sample is much larger than it actually is. In Table 13.4, for example, if the raw sampling weights were applied during analyses using a case weighting function in a software program, a single native English speaker from a public school in the sample would count as 336 students. Thus, most researchers typically apply an additional adjustment to the raw sampling weights to calculate what is known as a *relative sampling weight*. The relative sampling weight is simply the raw sampling weight divided by the mean raw sampling weight across all students, which adjusts the raw weight downward:

$$w_{rel} = \frac{w_{raw}}{\overline{w}_{raw}} \quad (6)$$

With the mean of the relative weights in the sample equal to 1.0, relative sampling weights preserve the sample size that is actually available during estimation and hypothesis testing. The relative sampling weights for the individuals in our example dataset are provided in Table 13.4 as well. Note that sampling weights can be further adjusted to compensate for other sampling design or data features beyond the disproportionate sampling across strata. For example, weights can also be used to adjust for the nonresponse rates among strata or to create samples that are more similar in structure to known population characteristics (referred to as post-stratification weight adjustments). These additional adjustments are beyond the scope of this chapter, but descriptions of such complex weights can be found in technical reports of most educational surveys.

Analysis of Example Data

For our illustrative example using the sample dataset, we can apply the traditional formula and estimation routines for a linear regression of Y on X in SAS using the code shown in Figure 13.2.

From this, we obtain estimates of the population parameters that do not account for any features of the survey design, neither the stratification nor the clustering. The unweighted estimate of β obtained from the sample data, displayed in Table 13.5, is equal to $b_{unweighted} = 0.088$.

To apply the relative sampling weights during analysis in SAS to produce a weighted estimate, the SAS code shown in Figure 13.3 can be applied, weighting the data by the students' final weights.

Also shown in Table 13.5, the application of the relative sampling weights adjusts the estimate of β from $b_{unweighted} = 0.088$ up to $b_{weighted} = 0.132$, shifting it in the direction of the true population value. Here, the weighted regression coefficient is estimated as

$$b = \frac{\sum w_i(x_i - \bar{x}_w)(y_i - \bar{y}_w)}{\sum w_i(x_i - \bar{x}_w)^2} \quad (7)$$

where the weighted values of the mean of X and Y are calculated generally as:

```
PROC REG;
MODEL Y_1 = X;
RUN;
```

Figure 13.2 SAS Syntax for Obtaining Traditional Sample Statistics in a Regression of Y on X

Table 13.5 Linear Regressions of English Reading Proficiency (Y) on Minutes of Reading (X)

Analysis	Parameter Estimate (b)	Standard Error (SEb)
Unweighted	0.088	0.070
Weighted	0.132	0.078
Weighted with linearization	0.132	0.119
Weighted with jackknife	0.132	0.056
Weighted with bootstrapping	0.131	0.120

```
PROC SURVEYREG;
WEIGHT REL_STUD_WT;
MODEL Y_1 = X;
RUN;
```

Figure 13.3 SAS Syntax for Obtaining Weighted Sample Statistics in a Regression of Y on X

$$\bar{y}_w = \frac{\sum w_i y_i}{\sum w_i} \tag{8}$$

The relative sampling weights reduce the negative bias in the estimate of the regression slope because they boost the weight of the native English speakers in public schools and shrink the weight of the oversampled groups. In our example, these groups include nonnative English speakers in public schools and both native and nonnative English speakers in private schools.

LIMITATIONS OF SAMPLING WEIGHTS

Even though the point estimate for β has been corrected by using weights during estimation, its associated standard error has not been adjusted for the fact that the sampling design is not a simple random sample. Additionally, when students have been selected into the sample at very different rates, there will be a large variation in the sampling weights across students that increases the standard error of the parameter estimate (Asparouhov & Muthén, 2007; Pfeffermann, 1993). Even though the weighted estimate of the parameter is closer to the population value on average, the larger confidence intervals surrounding it will result in a loss of precision for statistical tests (Korn & Graubard, 1995).

The effectiveness of the use of sampling weights at reducing bias in parameter estimates depends on the quality of the stratification variables that are used to select the sample. That is, the use of sampling weights reduces the bias associated with a parameter estimate to the degree that the stratification variables are *informative* (Asparouhov, 2006; Pfeffermann, 1993; Skinner, 1994). If the stratification variables are noninformative because they are not actually related to the outcome of interest, the unweighted estimate of the parameter will not be biased and the use of the sampling weights will only serve to unnecessarily increase the standard error of the estimate.

Model-Based Alternatives for Correcting Bias in Parameter Estimates

A model-based alternative to weighting is to include stratification variables as covariates in analyses (e.g., Pfefferman, 1993; Pfefferman, Skinner, Holmes, Goldstein, & Rasbash, 1998). In a regression analysis, for example, the disproportionate sampling design becomes *ignorable* for estimating the regression model if all of the stratification variables are included as predictor variables in the model. In our simple example, we could include school type and student type as predictors in the model to estimate a mean separately for public school students and private school students as well as native English speakers and nonnative English speakers, respectively. Interested readers are encouraged to perform such analyses themselves using the example data provided in Appendix 13.A.

Design-Based Approaches for Correcting Bias in Standard Error Estimates

Stratified, cluster, and multistage sampling designs typically lead to over- or underestimated standard errors for sampling distributions. Thus special methods for correcting the sampling variances are necessary. Popular approaches include linearization or replication techniques.

LINEARIZATION
In the *linearization* approach, linear functions are created to approximate sampling variance estimates for nonlinear functions (Kish & Frankel, 1974). In the context of this chapter, it is the variances of population parameter estimates that are nonlinear functions and are approximated by linear functions of the variances across the PSUs. Approximate linear estimates have been derived for a variety of model parameters under a number of complex sampling designs (Kalton, 1983). Software programs that can accommodate linearized estimates of sampling variances usually use just the sampling information from the first stage of the sampling process. For our example, the sampling variance will be a function of the variation in the regression coefficients for each PSU within each stratum. So imagine estimating the regression coefficient for each school (PSU) and then determining the variation in the regression coefficients across all public schools and, similarly, across all private schools. The sampling variance of the overall regression coefficient is then the pooled variation in the regression coefficient from the public and the private schools.

ANALYSIS OF EXAMPLE DATA
We illustrate the linearization approach here using our motivating example dataset. This requires us to further modify the weighted linear regression analysis in SAS as shown in Figure 13.4.

In this code, both a stratum indicator (school type) and cluster indicator (school) have been included, prompting SAS to produce a linearized estimate of the standard error associated with estimates. From this analysis, we obtain (1) weighted point estimates of the population parameters that account for the unequal selection probabilities across the strata as before but also

```
PROC SURVEYREG;
WEIGHT REL_STUD_WT;
STRATUM SCHOOL_TYPE;
CLUSTER J;
MODEL Y_1 = X;
RUN;
```

Figure 13.4 SAS Syntax for Obtaining Weighted Sample Statistics and Linearized Standard Error Estimates in a Regression of Y on X

(2) adjusted standard error estimates that account for the stratification and clustering. As shown in Table 13.5, the weighted parameter estimate is still $b_{\text{weighted}} = 0.132$, as in the previous weighted analysis, but now the standard error estimate has increased from SE (b_{weighted}) = 0.078 to SE ($b_{\text{weighted with linearization}}$) = 0.119 in the weighted analysis with linearization. This increase in standard error indicates that the parameter estimate is actually more imprecise once the complex sampling design for students is accounted for than the uncorrected estimate would suggest.

The difference in inferential decisions can be easily demonstrated using a confidence interval approach. For example, using the familiar 95% confidence interval formula for the population slope,

$$\hat{\beta} \pm t_{95\%} \, SE(\hat{\beta}) \tag{9}$$

we can construct such confidence intervals for the weighted estimation and the weighted analysis using linearization, both around a point estimate of $b_{\text{weighted}} = 0.132$. For the weighted analysis, the confidence interval for β ranges from −0.023 to 0.287. In contrast, for the weighted analysis with linearization, the confidence interval ranges from −0.104 to 0.368. Clearly, the latter interval is wider because the standard error is larger and thus represents the more conservative estimation case.

REPLICATION TECHNIQUES

Instead of using linearization techniques, replication techniques can be used to approximate the sampling variance associated with a parameter estimate by empirically creating a sampling distribution of the parameter estimate. Such techniques may be particularly useful if the software being utilized does not provide linearized estimates or if the data being used include some degree of nonnormality (Efron & Tibshirani, 1993). The most popular replication techniques include jackknifed, bootstrapped, and balanced repeated replication (Kish & Frankel, 1974; Rust & Rao, 1996; Sitter, 1992). These methods involve repeated sampling of subsets of students from the full sample of students to create what are referred to as replicate samples. The statistic of interest is then computed for each replicate sample, and the standard deviation of the estimate across replicate samples is used to approximate the standard error of the estimate.

JACKKNIFE ESTIMATION

In a simple application of a jackknife procedure, one PSU from the full data set is dropped and the statistic of interest is computed on the remaining data set. This process is repeated until all PSUs have been dropped once. The jackknife estimate of the statistic is simply the average of the values obtained across all replicates, and the approximated sampling variance can be obtained as the variance of the values of the statistic across replicate samples.

Jackknife replicate samples can be obtained in various ways depending on the particular sampling design used. In a single-stage design, a single observation can be dropped from the analysis (each observation is a PSU), whereas an entire cluster can be dropped in a multistage design. Given our example of a stratified sample with five PSUs (schools) selected in each stratum, five replicate samples are created for each stratum, with the first replicate sample not containing the first school, the second replicate sample not containing the second school (but containing the first), and so on (Lee, Forthoffer, & Lorimor, 1989).

Balanced Repeated Replication

The simplest application of a balanced repeated replication approach, known as *balanced half-sampling* (Canty & Davison, 1999), applies when a stratified sample contains just two observations within a larger unit, such as two students in a school or two schools in a district. In this case, one of the two observations from each stratum is selected to form a half sample and the statistic of interested is calculated. This process is repeated for each possible combination of half samples. Again, the balanced half-sampling estimate of the statistic is simply the average of the values obtained across all replicates, and the approximate standard error can be obtained as the standard deviation of the values of the statistic across all repeated replication samples. Balanced repeated replication samples can be constructed for more than two observations, but detailed descriptions are beyond the scope of this chapter.

Bootstrapping Estimation

In simple bootstrapping applications, random samples with replacement are taken from the original dataset. This means that the replicate sample could include the same PSU more than once and that the same set of PSUs could be selected across different replicate samples. Because the bootstrapping procedure does not control which PSUs are selected into the replicate sample—unlike the jackknife and balanced repeated replication procedures—each bootstrapping procedure provides less precision for the same number of replicate samples than either of the other two methods. Thus the bootstrapping procedure is usually repeated hundreds or thousands of times.

In bootstrapping, although each replicate sample often contains the same number of observations as the original dataset, some researchers have found that sampling (n-1) PSUs produces more appropriate sampling variance estimates (Efron & Tibshirani, 1993). Just as with jackknife and balanced replication estimation, the bootstrapped estimate of the statistic is simply the average of the values obtained across all replicates, and the approximate standard error can be obtained using the standard deviation of the values of the statistic across bootstrapped samples.

Analysis of Example Data

Specific details of the steps and computations of a jackknife analysis and bootstrap analysis are presented below and illustrated using the example dataset (a simple application of balanced repeated replication is not possible given that more than two PSUs were selected in each stratum). The SAS code for these analyses can be found in Appendix 13.B. In the first jackknife replicate sample, the first school (ID = 9) from the first stratum (public schools) is dropped from the analysis (i.e., observations are given weights equal to 0). Note that the remaining clusters in the first stratum have to be reweighted to account for the entire first stratum so that the overall sum of weights is equal to the sum of weights in that stratum before the cluster was dropped. Thus a rescaled weight is generated by multiplying the students' relative weight by a constant equal to the number of PSUs in the stratum over the number of PSUs less one. In our case, with 5 clusters per stratum, the students' relative weights in the remaining clusters will be inflated by 1.25. Therefore native English speaking students in the second school (ID = 31) who had original sample weights of 2.8 (see Table 13.4) will have weights of 3.5 and non-native English speakers in that school will have weights of .845 (1.25 times larger than their original weights of .7). This same weight rescaling will be made for all observations within the first stratum. The weights for the observations in the second stratum will remain in their original form because no PSUs were dropped from that stratum for the first replicate sample. This process is repeated to create a total of 10 replicate samples (i.e., until each PSU has been dropped once). For each replicate sample, Y is regressed on X and an estimate of β is obtained. The mean of the estimates across the 10 replicate samples is the jackknife estimate of β, and the standard deviation is used as the replication estimate of the standard error. For our sample, our 10 estimates of the regression coefficient were 0.137, 0.117, 0.001, 0.159, 0.234, 0.141, 0.130, 0.128, 0.135, and 0.136 for the replicate samples respectively. We thus find $b_{weighted}$ = 0.132 and SE ($b_{weighted\ with\ jackknife\ replication}$) = 0.056 in the weighted analysis with jackknife replication, as displayed in Table 13.5. Although we would normally expect the jackknife SE estimate to be larger than in the traditional analysis that does not account for the stratification and clustering, there is substantial instability with only 10 jackknife replicates in the analysis given our very small example dataset.

We also ran the same analysis using the bootstrapped resampling method of estimating the sampling variance. To obtain bootstrapped samples, we randomly select four of the five clusters (C-1) in each stratum with replacement. So, for example, in our first bootstrap sample, we sampled the following school IDs within the public school stratum: 31, 35, 35, and 42. Note that school ID 35 was selected twice for the sample, as can happen with sampling with replacement. For the private school stratum, the first bootstrap replicate contained the following school IDs: 75, 78, 94, and 94. Again, observations in the selected schools are reweighted to reflect their status in the replicate sample (the weight is set to 0 if the school was not selected into the replicate sample, or the weight is rescaled by 1.25 to adjust for the missing PSU). Using this first replicate sample, the regression is undertaken and we obtain a β estimate of 0.312. We carried out this process 500 times, regressing Y on X for each of the 500 replicate samples, and obtained β estimates ranging from −0.076 to 0.444, with an average of 0.131. The standard deviation of β across the replicates, or 0.120, is the estimate of the standard error associated with this estimate. The final results of the bootstrapping are displayed in Table 13.5.

LIMITATIONS OF DESIGN-BASED APPROACHES

The primary drawback of the use of linearization as well as replication techniques for practitioners is that these methods are not always available in standard statistical software packages. Instead, they must be carried out separately in specialized software packages for surveys, most of which cannot directly estimate more complex latent-variable models that may be of interest to researchers (though these features are becoming more popular). Additionally, replication techniques can become computationally demanding when the number of strata is large, strata contain a large number of clusters, students within clusters are subsampled, and so forth. As a compromise, some researchers (and software programs) apply replication techniques only at the first stage of the sampling design and ignore the sampling scheme within those primary sampling units to reduce the number and complexity of recalculations. For a discussion of more complex applications, the reader is referred to Canty and Davison (1999) and Sitter (1992).

Model-Based Alternative for Correcting Bias in Standard Error Estimates

The primary model-based alternative to linearization and replication techniques is a *multilevel modeling* technique. Many popular statistical models, such as regression models and some psychometric models, can be expressed as *hierarchical generalized linear models* (HGLM) (e.g., Kamata, 2001; Raudenbush & Bryk, 2002). Multilevel models directly incorporate the nested structure of the data by considering residual variance components at each level of the hierarchy. Given students nested within schools, for example, the model partitions residual variances into a between-school component, representing the variance of estimates at the school level, and a within-school component, representing the variance of estimates at the student level. Because the dependencies among observations within a cluster are explicitly incorporated in the model, variance estimates associated with model parameters are automatically adjusted. Furthermore, stratification variables can be included into the regression equations to additionally account for stratification and disproportionate sampling. Again, interested readers are encouraged to conduct such analyses using the example dataset.

Accommodating Complex Sampling Designs of Items in Analyses

The primary approach for calculating the uncertainty in estimates of student characteristics and estimates of sampling variance is known as *plausible values methodology*. Put simply, plausible values are student proficiency estimates that are based not only on the actual responses to items provided by the students but the covariate information for students as well (e.g., Mislevy, 1991; Rubin, 1987). Covariate information, including answers to certain background and demographic questions such as student gender, is used to improve the sparse informational value available in the actual student responses. Statistically speaking, proficiency estimates are treated as missing data whose values need to be *imputed* (i.e., filled in). The imputation is done using what is known as the *posterior distribution* of these parameters under a *Bayesian estimation framework*, which essentially characterizes the proficiency of each student as taking on a range of likely values. By using a range of likely values rather than a single point estimate, researchers are able to quantify more precisely the uncertainty in the estimate and to use it to compute accurate inferential statistics.

The proficiency scores for the latent variables are *plausible values* because they are probable yet not exact estimates of a student's latent variable scores. For each student there is one posterior distribution for his or her latent variable score, whose shape is influenced by his or her responses, covariate information, and prior information about his or her latent variable score if such information is available. Thus, if a sample consists of 5,000 students, the resulting analyses would be based on 5,000 posterior proficiency distributions for the 5,000 latent variable scores of the students.

Because each student proficiency estimate is captured through a posterior proficiency distribution, it is statistically advantageous to take multiple random draws (i.e., plausible values) from this distribution for each student. Subsequent analyses need to be conducted multiple times, once with each plausible value. Publicly available data sets often contain five plausible values for ability estimates of interest. An inspection of these values for each student shows that they will often vary less compared to how much each plausible value varies across the students. This makes sense, because student proficiencies typically differ much more across students than there is uncertainty about the proficiency of an individual student.

Generating plausible values is a relatively complex process and typically needs to be carried out by specialists who program the suitable routines (Mislevy, 1991; Thomas & Gan, 1997). However, once plausible values are drawn and included in datasets as variables, secondary analysts can use standard statistical tools to estimate subgroup and population characteristics appropriately. These analyses should be carried out repeatedly, once for each of the plausible values, and the resulting parameter estimates, their standard errors, and their covariance information should be averaged across the imputations.

Specifically, each analysis j yields an estimate of the parameter of interest ($\hat{Q}_j$). The population parameter of interest (Q) is simply estimated by the average value of the statistic ($\bar{\hat{Q}}$) across the repeated analyses with the different plausible values (m):

$$\bar{\hat{Q}} = \frac{1}{m} \sum_{j=1}^{m} \hat{Q}_j \tag{10}$$

The computation of the standard error for $\bar{\hat{Q}}$ is a bit more complicated because it has two sources. One component captures the *variation of* $\hat{Q}_j$ across the different plausible values analyses

$$VAR(\hat{Q}) = \frac{1}{m-1} \sum_{j=1}^{m} \left(\hat{Q}_j - \bar{\hat{Q}}\right)^2 \tag{11}$$

and the other component captures the *average variation of the sampling variances* across the different plausible values analyses:

$$\overline{VAR}(\hat{Q}) = \frac{1}{m} \sum_{j=1}^{m} VAR(\hat{Q}_j) \tag{12}$$

The sampling variance for $\bar{\hat{Q}}$ is then a weighted combination of these two components,

$$VAR(\bar{\hat{Q}}) = \overline{VAR}(\hat{Q}) + \left(1 + \frac{1}{m}\right) VAR(\hat{Q}) \tag{13}$$

and the square root of $VAR(\bar{\hat{Q}})$ is the standard error associated with $\bar{\hat{Q}}$.

Analysis of Example Data

Up until this point, we have worked with one estimate of each student's English language proficiency as the dependent variable in our regression analyses (Y_1). For the purpose of this section, we now consider that there are five dependent variables, each one representing one plausible value of proficiency (Y_1 through Y_5). Thus we have to repeat our simple linear regression model analysis five times and average the point estimates and standard errors for β using the formulas above. Note that we also have to accommodate the complex sampling of students in each analysis by incorporating weights and adjusting the standard error estimate using, for example, bootstrapping techniques.

The result of performing these analyses are shown in Table 13.6, where the sample statistics displayed for the first plausible value match the bootstrapping results presented earlier in this chapter.

The results displayed in Table 13.6 are similar but not identical across the five analyses, with coefficient estimates ranging from 0.029 to 0.223. The final estimate of the regression coefficient is equal to the average parameter estimate across the five analyses, or 0.143.

To calculate the final standard error associated with this estimate, the variance between the parameter estimates across analyses must be combined with the average sampling variance

Table 13.6 Example Using Plausible Values to Estimate Effect of Minutes of Reading on English Reading Proficiency

	Parameter Estimate ($b_{weighted}$)	Standard Error ($SE_{bootstrapped}$)	Sampling Variance ($SE_{bootstrapped})^2$
Plausible value 1	0.131	0.120	0.014
Plausible value 2	0.120	0.189	0.036
Plausible value 3	0.223	0.077	0.006
Plausible value 4	0.213	0.107	0.011
Plausible value 5	0.029	0.181	0.033
Final estimate	0.143	0.166	

within each analysis. The variance of the five parameter estimates is equal to 0.006, which is very small in this simple example. Squaring the standard error values presented in the table (i.e., converting the standard error values to sampling variances) and taking the average across the five yields 0.020. Combining these terms using the weighted average formula presented in Equation 13 equals 0.028. Taking the square root of this value yields 0.166, which is the desired standard error estimate associated with the slope parameter estimate across the five analyses. Therefore a 95% confidence interval around the final estimate of 0.143 ranges from −0.186 to 0.472. This interval is wider than the interval for the weighted estimation with bootstrapping based on only the first plausible value because we have accounted for the imprecision in measurement of our estimate of the dependent variable in the regression model.

Limitations of Plausible Values Methodology

An obvious limitation to the plausible values approach is its complexity. Thomas and Gan (1997) note that, by reducing the time and effort on the part of students, complex sampling designs for items shift demands onto the data analysts. First, measurement specialists will likely need to be employed to produce plausible values appropriately. Second, although secondary analysts can draw appropriate inferences from the plausible values using standard routines, they have to repeat their analyses multiple times and combine the results across analyses. In efforts to avoid the multiple runs for analyses using plausible values, researchers may be tempted to simply take the average of each student's plausible values and use this single value in a single analysis. This poor practice, however, fails to capture the variation across imputations that the plausible values methodology is designed to capture and will not produce variance estimates that account for the measurement uncertainty due to the complex sampling of items.

A second limitation of the complex sampling design for items more generally, and not plausible values per se, is that it does not yield reliable estimates of students' latent variable scores. Plausible values are the "best" estimates of student proficiencies, given sparse data to produce optimal comparisons of student groups at the aggregate level. This is the practical compromise that is made for educational surveys that serve predominantly system-monitoring functions, in that precise information about individual students for narrow domains is sacrificed for precise information about student groups for broader domains.

Conclusion

To correct for various aspects of a complex sampling design when using data from a large-scale educational survey, researchers will have to consider a variety of techniques and approaches.

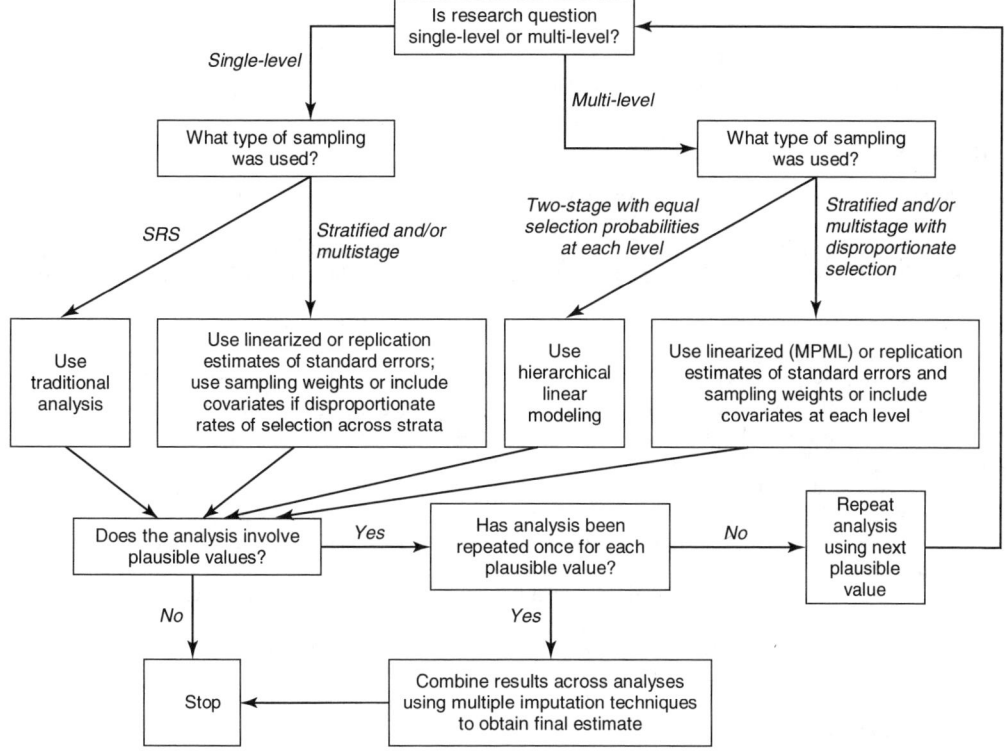

Figure 13.5 Flow Chart for Analyzing Complex Survey Data

From a design-based perspective, weighted estimation corrects for the impact of the sampling design for students in parameter estimation, whereas robust variance estimation techniques correct for the impact of the sampling design for students on standard error estimates. Alternative approaches to correct for the sampling design for students from a model-based perspective—namely, to include stratification variables as covariates to adjust parameter estimates and employ multilevel modeling techniques to produce design-consistent standard errors—are available as well. The plausible values approach accounts for a complex sampling design for items, allowing for the appropriate estimation of subgroup and population characteristics and their associated variances. Researchers faced with both complex sampling designs for students and items may have to consider corrections to all aspects of the design simultaneously during their analyses.

In closing, Figure 13.5 aims to walk researchers through all the decisions that must be made regarding adjustments to traditional analyses given complex sampling designs. It serves to summarize the questions that must be answered and provide recommended guidelines. The overarching recommendations and guidelines for accommodating complex sampling designs of students and items are to (1) understand what kind of sampling design was used and how it may impact model estimation, (2) consider the approach that best addresses the research question at hand (e.g., design-based versus model-based), and (3) carry out approaches to produce estimates of population parameters and their standard errors that are consistent with the sampling design.

Note

1. For simplicity in explanation and application, we ignore the fact that Y is a latent variable in our example; technically a latent regression equation is appropriate.

References

Asparouhov, T. (2006). General multi-level modeling with sampling weights. *Communications in Statistics: Theory and Methods, 35*(3), 439–460.

Asparouhov, T., & Muthén, B. (2007, July). *Testing for informative weights and weights trimming in multivariate modeling with survey data.* Proceedings of the 2007 JSM meeting, Section on Survey Research Methods, Salt Lake City, Utah.

Canty, A. J., & Davison, A. C. (1999). Resampling-based variance estimation for labour force surveys. *The Statistician, 48,* 379–391.

Childs, A., & Andrew P. (2003). Matrix sampling of items in large-scale assessments. *Practical Assessment, Research & Evaluation, 8*(16). Retrieved from http://PAREonline.net/getvn.asp?v = 8&n = 16

Efron, B., & Tibshirani, R. J. (1993). *An introduction to the bootstrap.* London: Chapman & Hall.

Frey, A., Hartig, J., & Rupp, A. A. (2009). An NCME instructional module on booklet designs in large-scale assessments of student achievement: Theory and practice. *Educational Measurement: Issues and Practice, 28,* 39–53.

Groves, R. M., Fowler, F. J., Couper, M. P., Lepkowski, J. M., Singer, E., & Tourangeau, R. (2004). *Survey methodology.* Hoboken, NJ: Wiley.

Hombo, C. M. (2003). NAEP and No Child Left Behind: Technical challenges and practical solutions. *Theory into Practice. 42,* 59–65.

Kalton, G. (1983). *Introduction to survey sampling.* Sage University Paper Series on Quantitative Applications in the Social Sciences, series no. 07-035. Beverly Hills, CA: Sage.

Kamata, A. (2001). Item analysis by the hierarchical generalized linear model. *Journal of Educational Measurement, 38,* 79–93.

Kish, L. (1965). *Survey sampling.* New York: Wiley.

Kish, L., & Frankel, M. R. (1974). Inference from complex samples. *Journal of the Royal Statistical Society, 36,* 1–37.

Korn, E. L., & Graubard, B. I. (1995). Examples of differing weighted and unweighted estimates from a sample survey. *The American Statistician, 49,* 291–295.

Lee, E. S., Forthoffer, R. N., & Lorimor, R. J. (1989). *Analyzing complex survey data.* University Paper series on Quantitative Applications in the Social Sciences, series no. 07-071. Beverly Hills, CA: Sage.

Mislevy, R. J. (1991). Randomization-based inference about latent variables from complex samples. *Psychometrika, 56,* 177–196.

Mislevy, R. J., Johnson, E. G., & Muraki, E. (1992). Scaling procedures in NAEP. *Journal of Educational Statistics, 17,* 131–154.

Muthén, B. O., & Satorra, A. (1995). Complex sample data in structural equation modeling. In P. V. Marsden (Ed.), *Sociological methodology* (pp. 267–316). Washington, DC: American Sociological Association.

Pfeffermann, D. (1993). The role of sampling weights when modeling survey data. *International Statisical Review, 61,* 317–337.

Pfefferman, D., Skinner, C. J., Holmes, D. J., Goldstein, H., & Rasbash, J. (1998). Weighting for unequal selection probabilities in multilevel models. *Journal of the Royal Statistical Society. Series B (Statistical Methodology), 60,* 23–40.

Raudenbush, S. W., & Bryk, A. S. (2002). *Hierarchical linear models: Applications and data analysis methods* (2nd ed.). Newbury Park, CA: Sage.

Rubin, D. B. (1987). *Multiple imputation for nonresponse in surveys.* New York: Wiley.

Rust, K. F., & Rao, J. (1996). Variance estimation for complex surveys using replication techniques. *Statistical Methods in Medical Research, 5,* 283–310.

Sitter, R. R. (1992). Comparing three bootstrap methods for survey data. *The Canadian Journal of Statistics, 20,* 135–154.

Skinner, C. J. (1994). Sample models and weights. *Proceedings of the Section on Survey Research Methods, American Statistical Association,* 133–142.

Thomas, N., & Gan, N. (1997). Generating multiple imputations for matrix sampling data analyzed with item response models. *Journal of Educational and Behavioral Statistics, 22,* 425–445.

Thomas, S. L., & Heck, R. H. (2001). Analysis of large-scale secondary data in higher education research: Potential perils associated with complex sampling designs. *Research in Higher Education, 42,* 517–540.

Von Davier, A. A., Carstensen, C. H., & von Davier, M. (2006). *Linking competencies in educational settings and measuring growth* (RR-06–12). Princeton, NJ: Educational Testing Service.

Appendix 13.A

Simple Example Dataset

SCHOOL ID	SCHOOL TYPE[a]	STUDENT TYPE[b]	STUDENT ID	X	Y_1	Y_2	Y_3	Y_4	Y_5	FINAL STUD PROB	FINAL STUD WT	REL STUD WT
9	0	0	15	133	100.978	120.191	94.014	93.534	107.607	0.003	336	2.8
9	0	0	53	101	95.188	106.012	77.376	111.545	108.060	0.003	336	2.8
9	0	0	61	131	100.671	101.663	110.808	90.374	80.769	0.003	336	2.8
9	0	0	73	101	97.683	116.301	113.766	94.312	102.696	0.003	336	2.8
9	0	0	109	117	94.365	102.901	100.421	96.427	95.551	0.003	336	2.8
9	0	1	125	145	77.244	85.740	128.262	76.384	84.618	0.012	84	0.7
9	0	1	127	127	89.847	102.103	145.869	120.375	98.201	0.012	84	0.7
9	0	1	128	116	70.225	103.025	95.412	96.804	100.409	0.012	84	0.7
9	0	1	140	86	85.432	79.798	73.314	52.071	58.041	0.012	84	0.7
9	0	1	144	122	91.204	87.339	82.552	105.017	104.389	0.012	84	0.7
31	0	0	4	94	92.129	98.594	99.411	90.607	87.227	0.003	336	2.8
31	0	0	35	143	93.256	98.563	91.460	99.373	64.725	0.003	336	2.8
31	0	0	67	121	108.310	76.737	105.102	98.248	100.191	0.003	336	2.8
31	0	0	76	118	81.793	113.322	116.396	121.908	88.974	0.003	336	2.8
31	0	0	110	133	70.891	61.818	72.715	103.183	87.977	0.003	336	2.8
31	0	1	133	117	111.339	102.359	107.803	138.915	74.374	0.012	84	0.7
31	0	1	143	89	70.934	77.048	104.070	83.059	85.450	0.012	84	0.7
31	0	1	145	83	77.584	90.886	96.316	100.238	89.107	0.012	84	0.7
31	0	1	149	106	80.779	66.566	77.062	85.428	101.547	0.012	84	0.7
31	0	1	150	80	45.673	81.202	52.165	76.884	52.249	0.012	84	0.7
35	0	0	51	168	118.107	117.849	104.805	127.303	109.748	0.003	336	2.8
35	0	0	63	166	123.765	132.608	140.688	132.423	128.061	0.003	336	2.8
35	0	0	75	124	116.255	127.723	118.676	135.329	129.576	0.003	336	2.8

(*Continued*)

Simple Example Dataset (Continued)

SCHOOL ID	SCHOOL TYPE[a]	STUDENT TYPE[b]	STUDENT ID	X	Y_1	Y_2	Y_3	Y_4	Y_5	FINAL STUD PROB	FINAL STUD WT	REL STUD WT
35	0	0	98	117	86.916	96.121	129.096	118.547	122.187	0.003	336	2.8
35	0	0	101	136	104.693	107.751	105.826	125.572	118.029	0.003	336	2.8
35	0	1	125	118	111.502	129.448	109.277	74.197	87.427	0.012	84	0.7
35	0	1	126	133	125.119	128.074	123.675	116.176	131.239	0.012	84	0.7
35	0	1	135	119	82.318	94.798	88.220	104.516	86.519	0.012	84	0.7
35	0	1	145	103	94.614	110.779	71.547	117.693	81.751	0.012	84	0.7
35	0	1	146	149	89.174	115.669	106.709	91.517	72.290	0.012	84	0.7
42	0	0	27	124	111.312	137.304	102.921	138.318	118.378	0.003	336	2.8
42	0	0	32	109	99.753	93.974	118.495	97.031	72.926	0.003	336	2.8
42	0	0	52	108	105.827	77.584	73.913	74.856	86.580	0.003	336	2.8
42	0	0	56	142	77.258	109.280	110.983	92.326	94.646	0.003	336	2.8
42	0	0	68	140	103.903	115.206	82.126	91.966	90.360	0.003	336	2.8
42	0	1	121	86	61.819	66.786	87.696	85.200	56.578	0.012	84	0.7
42	0	1	132	132	69.806	84.617	87.743	77.867	88.130	0.012	84	0.7
42	0	1	138	134	94.583	73.320	87.595	115.979	86.846	0.012	84	0.7
42	0	1	139	121	68.768	86.194	76.719	52.230	92.633	0.012	84	0.7
42	0	1	146	82	104.466	59.320	53.612	76.800	77.778	0.012	84	0.7
64	0	0	24	103	103.824	89.774	150.530	114.868	126.697	0.003	336	2.8
64	0	0	43	70	102.327	118.528	81.037	94.933	108.397	0.003	336	2.8
64	0	0	46	104	97.469	101.067	105.112	103.234	95.734	0.003	336	2.8
64	0	0	47	61	96.110	120.285	84.537	100.641	117.770	0.003	336	2.8
64	0	0	66	93	100.986	108.054	89.266	94.477	111.029	0.003	336	2.8
64	0	1	122	98	93.528	87.229	93.528	95.745	72.669	0.012	84	0.7
64	0	1	127	141	88.794	85.316	90.839	91.822	59.627	0.012	84	0.7
64	0	1	137	108	113.309	98.198	114.081	96.025	114.023	0.012	84	0.7
64	0	1	143	164	107.200	102.151	121.166	120.722	92.320	0.012	84	0.7
64	0	1	146	107	86.383	104.944	92.134	69.664	89.405	0.012	84	0.7
75	1	0	7	89	128.202	115.349	129.341	115.633	129.866	0.021	48	0.4

75	1	0	8	102	97.211	155.122	130.723	88.035	98.490	0.021	48	0.4
75	1	0	11	112	146.974	118.282	116.728	126.693	112.861	0.021	48	0.4
75	1	0	39	72	83.652	96.713	82.675	119.289	93.982	0.021	48	0.4
75	1	0	40	110	94.367	120.777	121.169	117.617	106.642	0.021	48	0.4
75	1	1	44	113	115.974	76.400	84.345	76.533	78.268	0.083	12	0.1
75	1	1	46	133	86.837	62.116	76.306	85.159	85.699	0.083	12	0.1
75	1	1	48	87	98.373	106.446	81.552	112.123	99.273	0.083	12	0.1
75	1	1	49	95	112.513	90.291	81.083	106.980	96.890	0.083	12	0.1
75	1	1	50	86	123.954	95.322	116.771	85.557	98.267	0.083	12	0.1
77	1	0	9	125	117.381	105.327	117.553	116.435	115.280	0.021	48	0.4
77	1	0	10	124	104.570	106.681	113.481	127.943	104.140	0.021	48	0.4
77	1	0	11	108	111.847	123.154	118.393	107.257	121.640	0.021	48	0.4
77	1	0	14	140	125.147	116.525	108.527	91.003	117.449	0.021	48	0.4
77	1	0	31	111	121.708	111.985	99.399	92.323	116.809	0.021	48	0.4
77	1	1	42	105	107.861	126.780	87.560	102.347	82.663	0.083	12	0.1
77	1	1	44	90	84.179	114.115	105.542	80.031	108.903	0.083	12	0.1
77	1	1	47	118	107.373	103.905	114.234	103.858	89.585	0.083	12	0.1
77	1	1	48	98	113.313	86.093	59.102	77.185	73.361	0.083	12	0.1
78	1	0	4	97	97.451	95.413	102.535	109.447	99.458	0.021	48	0.4
78	1	0	22	107	93.469	105.762	120.247	79.768	104.957	0.021	48	0.4
78	1	0	23	126	125.756	140.660	133.068	131.831	126.056	0.021	48	0.4
78	1	0	31	107	59.847	77.191	86.222	92.264	71.288	0.021	48	0.4
78	1	0	38	155	107.625	80.465	107.522	108.575	111.524	0.021	48	0.4
78	1	1	41	144	81.075	100.346	73.662	91.791	74.018	0.083	12	0.1
78	1	1	44	142	76.183	82.132	84.291	111.473	99.839	0.083	12	0.1
78	1	1	45	96	89.426	104.372	83.407	78.295	101.209	0.083	12	0.1
78	1	1	46	129	101.004	103.084	91.562	114.890	108.643	0.083	12	0.1
78	1	1	50	96	86.545	70.119	93.464	88.505	97.186	0.083	12	0.1
90	1	0	6	97	78.252	77.069	80.370	78.499	62.276	0.021	48	0.4
90	1	0	7	133	86.652	83.454	83.651	97.212	94.000	0.021	48	0.4
90	1	0	12	117	66.412	79.828	71.825	84.200	109.419	0.021	48	0.4

(*Continued*)

Simple Example Dataset (*Continued*)

SCHOOL ID	SCHOOL TYPE[a]	STUDENT TYPE[b]	STUDENT ID	X	Y_1	Y_2	Y_3	Y_4	Y_5	FINAL STUD PROB	FINAL STUD WT	REL STUD WT
90	1	0	26	164	106.740	86.951	91.635	110.747	104.513	0.021	48	0.4
90	1	0	33	165	90.192	83.485	74.308	101.656	69.398	0.021	48	0.4
90	1	1	41	167	95.935	73.468	92.160	67.589	86.589	0.083	12	0.1
90	1	1	44	150	96.067	119.753	94.949	92.209	71.304	0.083	12	0.1
90	1	1	46	145	90.212	79.453	90.285	103.554	106.806	0.083	12	0.1
90	1	1	48	100	88.302	83.475	83.309	96.816	71.849	0.083	12	0.1
90	1	1	49	113	92.134	50.416	54.514	80.607	89.278	0.083	12	0.1
94	1	0	18	130	100.295	99.130	109.091	128.857	118.448	0.021	48	0.4
94	1	0	21	155	84.678	98.482	124.870	106.618	89.590	0.021	48	0.4
94	1	0	32	179	114.847	132.325	104.045	106.875	84.668	0.021	48	0.4
94	1	0	34	81	109.086	112.852	114.540	121.164	114.117	0.021	48	0.4
94	1	0	35	151	106.446	139.854	112.290	99.238	127.389	0.021	48	0.4
94	1	1	41	137	74.362	92.945	76.767	67.536	69.570	0.083	12	0.1
94	1	1	43	146	128.571	104.739	113.203	111.411	89.872	0.083	12	0.1
94	1	1	48	132	103.837	100.197	76.617	89.390	101.288	0.083	12	0.1
94	1	1	49	130	81.144	91.700	83.810	85.168	89.237	0.083	12	0.1
94	1	1	50	155	90.242	60.788	97.171	80.405	95.498	0.083	12	0.1

[a] 0 = Public, 1 = Private

[b] 0 = Native English Speaker, 1 = Non-native English Speaker

Appendix 13.B

SAS Code for Generating and Applying Jackknife and Bootstrapping Techniques

```
**SAS syntax to run bootstrap replication with the Chapter data**;
PROC SORT DATA=final_sample; BY school_type j; *sort data by stratum, PSU*;
DATA STRAT_PSUS; SET final_sample; BY school_type j;
  IF FIRST.j; KEEP school_type j;   *list of stratum, PSU   *;
DATA STRATNUM; SET STRAT_PSUS; BY school_type j;
  RETAIN NUMPSU;
  IF FIRST.school_type THEN NUMPSU=0;
  IF FIRST.j THEN NUMPSU=NUMPSU+1;
  IF LAST.school_type;
  _NSIZE_=NUMPSU-1;
  KEEP school_type  _NSIZE_;    *provides data file of Stratum IDs and K-1*;

PROC SURVEYSELECT DATA=STRAT_PSUS METHOD=URS SAMPSIZE=STRATNUM SEED=8167
  OUT=SELECTED_PSUS REP=500;
  STRATA school_type; RUN;     *requests 500 stratified samples of PSUs be drawn
            *(based on school_type) with replacement, using the
            *(K-1) sample sizes contained in File STRATNUM. *;
PROC SORT DATA=SELECTED_PSUS; BY school_type j;

DATA ADD_NMINUS1;
  MERGE SELECTED_PSUS STRATNUM; BY school_type;
  WEIGHTSCALE=(_NSIZE_+1)/(_NSIZE_);
            *creates a constant for each stratum to be applied
            *to scale weights from selected PSUs*;
RUN;

%MACRO BOOT;
%DO B=1 %TO 500;   ***run for as many BOOTSTRAP SAMPLES that you have*;
DATA PSU_REP;
  SET ADD_NMINUS1;
  IF REPLICATE=&B; *selects appropriate PSUs given bootstrap sample number*;
  RUN;

DATA ALLDATA;
  MERGE PSU_REP (IN=A) final_sample; BY school_type j; IF A;
        *only records that match with the selected bootstrap PSUs
        *are included in this analysis*;
  NEWWEIGHT=WEIGHTSCALE*final_stud_wt;  *weights are adjusted by K/(K-1)*;
        *next, I write out model variables to a text file *;
  DO K=1 TO NUMBERHITS;
    OUTPUT;
  END;
RUN;

PROC REG DATA=alldata OUTEST=REG_RESULTS NOPRINT; WEIGHT newweight;
  Model Y_1= X; Model Y_2= X; Model Y_3= X; Model Y_4= X; Model Y_5= X; RUN; QUIT;

DATA BOOT_RESULTS;
  SET REG_RESULTS;
  RETAIN BETA_Y1_X BETA_Y2_X BETA_Y3_X BETA_Y4_X BETA_Y5_X .;
```

```
IF _DEPVAR_='Y_1' THEN BETA_Y1_X = X;
ELSE IF _DEPVAR_='Y_2' THEN BETA_Y2_X = X;
ELSE IF _DEPVAR_='Y_3' THEN BETA_Y3_X = X;
ELSE IF _DEPVAR_='Y_4' THEN BETA_Y4_X = X;
ELSE IF _DEPVAR_='Y_5' THEN BETA_Y5_X = X;
BOOT=&B;
IF _DEPVAR_='Y_5' THEN OUTPUT;
RUN;

PROC DATASETS; APPEND BASE=ALL_BOOT_RESULTS  DATA=BOOT_RESULTS; quit;
%END;
%MEND;

%BOOT;
PROC MEANS DATA=ALL_BOOT_RESULTS; VAR  BETA_Y1_X BETA_Y2_X BETA_Y3_X BETA_Y4_X BETA_Y5_X ;
RUN;
```

SAS syntax to run jackknife replication with the Chapter data;

```
PROC SORT DATA=final_sample; BY school_type j; *sort data by stratum, PSU*;
DATA STRAT_PSUS; SET final_sample; BY school_type j;
  IF FIRST.j; KEEP school_type j;   *list of stratum, PSU   *;
DATA STRATNUM; SET STRAT_PSUS; BY school_type j;
  RETAIN NUMPSU;
  IF FIRST.school_type THEN NUMPSU=0;
  IF FIRST.j THEN NUMPSU=NUMPSU+1;
  IF LAST.school_type;
  _NSIZE_=NUMPSU-1;
  WEIGHTSCALE = NUMPSU/_NSIZE_;
  KEEP school_type _NSIZE_ WEIGHTSCALE;      *provides data file of Stratum IDs and K-1 and weight inflation*;

DATA FINAL_SAMPLE_JACKWEIGHTS;
  MERGE FINAL_SAMPLE STRATNUM; BY school_type;

  **hard coded the school ID values here to create JACK weights **;
  IF SCHOOL_TYPE=0 AND J=9 THEN JACK1=0; ELSE JACK1=WEIGHTSCALE*FINAL_STUD_WT;
  IF SCHOOL_TYPE=0 AND J=31 THEN JACK2=0; ELSE JACK2=WEIGHTSCALE*FINAL_STUD_WT;
  IF SCHOOL_TYPE=0 AND J=35 THEN JACK3=0; ELSE JACK3=WEIGHTSCALE*FINAL_STUD_WT;
  IF SCHOOL_TYPE=0 AND J=42 THEN JACK4=0; ELSE JACK4=WEIGHTSCALE*FINAL_STUD_WT;
  IF SCHOOL_TYPE=0 AND J=64 THEN JACK5=0; ELSE JACK5=WEIGHTSCALE*FINAL_STUD_WT;
  IF SCHOOL_TYPE=1 AND J=75 THEN JACK6=0; ELSE JACK6=WEIGHTSCALE*FINAL_STUD_WT;
  IF SCHOOL_TYPE=1 AND J=77 THEN JACK7=0; ELSE JACK7=WEIGHTSCALE*FINAL_STUD_WT;
  IF SCHOOL_TYPE=1 AND J=78 THEN JACK8=0; ELSE JACK8=WEIGHTSCALE*FINAL_STUD_WT;
  IF SCHOOL_TYPE=1 AND J=90 THEN JACK9=0; ELSE JACK9=WEIGHTSCALE*FINAL_STUD_WT;
  IF SCHOOL_TYPE=1 AND J=94 THEN JACK10=0; ELSE JACK10=WEIGHTSCALE*FINAL_STUD_WT;


%MACRO JACK;
%DO J=1 %TO 10;   ***run for as many jackknife weights that you have*;
 PROC REG DATA=final_sample_jackweights OUTEST=REG_RESULTS NOPRINT; WEIGHT jack&J;
    Model Y_1= X; Model Y_2= X; Model Y_3= X; Model Y_4= X; Model Y_5= X; RUN; QUIT;

DATA JACK_RESULTS;
 SET REG_RESULTS;
 RETAIN BETA_Y1_X BETA_Y2_X BETA_Y3_X BETA_Y4_X BETA_Y5_X .;
 IF _DEPVAR_='Y_1' THEN BETA_Y1_X = X;
 ELSE IF _DEPVAR_='Y_2' THEN BETA_Y2_X = X;
 ELSE IF _DEPVAR_='Y_3' THEN BETA_Y3_X = X;
 ELSE IF _DEPVAR_='Y_4' THEN BETA_Y4_X = X;
```

```
ELSE IF _DEPVAR_='Y_5' THEN BETA_Y5_X = X;
JACK=&J;
IF _DEPVAR_='Y_5' THEN OUTPUT;
RUN;

PROC DATASETS; APPEND BASE=ALL_JACK_RESULTS  DATA=JACK_RESULTS; quit;

%END;
%MEND;
%JACK;
PROC MEANS DATA=ALL_JACK_RESULTS; VAR  BETA_Y1_X BETA_Y2_X BETA_Y3_X BETA_Y4_X BETA_Y5_X ;
RUN;
```

14

Taking Atypical Response Patterns Into Account
A Multidimensional Measurement Model From Item Response Theory

Gilles Raîche, David Magis, Jean-Guy Blais, and Pierre Brochu

> **Introduction**
> **Formulation of Logistic Models**
>   Likelihood Function of Response Patterns and Estimation
>   Methods of Ability Level
>   Estimation Methods of Item Parameters
> **Person-Characteristic Curves**
> **Multidimensional Models of Person-Characteristic Curves**
> **Estimation of Person Parameters**
> **Examples of Application**
> **Example of the Application to the PISA Data (2003)**
> **Conclusion**

Introduction

Large-scale studies in education have made a significant mass of relative data available relating to ability levels in diverse disciplines among the student populations of several countries. These surveys have also provided diverse contextual data specific to the students, their parents, their teachers, and their school or education system. These data permit us to study the relationship between contextual variables and the academic performance of the students. It is this kind of material that makes information regarding international studies and programs available to us—for example, PISA, TEIMS, PIRLS, and PPCE (in Canada specifically).[1] The nature of these data and their acquisition design make it necessary to apply modern analysis methods, based for the most part on models that result from item response theory (IRT). More specifically, these models concern the multidimensional disciplinary ability levels of the students.

In this chapter, we describe current models from IRT intended for responses of a dichotomous nature and the characteristic curves of associated items: the Rasch model and the two-, three-, and four-parameter logistic models. Second, and what constitutes the focus of this chapter, we present multidimensional models of measurement in the spirit of characteristic curves, proposed by Trabin and Weiss (1983) with regard to person parameters, which allow for consideration of the shape of certain characteristic curves by atypical individuals who exhibit personal pseudoguessing, inattention, and fluctuation. Because the person parameters are directly incorporated into these measurement models, these are much more useful in secondary analyses aimed at analyzing atypical response patterns than the previously proposed common detection indices. During primary analysis we may obtain less biased estimates regarding the ability level of the individual, although this has yet to be verified by subsequent research. However, it must be noted that the sampling structure applied in these investigations and the management design will render the estimation of the item parameters more complex.[2]

Formulation of Logistic Models

Several item response models have been proposed since the formal introduction of IRT by Lord in 1952 and the subsequent work of Rasch (1960) on the testing of cognitive performance and intelligence. A large part of this modeling applies solely to responses of a dichotomous nature, whereas others take responses of a polytomous nature into account (Andrich, 1978; Master, 1982; Samejima, 1969), ordered or not (Bock, 1972; Samejima, 1969). In this chapter, however, we deal only with models that apply to dichotomous responses. Models aimed at polytomous responses require much more development, and the additional person parameters implied are not necessarily equivalent to the one related to dichotomous responses.

One of the models to be applied to dichotomous responses is the four-parameter logistic response model (4PL), represented by Equation 1. The 4PL (Barton & Lord, 1981; McDonald, 1967) is particularly important here because the multidimensional item response model proposed later in this paper is a formal extension of this model. In the 4PL, one parameter of inattention takes d_i account of the upper asymptote of the item characteristic curve. This parameter corresponds to the probability that a person whose ability level is very high fails in an item where the item difficulty level is lower than his or her own ability level. This model is appropriate when it is considered that the person whose ability level is very high can be inattentive and can respond incorrectly to certain items that should be easy for them. Equation 1 allows for calculation of the probability P_{ij} that a subject j having an ability level θ_j can obtain a good response ($x_{ij} = 1$) to an item i with difficulty level b_i, discrimination power a_i, pseudoguessing c_i, and inattention d_i.

$$P_{ij} = P(x_{ij} = 1 | \theta_j, a_i, b_i, c_i, d_i) = c_i + \frac{(d_i - c_i)}{1 + e^{-a_i(\theta_j - b_i)}} \qquad (1)$$

As can be seen, each of the logistical models considered here can be hierarchically realized by simplifying the one with the more significant number of parameters. In this way the three-parameter model is achieved by fixing the d_i parameter of inattention at 1. The two-parameter model is achieved by fixing the c_i parameter of pseudoguessing at 0, while the one-parameter model indicates that the a_i parameter of discrimination is the same for all items in the same test, generally to 1. It should be noted, however, that the pseudoguessing and inattention item parameters are by design generally rather difficult to estimate. Thus we must deal with problems of correlation between these two parameters and the other item parameters. Also, it is necessary to have enough respondents with ability levels that are significantly inferior to the item

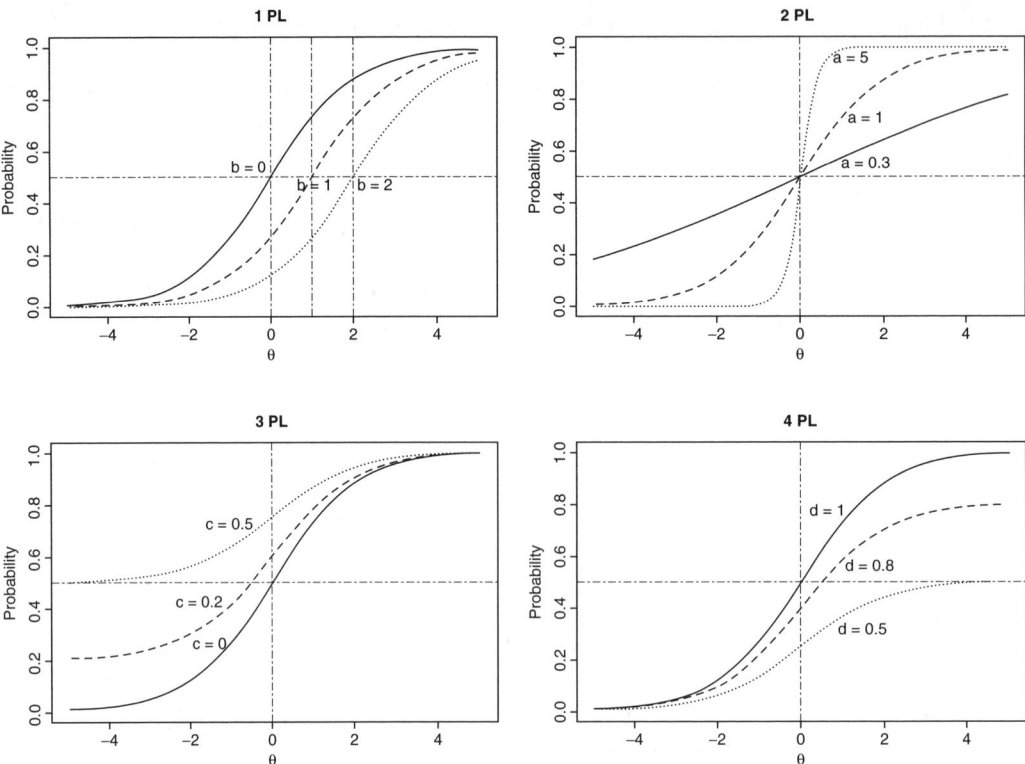

Figure 14.1 Examples of Item Characteristic Curves for the One-, Two-, Three-, and Four-Parameters Logistic Models Resulting from IRT (Dichotomous Responses)

difficulty level to allow for an estimate of pseudoguessing. Conversely, it is necessary to have enough respondents with ability levels significantly superior to the item difficulty level to enable estimation of the inattention parameter.

Figure 14.1 presents examples of item characteristic curves from these four item response models. More specifically, the lower right section of Figure 14.1 presents three examples of such items from a 4PL model, the parameter of inattention varying between 0.5 and 1.[3] At the time this model was proposed, the estimation methods used posed significant problems of instability in the calculations, mainly problems related to the existence of local maximums. Current Bayesian methods, without resolving all the problems, now permit us to reconsider the estimation.

Likelihood Function of Response Patterns and Estimation Methods of Ability Level

The likelihood function of the responses patterns Xj at the ability level θ_j and the parameters of the n items ai, bi, ci, and di, according to the chosen model, are illustrated by Equation 2. This equation also expresses the principle of strong local independence according to which, at a constant skill level value, the probability of obtaining a response from an item in the test $P_{ij}^{x_{ij}} Q_{ij}^{1-x_{ij}}$ is independent of the probability of obtaining a response to another item in the same test.

$$P_j = P(X_j | \theta_j, a_i, b_i, c_i, d_i) = \prod_{i=1}^{n} P_{ij}^{x_{ij}} Q_{ij}^{1-x_{ij}} \quad (2)$$

Proceeding from this function, where $Q_{ij} = 1 - P_{ij}$, the ability level of individuals can be estimated. The most current methods of estimation are based on the mode (maximum likelihood) of the associated likelihood function (Lord, 1952) or on the mathematical expectation of the ability level (Bock & Mislevy, 1982). From Figure 14.2, one can see the associated likelihood function in the response patterns of four different persons. The discrimination parameter is set at 1 for the five items, while the difficulty parameter varies from –2 to 2 by a step of 1 and the pseudoguessing parameter varies from 0 to 0.3 by a step of 0.075. Since only five items are considered in this fictitious test, these curves, excepting the first response pattern, do not present a clear overall maximum. So, it is difficult to estimate from the mode the most likely value of the ability level for each of the three other response patterns considered here.

The estimate of the ability level is thus obtained from the mode of the likelihood function, more specifically by calculating the value that cancels out the first derivative of this function. To simplify the calculations, it is generally preferable to locate the value that cancels the first derivative of the logarithm of Equation 2. Traditionally this calculation is done by using the Newton-Raphson method (Hambleton & Swaminathan, 1985, pp. 75–99) or the Fischer score (Skrondal & Rabe-Hesketh, 2004, pp. 180–182) when the mathematical expectation of the information taken from the Fischer method is preferred over the observed value. Equation 3 represents the function associated with the calculation of the maximum likelihood:

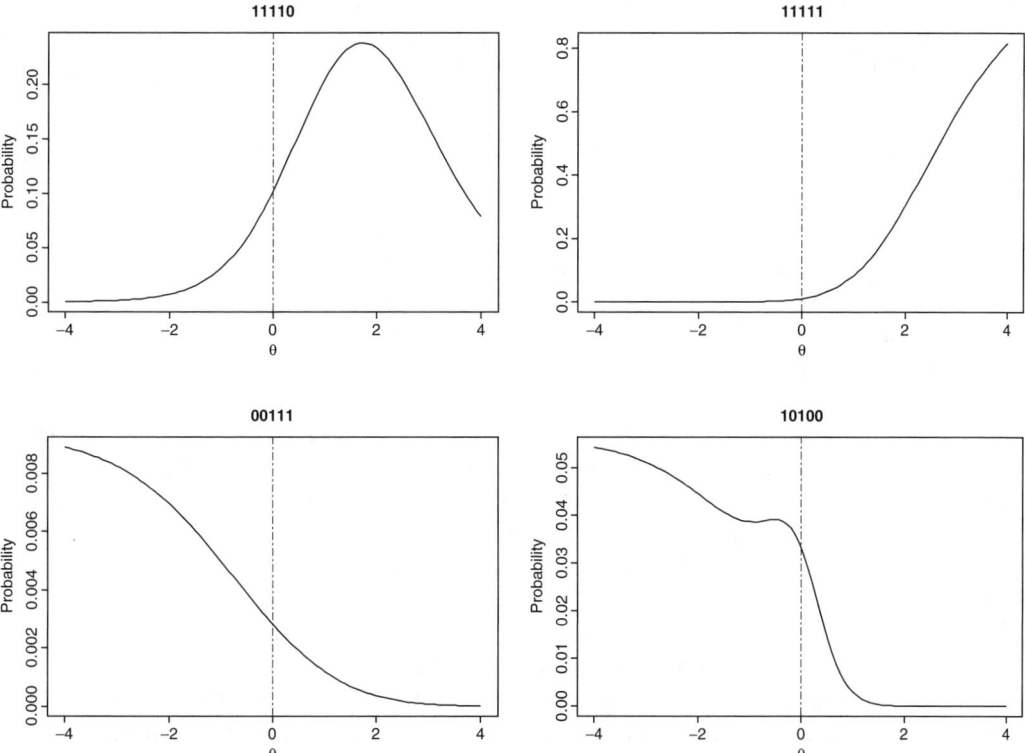

Figure 14.2 Functions of Likelihood of Patterns of Response Without A Priori Distribution

$$\theta_{ml} \equiv l(P_j)' = 0 \tag{3}$$

where the apostrophe represents the differentiation operator in relation to the ability level.

To offset the difficulty of estimating the ability level in potential cases where multiple modes exist, Bayesian methods have been proposed (Birnbaum, 1969). In a Bayesian context, the interest focuses on the a posteriori distribution illustrated by Equation 4.

$$P_j = P(X_j | \theta_j, a_i, b_i, c_i, d_i) = f(\theta_j) \prod_{i=1}^{n} P_{ij}^{x_{ij}} Q_{ij}^{1-x_{ij}} \tag{4}$$

As before, in order to estimate with maximum likelihood, methods of cancelling the first derivative of this function are used to determine the mode of the likelihood function. Equation 5 illustrates the first derivative of the likelihood function to be canceled.

$$\theta_{map} \equiv l(f(\theta_j))' + l(P_j)' = 0. \tag{5}$$

In Equation 4, it can be seen that the multiplication of the likelihood function arising in Equation 2 by an a priori probability is a function of the ability level. Generally it is an informative a priori distribution $f(\theta)$, often a Gaussian distribution $N(\mu, \sigma^2)$. When the a priori distribution is noninformative and uniform on a fixed interval where $(\theta) = c$, so is therefore a constant, then the a posteriori distribution simply corresponds to the likelihood function expressed in Equation 6. Besides the fact that this distribution is limited at the upper and lower extremities, in practice it is equivalent to the likelihood function by a maximum likelihood encountered previously in Equation 2.

$$P_j = P(\theta_j | X_j, a_i, b_i, c_i, d_i) = c \prod_{i=1}^{n} P_{ij}^{x_{ij}} Q_{ij}^{1-x_{ij}} = P(X_j | \theta_j, a_i, b_i, c_i, d_i) \tag{6}$$

Figure 14.3 illustrates the a posteriori likelihood function associated with the same patterns of responses observed in Figure 14.2 when the a priori distribution is Gaussian. Note that all the curves display a unique local maximum and bring this close to the mean of the a priori distribution, which is equal to 0. Consequently, the estimation of the ability level by a posteriori maximum likelihood method is clearly advantageous to avoid multiple local maximums (Magis & Raîche, 2010).

The maximum likelihood a posteriori estimation method is based on asymptotic developments where the number of administered items is taken as infinite. In practice, the number of items is limited (rarely more than 100) and the application of methods based on asymptotic developments unfortunately gives rise to bias in estimation. Other methods of estimating the ability level have been proposed to offset this problem. One of these is Warm's (1989) weighted maximum likelihood, inspired by the work of Lord (1983) with regard to the reduction in bias with the estimations of the ability level. The a priori function is replaced by a non informative function, which allows the estimator's bias to be asymptotically canceled. Where one- and two-parameter models are considered, Magis and Raîche (2011) have shown that Warm's method does in fact correspond to usage of Jeffreys's (1961) a priori function, a fact that was also underlined by Warm (1989) and Hoijtink & Boomsma (1995) for the one- and two-parameters item response logistic models respectively. This noninformative a priori function simplifies

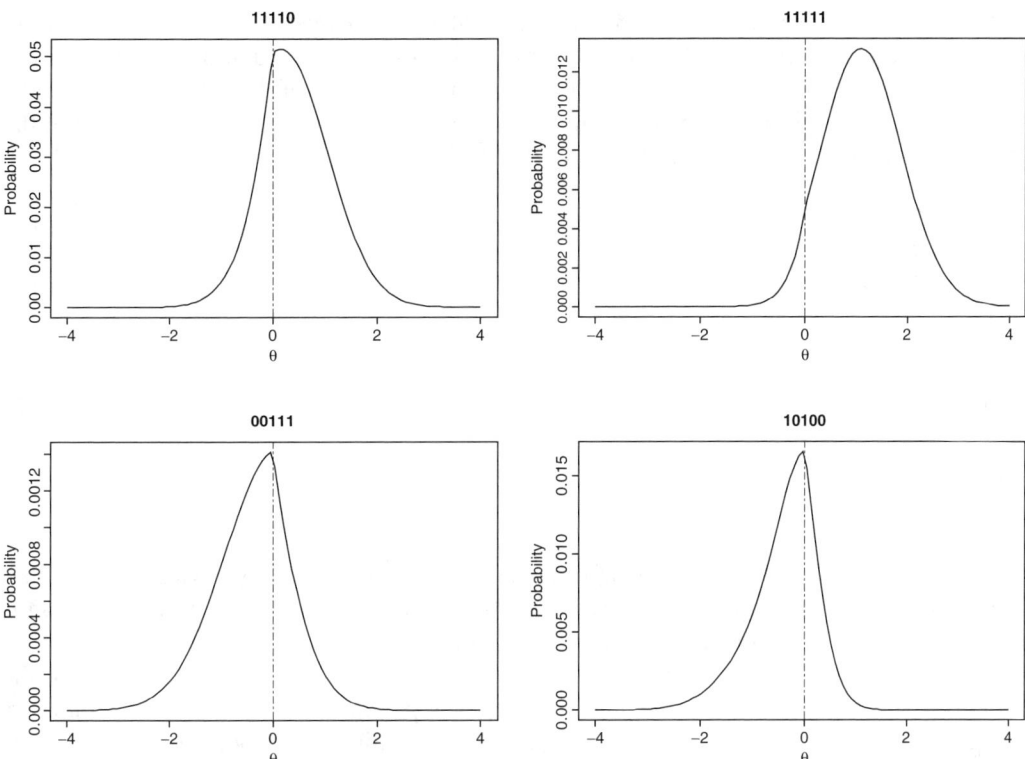

Figure 14.3 Functions of Likelihood of Patterns of Responses With A Priori Distribution

calculations and allows us to more easily envisage the implementation of other item response models, such as ordered and nominal polytomic models. Unfortunately models with more than two parameters no longer show this equivalence between the Jeffrey's a priori function and the Warm's weighted maximum likelihood. The function to be cancelled then takes the form of Equation 7.

$$\theta_{warm} \equiv \frac{J(\theta_j)}{2I(\theta_j)} + l(P_j)' = 0 \qquad (7)$$

where

$$J(\theta) = \sum_{i=1}^{n} \frac{P_i'(\theta)P_i''(\theta)}{P_i(\theta)Q_i(\theta)} \qquad (8)$$

and

$$I(\theta) = \sum_{i=1}^{n} \frac{[P_i'(\theta)]^2}{P_i(\theta)Q_i(\theta)} \qquad (9)$$

Equation 9 corresponds to the expected Fischer information.

Last, estimation methods have been proposed that are not based on calculation of the mode of the likelihood function. The most used is probably the expected a posteriori (EAP) estimation method of Bock and Mislevy (1982; Baker & Kim, 2004). The expected a posteriori estimation method looks like maximal likelihood a posteriori insofar as it used an a priori distribution and also sets out a Bayesian formulation. It is based on the calculation of the mean rather than the mode. Equation 10 illustrates the function used. In practice a numerical approximation of the integrals is carried out (Equation 11) (Baker & Kim, 2004, p. 193).

$$\theta_{eap} = \frac{\int_\theta \theta f(\theta) P_j \, d\theta}{\int_\theta f(\theta) P_j \, d\theta} \tag{10}$$

$$\theta_{eap} = \frac{\sum_\theta \theta f(\theta) P_j}{\sum_\theta f(\theta) P_j} \tag{11}$$

Estimation Methods of Item Parameters

The estimation of the item parameters from IRT item response models issues a particular challenge given that, in the majority of cases, the ability level of the person is unknown. Three families of solutions to this problem have been envisaged.

The first solution consists in maximizing the likelihood of all the response patterns of the persons X, making them conditional jointly on the item parameters and the person parameters concerned (Equation 12). This involves using the joint maximum likelihood estimation (JMLE) method proposed by Lord (1952) and Birnbaum (1968).

$$P = P(X \mid \theta, a, b, c, d) = \prod_{j=1}^{N} \prod_{i=1}^{n} P_{ij}^{x_{ij}} Q_{ij}^{1-x_{ij}} \tag{12}$$

Since, at the outset, neither the item parameters nor the person parameters are known, the JMLE method consists in fixing the arbitrary values beforehand, whether to the parameters of the items or persons. Generally it is preferred to fix the person parameters by calculating the z score linked to the number of correct responses for each person. Therefore it is possible to obtain a first estimate of the item parameters by maximum likelihood. This first estimate is then used to get the second estimate of the ability level of the persons by maximum likelihood. The process is repeated until the estimates are not significantly more different than those in the previous iteration. Given its nature, it probably would have been preferable to describe this method of estimation as more of an alternating than a joint one (van der Linden & Hambleton, 1997). Strandmark and Linn (1987, p. 361) make use of the cyclic maximum likelihood qualifier. Variations in this method have been proposed. For example, at each iteration it is possible to replace the maximum likelihood estimation method with maximum likelihood a posteriori. It is also possible to use the expected a posteriori method during estimation of the ability level.

Unfortunately the JMLE method presents a significant problem on the theoretical level. In fact, this estimation method theoretically creates a bias that is difficult to monitor in the estimation of parameters of item and person. Also, estimates are affected in such a way that they do not approach their real values when the number of persons approaches infinity (Baker & Kim, 2004). To offset these difficulties, estimation methods have been proposed that do not require an estimation of ability level. One method consists of applying a theoretical probability distribution, $f(\theta)$, of the ability level and then estimating the item parameters according to this probability distribution rather than according to the ability level of each of the persons. Therefore the focus is now on the marginal probability distribution of the response patterns and the method is then described as an estimation by marginal maximum likelihood (MML) (Bock & Lieberman, 1970; Embretson & Reise, 2000; van der Linden & Hambleton, 1997).

The marginal probability of a response pattern, j, whatever the level of ability of the person, is represented by Equation 13. The maximization of the function $P = \prod_{j=1}^{N} P_j$ on the entirety of persons is thus independent of the ability level of each person.

$$P_j = P(X_j | a, b, c, d) = \int_{-\infty}^{\infty} \prod_{i=1}^{n} P_{ij}^{x_{ij}} Q_{ij}^{1-x_{ij}} f(\theta) d\theta \tag{13}$$

A third method allows us also to estimate the item parameters without knowing the value of the ability level of each of the persons. This involves the conditional maximum likelihood estimation method (CML), suggested by Rasch (1961) and developed in more detail by Andersen (1972). The probability of getting a response pattern conditional on the total score is represented by Equation 14. This involves maximizing $P = \prod_{j=1}^{N} P_j$, as in the case of maximum marginal likelihood. Moreover, this method presents the advantage of not having to put forward a hypothesis with regard to the probability distribution of the ability level and of only having to depend on the number of correct responses, rj, taken from each person. Estimation by conditional maximum likelihood can, however, be used when the estimator of the ability level is a sufficient statistic, which completely explains the number of correct responses achieved by each person. This is notably the case with modeling based on the Rasch model, where there is neither a parameter of pseudoguessing nor one of inattention, and where the discrimination parameter is constant (at 1) for all items. The one-parameter logistic model responds to these requirements.

$$P_j = P(X_j | \theta_j, b_i) = P(r_j | b_i) P(X_j | r_j, b_i) \tag{14}$$

A more recent and promising approach involves Monte Carlo Markov chains, also using mathematical expectation as an estimator of ability level (Albert, 1992; Patz & Junker, 1999a, 1999b). In fact, this Bayesian method of estimation represents rather a body of methods whose development has spurred a lot of interest. In a typical Bayesian approach, values are calculated that maximize the a posteriori probability of item parameters and respondents conditional on the data, $P(\theta, a, b, c, d | X)$ more than the probability of data conditional on the items parameters and persons, $P(X | \theta, a, b, c, d)$. Equations 15 and 16 illustrate the functions that are used to allow for estimation of the parameters of items and persons.

$$P(\theta_j, a_i, b_i, c_i, d_i | X) = \frac{P(\theta_j, a_i, b_i, c_i, d_i) P(X | \theta_j, a_i, b_i, c_i, d_i)}{P(X)} \tag{15}$$

Where $P(X)$ is expressed by a multiple integral whose complexity is dependent on the number of parameters to be estimated.

$$P(X) = \int_{\theta} \int_{a} \int_{b} \int_{c} \int_{d} P(\theta_j) P(X | \theta_j, a_i, b_i, c_i, d_i) d\theta da db dc dd \tag{16}$$

Because this integral cannot be computed by algebraic means, Monte Carlo techniques of integration are applied. In addition, given that the structure of covariance between the parameters is difficult if not impossible to model, their interdependence is monitored using Markov chains. This is why these are described as Monte Carlo Markov chain methods.

Person-Characteristic Curves

The models presented up to now take only one parameter of the person into account; that is, the ability level. However, other models that factor in more than one person parameter are possible. This is why they are described as being multidimensional with regard to the person parameters. For example, even in 1967, McDonald proposed a multidimensional model where he simultaneously took several ability levels into account ($\theta_1, \theta_2, \cdots, \theta_N$) in a manner similar to those found in classic linear exploratory and confirmatory factor analysis.

It is also possible to approach multidimensional models of person parameters that take parameters other than ability levels into account, whether one-dimensional or multidimensional. In light of this, certain theorists—among them Carroll (1983), Ferrando (2004, 2006), Levine and Drasgow (1983), Strandmark and Linn (1987), and Trabin and Weiss (1983)—were interested in the person-characteristic curves (PRCs) that took fluctuations in the ability level of the person into account as well as his or her personal pseudguessing and inattention.

Another insightful illustration of these additional personal parameters can be provided by person response curves such as those proposed by Trabin and Weiss (1983). To this effect, Figure 14.4 shows the representative curves of the probability of gaining a correct response by four persons according to the difficulty level of the item given to them. The curve of a regular pattern shows that the person has a zero probability of getting a correct response to a very difficult item and is certain to get a correct response to a very easy item. The slope of the curve is fairly important, as it indicates that the probability of a correct response to an item is strongly affected by the difficulty of the items, which is desirable.

The person curve, which shows inattention, indicates, as already seen, that this person has a zero probability of achieving a correct response to a very difficult item but, nonetheless, has a probability equal to only 0.8 of achieving a correct response to a very easy item. The person curve, which displays the behavior of pseudoguessing, indicates that this person has a probability equal to around 0.4 of achieving a correct answer to a difficult item. This value is greater than the 0 value seen earlier.

Finally a fourth curve characterizes a person whose ability level fluctuates within the test. For this person the variation in item difficulty level has less effect on the probability of achieving a correct response to the item, as this is dependent on his or her temporary ability level rather than on the difficulty level of the item.

These person-characteristic curves differ from one another with regard to four personal parameters: ability level, θ; fluctuation, S; pseudoguessing, χ; and inattention, δ. It must be noted that, in order to preserve notational coherence with the symbols used for the item parameters, Greek letters are used to identify the person parameters. This is not the case, however, for personal fluctuation; the explanation for this is presented later from the proposed item response model.

Multidimensional Models of Person-Characteristic Curves

Levine and Drasgow (1983) proposed a model that takes fluctuation in the ability level into account concurrently with the item parameters of the three-parameter model: the Gaussian

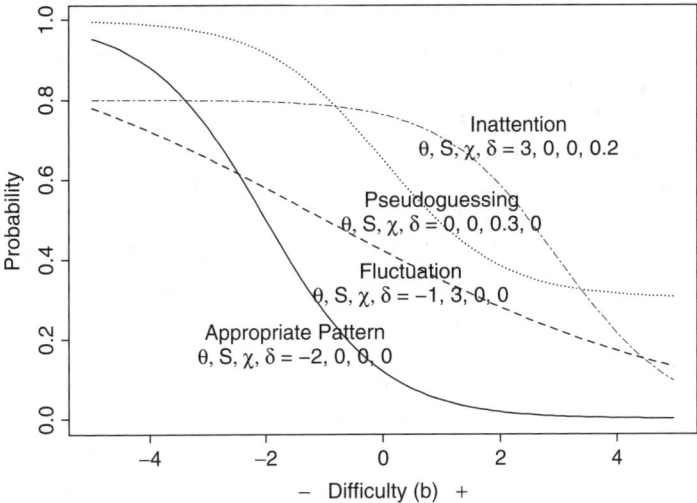

Figure 14.4 Persons Characteristic Curves as Per Four Profiles

model also recently studied by Ferrando (2004, 2006). The introduction of additional person parameters has also been done from a generalized logistical model by Strandmark and Linn (1987). They proposed adding a personal parameter of pseudoguessing and another of personal discrimination. None of these models, however, allow for the personal parameters we are concerned with here to be taken into account at the same time. Also, the way in which these authors deal with the parameters is somewhat limited. For example, Strandmark and Linn considered a model where the discriminations of the person and the item are multiplied when, in fact, the addition of two variances should be carried out, as seen in Equations 17 and 18 below. In addition, in reality the Ferrando model limits itself in considering only the difficulty parameter and not the other items parameters. It therefore seems appropriate to introduce a new proposal.

Considering the items parameters already approached and the new personal parameters, Equations 17 and 18 can represent a logistic model of four-person and four-item parameters. This modeling has previously been proposed by Raîche, Magis, and Blais (Blais, Raîche & Magis, 2009; Raîche, Magis & Blais, 2008, 2009). As previously indicated, the relationship between the symbols associated with the parameters of items and of persons can now be observed.

$$P_{ij} = P(x_{ij} = 1 | S_j, \theta_j, \chi_j, \delta_j, s_i, b_i, c_i, d_i) \tag{17}$$

$$P_{ij} = (\chi_j + c_i) + \frac{\delta_j + d_i - (\chi_j + c_i)}{1 + e^{\frac{(\theta_j - b_i)}{\sqrt{S_i^2 + S_j^2}}}} \tag{18}$$

The personal parameters of pseudoguessing and inattention vary from 0 to 1, as is the case with the corresponding item parameters. The fluctuation parameter of person S and the standard deviation of item s vary between 0 and $+\infty$. In the case of the inattention parameter, which is a person parameter, this, unlike the item parameter, is actually equal to the complement of maximal probability that a person will achieve a correct response to an item of low difficulty. A person whose pseudoguessing parameter is higher may tend to achieve a correct response to difficult items more often than anticipated: owing to plagiarism for example. Conversely a person whose inattention parameter is higher may tend to achieve a correct response to easy items less often than anticipated. A student who proceeds carelessly when the items are rather easy for him would be representative of this kind of behavior.

The reader will also note that this model does not formally use the item discrimination parameter. In fact, to be able to distinguish between the discrimination parameters of items and persons, these parameters must be reformulated, as Thurstone (1927) suggested. More specifically, these parameters can also be viewed as standard deviations; in this form, their variances are additive. Equation 19 illustrates this situation. The discrimination is, in fact, equal to the inverse of the square root of the sum of the variance resulting from the item s^2 and from the person S^2. The proposed model allows us to make this distinction and thus to estimate these parameters separately. It is also for this reason that the labeling of personal fluctuation (standard deviation) is applied, rather than personal discrimination, as did Strandmak and Linn (1987), which limited the range of their model.

$$a = \frac{1}{\sqrt{s_i^2 + S_j^2}} \tag{19}$$

Of course it is possible to consider simplified models where just one, two, or three person parameters are used simultaneously. As a result, a model where only the ability level and the personal fluctuation are considered, while fixing the item parameters, as per the Rasch model, would simplify to the representation proposed by Ferrando.

Estimation of Person Parameters

All the methods previously presented can theoretically be used to achieve the estimation of the parameters of items and persons. However, certain of these currently present rather significant difficulties, whereas others are just relatively simple extensions to be implemented.

Thus the simultaneous estimation of the item and person parameters can be carried out by joint maximal likelihood. Meanwhile it has already been emphasized that the problems are created by bias and inconsistency in the estimation of item parameters, thus limiting its usage. Furthermore, the CMLE method cannot be used, as the model we are considering here does not offer sufficient estimates, as is the case with models stemming from the Rasch model. Marginal maximum likelihood estimation could be of interest, but the necessary number of quadrature points to approximate the four-dimensional integrals implied by the four-person parameters seem to seriously limit the use of this method. In fact, the use of at least 20 quadrature points for each of the dimensions implied, in total 20^4 quadrature points, would be necessary. The most promising method seems to be the one based on the Monte Carlo Markov chains. With the flexibility of available software, it is relatively easy to implement and rather free with regard to the prior probability distributions that can be used. Nonetheless, the use of this method will require much scrutiny to study the behavior of the estimates and their statistical properties.

Despite the difficulties raised with regard to the estimation of item parameters, it is possible that these problems are of little importance when we consider that their estimation could be gained quite simply from unidimensional one-, two-, three-, or four-parameter logistic models.

The item parameters estimated in this manner would represent their average value when person parameters of the entire population had been taken into account. In fact, the estimation of the additional three-person parameters implies that, within the proposed multidimensional model, this estimation will not be of importance except in identifying or correcting the estimation of the ability level of the person whose patterns differ considerably from the expected response patterns of persons from the reference population.

Contrary to the estimation of item parameters, the estimation of person parameters is relatively simple to achieve by the usual estimation methods: maximum likelihood, maximum likelihood a posteriori, weighted maximum likelihood, or expected a posteriori. As previously noted with the estimation of item parameters using marginal maximum likelihood, it must be emphasized again that the number of quadrature points increases considerably with the growth in the number of person parameters; therefore, the expected a posteriori method appears less suitable. This is why the first three estimation methods are preferred.

The estimation methods by maximum likelihood and maximum likelihood a posteriori are currently implemented into the online package *irtProb* (Raîche & Magis, 2009) available on the website of the *R* software.[4]

Despite the level of complexity of Equation 18, the estimation of the person parameters by the method of maximum likelihood does not generally appear to cause too many problems. With regard to the method of maximum likelihood a posteriori, its implementation currently limits a priori distribution $N(0, 1)$ solely on the ability parameter. Subsequent versions of the *irtProb* package will also consider prior distributions suited to the personal parameters of fluctuation, pseudoguessing, and inattention. More promising however, is the introduction of Jeffreys's (1961) noninformative functions for all person parameters, which should yield more flexibility to take in account a priori simultaneously for all the person parameters. The use of these functions should allow us to come closer to the target with less biased estimation through Warm's (1989) weighted maximum likelihood.

Examples of Application

To illustrate the application of this new multidimensional model and put it to the test, four examples are presented here. For each one, 300 response patterns to 60 items are simulated. With regard to the item parameters, the difficulty level varies from −4 to +4, the standard deviation is equal to 1, and both pseudoguessing and inattention are equal to 0. In all cases, the ability level is fixed at −1 and estimation of the person parameters is achieved by maximum likelihood a posteriori by using a prior distribution $N(0,1)$. The first example illustrates a situation where the additional person parameters are all equal to 0—a situation that, here, corresponds strictly to the simple unidimensional one-parameter logistic model. In the following three examples, the personal parameters of fluctuation, pseudoguessing, and inattention are individually manipulated to take on the following values respectively: 0.5, 0.3, and 0.3. All the calculations were made with the aid of the online package *irtProb*, the source code for which is available in Appendix 14.A.

In the right-hand column of Table 14.1, it can be seen that, when the estimation is made according to the one-parameter logistic model, the estimated value of the ability level, θ, enables the real value to be regained with small bias (only −0.06). The estimation of this same person parameter using the multidimensional model is less precise but is still very satisfactory, displaying an error of −0.1. The standard error of the estimator ($S_\theta = 0,26$) is also equal to the value computed from the one-parameter logistic model. The estimated values of the personal parameters of fluctuation, S, pseudoguessing, χ, and inattention, δ, are also very close to the

Table 14.1 Example of the Estimation of Person Parameters When the Personal Parameters of Fluctuation, Pseudoguessing, and Inattention Are All Equal to 0

	θ	S	χ	δ	Θ_{1PL}
Real value	−1.00	0.00	0.00	0.00	−1.00
Estimated value	−0.90	0.06	0.00	0.02	−0.94
Empirical standard error	0.26	0.14	0.01	0.04	0.26

Table 14.2 Example of the Estimation of Person Parameters When the Personal Fluctuation Parameter Is Equal to 0.5

	θ	S	χ	δ	Θ_{1PL}
Real value	−1.00	0.50	0.00	0.00	−1.00
Estimated value	−0.83	0.21	0.01	0.04	−0.92
Empirical standard error	0.32	0.27	0.02	0.06	0.29

real values. It appears that, even under these conditions, the multidimensional model allows sufficiently precise values of all the person parameters to be achieved.

In the second example, fixing it at only 0.5 for all subjects changes the personal fluctuation parameter. This value will have an average impact on the total discrimination level as, according to Equation 19, this reduces the effective discrimination from 1 to $=\frac{1}{\sqrt{1^2 + 0.5^2}}$ (i.e., 0.89). The standard error of the ability level estimator should then be greater than that observed in the previous example. Table 14.2 shows the results; the estimation of the ability level according to one-parameter logistic model is marginally affected by this condition and its standard error is mildly increased from 0.26 to 0.29. However, when the multidimensional model is applied, the standard error of the estimator of the ability level is now equal to 0.32 and the error of estimation is greater than that observed in the unidimensional model. This could lead us to think that the multidimensional model was less efficient than the simpler unidimensional model. But the multidimensional model shows us that the person fluctuation parameter is greater than 0 and that one must be cautious in the use of the estimation of the ability level. This means that the multidimensional model can prove extremely useful in detecting any potential problems that may arise.

In Table 14.3 we can observe the results achieved when the personal pseudoguessing parameter is fixed at 0.3. This scenario is encountered again when the persons to whom the test is given try to fraudulently improve their scores in the test. If this potential problem is not considered and an estimation of the ability level of persons in line with the unidimensional model is done, the ability level of the persons is sharply underestimated. Attempts to increase scores on the test are therefore successful. But when the multidimensional model is applied, an estimated value of the ability level approaches the real value. Additionally, the estimated value of the personal pseudoguessing parameter (0.25) is more reflective of the real value (0.3) with an overall satisfactory standard error (0.10). It can also be seen here that the personal fluctuation parameter shows a value equal to 0.21. This appears very predictable as, where the personal pseudoguessing parameter has a value greater than 0, a fluctuation occurs in the ability level. In other words, these two personal parameters should correlate. Looking at the results achieved, the multidimensional model once again demonstrates its superiority to the unidimensional model.

Table 14.3 Example of the Estimation of Person Parameters When the Personal Pseudoguessing Parameter Is Equal to 0.3

	θ	S	χ	δ	Θ_{1PL}
Real value	−1.00	0.00	0.30	0.00	−1.00
Estimated value	−0.61	0.21	0.25	0.01	0.47
Empirical standard error	0.43	0.33	0.10	0.03	0.37

Table 14.4 Example of the Estimation of the Persons Parameter When the Personal Inattention Parameter Is Equal to 0.3

	θ	S	χ	δ	Θ_{1PL}
Real value	−1.00	0.00	0.00	0.30	−1.00
Estimated value	−0.90	0.06	0.00	0.31	−1.81
Empirical standard error	0.42	0.15	0.01	0.13	0.35

Finally, the fourth example illustrates a situation where the persons to whom the test is given are either inattentive or try to perform badly in the test so as to artificially reduce their estimated ability level. To recreate this scenario, the personal inattention parameter is fixed at 0.3. Table 14.4 lets us see that, in this situation, use of the unidimensional model ensures that the estimated value of the ability level is sharply underestimated (−1.81 rather than −1). However, the multidimensional model allows us to achieve an estimated value that is closer to its real figure. It also enables us to reach a value that is much closer to the real value of the personal inattention parameter. This result is somewhat impressive, as we would have thought it difficult to achieve the estimation of the personal parameters in this scenario, since the persons concerned have a relatively weak ability level.

Example of the Application to the PISA Data (2003)

Another example is proposed to illustrate the application of this multidimensional model to actual data taken from the results of 31 items in mathematics. This is from the first booklet produced on the occasion of the 2003 PISA large-scale survey in Canada. To avoid using patterns containing missing data, only 2,182 out of a possible 27,953 observations with no missing data are used.[5] In this way, coding missing items response as 0 or even using response patterns of different lengths is avoided. The results achieved will therefore be more easily comparable with one another. It must also be emphasized that, among the 31 items making up the first booklet, three show polytomous responses: they were reclassified as dichotomous to allow for application of a one-parameter model in the Rasch design. The items parameters are found in the technical manual from PISA 2003 (Organisation for Economic Co-operation and Development, 2005, pp. 412–413) and in the source code of the appendix 14.B to this chapter

In Table 14.5, the person parameters that were estimated for the first 10 respondents can be seen. Not one single case shows a personal fluctuation parameter greater than 0. These 10 response patterns do not appear, then, to be affected by a problem of fluctuation of the ability level in the test. But respondents 71 to 92 show pseudoguessing parameters of 0.33 and 0.40, which leads us to believe that they tried to artificially increase their score. With respect to the inattention parameter, the results achieved indicate that only respondent 55 ($\delta = 0.46$) could have been inattentive during the test or tried to deliberately reduce his score. A calculation of the percentiles associated with the parameters of personal fluctuation, pseudoguessing, and

Table 14.5 Example of the Estimation of the Person Parameters from Results in Mathematics Achieved at the 2003 PISA in Canada. (First 10 observations without missing data from a total of 2,182 observations)

Observation	θ	S	χ	δ
23	0.65	0.00	0.00	0.00
24	−0.04	0.00	0.00	0.01
28	−0.21	0.00	0.00	0.07
55	−0.35	0.00	0.00	0.46
57	0.43	0.00	0.04	0.00
68	−0.26	0.00	0.00	0.19
70	−0.49	0.00	0.00	0.00
71	0.31	0.00	0.40	0.00
74	−0.06	0.00	0.00	0.00
92	0.51	0.00	0.33	0.00

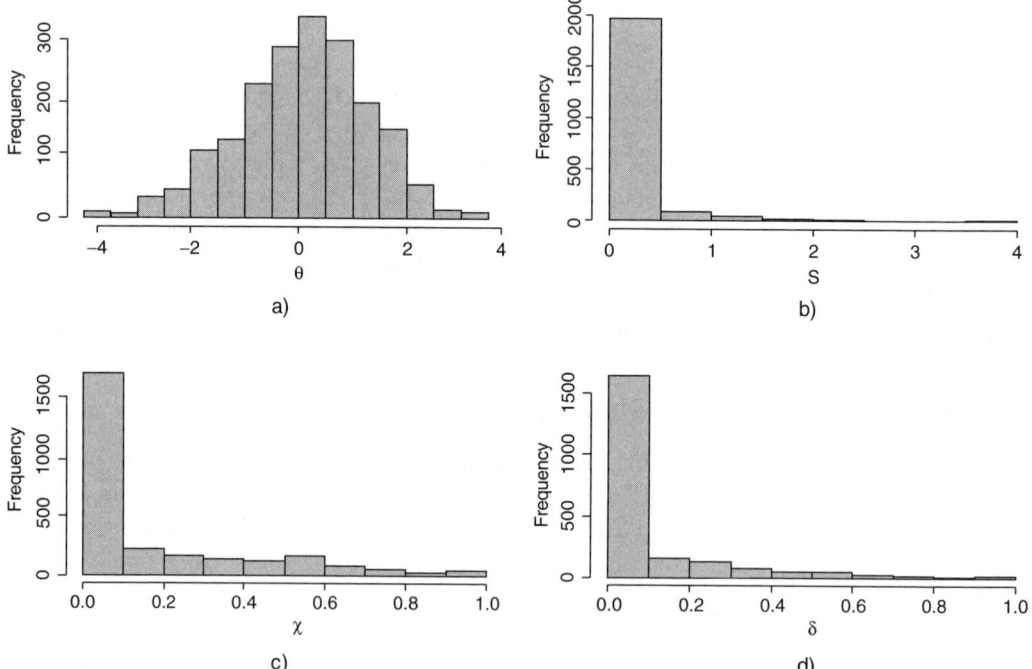

Figure 14.5 Distribution of the Four-Person Parameters in a Sample of Results Obtained in Mathematics From PISA in 2003 in Canada

inattention indicates that the nominal threshold of 0.5 for a type I error is respectively equal to 0.62, 0.54, and 0.33.[6] These would be the critical values to monitor in the context of the administration of items from the booklet. It must be emphasized that only respondent 55 shows such a high value, which concerns only the personal inattention parameter.

Figure 14.5 allows us to observe the distribution of the four person parameters from frequency histograms. Besides a mostly Gaussian probability distribution of the ability level, the majority of estimators associated with the three other person parameters show strongly asymmetrical

Table 14.6 Descriptive Statistics and Pearson Correlations Between the Estimated Values of the Person Parameters From the Results in Mathematics Achieved by 2003 PISA in Canada (Solely Observations With No Missing Data Where n = 2,182)

	θ	S	χ	δ
Θ	1.00	−0.03	0.28	−0.31
S	−0.03	1.00	0.17	0.06
X	0.28	0.17	1.00	−0.20
Δ	−0.31	0.06	−0.20	1.00
Average	0.03	0.02	0.16	0.09
Median	0.03	0.02	0.00	0.00
SD*	0.47	0.55	0.24	0.18
Minimum	−1.49	0.00	0.00	0.00
Maximum	1.27	4.00	1.00	1.00

*SD, standard deviation.

distributions concentrated around 0. The majority of the 2,182 respondents studied seem, then, to display an appropriate pattern of responses and to have responded honestly in the test in accordance with the model studied. This finding is rather reassuring with regard to the quality of the results achieved in this large-scale enquiry.

Finally, Table 14.6 concurrently displays the descriptive statistics relative to the four estimators of the person parameters and the Pearson correlations between these estimators. First of all and in line with the features of descriptive statistics, note that the estimator of the ability level displays, as expected, an average close to 0, but that the range of the values associated with this is relatively limited (between −1.49 and 1.27). These results do not allow us make a judgment on the relationship between the extreme values of the estimator of the ability level and the estimators of other person parameters. This limited range is explained quite simply by the use of the new model. Indeed, when only the ability level is estimated from the simpler unidimensional Rasch model without factoring in the three additional personal parameters, the range of the ability level varies between −4.0 and 3.88—that is, values that thus cover the probable scale of the ability level. Application of the multidimensional model therefore tends to compress the scale of the estimated values of the ability level around the a priori average, which here is uniformly equal to 0.

The median of the estimates of the additional three-person parameters is located around 0; but, in the case of the mean of the parameter estimates of pseudoguessing and inattention, the average is noticcably greater than the median (i.e., a reflection of the asymmetry of their frequency distribution, previously seen in Figure 14.5). Last, it is noted that the maximal value of personal fluctuation is very important (i.e., 4). After verifying the data, it is a matter of being in a position where there are only 14 respondents.

As far as the correlations between estimates go, the higher the estimate of ability level, the higher the estimate of the parameter of pseudoguessing. This could be explained by the fact that the ability level would be underestimated when an instance of pseudoguessing occurs with the respondent. A reverse relationship is observed with regard to the inattention parameter estimator. In this last case, an instance of inattention results in an underestimation of the ability level. The correlation between the estimates of the parameters of pseudoguessing and inattention is negative, emphasizing that the more a respondent displays instances of inattention, the less pseudoguessing there is. Finally, the personal fluctuation estimate is virtually unrelated to the ability level estimator. However, the personal fluctuation estimate shows a weak positive correlation with the pseudoguessing parameter estimator; but, as outlined above, the fact that the range of the ability level estimator is rather restricted probably limits the interpretations associated with these correlations.

Conclusion

The aim of this chapter was to present a multidimensional logistic item response model that, aside from the usual items parameters, integrated additional person parameters—of fluctuation, pseudoguessing, and inattention—thus suggesting a multidimensional model comprising additional person parameters. Prior to this presentation, however, the unidimensional logistic item response models with one, two, three, or four parameters were described. Then the methods of estimating the item and person parameters were presented. This, then, allowed the introduction of the person-characteristic curves in the spirit of Trabin and Weiss (1983). It was then possible to propose a multidimensional model of person parameters associated with the person-characteristic curves and thereby to suggest methods of estimating these additional parameters. Following this, the effectiveness of these methods of estimation and the usefulness of the multidimensional model were illustrated by four rather simple examples where each of the new person parameters was individually controlled. As previously emphasized, the use of this multidimensional person-parameter model will necessitate many more studies to analyze the behavior of estimators and to learn their statistical properties. Another example allowed for implementation of the PISA data from Canada in 2003.

Multidimensional modeling has proven to be very efficient under all conditions of the experiments in this chapter. Thus it was possible to achieve a better estimation of the ability level and to estimate the additional person parameters. This model could also prove to be very useful in correcting the estimated value of the ability level when persons try to artificially increase or reduce their test score. It could also be very relevant in allowing detection of appropriate response patterns. As Ferrando (2004) showed, the value of the Pearson correlation between the personal fluctuation parameter and the index of detection of inappropriate response patterns l_z^* proposed by Snijders (2001) is very high, which indicates that these two statistics roughly measure the same thing. In addition to this, certain work carried out by Béland, Raîche, Magis, and Brassard (2009) shows that the personal parameters of pseudoguessing and of inattention allow the detection of behaviors inappropriate to a test different from those detected in the majority of detection indexes (infit, outfit, caution indices, Guttman errors, etc.) (Kabaratsos, 2003; Meijer & Sijtsma, 2001; Raîche & Blais, 2003, 2005). These two additional parameters could then be used as new indices (pseudoguessing and inattention) of detection, mainly with regard to anticipated behaviors of intentional over- and underperformance. It could also be interesting to apply this approach to the identification of subpopulations; for example, to determine whether boys with an increased ability level display more instances of inattention than girls.

Also, because the person parameters are directly incorporated into these measurement models, these are much more useful in secondary analysis to analyze atypical response patterns than the normal indexes of detection proposed previously (for example, Lz, infit, outfit, caution indices, Guttman errors, etc.). This implies, however, that it will be necessary to improve estimation either by marginal maximum likelihood or by Monte Carlo Markov chains. In the first case, the challenges of numeric multidimensional integration will have to be removed, whereas in the second case it will have to be established which are the most appropriate functions of an a priori probability distribution for each of the additional person parameters. During the primary analysis, we will also be able to obtain estimates containing less bias of the person ability level. It must be noted, however, that the sampling structure appropriate to these enquiries (Mislevy,

1991; Mislevy, Beaton, Kaplan, & Sheehan, 1992) will make the estimation of items parameters much more complex and that the use of contextual information (Mislevy & Sheehan, 1989) will then be used to improve the estimation of the person parameters. Finally, to respond to the needs of large-scale studies, extensions specific to polytomous, nominal, and ordered item responses will have to be developed.

Notes

This research was made possible thanks to funding from the Social Sciences and Humanities Research Council of Canada (SSHRC), from the *Fonds québécois de la recherche sur la société et la culture* (FQRSC), and a research grant from the *Fonds national de la Recherche Scientifique* (FNRS, Belgium). The research was undertaken at the *Centre sur le développement et les applications en mesure et évaluation* (Cdame) at the Université du Québec à Montréal.

We thank the University of Liège's English Translation Service in Belgium for the support given in translating this chapter from French to English.

1. Programme international pour le suivi des acquis/Programme for International Student Assessment: www.pisa.oecd.org; Tendances de l'enquête internationale en mathématiques et en sciences: *timss.bc.edu*; Programme international de recherche en lecture scolaire: *pirls.bc.edu*; Programme pancanadien d'évaluation: www.cmec.ca/Programs/Iassessment/pancan/Pages/default_fr.aspx

2. The sampling is often carried out in a random manner on two levels (for the schools and the students) or randomly for the schools and in accordance with a full class group. The application is carried out, for the most part, in line with a model based on rotating groups of items where identical booklets are given to different students.

3. Frequently this situation is encountered when items are presented to students according to an increasing level of difficulty. Students with a higher ability level will at times tend to give less attention to easy items at the start of the test (inattention) in the same way that students of lesser ability tend more to guess the answer to difficult items at the end of the test (pseudoguessing).

4. Available on the CRAN R website: http://cran.r-project.org/web/packages/irtProb/

5. The large amount of missing data is explained by the administration of blocks of items (booklets), previously mentioned, where all the students do not respond to all the test questions.

6. The number of observations associated with this percentile is equal to 110 (i.e., 2,182 × 0.05).

References

Albert, J. H. (1992). Bayesian estimation of normal ogive item response curves using Gibbs sampling. *Journal of educational statistics, 17*, 251–269.

Andersen, E. B. (1972). The numerical solution of a set of conditional estimation equations. *Journal of the Royal Statistical Society*, Series B, *34*, 42–54.

Andrich, D. (1978). A rating formulation for ordered response categories. *Psychometrika, 43*, 561–573.

Baker, F. B., & Kim, S.-H. (2004). *Item response theory: Parameter estimation techniques*. New York, NJ: Dekker.

Barton, M. A., & Lord, F. M. (1981). *An upper asymptote for the three-parameter logistical item-response model*. Research bulletin 81–20. Princeton, NJ: Educational Testing Service.

Béland, S., Raîche, G., Magis, D., & Brassard, P. (2009, July). *Correlates of personal fluctuation, pseudo-chance, and inattention subject parameters: Relations with parametric and non-parametric person fit indices*. Paper presented at the international meeting of the Psychometric Society, Cambridge, UK.

Birnbaum, A. (1968). Some latent trait models and their use in inferring an examinee's ability. In F. M. Lord & M. R. Novick (Eds.), *Statistical theories of mental test scores*. Boston: Addison-Wesley.

Birnbaum, A. (1969). Statistical theory for logistical mental test models with a prior distribution of ability. *Journal of Mathematical Psychology, 6*, 258–276.

Blais, J.-G., Raîche, G., & Magis, D. (2009). La détection des patrons de réponses problématiques dans le contexte des tests informatisés. In J.-G. Blais (Ed.), *Évaluation des apprentissages et technologies de l'information et de la communication. Enjeux, applications et modèles de mesure*. Ste-Foy, Québec: Presses de l'Université Laval.

Bock, R. D., & Lieberman, M. (1970). Fitting a response model for *n* dichotomous scored items. *Psychometrika, 35*, 179–197.

Bock, R. D., & Mislevy, R. J. (1982). Adaptive EAP estimation of ability in a microcomputer environmemt. *Applied Psychological Measurement, 6*(4), 431–444.

Carroll, J. B. (1983). The difficulty of a test and its factor composition revisited. In H. Wainer & S. Messick (Eds.), *Principals of modern psychological measurement: A festschrift for Frederic Lord*. Mahwah, NJ: Erlbaum.

Embretson, S. E., & Reise, S. P. (2000). *Item response theory for psychologists*. Mahwah, NJ: Erlbaum.

Ferrando, P. J. (2004). Person reliability in personality measurement: An item response theory analysis. *Applied Psychological Measurement, 28*(2), 126–140.

Ferrando, P. J. (2006). Implications of person fluctuation for the stability and validity of test scores. *Methodology, 2*(4), 142–148.

Hambleton, R. K., & Swaminathan, H. (1985). *Item response theory: Principles and applications*. Boston, MA: Klüwer.

Hoijtink, H., & Boomsma, A. (1995). On person parameter estimation in the dichotomous Rasch model. In G. H. Fischer & I. W. Molenaar (Eds.), *Rasch model: Foundations, recent developments, and applications*. New York: Springer.

Jeffreys, B. (1961). *Theory of probability* (3rd ed.). Oxford, UK: Clarendon.

Kabaratsos, G. (2003). Comparing the aberrant response detection performance of thirty-six fit statistics. *Applied Measurement in Education, 16*, 277–298.

Levine, M. V., & Drasgow, F. (1983). Appropriateness measurement: validating studies and variable ability models. In D. J. Weiss (Ed.), *New horizons in testing: Latent trait test theory and computerized adaptive testing*. New York: Academic Press.

Lord, F. M. (1952). A theory of test scores. *Psychometric Monographs, 7*.

Lord, F. M. (1980). *Applications of item response theory to practical testing problems*. Mahwah, NJ: Erlbaum.

Lord, F. M. (1983). Unbiased estimators of ability parameters, of their variance, and of their parallel-forms reliability. *Psychometrika, 48*, 233–245.

Magis, D., & Raîche, G. (2010). An iterative maximum *a posteriori* estimation of proficiency level to detect multiple local likelihood maxima. *Applied Psychological Measurement, 34*, 75–90.

Magis, D., & Raîche, G. (2011). When do Bayesian modal and weighted likelihood estimation of ability correspond? A note on their relationships under logistic IRT models. *Psychometrika*. DOI: 10.1007/S11336-011-9233-5

Master, G. N. (1982). A Rasch model for partial credit scoring. *Psychometrika, 47*, 149–174.

McDonald, R. P. (1967). Non-linear factor analysis. *Psychometric Monograph, 15*.

Meijer, R. B., & Sijtsma, K. (2001). Methodology review: Evaluating person fit. *Applied Psychological Measurement, 25*(2), 107–135.

Mislevy, R. J. (1991). Randomization-based inference about latent variables from complex samples. *Psychometrika, 56*(2), 177–196.

Mislevy, R. J., Beaton, A. E., Kaplan, B., & Sheehan, K. M. (1992). Estimating population characteristics from sparse matrix samples of item responses. *Journal of Educational Measurement, 29*(2), 133–161.

Mislevy, R. J., & Sheehan, K. M. (1989). The role of collateral information about examinees in item parameter estimation. *Psychometrika, 54*(4), 661–679.

Organisation for Economic Co-operation and Development. (2005). *PISA 2003 technical report*. Paris: Author.

Patz, R. J., & Junker, B. W. (1999a). A straightforward approach to Markov Chain Monte Marlo methods for item response models. *Journal of Educational and Behavioural Statistics, 24*, 146–178.

Patz, R. J., & Junker, B. W. (1999b). Applications and extensions of MCMC in IRT: Multiple item types, missing data, and rated responses. *Journal of Educational and Behavioural Statistics, 24*, 342–366.

Raîche, G., & Blais, J.-G. (2003). Efficacité du dépistage des étudiantes et des étudiants qui cherchent à obtenir un résultat faible au test de classement en anglais, langue seconde, au collégial. In J.-G. Blais & G. Raîche (Eds.), *Regards sur la modelling de la mesure en éducation et en sciences sociales*. Ste-Foy, Québec: Presses de l'Université Laval.

Raîche, G., & Blais, J.-G. (2005, July). *Characterization of the distribution of the Lz index of person fit according to the estimated proficiency level*. Paper presented at the international meeting of the psychometric Society, IMPS05, Tilburg, The Netherlands [ERIC DOCUMENT NO ED490515].

Raîche, G., & Magis, D. (2009). *irtProb 1.0. Utilities and probability distributions related to multdimensional person item response models*. Retrieved from http://cran.r-project.org/web/packages/irtProb.

Raîche, G., Magis, D., & Blais, J.-G. (2008, July). *Multidimensional item response theory models integrating additional inattention, pseudo-chance, and discrimination person parameters*. Paper presented at the international meeting of the Psychometric Society, Durham, NH.

Raîche, G., Magis, D., & Blais, J.-G. (2009). *Multidimensional fluctuation, pseudo-chance and carelessness IRT person parameters models*. Paper presented at the international meeting of the Psychometric Society, Cambridge, UK.

Rasch, G. (1960). *Probabilistic models for some intelligence and attainment tests*. Copenhagen: Danish Institute for Educational Research.

Rasch, G. (1961). *On general laws and the meaning of measurement in psychology: Proceedings of the fourth Berkeley symposium on mathematical statistics and probability. Vol. 4.* Berkeley, CA: University of California Press.
Samejima, F. (1969). Estimation of ability using a response pattern of graded scores. *Psychometric Monograph, 17.*
Skrondal, A., & Rabe-Hesketh, S. (2004). *Generalized latent variable modeling: Multilevel, longitudinal, and structural equation models.* Boca Raton, FL: Chapman & Hall.
Snijders, T. (2001). Asymptotic null distribution of person fit statistics with estimated person parameter. *Psychometrika, 66*(3), 331–342.
Strandmark, N. L., & Linn, R. L. (1987). A generalized logistical item response model parameterizing test score inappropriateness. *Applied Psychological Measurement, 11*(4), 355–370.
Thurstone, L. L. (1927). A law of comparative judgment. *Psychological Review, 34,* 273–286.
Trabin, T. E., & Weiss, D. J. (1983). The person response curve: fit of individuals to item response theory models. In D. J. Weiss (Ed.), *New horizons in testing. Latent trait test theory and computerized adaptive testing.* New York: Academic Press.
Van der Linden, W. J., & Hambleton, R. K. (1997). Item response theory: Brief history, common models, and extensions. In W. J. van der Linden & R. K. Hambleton (Eds.), *Handbook of modern item response theory.* New York: Springer.
Warm, T. A. (1989). Weighted likelihood estimation of ability in item response theory. *Psychometrika, 54*(3), 427–450.

Appendix 14.A

R Source Code Used to Produce the Results of Four Examples

```
# CREATION OF A FUNCTION TO ESTIMATE THE PERSONS PARAMETERS
# AND TO PRODUCE A SUMMARY OF THE SIMULATIONS
estimation <- function(X,b,s,c,d,m=0,model,prior="normal") {
 if (model =="T") {
  personParameters <- data.frame(apply(X, 1, m4plEstimate, b=b,
                                        s=s, c=c, d=d, m=0,
                                        model=model, prior=prior))
  colnames(personParameters) <- "T"
 }

 if (model != "T") {
  personParameters <- data.frame(t(apply(X, 1, m4plEstimate, b=b,
                                         s=s, c=c, d=d, m=0,
                                         model=model, prior=prior)) )
 }

 results <- rbind(round(c(mean=mean(personParameters, na.rm=TRUE)),2),
                  round(c(se=sd(personParameters, na.rm=TRUE)),2))
 colnames(results) <- colnames(personParameters)
 rownames(results) <- c("Estimator", "Standard.Error")
 return(results)
}
```

```
# INITIALISATION
require(irtProb)
nItems     <- 60
rep        <- 300
nSubjects  <- 1
# Item Parameters
a          <- rep(1.702,nItems)
b          <- seq(-4.4,length=nItems)
c          <- rep(0,nItems)
d          <- rep(1,nItems)
# Persons parameters of that should be modified to allow production of
tables 1 to 4
theta      <- seq(-1,-1,length=nSubjects)
S          <- runif(n=nSubjects,min=0.0,max=0.0)
C          <- runif(n=nSubjects,min=0.0,max=0.0)
D          <- runif(n=nSubjects,min=0.3,max=0.3)
# Simulation of patterns of response
set.seed(seed = 100)
X          <- ggrm4pl(n=nItems, rep=rep,
                      theta=theta, S=S, C=C, D=D,
                      s=1/a, b=b,c=c,d=d)
# MODELLING
# Estimation of the item parameters and summary of simulations
# Unidimensional modelling
estimation(X,b=b,s=1/a,c=c,d=d,m=0,model="T",  prior="normal")
# Multidimensional modelling
estimation(X,b=b,s=1/a,c=c,d=d,m=0,model="SCD",prior="normal")
```

Appendix 14.B

R Source Code Used to Produce the Results of the Example From the PISA

```
# THIS CODE AND THE DATA FILE ARE LOCATED ON THE FOLLOWING WEBSITE:
# http://www.er.uqam.ca/nobel/r17165/RECHERCHE/COMMUNICATIONS/2010/
# LOADING OF PACKAGES
if (length (which((.packages(all = TRUE)) == "irtProb"))  == 0)
 {install.packages("irtProb",  dependencies=T)}
require(irtProb)

# READING DATA FOR THE 2182 RESPONDENTS WITHOUT MISSING INFORMATION IN 31
ITEMS OF BOOKLET 1
X <-
```

```
read.table(file="http://www.er.uqam.ca/nobel/r17165/RECHERCHE/COMMUNICATIONS/
2010/PISA_2003_SIMON.dat")

# INITIALISATION OF ITEM DIFFICULTY PARAMETER
# FOR 31 ITEMS OF BOOKLET 1
b <- c(
  -1.496,  0.432, -0.666,  1.235, -1.491,
   0.641, -0.906,  1.114,  0.578,  0.494,
   1.982,  0.680, -1.821,  1.462,  0.001,
  -0.879,  0.272,  0.074, -0.582, -0.569,
   0.026,  0.257,  0.098,  0.846, -1.307,
   1.389, -3.077, -0.968, -1.156,  1.563,
   1.033)

# ESTIMATION OF PERSON PARAMETERS
persons <- m4plPersonParameters(x=X, b=b, s=1, c=0, d=1, m=0,
                                model="SCD",
                                prior="uniform", more=FALSE)

# RESULTS
# Table 6
# Displaying parameters of persons for the first 10 respondents
round(persons[1:10,], 2)
# Quantiles at threshold 0.05
quantile(x=persons$S, probs=1-0.05)
quantile(x=persons$C, probs=1-0.05)
quantile(x=persons$D, probs=1-0.05)
# Table 7
# Descriptive statistics and Pearson round(cor(persons),3)
mean(persons);sd(persons);summary(persons)
# Figure 6
# Frequency histograms
par(mfrow=c(2,2))
 hist(persons$T, main="", xlab=expression(theta),
      ylab="Frequency", sub="a)")
 hist(persons$S, main="", xlab=expression(S),
      ylab="Frequency", sub="b)")
 hist(persons$C, main="", xlab=expression(chi),
      ylab="Frequency", sub="c)")
 hist(persons$D, main="", xlab=expression(delta),
      ylab="Frequency", sub="d)")
par(mfrow=c(1,1))
```

15
Missing Data
Issues and Treatments

Michel Rousseau

> *Introduction*
> *Definition, Classification, and Mechanisms*
> *Prevention*
>   Target Population
>   Measurement Tools
>   Data-Entry Procedure
> *Diagnosis*
>   Calculation of the Missing Data Ratio
>   Identification of the Mechanism
> *Treatment*
>   Treatment Methods: An Example
>   Complete Case Methods
>   Imputation Methods
>   Model-Based Methods
> *Conclusion*

We thank Hugo Cantin for translating this chapter from French to English.

Introduction

More than 30 years ago, Rubin (1976) demonstrated the negative impact of missing data in a database on the validity of results. Results from large-scale education assessments can therefore be invalid if missing data are not treated correctly. Some authors, such as Fichman and Cummings (2003) and Enders (2004), mention that in spite of the potential bias caused by missing data, very few scientific papers identify the methods by the researchers to compensate for those missing data. This is even more relevant in the context of studies in education. This chapter provides an overview of the issue and suggests treatment steps: prevention, exploration of the data file, and ultimately the application of a treatment method if necessary. It addresses, from a global point of view, the issue of missing data. However, all aspects of this problem cannot be addressed in a single chapter.

Definition, Classification, and Mechanisms

The term *missing data* refers to a situation where information is missing in a database. For instance, if we ask students to state the number of minutes they spent doing their homework last week, everyone should, in principle, be able to provide this information, even those who did not do any homework. If, however, the same students are asked a question on the importance of parental support, students who did not do their homework would not be able to answer. For the first question, any information that was not observed would be considered missing and some form of treatment would have to be applied, such as the imputation of an expected value. For the second question, it would not be appropriate to apply a treatment, such as the imputation of an expected value, to information that was not observed.

Van der Kamp and Bijleveld (1998) have identified three types of missing data in quantitative research: missing subjects, missing occasions, and missing values. Missing subjects are subjects that have been selected to participate in a research project who, for various reasons, do not. Such missing data include individuals who refuse to participate in or to answer a survey, those who could not be contacted at the time of recruitment, and those who were not available or could not participate. Any subject who was removed without a reasonable motive from a sample by the research team, who provided abnormal answers, or whose behavior suggests that his or her answers are invalid could also be considered a missing subject. For such missing data, the information in the database will be missing for specific subjects in all variables being considered in a research project. Therefore, the representativeness of the sample as compared with the target population will be affected, thus limiting the capacity to generalize the results. That is, the external validity of a research project is threatened by the presence of missing data of this type.

Missing occasions are found in situations where longitudinal research designs are used. Such missing data occur when subjects participate in a measurement occasion but, for various reasons, do not take part in all measurement occasions planned in the longitudinal design. Missing occasions can occur because individuals have moved to another area, died, or refused to continue to participate in the research. This causes data to be available for at least one measurement period and to be missing for at least one measurement period. As for missing subjects, such missing data can affect the representativeness of a sample. However, contrary to missing subjects, information on the variables of interest to the study remains available. This allows, among other things, for the evaluation of differences between subjects with missing occasions and subjects where data are fully available (Van der Kamp & Bijleveld, 1998).

Finally, even though some individuals agree to participate in a survey and on every occasion of a longitudinal study, they can still yield missing values—the third type of missing data. For such missing data, information is available for some of the variables studied but missing for others. Missing values can occur when individuals refuse to provide information, are unable to, or simply forget to answer questions. Such missing data will likely cause problems for the statistical analysis of the results, since most statistical analysis methods are designed to process complete, rectangular data sets (Little & Rubin, 2002). Generally speaking, for statistical analysis software to correctly perform its task, the data must be available for all subjects and all variables.

However, some statistical analysis methods can be used with incomplete matrices. This is addressed in detail later in this chapter.

In addition to these three types of missing data, three mechanisms that can cause missing data to occur are considered. Data can be missing completely at random (MCAR), missing at random (MAR), or not missing at random (NMAR). The definition of these three mechanisms is explained below using the basic principles of sampling.

Data can be missing completely at random (MCAR) if, in a database, the probability of observing a missing value is independent of the value itself or of any other variable. For example, a subject could be sick the day a measurement is taken or could forget to answer some questions after being distracted. MCAR situations are akin to a simple random sampling. For this sampling mechanism, each individual has the same probability of being selected, and subject selection does not depend on any specific individual characteristic. This random selection mechanism ensures that statistics calculated based on these samples are representative of the parameters of the population studied.

Data will be missing at random (MAR) if, in a database, the probability of observing a missing value is independent of the value itself but dependent on another variable. For instance, boys could be more likely than girls to refuse to participate in a research project. For the postulate of a random mechanism to be verified, a completely random mechanism must cause missing values to occur for each of the subgroups (boys and girls in our example). MAR data can be likened to a stratified random sampling. The random nature of the sampling ensures the representativeness of statistics as compared with the parameters of the population even though some adjustments to the estimation of the parameters are necessary.

Finally, data will not be missing at random (NMAR) if the probability of observing a missing value is dependent on the value itself. For example, students who spend less time doing homework are less likely to answer a question on the time spent at home doing homework and studying. For this last mechanism, the situation can be likened to a nonprobabilistic sampling, since certain specific characteristics of the subjects will determine whether a given subject will be part of a sample. For this type of sampling, the estimation of the parameters of the population from the statistics obtained for a sample will very likely be biased.

A final classification, specific to academic performance tests, has been suggested by Lord (1980). This involves unreached items and omitted items. These two types are missing values. However, they are caused by two specific issues: items not reached are those for which an individual was unable to read the statement owing to the time limit imposed on the measurement, and omitted items are items for which the statement was read by a subject who still did not provide an answer. Generally, these two types of missing values are identified by their position in a test as well as by the way in which they must be processed. Unreached items are a block of unanswered items located at the end of a test. Since the lack of answers is due to time constraints and has nothing to do with abilities, they should not be considered in the estimation of the score of an individual subject (Lord, 1980). Omitted items are spread out in a test and must be processed, since the subject had a chance to give the answer.

Prevention

Any treatment method, however efficient, will not completely remove the bias caused by missing values (Allison, 2001). In the planning of a large-scale survey, certain specific factors must be considered because adequate planning can reduce the likelihood of missing data. It is therefore important to pay attention to some aspects of the target population, as well as to the tools being used and the data-entry procedure.

Target Population

Target populations in large-scale academic performance surveys are said to be captive, since the measurements are usually taken during class and participation is often mandatory. For some surveys, questionnaires are administered to a sample student population; for others, all students are required to participate. This reduces the number of potential missing subjects or occasions but cannot prevent missing values.

Therefore it becomes important to review the specific characteristics of certain student subgroups where missing values are more likely to occur. This is especially true for students with reading problems, who will need more time to answer the questions. They are more at risk of being unable to provide the answers owing to the limited time available for the administration of the questionnaires. In Lord's classification, such questions would be considered "not reached" items, since the lack of time combined with the reading problems would explain the missing answer. It would seem appropriate to not consider these items in calculating the scores of these students. Moreover, the level of language used to frame the question could be too difficult for these students, causing them to misunderstand instructions, the wording of questions, or the choices provided for multiple answers. This could lead to a drop in motivation or frustration, which would in turn influence the response rate of students with reading problems (Bradburn, 1992). Finally, specific students could be more likely to react to the nature of the information required because of their age, gender, or socioeconomic status.

A pilot survey on the questionnaires, used with a reduced and representative sample of the target population, allows for the identification of potential problems. A review of the level of language needed to fill the questionnaire with a group composed of specialists can also help to eliminate these issues. When the survey addresses issues that can be potentially sensitive to some populations or subpopulations, the privacy guarantee can also help to reduce nonresponse problems (Singer, van Thurn, & Miller, 1995). It must be mentioned that the sensitivity of the subjects is very likely related to cultural aspects specific to particular populations. In the same manner, the level of confidence in the privacy guarantee may vary from one population to the other.

Measurement Tools

In large-scale surveys, the questionnaire is the main data-collection tool. Apart from the content of questions that may be sensitive to some students, the length of questionnaires is another aspect that can influence nonresponse. In addition to the time constraints they represent for students with reading problems, heavy information output requirements can discourage students who are already less motivated to answer all the questions found in the tools.

As for the length of the questionnaires, special care must be taken to select only the key variables of interest and not to add variables "just in case" the information could prove useful. Also, the rating scales must be as short as possible. However, there are not only negative aspects to a longer questionnaire: it provides more information, which improves the efficiency of some methods of treating missing data, especially imputation methods. The need for information must be balanced with the burden placed on those who are required to answer the questionnaires.

Finally, the look and feel of the questionnaire can also influence nonresponse (Dillman, 2000). For instance, the use of small characters or the lack of spacing between questions could cause some subjects to inadvertently skip questions or to answer the right question in the wrong field. The general visual aspect of a questionnaire can increase its readability and overall appeal.

Data-Entry Procedure

When many questionnaires are to be entered in a database, it is only natural to try to automate the procedure—for instance, using scan sheets or questionnaires formatted with predefined fields. Compared with manual data entry, automated procedures can greatly reduce the risk of encountering missing values. Operations such as training data-entry agents and controlling the quality of the work can improve the quality of the data-entry process. Using web or software applications to administer questionnaires is another way of controlling for missing data.

Diagnosis

Calculation of the Missing Data Ratio

Diagnosis begins with calculation of the ratio of data missing in the database. This ratio allows researchers to get a detailed picture of the database and supports the decisions taken regarding the methods chosen to address the issue. For example, if the response rate of a variable in the database is too low, the researchers could decide to eliminate it from the analysis model instead of risking the use of a strongly biased variable in the model. Even if, at first glance, this dimension seems simple enough, calculation of the ratio can be complex, since the various types of missing data—including subjects, occasions, and values as well as both sides of a matrix, subjects, and variables—must be taken into consideration.

Participation or response rate is one of the first aspects to consider: it concerns missing subjects. The participation rate is obtained by dividing the number of subjects who participated in the survey by the total number of participants expected. Even if students are required to take part in a survey, a certain proportion could be sick or might decide not to show up if the results will not affect their grades (e.g., for the PISA or TIMSS). For these two studies, a replacement sample has been planned to address these situations, but even this sample is not without its problems. In 2000, PISA results obtained in the Netherlands have been removed from the international comparisons of the study because the response rate was too low.

Once the data have been entered into a database, the missing data ratio can be examined in a number of ways. For subjects, it is possible to calculate the amount of missing data for each individual in the database and thus to identify subjects with missing data in one or more fields. For variables, it is possible to calculate the amount of missing data per variable and to identify the variables where data are missing in at least one field. The ratio must be considered both from a subject and variable point of view to fully elucidate the cause of the problem and make decisions regarding the treatment method. For example, a study of the situation could identify a number of subjects sharing some characteristics for whom a great quantity of data are missing. Also, certain variables that are deemed sensitive could be removed if too many data are missing. This type of solution could not be applied to situations where missing data are not concentrated in a specific subgroup of subjects or variables.

The ratio of missing data in a database will be calculated using the total number of possible observations. For example, if a database has 500 subjects and 10 variables, the total number of possible observations will be 5,000 (500 × 10). The number of missing observations in the database will be divided by this number of possible observations. If the database has 300 missing observations, the missing data ratio will be 6% (300/5,000). Note that the calculation of the missing data ratio does not take into account the selection probability of individuals, since the diagnosis of the problem is performed on the sample regardless of a generalization to a specific population.

Identification of the Mechanism

The mechanism behind missing data is one of the most important aspects of the identification of the appropriate treatment method. However, this operation remains limited, since it allows the detection only of the absence of a completely random mechanism (McKnight, McKnight, Sidani, & Figuerdo, 2007). Little (1988) proposed a general identification method based on a chi-square test. This method, implemented in SPSS among other software, allows the testing of the null hypothesis, according to which a completely random mechanism explains missing values in a database. If the value of chi square is statistically significant, the null hypothesis must be rejected and the researcher must conclude that data are missing at random (MAR) or not missing at random (NMAR).

Making a distinction between these two mechanisms is difficult. In general, if a researcher has control over the occurrence of missing data, it is appropriate to consider a random mechanism as plausible (Schafer, 1997). If a researcher cannot control this mechanism, it is then appropriate to consider the missing data as being NMAR. In other circumstances, access to additional external information is required to test whether data are MAR or NMAR. This information can include, for example, parameters from previous studies or data from the monitoring of subjects for whom data are missing.

Treatment

The major issue with missing data is that most statistical analysis methods have been developed to deal with complete matrices. Therefore, before proceeding with the statistical analysis, some kind of treatment must be applied to a matrix containing missing data, even though the researcher will not always be aware that a treatment has been used. These various treatment methods can be divided into three categories: complete case methods, imputation methods, and model-based methods.

Treatment Methods: An Example

In order to demonstrate the impacts of missing data treatment methods on results of analysis, the same example is used for the entire section on the presentation of these treatment methods. A database contains 250 subjects and four variables: (1) the results of a science test (*science*), (2) raising of awareness on environmental issues (*envir*), (3) the pleasure provided by science (*pleasure*), and (4) the socioeconomic status of the family (*ses*). A regression model is used to attempt to predict the results of the science test in relation to the three other variables in the database. Descriptive statistics, along with the regression coefficient, are included in Table 15.1.

Table 15.1 Descriptive Statistics and Regression Coefficients for the Entire Sample

Variable	Average	Standard Deviation	Nonstandard Regression Coefficient (B)	Standard Error of Coefficient B
Intercept			514.46	4.65
science	526.12	89.31		
envir	0.154	1.00	27.65	5.06
pleasure	0.103	1.14	22.27	4.43
ses	0.201	0.815	25.38	5.77

266 • Michel Rousseau

These data are taken from the Canadian sample of the 2006 PISA. The regression model allows for prediction of 37.4% of the variance of the science test results. All regression coefficients are statistically significant at P <0.05.

Using this database, a NMAR mechanism has been simulated for the three independent variables. For *envir* and *ses*, the smaller the value for a given student, the higher its chances of being deleted. For *pleasure*, the opposite relationship was used to delete values. For each variable, 20% of the values were deleted.

Complete Case Methods

The simplest way of treating missing data is to remove from the statistical analysis all subjects where at least one value is missing for the variables included in our analysis. For example, in the analysis of a regression model including three independent variables, subjects with at least one missing value on either the dependent variable or one of the three independent variables will be removed from the analysis. This method is called listwise deletion; very often it is the default option of statistical analysis software.

From a practical point of view, this method limits the possibility of comparing analysis results, since subjects, on whom the calculations will be performed, will tend to vary according to the response rate of variables included in the analysis model. For instance, if we want to compare the prediction quality of a model using two independent variables instead of all three and we remove a variable with a low response rate, the database used to calculate the parameter estimates for both models will not be the same, thus limiting the validity of the comparisons. Another practical limitation of this method is that it will tend to reduce the statistical power, which is directly influenced by the size of the sample.

Table 15.2 shows the descriptive statistics obtained by the use of both complete case methods presented. For *envir* and *ses*, since the simulated nonrandom mechanism mostly deleted

Table 15.2 Descriptive Statistics and Regression Coefficients Obtained via the Listwise and Pairwise Deletion Methods

	Listwise Deletion	Pairwise Deletion
Average		
envir	0.383	
pleasure	−0.175	
ses	0.356	
Standard deviation		
envir	0.923	
pleasure	1.049	
ses	0.786	
Nonstandard regression coefficient (B)		
B_0 – Intercept	516.21	510.07
B_1 – envir	23.72	24.52
B_2 – pleasure	27.05	24.85
B_3 – ses	24.72	30.93
Standard error of coefficient B		
se_0 – Intercept	7.91	7.06
se_1 – envir	7.70	6.64
se_2 – pleasure	6.77	5.96
se_3 – ses	9.65	7.60

small values, averages obtained with the listwise deletion method were higher than for complete data. The opposite is true for *pleasure*. Also, standard deviations are lower for these three variables.

The objective of the second method, called pairwise deletion, is to build a correlation or variance/covariance matrix calculated using the available data for each pair of variables. Consequently the number of subjects by correlation or covariance coefficient will vary based on the distribution of the missing data in the database. Instead of performing a statistical analysis on the matrix, this correlation or covariance matrix will provide a basis for the analysis. For example, factorial analyses are performed using the correlation matrix. The practical limitation of this method lies in the fact that there is a high risk of obtaining a matrix that will not be positive and adequately defined (Enders, 2001), therefore preventing further analysis.

Table 15.2 also shows the regression coefficients and the standard errors of these coefficients, obtained after the application of the listwise and pairwise deletion methods. Compared with results provided by complete data, the predicted variance proportion is smaller for the listwise deletion method (28.9%) as well as for the pairwise deletion method (33.2%). As for the value of regression coefficients, the values obtained using complete data differ. Finally, since the number of subjects used is smaller, standard errors of coefficients are higher than with complete data. However, all coefficients of the regression model remain statistically significant.

In addition to the practical limitations, the real efficiency of complete case methods must be put into question. As shown in the last example, parameter estimates obtained after the application of these treatment methods are valid only when missing data are MCAR.

Imputation Methods

Imputation methods replace missing data in a matrix with plausible values. A value is said to be plausible when it represents a value that would have been observed if data had been complete. A wide range of imputation strategies have been developed; they can be divided in two major categories: simple and multiple.

SIMPLE IMPUTATION METHODS

There are a variety of simple imputation methods, divided in explicit and implicit methods (Little & Rubin, 2002). Explicit methods use a distribution of predicted values based on a formal statistical model, whereas implicit methods rely on an algorithm for which the properties of the statistical model are not known.

EXAMPLES OF EXPLICIT METHODS

Various examples of explicit single imputation methods are described in this section, including intersubject, intrasubject, and a combination of both.

INTERSUBJECT METHODS

These methods replace missing values on a variable using the distribution of values observed for this variable. One of the most common methods (Roth, 1994) consists in replacing any missing value on a variable with the average value observed for this variable. Despite its popularity, this method is not efficient (McKnight et al., 2007). By replacing the missing values with a constant, the variance of this variable is automatically reduced. This reduction will increase with the proportion of missing values. Consequently standard errors and correlation estimates of this variable with other variables will be biased. Also, this treatment method will provide biased average estimates when data are not MCAR. Finally, this procedure can be applied only to continuous

Table 15.3 Descriptive Statistics and Regression Coefficients Obtained by Mean Imputation and Regression Imputation

	Mean Imputation	Regression Imputation
Average		
envir	0.383	0.340
pleasure	−0.175	−1.471
ses	0.356	0.359
Standard deviation		
envir	0.835	0.896
pleasure	0.950	1.047
ses	0.712	0.781
Nonstandard regression coefficient (B)		
B_0 – Intercept	509.00	510.74
B_1 – envir	25.51	26.40
B_2 – pleasure	27.00	26.43
B_3 – ses	33.92	28.67
Standard error of coefficient B		
se_0 – Intercept	5.99	5.51
se_1 – envir	5.93	5.45
se_2 – pleasure	5.29	4.70
se_3 – ses	6.89	6.15

variables. Other methods, such as using the median value, can also be used to allocate missing values from the distribution of observed values for a variable. These various approaches share the same limitations as the imputation by replacement of the average of a variable.

Table 15.3 shows the descriptive statistics obtained after the application of the mean imputation. The averages obtained for the three variables are identical to those observed after the application of the listwise deletion method. The values observed in standard deviations are lower than those for complete data. The variance proportion, as explained by the regression model, is now 29.1%. As is the case with complete case methods, the regression coefficient values differ from what is observed with complete data.

Intrasubject Methods

Intrasubject methods are similar to intersubject methods, but a missing value on a variable for a given subject will be allocated using values observed in other variables for this same subject. These methods are essentially used for scales containing several items. Since these items are considered as sharing a common latent variable, information available on other items may be used to allocate the missing data on a specific item. Usually the average of other items is used to allocate the missing value. This procedure is criticized and with it, compared with other methods, biases would be stronger when data are NMAR (Rousseau, 2006).

Inter- and Intrasubject Methods

These methods are improvements over the methods described above since they allow for a greater amount of information to be taken in consideration in the imputation of the missing values. In addition to accounting for the values observed for a variable, they also consider the relationships between this variable and other variables contained in the database. The most common methods of this type are conditional mean imputation and regression model imputation.

Conditional mean imputation consists in regrouping subjects into subgroups defined by one or more variables theoretically associated with the variable for which missing data are to be imputed. For instance, if the gender is theoretically associated with the variable for which missing data are to be replaced, a mean value of this variable will be calculated for boys, and all missing values for boys will be replaced by this mean value. The same procedure will be applied to girls. This method will reduce sample variance for this variable, which will result in standard errors and correlation values being less biased.

Regression model imputation consists in predicting a missing value using a regression equation that includes a certain number of independent variables. A regression model must be developed for each variable with missing values, and regression coefficients will be calculated using complete cases for the variables included in the model. Imputation of missing values will be performed using the regression coefficients of the model. Normally a new regression model must be built for each variable in the database for which missing values must be replaced. The choice of variables to include in the regression model is an issue that could limit the efficiency of this treatment method. This choice can be based on theoretical or empirical considerations by identifying the variables with the strongest ties to the one for which values must be assigned. Basing the choice of variables on purely empirical considerations increases the risk of making imputation errors and allocating improbable values. Also, variables selected for the regression model must not be used in future statistical analyses, since they will artificially increase the relationships between variables. Finally, the procedure can be cumbersome in situations where the number of variables is high.

Inter- and intrasubject methods are valid only if data are MCAR, and even when this mechanism is present, they tend to bias the standard errors of the parameter estimates, since the variability of the estimations is decreased. This issue can be controlled by drawing an allocated value from the distribution of possible values instead of its center (Little & Rubin, 2002). For example, if a regression model is used to allocate a missing value, instead of using the value predicted by the regression model, the value will be drawn from a distribution of possible values for which the predicted value is an average. Even if this procedure provides a more accurate estimation of standard errors, these errors will be biased if missing data are not MCAR.

Table 15.3 shows the statistics obtained after applying the regression imputation method. Averages for three variables are lower than averages provided by complete data. As for other treatment methods, averages obtained after using the regression imputation method are higher for *envir* and *ses* variables while the average for *pleasure* is lower. Also, values for standard deviations are slightly less higher than for complete data. As for the regression model tested, the predicted variance percentage is of 33.6% for this imputation method. Regression coefficient values are different, notably the intercept value and the coefficient of variables *pleasure* and *ses*. Finally, regression coefficients for *envir* and *pleasure* are statistically significant, which is no longer the case for *ses*.

Examples of Implicit Methods
Unlike explicit methods, implicit methods do not use a mathematical model to allocate missing values, thus making their impacts more difficult to estimate.

Hot-deck and Cold-deck Methods
The terms *hot-deck* and *cold-deck* date back to the time when computers used punched cards. The imputation of missing values for a subject based on those available in a database is called *hot-deck imputation*. If the imputation is performed using subjects from another database, it will instead be called a cold-deck imputation. There are several approaches to both hot-deck and cold-deck imputation. The methods seek to identify, based on the available subjects, potential donor subjects from which a value will be drawn to allocate a missing value on a variable. The methods differ by the way they identify potential donor subjects and select the value to allocate.

These treatment methods are only efficient if data are MCAR (McKnight et al., 2007). If data are MAR and the mechanism is known, these methods can be used, but they must take the mechanism explaining missing data into account. However, knowledge of this mechanism is a rare occurrence. In other circumstances, there will be an unpredictable bias on parameter estimates. Moreover, the application of these methods, especially a hot-deck method, could decrease the variability of value distribution, since allocated values are replaced by values already in the database. This decrease in variability will affect standard errors of estimates, even though this bias will probably be lower than for methods such as mean imputation.

The various simple imputation methods share a common limitation: a reduction of the variance, which affects the standard error of parameter estimates even in accurate imputation models. This causes significance tests to be too liberal, with null hypotheses being rejected too easily. Also, these treatment methods can be treacherous, as some researchers will tend to "forget" that they are working with an incomplete matrix and that their imputation mechanism of choice could create strong biases in statistical analysis results.

Rubin (1987) suggested using the multiple imputation method to address the limitations associated with simple imputation methods, notably to control biases related to the estimation of standard errors. The next section describes the multiple imputation method, which is fast becoming the method of choice to treat missing data (McKnight et al., 2007).

Multiple Imputation Methods

Multiple imputation shares similarities with simple imputation methods, such as regression imputation. This last method replaces a missing value with a value predicted using a specific model. As for all regression models, it is not without errors, meaning that the value predicted, and therefore imputed, is not necessarily the value expected. Multiple imputation accounts for this uncertainty when values are allocated based on a theoretical data distribution model (Schafer & Graham, 2002). In order to predict a value for any missing data, multiple imputation, instead of providing a single matrix, will generate m plausible matrices. These m matrices contain the same observed data, but the values of imputed data can be different. This variability between the predicted values of m matrices reflects the uncertainty associated with imputation (Fichman & Cummings, 2003). One of its key advantages is that it enables, later on, the use of "traditional" statistical analysis methods (Schafer & Graham, 2002), but with m identical analyses instead of a single one. These m analyses are then combined, and the variability of parameter estimates is considered in the calculation of standard errors, which makes significance tests more conservative.

Parameter estimates obtained with the m analyses are combined using relatively simple operations, defined by Rubin (1987). In this method, Q represents the parameter of interest of a population, such as the mean. If a sample can use all available data, the parameter estimate of the parameter will be $\hat{Q}$, with $\sqrt{U}$ being the standard error for this estimate. If m allocated matrices are used, $\hat{Q}$ and $\sqrt{U}$ cannot be calculated directly, and m versions of these two statistics are generated.

According to the method suggested by Rubin (1987), the combined estimate $\overline{Q}$ of the parameter will simply be the average m of estimates $\hat{Q}$, or

$$\overline{Q} = m^{-1} \sum_{j=1}^{m} \hat{Q}^{(j)} \tag{1}$$

The variance of the combined estimate $\overline{Q}$ is divided in two parts: intraimputation variance, which is an average of the variances:

Table 15.4 Regression Coefficient Average

	1	2	3	4	5	Average
B_0 – Intercept	510.35	511.23	512.80	511.98	511.35	511.54
B_1 – envir	26.92	27.90	23.87	28.88	26.41	26.80
B_2 – pleasure	24.27	27.56	25.26	26.26	24.90	25.65
B_3 – ses	26.13	26.66	28.18	29.80	27.94	27.74

Table 15.5 Intraimputation Variance

	1	2	3	4	5	Intraimputation Variance
B_0 – Intercept	5.44	5.31	5.24	5.37	5.35	5.34
B_1 – envir	5.30	4.96	5.30	5.14	5.27	5.19
B_2 – pleasure	4.77	4.67	4.87	4.78	4.73	4.76
B_3 – ses	5.90	6.07	5.99	6.10	6.30	6.07

Table 15.6 Interimputation Variance

	1	2	3	4	5	Interimputation Variance
B_0 – Intercept	−1.19	−0.31	1.26	0.44	−0.19	0.83
B_1 – envir	0.12	1.10	−2.93	2.08	−0.39	3.57
B_2 – pleasure	−1.38	1.91	−0.39	0.61	−0.75	1.66
B_3 – ses	−1.61	−1.08	0.44	2.06	0.20	2.06

$$\overline{U} = m^{-1} \sum_{j=1}^{m} U^{(j)} \tag{2}$$

and interimputation variance:

$$B = (m-1)^{-1} \sum_{j=1}^{m} \left[\hat{Q}^{(j)} - \overline{Q} \right]^2 \tag{3}$$

The total variance is the corrected sum of both components of the variance:

$$T = \overline{U} + (1 + m^{-1})B \tag{4}$$

The total standard error is equal to the square root of T. This standard error is used for building a confidence interval around the combined estimate $\overline{Q}$.

Table 15.4 shows the regression coefficients obtained for five imputed values matrices. Also, the last column of the table shows the average for all five matrices. In this example, estimate $\overline{Q}$ of the intercept is equal to the average of the five values, or 511.54.

Tables 15.5 and 15.6 present the intraimputation variance $\overline{U}$ and interimputation variance B obtained for five imputed values matrices. For the intercept estimate, the intraimputation variance is equal to the average of the variances, or 5.34, and the interimputation variance B is equal to 0.83. The total variance T is 6.34 for a standard error of 2.52.

The validity of results provided by the combination procedure defined by Rubin relies on the efficiency of the process used to obtain the complete matrices. Schafer (1997) developed a method for performing this operation. Starting with the hypothetical case of a researcher who collected, from a sample of subjects, information from three variables, Y1, Y2 et Y3, for which it is supposed that the joint distribution in the population is a normal distribution. As in the majority of research projects, data are missing for variable Y3 for a certain number of participants. The sample can then be split into two subgroups: subgroup A includes subjects for whom information is complete, and subgroup B includes subjects for whom Y3 data are missing. Normally, the population parameters are not known for these three variables. If they were known, however, as in Monte Carlo procedures, for example, the multiple imputation would be performed in the manner described below:

Subgroup A requires no imputation. For subgroup B, a linear regression analysis is performed first, with Y3 as a dependent variable and Y1 and Y2 as independent variables. The Y1 and Y2 values of subjects for which Y3 data are missing are then used to predict the missing Y3 value. Value $\hat{Y}_3$ is allocated by adding another value taken from the distribution of residual values to the predicted value. This replacement procedure is repeated m times, depending on the number of matrices deemed necessary.

In a real situation, the population parameters are not known, so there is no choice but to try to estimate them. It would be possible, for example, to estimate these parameters using data from subgroup A, where all the necessary information is present. However, this procedure is not ideal, as it does not account for all the data in the database. However, more adequate approaches have been developed, such as those based on maximum likelihood, which allow the distribution of all three variables to be considered (Schafer, 1997). The EM (*expectation-maximization*) algorithm is one of the most common estimation methods for these specific cases (Schafer & Graham, 2002; Little & Rubin, 2002).

Once the parameter estimates of the regression model are identified, the researcher will be able to use these estimates to replace missing values—an operation that will be repeated m times. Surveys such as the PISA perform five different imputations.

This simple example gives a good idea of the way multiple imputation works. However, a real research situation is a lot more complex, so a third subgroup, subgroup C, will be added. It includes subjects for which Y1 and Y2 data are missing. In this situation, in addition to predicting the value of Y3 for subgroup B, values for Y1 and Y2 will also have to be predicted simultaneously for subgroup C.

If the joint distribution parameters are known for these three variables, imputation will be easy. In this example though they are unknown, and therefore have to be estimated. Joint distribution parameters of variables Y1, Y2, and Y3 must be estimated using all of the data present for subgroups A, B, and C. Maximal likelihood estimators, such as those provided by algorithm EM, will use all the information available for the three variables. This algorithm is incidentally recognized as an efficient missing data treatment method (Schafer & Graham, 2002).

Using the joint distribution parameter estimates of the three variables, it is possible to perform a multiple imputation for subgroups B and C. To this end, Rubin (1987) suggests an operation inspired by the Bayesian approach, which involves drawing distribution parameter values at random from an a posteriori distribution of these parameters, obtained via the likelihood of observed data function and an a priori distribution. Schafer (1997) developed the data augmentation method, which allows such an operation to be performed. This method is a procedure based on a Markov chain simulation (Sinharay, Stern, & Russel, 2001). First, missing data are replaced by plausible values drawn at random from the distribution defined by EM estimates. Distribution parameters are then estimated again using this first complete matrix. This iteration is repeated until the model is consistent, meaning until only minor differences are observed in parameter values (Sinharay et al., 2001). This is a Markov chain procedure, which can be repeated indefinitely, each iteration generating a plausible matrix. However, only when the model has achieved consistency is it appropriate to use the matrices obtained via this method (Schafer, 1997).

It is important to specify that the data augmentation method developed by Schafer (1997) is based on the postulate of the multivariate normal distribution of $Y1$, $Y2$, and $Y3$. This postulate generally does not always apply to real data, especially when data are ordinal, which is the case for answers to a Likert-type scale, for example. It seems that this method is efficient even when data do not fit this postulate perfectly and that the sample is small (Graham & Schafer, 1999). Also, Schafer and Graham (2002) report that this method, based on a normal model, has proven its efficiency in a variety of situations. However, in some cases, use of the multivariate normal distribution model is not recommended at all, as for nominal and therefore nonordinal category variables.

However, this imputation method relies on the postulate that data are missing at random (Schafer, 1997). Its efficiency cannot be guaranteed when data are not missing at random (Pigott, 2001; Schafer & Graham, 2002). Some specific treatment methods are proposed for data not missing at random, but these remain experimental for the time being (Sinharay et al., 2001). Also, with no commercial software currently supporting procedures of this type, they remain rather uncommon. According to some researchers, multiple imputation would be robust even for data not missing at random (King, Honaker, Joseph, & Scheve, 2001). Fichman and Cummings (2003) state that it remains more adequate than the listwise deletion method. Nevertheless, additional research must be conducted to assess the robustness of multiple imputation with regard to the refutation of the postulate for data missing at random.

Multiple imputation provides many benefits. First, as in simple imputations, analyses can be performed using the most common analysis methods and software, such as SAS or SPSS. This allows the imputation model to be separated from the analysis model (Pigott, 2001). Also, when applied correctly, this method enables the efficient resolution for most statistical analyses of issues caused by missing data (Schafer & Graham, 2002).

Second, it is not necessary to reallocate values with each new analysis. Contrary to some missing data treatment methods, multiple imputation does not make any distinction between independent and dependent variables. The imputation model preserves the key characteristics of the joint distribution, such as averages,, and correlations. Therefore a method that keeps these characteristics in a matrix maintains the linear relationships that tie each variable to the others (Schafer & Graham, 2002). In complementary analyses, any variable can be considered as dependent or independent.

Third, it is possible to use distributions other than the multivariate normal distribution to create the m allocated databases. This method allows the verification of the impact of the distribution on the results and reflects some uncertainty as to the distribution characteristics used for the imputation.

Finally, a relatively low number of allocated matrices are required to provide accurate parameter estimates. For example, with a 50% missing data ratio, the use of 10 such sets will ensure an efficiency of 95% (Schafer & Graham, 2002). This is a general efficiency rate that does not consider all the factors related to the specifications of the survey. For more information on the operations required to estimate the efficiency of the number of matrices, see Schafer and

Graham (2002). In most cases, three to five allocated matrices would be enough to yield excellent results (Sinharay et al., 2001).

Model-Based Methods

These treatment methods are not intended to replace missing values but to estimate parameters using the information observed, even if this information is incomplete. The most common procedure is the maximum likelihood (ML) method (McKnight et al., 2007). It must be noted that this procedure has not been developed to treat specific cases of missing data but that among its features is the ability to estimate unbiased model parameters using an incomplete matrix if the data are MAR (Allison, 2001). ML is found in most commercial statistical software, such as SPSS or SAS. This procedure is used, among other things, to estimate the parameters of structural equation and multilevel models or the parameters of items in the item response theory.

Real-life situations rarely allow the use of a simple ML procedure. Missing data patterns do not have the specific format required to apply the factorization of the likelihood function (Little & Rubin, 2002). In these situations, estimates are provided by the expectation-maximization (EM) method. It is an iterative method that consists in (1) replacing missing data using an estimate of these values; (2) estimating model parameter values; (3) replacing, once again, the missing values using the parameters provided in the second phase; and (4) reestimating model parameter values until consistency is achieved—that is, until the values of the model parameters tend to remain the same. The EM method is therefore considered an iterative process. It can be used when the statistical analysis is not based on a ML method (e.g., a partial least-squares regression analysis). A first step would be to build a variance-covariance matrix using the EM method and then to estimate the regression model parameters via this matrix.

Conclusion

Since missing data and an inadequate treatment are likely to bias the results of a study, the issue must be addressed when the results are released, whether in an internal or a public report or in papers published in professional and scientific journals. In writing a paper, a researcher must identify the scope of the issue, the solutions used to address the issue, and the possible impacts on the results of the study. This information must allow readers to pass critical judgment on the probable biases related to missing data.

More specifically, it is important to clearly identify whether missing data are present in the published study. Missing data must be identified by type (subject, occasion, or value), and all types that can potentially be encountered must be mentioned. A researcher must not focus on a single type of data and forget about the likelihood of other missing data types being present. For example, the researcher could include the ratio of missing subjects in his or her report without addressing the missing values in his or her database. The ratio of missing data of each type must also be identified, since the biases may be higher as this ratio increases. The ratio affects biases, since data are usually not missing at random. The researcher can also study the reasons behind missing data. These reasons could help determine whether data are more likely to be MCAR, MAR, or NMAR.

Clearly identifying the treatment method used is important. The method or methods selected must be supported by theoretical and empirical arguments. Finally, based on all previous information, the discussion must include a section on the impact of missing data and of the solutions applied on the results and findings of the study.

References

Allison, P. D. (2001). *Missing data.* Sage University papers series on quantitative applications in the social sciences (pp. 7–136). Thousand Oaks, CA: Sage.
Bradburn, N. M. (1992). A response to the nonresponse problem. *Public Opinion Quarterly, 56,* 391–397.
Dillman, D. A. (2000). *Mail and Internet survey: The tailored design method.* Hoboken, NJ: Wiley.
Enders, C. K. (2001). The performance of the full information maximum of likelihood estimator in multiple regression models with missing data. *Educational and Psychological measurement, 61,* 713–740.
Enders, C. K. (2004). The impact of missing data on sample reliability estimates: Implications for reliability reporting practices. *Educational and Psychological Measurement, 64,* 419–436.
Fichman, M., & Cummings, J. N. (2003). Multiple imputation for missing data: Making the most of what you know. *Organizational Research Methods, 6,* 282–308.
Graham, J. W., & Schafer, J. L. (1999). On the performance of multiple imputation for multivariate data with small sample size. In R. Hoyle (Ed.), *Statistical strategies of small sample research.* Thousand Oaks, CA: Sage.
King, G., Honaker, J., Joseph, A., & Scheve, K. (2001). Analyzing incomplete political science data: An alternative algorithm for multiple imputation. *American Political Science Review, 95,* 49–69.
Little, R. J. A. (1988). A test of missing completely at random for multivariate data with missing values. *Journal of the American Statistical Association, 83,* 1198–1202.
Little, R. J. A., & Rubin, D. B. (2002). *Statistical analysis with missing data* (2nd ed.). Hoboken, NJ: Wiley.
Lord, F. M. (1980). *Applications of item response theory to practical testing problems.* Mahwah, NJ: Erlbaum.
McKnight, P. E., McKnight, K. M., Sidani, S., & Figuerdo, A. J. (2007). *Missing data: A gentle introduction.* New York: Guilford Press.
Pigott, T. D. (2001). A review of methods for missing data. *Educational Research and Evaluation, 7,* 353–383.
Roth, P. L. (1994). Missing data: A conceptual review for applied psychologists. *Personal Psychology, 47,* 537–560.
Rousseau, M. (2006). *L'impact des méthodes de traitement des valeurs manquantes sur les qualities psychométriques d'échelles de mesure de type Likert.* Thèse de doctorat présenté à la Faculté des sciences de l'éducation de l'Université Laval.
Rubin, D. B. (1976). Inference and missing data. *Biometrika, 20,* 159–183.
Rubin, D. B. (1987). *Multiple imputation for nonresponse in surveys.* Hoboken, NJ: Wiley.
Schafer, J. L. (1997). *Analysis of incomplete multivariate data.* New York: Chapman and Hall.
Schafer, J. L., & Graham, J. W. (2002). Missing data: Our view of the state of the art. *Psychological Methods, 7,* 147–177.
Singer, E., van Thurn, D. R., & Miller, E. R. (1995). Confidentiality assurances and response. A quantitative review of the experimental literature. *Public Opinion Quarterly, 59,* 66–77.
Sinharay, S., Stern, H. S., & Russel, D. (2001). The use of multiple imputation for the analysis of missing data. *Psychological Methods, 6,* 317–329.
Van der Kamp, L. J. T., & Bijleveld, C. C. J. H. (1998). Methodological issues in longitudinal research in Bijleveld, C. C. J. H. & Van der Kamp, L. J. T. (Eds.), *Longitudinal data analysis* (pp. 1–45). London: Sage.

16
Measurement and Statistical Analysis Issues With Longitudinal Assessment Data

Bruno D. Zumbo, Amery D. Wu, and Yan Liu

Introduction
Measurement Issues
  Temporal Measurement Invariance
  Standardization
  Vertical Scaling
Statistical Analysis Issues
  Data Collected Over Two Periods in Time
  Data Collected Over More Than Two Periods in Time
Conclusion

Introduction

To study the time-related change in educational achievement, scores on knowledge tests, or personal attributes is a primary reason for collecting longitudinal data. Change is a fundamental concept in educational, sociological, and psychological settings. For some areas of research, such as developmental psychology or areas involving program evaluation, change is a central aspect of study. In other areas, change may not be the central aspect of study, but it can still be of concern. The term *longitudinal* is sometimes used to suggest situations in which change is investigated over long periods of time (e.g., decades), but we are using the term more generally to describe any setting in which one is interested in change and in which (1) the same people are observed repeatedly over time, (2) commensurable measurements (including parallel tests) are used, and (3) the timing for each measurement is known (Lloyd, 2010; McArdle & Nesselroade, 2003).

There is now a vast methodological and statistical research literature going back to the early 1950s addressing issues of measurement, research design, and analysis of longitudinal data. For recent reviews and developments see, for example, Bryk and Raudenbush (1987); Lloyd (2010); McArdle and Nesselroade (2003); Raudenbush (2001); Singer and Willett (2003); Willett and Singer (1991); Wu, Liu, Gadermann, and Zumbo (2010); Zimmerman (2009); and Zumbo (1999). Given the vast literature, our purpose is to discuss some lingering issues in the methodological literature that are reflective of our program of research. These topics were selected because they cut across matters of measurement and statistical analysis in commonly encountered longitudinal studies of educational and psychological phenomena, and they demonstrate some of the fundamental and lingering issues in the field.

The chapter is divided into two broad sections, with subsections. The first section, titled Measurement Issues, has three subsections: (1) Temporal Measurement Invariance, (2) Standardization, and (3) Vertical Scaling. The second section, titled Statistical Analysis Issues, is divided into two subsections: (1) Data Collected Over Two Periods in Time and (2) Data Collected Over More Than Two Periods in Time, the latter of which is also subdivided into three sections titled (i) Hierarchical Linear Models, (ii) Structural Equation Models, and (iii) Multiple-Indicators Latent Growth Model.

We chose to discuss the measurement issues first because they apply, at least in principle, to all of the statistical analysis methods. The three measurement topics are interrelated and, in essence, deal with the matter of what are the necessary measurement properties to be able to compare scores over time. The temporal invariance subsection addresses the following two questions: How does one determine if he or she is measuring the same (or commensurable) variable over time? And, if one measures the same variable but differently over time, how can one link the scales on a common metric to allow comparisons of those different measures over time? It makes no sense to consider change, at least of the quantitative variety of change, if one is not measuring the same variable in the same manner with the same respondents over time. We do not address the case of qualitative change over time. Instead, as is the case in mainstream measurement and methodological literature, our focus is on whether the level of a quantitative variable(s) increases or decreases over time and whether it does so systematically. The second subsection addresses the matter of transforming the scores to make them appear to be on the same metric by applying a linear transformation (e.g., a z-score transformation) and the limitations of doing so. The final subsection provides a brief overview of psychometric methods for linking vertical scales.

The statistical analysis section first deals with longstanding matters of how one should study change when only two time points of data are collected. Some would argue that two time points of data is simply insufficient to do anything at all, whereas we present a more balanced view that if difference scores make sense from a subject matter perspective and if the corresponding analysis is likely to have appropriate statistical power, there is no reason to avoid their use. The second statistical analysis section provides brief descriptions of widely used statistical methods for the analysis of longitudinal data from more than two points in time: hierarchical linear models, structural equation models, and multiple-indicators latent growth models. These three methods all focus on the analysis of the trajectories of change.

Measurement Issues

Temporal Measurement Invariance

The issue of *temporal measurement invariance* is often neglected in longitudinal studies. We have found that this lack of concern for temporal measurement invariance is due to the (incorrect) belief that using the same instrument over time is sufficient to warrant comparability. However, the investigation of temporal measurement invariance examines whether the metric of the outcome variables remains the same when measured at multiple time points on the same group of individuals. The purpose is to examine whether the scores of the outcome variables are confounded by a temporal change in the scale of measurement. Establishing temporal measurement invariance is the prerequisite for analyzing change. Temporal measurement invariance provides evidence that the studied construct is measured on the same metric over time; hence cross-time comparison is warranted and the results and interpretations are not biased by a lack of measurement invariance.

The testing of measurement invariance is an elementary topic that is not described in detail herein because several descriptions are widely available in the literature. For example, Brown (2006, pp. 252–266) provides a detailed description of the technical and statistical issues involved, as well as an example using software such as *Mplus* and LISREL, in testing temporal measurement invariance using structural equation modeling. The key point is that one is testing competing (nested) structural equation models using single-group-parameter constraints. Furthermore, prespecified correlated measurement errors are needed in the model to capture the obvious temporal extracovariation induced by using the same (or parallel) measure over time. Brown also addresses the important matter of whether one should specify intercept terms and equality of error variances over time. Although introductory descriptions of testing longitudinal measurement invariance have been widely available for some time, it is noteworthy, as Brown himself states, that this type of invariance testing is rarely addressed in the applied literature. The reader should note that the matter of testing and modeling temporal invariance is also discussed below in the section on the multiple-indicators latent growth model.

We have found, in our experience, that researchers often assume temporal comparability when the measures are different over time. However, changing the observed indicators over time is one of the most frequent sources of lack of measurement invariance. Researchers often modify their instrument over time by changing the content and/or the response format. Examples of such practice might be using a four-point Likert response format at time one and a six-point response format at time two, as well as dropping or adding items to the instrument. In these cases, a longitudinal study based on the observed total score of the modified items would be meaningless because cross-time total scores are clearly on different metrics (e.g., the range of the total score would be different across time).

Standardization

Standardization (transformation to z scores) is one appealing and intuitive way to solve the problem of lack of temporal measurement invariance due to change in the instrument or when there is a concern about a change in metric over time. This normative transformation converts the outcome variables at each time point into z scores, with a mean of zero and standard deviation of one. The z scores make the outcome scores appear to be on the same metric across time and seemingly comparable over time. However, this solution is not appropriate for studying change in the observed outcome variables because standardization may change the shape of the observed trajectories of the original observed scores (Willet, Singer, & Martin, 1998).

This problem is caused in part by unequal variances, hence standard deviations, of the observed outcome variables over time. Although standardization of the observed data at each time point into z scores transforms the cross-time raw outcome scores into a seemingly common z scale and makes the comparison appear feasible, it may greatly distort the temporal pattern and shape of the observed trajectories. For example, imagine that an individual's raw total outcome scores across four time points are 10, 12, 14, and 16. The four time points each happen to have a mean of zero and standard deviations of 5, 6, 7, and 8, respectively. This individual's raw total scores clearly indicates a linear increment in the observed trajectory; however, their corresponding z scores will all be 2, indicating a flat growth trajectory. The phenomenon of unequal cross-time variances is very common with real longitudinal data. This limitation of z-score transformations applies to both the two time-point analyses (Zumbo, 1999) and trajectories.

Vertical Scaling

A common question in large-scale educational assessment settings is something akin to this: How much more proficient are our students in mathematics (or reading) now in Grade 7 than they were 2 years ago in Grade 5? That is, how much growth has there been in mathematics (or reading) proficiency? Interestingly, to measure this type of change, our tests must also change, because our instruments for measuring mathematics (or reading) achievement will provide valid and reliable information if they are tailored to a particular grade. Therefore, in many educational contexts, measures need to be different across the grades to be able to measure change across the grades. One can easily imagine that a Grade 7 mathematics test should, by definition, be more difficult (for Grade 5 students) than a grade-appropriate Grade 5 test. Therefore it is difficult to use the same tests across all the grades to accurately capture the growth of students' achievement performance. Although mathematics ability is used for all grades, the construct under study is not exactly the same across grades; correspondingly, each grade represents a different population.

Vertical scaling refers to a measurement process of putting scores from different test levels (e.g., Grade 3 to Grade 8) onto a common developmental scale, which is often used to assess the growth of students' academic performance over the course of their schooling. The use of vertical scaling becomes involved with many issues, such as the definition and type of construct/domain being measured, definition of growth, designs for data collection, test scoring, and comparisons of scaling results (i.e., between-grade differences and within-grade variability) (Kolen & Brennan, 2004). Given our space limitations relative to the vast literature on vertical scaling, only overall orienting remarks on this topic are provided here. For detailed discussion of the issues in vertical scaling, see, for example, Harris (1991, 2007); Harris, Hendrickson, Tong, Shin, and Shyu (2004); Holland (2007); Patz and Hanson (2002); and Patz and Yao (2006, 2007).

Given the nature of students' academic growth, Holland (2007) points out that tests designed for vertical scaling typically involve similar constructs, different difficulty, and different populations of examinees. The constructs being measured in a vertical scale are allowed to have both quantitative and qualitative change over time/across grades (i.e., different difficulty levels and different subtopics). However, one will need to consider whether a vertical scale is meaningful for deriving a common scale across grades on one subject matter when the subject has qualitative change.

Vertical scales may be more reasonable for subjects that are taught and learned continuously, like reading and mathematics, whereas it may not be appropriate for a subject such as science because the content of the subject changes from one grade to another, such as life science at one grade level and earth science at the next (Lissitz & Huynh, 2003; Young, 2006). Hence it seems more sensible to apply a vertical scale to an academic subject that has certain amount of overlap on content between adjacent grades, which can justify the interpretation of differences between different test levels as growth.

Kolen and Brennan (2004) provide two conceptual definitions of growth: (1) the *domain definition*, by which the domain includes content taught across all grade levels and growth is defined over the entire range of test content covered by all grade levels, and (2) the *grade-to-grade definition*, which defines growth over the content that is taught at a specific grade level. Using the domain definition, grade-to-grade growth refers to the change in scores from one grade to the next over the entire domain of content; using the grade-to-grade definition, grade-to-grade growth is the change in scores from one grade to the next over the content taught in a specific grade level. Generally the definitions of growth are operationally defined by a combination of data collection designs, the characteristics of the score scale, and statistical methods used for conducting the scaling.

In the context of vertical scales, the test content is different across different grades, and items are different too, so the temporal measurement invariance cannot be examined by conventional factor analysis and covariance modeling approaches. Instead, vertical scales are usually constructed through a common-item nonequivalent groups design, in which a set of items from one grade is embedded into the adjacent grade, providing a mechanism to estimate change in academic performance between two consecutive grade levels (Kolen & Brennan, 2004). It is expected that the response to the common items will be consistent between the two grades. However, it rarely happens that the parameter estimates of all common items are invariant between adjacent grades in operational work. Holland (2007) also pointed out that students from different grades represent different populations and that the construct being measured is similar but not the same for adjacent graders.

Statistical Analysis Issues

It is helpful to organize the statistical analysis issues by the number of measured time points: two or more than two.

Data Collected Over Two Periods in Time

When data are collected over two time periods, a common index of change is the (simple) difference score—for example, score at time two minus the score at time one. As Cattell (1982) and Zumbo (1999) state, there is such doubt in research practice about the reliability of difference scores that granting agencies, journal editors, reviewers, and committees of graduate students' theses have been known to deplore their use. Our purpose is to make the case that difference scores can be useful and that data collected at two time points can be analyzed.

It should be emphasized, at this point, that we do not intend to suggest that difference scores (also called change or gain scores) should be ubiquitously used in research settings. The reliability of differences scores, like that of all test scores, depends on the experimental procedures and on the proper use of the instruments by the investigator. This presentation—like those of Thomas and Zumbo (2012), Zimmerman and Williams (1982a, 1982b), and Zumbo (1999)—indicates that difference scores can be reliable and valid and that it would be premature to discard or altogether ban such measures in research and evaluation. Clearly, in their advocacy for the difference score, neither Thomas and Zumbo nor Zimmerman and Williams nor Zumbo encourage its use indiscriminately. Nevertheless more recent literature suggests that, to a large extent, the intuition of researchers in many fields who believe that the simple change score can be a substantively meaningful index is well founded (see Zumbo, 1999, for a review).

This avoidance of the difference score is somewhat puzzling, given that commonly accepted statistical tests with repeated-measures ANOVA involve difference scores (Huck & McLean, 1975; Maxwell & Howard, 1981). This discrepancy in recommendations and practice is an interesting vantage point from which to discuss the reliability of difference scores. Thomas and Zumbo (2012) examined difference scores from the point of view of reliability and repeated-measures ANOVA. Like others working from within a strictly classical test theory psychometric point of view, they demonstrated that difference scores should not be assessed in terms of reliability and that the abolition of difference scores in research practice is totally unwarranted.

As Thomas and Zumbo (2012) state, the belief that difference scores should be abolished or banned stems from the observation that the reliability of difference scores is less, often much less, than the reliability of the two base measures themselves. They go on to demonstrate that this belief cannot be logically supported by an appeal to reliability theory. In fact, to prohibit difference scores is to prohibit one of the most popular experimental designs in the educational, social, behavioral, and life sciences fields—namely, the repeated-measures design.

From the viewpoint of repeated-measures ANOVA, Thomas and Zumbo showed that the classical definition of reliability leads to the paradoxical situation of zero reliability in combination with a powerful repeated-measures test; a finding first demonstrated by Overall and Woodward (1975) for the paired-samples Student t-test. However, from the viewpoint of repeated-measures ANOVA, they demonstrated that the paradox arises from an inappropriate application of the classical definition. Given the importance to both practitioners and theoreticians of the derivation of simple generalization of the definition of reliability that removes the paradox entirely, Thomas and Zumbo's (2012) mathematical results are summarized herein.

Thomas and Zumbo show that the typical classical repeated-measures analysis corresponds to the case of zero reliability of the difference score. However, a repeated-measures analysis is based on contrasts among the observed scores, and when there are only two repeated measures levels, the only contrast available is the difference score. Unlike difference scores, however, paradoxically, few researchers object to repeated measures designs. The paradox is not restricted to the two-level case. A similar analysis reveals that the reliability of all contrasts in a multilevel repeated-measures setup will be zero.

Thomas and Zumbo go on to show that the source of the apparent paradox can be revealed by examining the difference score equation $y_1 - y_2 = (T_1 - T_2) + (\varepsilon_1 - \varepsilon_2)$ wherein T denotes the true scores and ε the errors for the two time points. From this equation, it can be seen that the typical participant (person) random effect in the repeated-measures ANOVA has canceled. This is the beauty of a repeated-measures design: each subject acts as her or his own control. However, a corollary of this cancellation is that the true score in the measurement model described above is now the fixed effect $T_1 - T_2$, that is, a constant. But the variance of a constant is zero, so that when the classical reliability formula is applied to this equation, the result is zero reliability. But repeated-measures designs are not analyzed using considerations of reliability. The standard approach for the repeated-measures model would be to estimate the fixed effect $T_1 - T_2$ using the difference of the sample means of the time one and two observed scores and to then test this effect using an estimate of the variance of $\varepsilon_1 - \varepsilon_2$, namely the sample variance of the difference scores, $y_1 - y_2$.

Thomas and Zumbo resolve the reliability paradox by showing that a generalized definition of reliability yields the noncentrality parameter of the repeated-measures test, an entirely logical and intuitively reasonable result. In short, their mathematical results have shown that evaluating the utility of repeated-measures ANOVA by applying the classical definition of reliability to difference scores leads to an apparent paradox. Repeated-measures ANOVA can have arbitrarily high power even though the "reliability" of its difference scores is zero. This well-known paradox can be resolved by a minor modification to the definition of reliability. However, the redefinition of reliability is not the real issue. The real issue is that difference scores should not be assessed in terms of reliability and that to ban difference scores as a result of such assessments is totally unwarranted. The arguments used by Thomas and Zumbo can be extended to cover other analyses in which difference scores might be used (e.g., multiple linear regression), although details are omitted. The conclusion is the same: classical reliability is an inappropriate way of assessing the utility of difference scores. If difference scores make sense from a subject matter perspective and if the corresponding analysis is likely to have appropriate power, there is no reason to avoid their use.

Data Collected Over More Than Two Periods in Time

Difference scores, however, are often not appropriate when data are observed at more than two time points. In this case, one needs statistical analysis methods that focus on the trajectory created by the multiple tests scores. There are several expository discussions of statistical methods for the analysis of data collected over more than two periods in time (e.g., Singer, 1998; Singer & Willett, 2003); but for the sake of completeness we briefly describe three methods for the analysis of such data: hierarchical linear models, structural equation models, and the multiple-indicators latent growth model.

HIERARCHICAL LINEAR MODELS

The driving conceptual force behind the use of the hierarchical linear model (HLM) for the analysis of data from more than two time periods is that one can estimate the parameters of a trajectory (i.e., a curve), which represents the change over time in our variable of interest by treating it as a sample of samples (i.e., random effect). In this way, one can think of the different levels of an HLM capturing the intra- and intersubject variation.

As per typical HLM, one begins with an unconditional model. Following conventional notation, the multilevel formulation of the unconditional change/growth model is shown below.

$$Level\ 1: Y_{ij} = \pi_{0i} + \pi_{1i}(TIME_{ij}) + r_{ij}, \quad r_{ij} : N\left[0, var(r_{ij})\right] \tag{1}$$

$$Level\ 2: \pi_{0i} = \beta_{00} + u_{0i}, \tag{2}$$

$$\begin{aligned} &Level\ 2: \pi_{1i} = \beta_{10} + u_{1i}, \\ &u_{0i}\ N \sim 0 \quad var(u_{0i}) \quad cov(u_{0i}, u_{1i}) \\ &u_{1i}\ N \sim 0 \quad cov(u_{0i}, u_{1i}) \quad var(u_{1i}) \end{aligned} \tag{3}$$

It should be noted that assuming that the measurements are taken at equal intervals, time is usually coded as 0, 1, 2,..., p, where p denotes the number of times the data are collected minus one. See Biesanz et al. (2004) for a discussion of the role of coding time in estimating and interpreting HLM models.

In the widely used language of HLM, the level 1 model, Equation 1, represents the change trajectory for individual i at times j, the repeated measures. Therefore, each individual i's Y-score (e.g., their mathematics achievement score or their self-concept score) at time j is a function of the intercept (i.e., initial status, π_{0i}), the slope (i.e., the rate of change, π_{1i}), and a time-specific residual term (r_{ij}), which is the deviation between an individual's observed data points and their estimated linear trajectory. The residual term is normally distributed with a mean of zero and a variance denoted, $var(r_{ij})$. In turn, Equation 2 describes the individual intercepts as a function of the average initial status (β_{00}) across individuals plus an individual deviation (u_{0i}) from this average. Likewise, in Equation 2 individual rates of change are expressed as a function of the average rate of change (β_{10}) across individuals and a residual (u_{1i}). The residual terms in Equations 2 and 3 are also normally distributed, with a zero mean and estimated variance components $var(u_{0i})$ and $var(u_{1i})$, and covariance $cov(u_{0i}, u_{1i})$. The equation that is actually fit by software is not that in Equations 1 to 3 per se but rather a combined model arrived at by combining Equations 1 to 3:

$$Y_{ij} = \beta_{00} + \beta_{10}(TIME_{ij}) + u_{1i}(TIME_{ij}) + u_{0i} + r_{ij},$$

and the variance and covariance terms specified above.

Equations 1 through 3 allow one to estimate the average initial status and the average rate of change (and, of course, appropriate statistical tests can be performed to test their respective statistical significance). Likewise, one is able to estimate and test the variance components captured by the variance component terms in Equations 1 to 3.

Equations 1 to 3 are unconditional models in the sense that there are no individual level predictors or covariates in Equations 2 and 3. These initial equations are sufficient to describe the change trajectories; but if one wants to explore correlates or explanatory variables for the individual differences in change, one needs predictor variables, which we denote as X_q, q = 1, 2, 3,…, k for k potential predictors, added to Equations 2 to 3.

$$\text{Level 1}: Y_{ij} = \pi_{0i} + \pi_{1i}(TIME_{ij}) + r_{ij}, \quad r_{ij} : N[0, var(r_{ij})] \qquad (4)$$

$$\text{Level 2}: \pi_{0i} = \beta_{00} + \beta_{01}X_1 + u_{0i} \qquad (5)$$

$$\text{Level 2}: \pi_{1i} = \beta_{10} + \beta_{11}X_1 + u_{1i}$$
$$u_{0i} \, N \sim 0 \quad var(u_{0i}) \quad cov(u_{0i}, u_{1i})$$
$$u_{1i} \, N \sim 0 \quad cov(u_{0i}, u_{1i}) \quad var(u_{1i}) \qquad (6)$$

There are several issues regarding centering the explanatory variables, sample size, and specifying the appropriate covariance matrix over time that our brief discussion cannot address. See Singer and Willett (2003) for more details.

STRUCTURAL EQUATION MODELS

Longitudinal data can also be analyzed using the structural equation modeling (SEM) framework. Broadly speaking, SEM uses latent variables to account for the relations between the temporally repeated outcome variables. The temporally repeated outcome variables can either be observed variables or latent variables that are themselves indicated by a set variable observed over time.

Unlike the multilevel approach that models time as an independent variable, the SEM approach models time as the parameters (i.e., time scores or loadings) for the growth factors. The growth factors (i.e., random effects) are indicated by the temporally repeated outcome variables. The time score parameters for the growth factors can either be fixed to specify a particularly assumed growth function or be freely estimated if no particular growth curve is assumed. A simple linear curve, for example, will entail two growth factors: intercept and slope. The intercept growth factor estimates the amount of the outcome variable at the time when the time score is fixed at zero, which is typically specified at the time point when the outcome variable is first or last collected. Explanatory variables, which can either be observed or latent, can be incorporated to explain the variation in the growth factors.

Note that SEM takes a multivariate approach to growth modeling such that the temporally repeated outcome variables are treated as a multivariate outcome vector. In contrast, multilevel modeling usually takes a univariate approach, where the temporally repeated outcome variables are treated as a single outcome for which repeated measures are nested within individuals. As a result, the SEM approach does not constitute one level for modeling the intraindividual growth over time, leading to the number of levels being one less than the conventional multilevel models. The SEM approach allows a variety of flexibilities for modeling growth and change, such as the ease with modeling correlated residual variances and freely estimated growth function, and so on.

Table 16.1 Equations for the Three-Phase MIML Model

Phase-1 Measurement Model

$$Y_{ijt} = \tau_{jt} + \lambda_{jt} F_{it} + r_{ijt} \qquad (7)$$

i = individuals, j = observed indicators, t = time points

Y_{ijt} = observed response variables/indicators

τ_{jt} = intercept of indicators

λ_{jt} = factor loadings

F_{it} = latent factor score across time points

r_{ijt} = residual for Y_{ijt}

Phase-2 Latent Growth Model (Intraindividual Model)

$$F_{it} = \eta_{0i} + b_t \eta_{1i} + \varepsilon_{it} \qquad (8)$$

η_{0i} = intercept growth factor

η_{1i} = slope growth factor

b_t = time score

ε_{it} = residual for F_{it}

Phase-3 Growth Prediction Model (Interindividual Model)

$$\eta_{0i} = \alpha_0 + \gamma_0 X_i + \varsigma_{0i} \qquad (9)$$

$$\eta_{1i} = \alpha_1 + \gamma_1 X_i + \varsigma_{1i} \qquad (10)$$

X_i = time-invariant predictors

γ_0 and γ_1 are regression coefficient of predictors

ς_{01} = residual for η_{0i}

ς_{02} = residual for η_{1i}

MULTIPLE-INDICATORS LATENT GROWTH MODEL

Following the HLM and SEM approaches, we describe the multiple-indicators latent growth model (multiple-indicators LGM), a SEM approach for analyzing longitudinal data. Conceptually, the structure of the multiple-indicators LGM consists of three phases. Phase 1, the *measurement model*, defines the scaling relationship between the observed indicators and the latent variable, of which the change over time is studied. Phase 2 adds the *latent growth model* to the phase 1 model. The latent growth model captures the intraindividual change in the latent variables over time. Phase 3 adds the *interindividual model* to the phase 2 model. The interindividual model predicts the interindividual differences in growth. Using the notation and approaches developed by Bengt Muthén and Linda Muthén, and implemented in the M*plus* software (Muthén & Muthén, 2007), Table 16.1 provides the mathematical equations for the multiple-indicators LGM and Figure 16.1 depicts the equations graphically in path diagrammatic language.

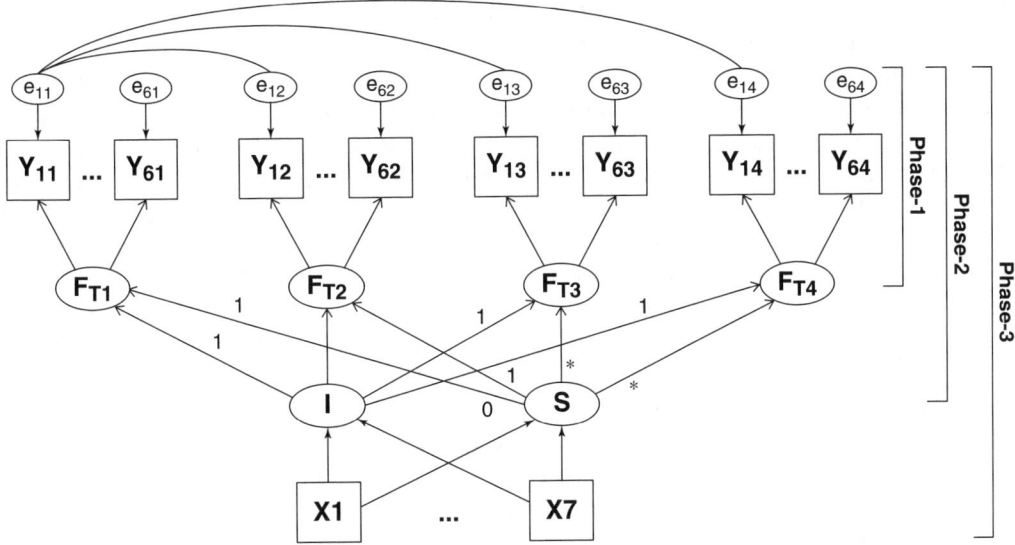

Figure 16.1 A Path Diagram for the 3-Phase MIML Model

PHASE 1: THE MEASUREMENT MODEL

The addition of a measurement model to a traditional growth model brings several advantages (see Equations 7 to 10 in Table 16.1 and Figure 16.1). First, it simultaneously incorporates multiple indicators into one model, which, as a result, allows growth inferences to be made about the latent variable rather than the observed variables. The latent outcome variables, F_{T1}, F_{T2}, F_{T3}, and F_{T4}, are depicted as ovals in Figure 16.1. The observed variables define the operational meaning of the latent variable. Therefore incorporating multiple observed variables enables researchers to model growth and change in the latent variable, which are corrected from systematic measurement errors.

Furthermore, embedding a measurement model allows for the investigation and calibration of measurement invariance over time. In the multiple-indicators LGM, the outcome measures of interest are the latent variables. Thus measurement invariance is investigated at the latent variable level through its measurement model. Establishing temporal measurement invariance is the prerequisite for analyzing change in the latent growth curve in phase 2.

In the SEM framework, the multigroup confirmatory factor analysis (MG-CFA) technique is used for testing measurement invariance across temporal groups prior to a growth study being carried out. Recent developments have come to an agreement that, at the very least, investigation of measurement invariance should (1) be based on the mean and covariance structure (MACS) of the observed variables (Little, 1997; Meredith, 1993; Wu, Li, & Zumbo, 2007) and (2) meet the condition of *strong invariance*—that is, cross-sample equality of the indicator intercepts and the factor loadings (e.g., Little, 1997; Meredith, 1993; Wu, Li, & Zumbo, 2007).

An indicator intercept is the value of an estimated observed variable when the latent variable is zero; it is the scaling constant (i.e., location) of the latent variable for the observed indicator. In a longitudinal study, testing of the equality of the indicator intercepts involves an investigation of whether the scaling constant remains the same for the observed indicators *across all time points*. Factor loadings represent the expected change in an observed variable per unit change in the latent variable. In a longitudinal study, however, testing the equality of the factor loadings involves an investigation of whether the scaling unit of the latent variable remains the same for the observed variables *across all time points*.

Embedding a measurement model may resolve the problem of lack of measurement invariance due to changes made to the instrument over time. To achieve this, MG-CFA strict measurement invariance is specified based on the mean and covariance structure of the z scores. The problem of standardization in distorting observed trajectories will not occur if the study of the growth trajectory is at the latent variable level. This is because standardizing does not alter the overall distribution of the raw outcome scores. That is, the overall distributions of the raw outcome scores and of the z scores will remain the same. For a latent growth model like the multiple-indicators LGM, the actual data for the measurement model is the mean and covariance structure (i.e., MACS) among the observed variables rather than the raw scores per se. Despite the fact that the means and covariances may change in magnitude, the structure will remain identical whether it was calculated based on the raw scores or the z scores. Namely, individuals' scores on the latent outcome variable created on the basis of the mean and covariance matrix of the z scores would remain consistent with those of the raw scores (Cronbach, 1990, p. 121; Gorsuch, 1983, p. 299). If the strict invariance model fits well to the mean and covariance structure of the z scores, lack of measurement invariance is disapproved and the modeling can move to the next phase.

PHASE 2: THE LATENT GROWTH MODEL (INTRAINDIVIDUAL MODEL)

In phase 2, the latent growth model is added to the phase 1 model. The latent variables that define individuals' change over time are referred to as the *intercept growth factor* and the *slope growth factor* (Muthén & Muthén, 2007). The intercept growth factor (denoted as η_{0i} in Equation 8 and depicted as the letter I in an oval in Figure 16.1) represents the estimated status of individuals' growth curve at the time point when the time score is zero (i.e., b_t equals zero in Equation 8), which is usually specified to be at the first time point indicating the estimated initial status of the latent outcome variable. The loadings (i.e., weights) of the intercept growth factor for each of the latent outcome variables ($F_{T1}-F_{T4}$) are fixed to be one. The mean and variance of the intercept growth factor indicate the central tendency and variation in the estimated value of the latent outcome variables when the time score is zero. It should be noted that other growth factors than the slope growth factor can also be modeled. For example, with sufficient time points, a higher-order polynomial curve (such as a quadratic growth factor) can be incorporated to capture the nonlinear trend in the observed trajectories.

When a linear curve is modeled, the slope growth factor (denoted as η_{1i} in Equation 8 and depicted as the letter S in an oval in Figure 16.1) represents the increase in the latent outcome variable for a time score increase of one unit (i.e., the constant growth rate of each individual over all time points). The mean and the variance of the slope growth factor indicate the central tendency and variation of the growth rate over individuals. Covariance between the intercept and growth factors indicates how the initial status and the growth rate are related. For example, a negative covariance indicates that the higher the individual's initial status, the slower the individual's growth rate.

Time scores denoted as b_t in Equation 8 (i.e., loadings for the slope growth factor), in essence, are the weights assigned to the slope growth factor in order to predict the latent outcome variable at a specific time point. They are parameters in the multiple indicators LGM and can either be fixed or freely estimated to determine the shape of the growth curve. Note that a minimum of four time points is recommended for using free time score to capture the nonlinear growth, and two of the time scores need to be fixed for the purpose of model identification; typically, the scores are set to be 0 and 1 for the first two time points ($b_1 = 0$ and $b_2 = 1$). Fixing the first two time scores to 0 and 1 specifies the time elapsed between the first and second time points to be the unit time interval for interpretation. Note that a minimum of four time points is recommended for growth models for two reasons: (1) it is not possible to make the model identify enough parameters in the growth model with less than four time points and (2) data with four time points give more power. For more information, see Muthén (1999).

Freeing the time scores allows the model to better trace the data curve rather than imposing a prespecified curve, which may turn out to fit poorly when the observed data show no clear patterns or follow no familiar curves. As an example, let us consider data collected at four time points with 6-month equal intervals. If the first two time scores are fixed to 0 and 1 and the last two are freely estimated to be 3.5 and 0.2, they can be interpreted as follows: if the amount of change during the first 6 months was scaled to be 1, the expected change at the third time point would be 3.5 and the expected change at the fourth time point would be 0.2. In other words, compared with the first interval growth rate of 1, we expect a growth rate 2.5 times faster than the first interval during the second interval (3.5–1 = 2.5) but an even faster decrease in the growth rate of –3.3 during the third interval (0.2–3.5 = – 3.3). These two free time scores reveal that the growth curve may not fit well to a particular known function such as a linear or quadratic; it reached a high peak at the third time point but a sharp decline at the fourth time point.

It is very important not to interpret the mean of the slope growth factor as a constant rate of change over all time points or over the study period but as the rate of change for a time score change of 1. Namely, the slope growth factor mean is the change in the latent outcome variable for a one unit change in the time score. So if the unit time interval is scaled to occur between the first and second time points (6 months in our example), by fixing the first two time scores to 0 and 1 and freeing the last two, the growth factor mean is the change in the outcome variable for the first 6 months. Thus the growth factor mean is the estimated mean difference between the latent outcome variables at the first and second time points. If the unit time interval is scaled to occur between the first and last time points (24 months in our example), by fixing the first and last time scores to 0 and 1 and freeing the middle two time scores, the growth factor mean is the change in the outcome variable for the 24 months.

PHASE 3: THE GROWTH PREDICTION MODEL (INTERINDIVIDUAL MODEL)
In phase 3, the growth prediction model is added to the phase 2 model. The growth prediction model is formulated by including time-varying and/or time-invariant predictors into the model to examine the relationship between the predictors and the intercept growth factor as well as between the predictors and the slope growth factor (see Equations 9 and 10 and Figure 16.1). Time-invariant predictors depict individuals' static status (e.g., gender), whereas time-varying predictors are variables of which the values vary across time, hence they may have different predictions on the growth factors (e.g., health condition). In addition, the SEM approach allows the flexibility of incorporating both observed and latent predictors. For instance, a researcher may be interested in observed predictors such as gender and age as well as latent predictors, such as personality traits.

Conclusion

The present review of the voluminous literature on the measurement and analysis of longitudinal assessment data points to the fact that tremendous advances are being made on the technical and conceptual fronts. On the measurement front, this chapter points to temporal measurement invariance, standardization, and vertical scaling. These overarching issues need to be addressed before one moves to the matter of statistical analysis or reporting. Longitudinal assessments made over two time points are criticized in the technical literature because two measurement points do not allow one to analyze trajectories of change. However, these two-wave (two-time-point) designs are still very commonly used and, in certain circumstances, difference scores are appropriate methods. Two-wave data are meant to address the matter of the "amount of change" rather than the "rate of change," which is more appropriately dealt with by multiwave designs (with more than two time points). When one has multiwave longitudinal assessment data, one can use hierarchical linear models (HLM), structural equation, and multiple indicators latent growth models.

In an extremely influential paper, Cronbach and Furby (1970) asked a very important question, which has shaped the assessment literature until very recently. They asked: How should we measure change—or should we? As Zumbo (1999, p. 298) responds, how we should measure change depends, of course, on the research question. If one is interested in change over a long period of time, then there are many exciting methodologies such as hierarchical linear modeling, structural equation modeling, and multiple-indicators latent growth models. If, however, the research question involves two points in time, difference scores may be quite appropriate. And should we measure change? Of course we should. Change is a fundamental and pervasive concept, which we now have the methodological machinery to address.

References

Biesanz, J. C., Deeb-Sossa, N., Papadakis, A. A., Bollen, K. A., & Curran, P. J. (2004). The role of coding time in estimating and interpreting growth curve models. *Psychological Methods, 9,* 30–52.

Brown, T. A. (2006). *Confirmatory factor analysis for applied research.* New York: Guilford Press.

Bryk, A. S., & Raudenbush, S. W. (1987). Application of hierarchical linear models to assessing change. *Psychological Bulletin, 101,* 147–158.

Cattell, R. B. (1982). The clinical use of difference scores: Some psychometric problems. *Multivariate Experimental Clinical Research, 6,* 87–98.

Cronbach, L. J. (1990). *Essentials of psychological testing* (5th ed.). New York: HarperCollins.

Cronbach, L., & Furby, L. (1970). How should we measure change—Or should we? *Psychological Bulletin, 74,* 68–80.

Gorsuch, R. L. (1983). *Factor analysis* (2nd ed.). Hillsdale, NJ: Erlbaum.

Harris, D. J. (1991). A comparison of Angoff's design I and design II for vertical equating using traditional and IRT methodology. *Journal of Educational Measurement, 28,* 221–235.

Harris, D. J. (2007). Practical issues in vertical scaling. In N. J. Dorans, M. Pommerich, & P. W. Holland (Eds.), *Linking and aligning scores and scales.* New York: Springer.

Harris, D. J., Hendrickson, A. B., Tong, Y., Shin, S., & Shyu, C. (2004, April). *Vertical scales and the measurement of growth.* Paper presented at the annual conference of the National Council of Measurement in Education, San Diego, CA.

Holland, P. W. (2007). A framework and history for score linking. In N. J. Dorans, M. Pommerich, & P. W. Holland (Eds.), *Linking and aligning scores and scales.* New York: Springer.

Huck, S. W., & McLean, R. A. (1975). Using a repeated measures ANOVA to analyze the data from a pretest-posttest design: A potentially confusing task. *Psychological Bulletin, 82,* 511–518.

Kolen, M., & Brennan, R. (2004). *Test equating, scaling, and linking: Methods and practices* (2nd ed.). New York: Springer.

Lissitz, R. W., & Huynh, H. (2003). Vertical equating for state assessments: issues and solutions in determination of adequate yearly progress and school accountability. *Practical Assessment, Research, & Evaluation, 8(10).* Retrieved from http://PAREonline.net/getvn.asp?v=8&n=10

Little, T. D. (1997). Mean and covariance structures (MACS) analyses of cross-cultural data: Practical and theoretical issues. *Multivariate Behavioral Research, 32,* 53–76.

Lloyd, J. E. V. (2010). Construct commensurability and the analysis of change. *Educational and Psychological Measurement, 70,* 252–266.

Maxwell, S. E., & Howard, G. S. (1981). Change scores—Necessarily anathema? *Educational and Psychological Measurement, 41,* 747–756.

McArdle, J. J., & Nesselroade, J. R. (2003). Growth curve analysis in contemporary psychological research. In J. Schinka & W. Velicer (Eds.), *Comprehensive handbook of psychology: Research methods in psychology* (Vol. 2, pp. 447–480). New York: Wiley.

Meredith, W. (1993). MI, factor analysis and factorial invariance. *Psychometrika, 58,* 525–543.

Muthén, L. K. (1999, October 29). Retrieved from http://www.statmodel.com/discussion/messages/14/20.html#POST16727

Muthén, L. K., & Muthén, B. O. (2007). *Mplus user's guide* (5th ed.). Los Angeles: Muthén & Muthén.

Overall, J. E., & Woodward, J. A. (1975). Unreliability of difference scores: A paradox for the measurement of change. *Psychological Bulletin, 82,* 85–86.

Patz, R. J., & Hanson, B. (2002). *Psychometric issues in vertical scaling.* Paper presented at the annual meeting of the National Council on Measurement in Education, New Orleans, LA.

Patz, R. J., & Yao, L. (2006). Vertical scaling: Statistical models for measuring growth and achievement. In S. Sinharay & C. Rao (Eds.), *Handbook of statistics, 26: Psychometrics.* Amsterdam: North Holland.

Patz, R. J., & Yao, L. (2007). Methods and models for vertical scaling. In N. J. Dorans, M. Pommerich, & P. W. Holland (Eds.), *Linking and aligning scores and scales.* New York: Springer.

Raudenbush, S. W. (2001). Comparing personal trajectories and drawing causal inferences from longitudinal data. *Annual Review of Psychology, 52,* 501–525.

Singer J., & Willett, J. (2003). *Applied longitudinal data analysis: Modeling change and event occurrence.* Oxford, UK: Oxford University Press.

Singer, J. D. (1998). Using SASPROCMIXED to fit multilevel models, hierarchical models, and individual growth models. *Journal of Educational and Behavioral Statistics, 23,* 323–355.

Thomas, D. R., & Zumbo, B. D. (2012). Difference scores from the point of view of reliability and repeated measures ANOVA: In defense of difference scores for data analysis. *Educational and Psychological Measurement, 72,* 37–43.

Willett, J. B., & Singer, J. D. (1991). From whether to when: New methods for studying student dropout and teacher attrition. *Review of Educational Research, 61,* 407–450.

Willett, J. B., Singer, J. D., & Martin, N. M. (1998). The design and analysis of longitudinal studies of psychopathology and development in context: Statistical models and methodological recommendations. *Development and Psychopathology, 10,* 395–426.

Wu, A. D., Li, Z., & Zumbo, B. D. (2007). Decoding the meaning of factorial invariance and updating the practice of multi-group confirmatory factor analysis: A demonstration with TIMSS data. *Practical Assessment, Research, and Evaluation, 12,* 1–26.

Wu, A. D., Liu, Y., Gadermann, A. M., & Zumbo, B. D. (2010). Multiple-indicator multilevel growth model: A solution to multiple methodological challenges in longitudinal studies. *Social Indicators Research: International Interdisciplinary Journal for Quality of Life Measurement, 97,* 123–142.

Young, M. J. (2006). Vertical Scales. In S. M. Downing & T. M. Haladyna (Eds.), *Handbook of test development.* Mahwah, NJ: Erlbaum.

Zimmerman, D.W. (2009). The reliability of difference scores in populations and samples. *Journal of Educational Measurement, 46,* 19–42.

Zimmerman, D. W., & Williams, R. H. (1982a). Gain scores in research can be highly reliable. *Journal of Educational Measurement, 19,* 149–154.

Zimmerman, D. W., & Williams, R. H. (1982b). The relative error magnitude in three measures of change. *Psychometrika, 47,* 141–147.

Zumbo, B. D. (1999). The simple difference score as an inherently poor measure of change: Some reality, much mythology. In Bruce Thompson (Ed.). *Advances in Social Science Methodology* (Vol. 5, pp. 269–304). Greenwich, CT: JAI Press.

Index

accommodating complex sampling designs of students 218–26; balanced repeated replication 224; bootstrapping estimation 224, 235–7; design-based approaches for correcting bias in parameter estimates 218–22; design-based approaches for correcting bias in standard error estimates 222–5; jackknife estimates 223–4, 235–7; linearization 222; model-based approaches for correcting bias in parameter estimates 222; model-based approach for correcting bias in standard error estimates 226; replication techniques 223; SAS code for jackknife and bootstrapping techniques (appendix) 235–7; *see also* complex person and item sampling

accommodating special needs 125–40; accommodation interactions 129; adaptations of tests 126; alternate responding 130; alternate test presentation 130–1; appropriate accommodation 126, 127–9; appropriateness and effectiveness 131–32; clarity in practice 136; computer delivery 126; construct-irrelevant variance (CIV) 128–9; effectiveness research on 126, 129–31; English language learners (ELLs) 126; enlarged print 128; extended time 129–30; future research on 132–4; Individualized Education Plan (IEP) 127; interaction hypothesis 129; modifications of tests 126; National Center on Educational Outcomes (NCEO) 134, 136; oral directions 126; oral presentation of test items 126; practical implications 132; practice upgrading 136–7; students with disabilities (SWDs) 126, 127; test development using universal design 134–6; training 137; universal design for assessments (UDA) 134–6; validity of measurement inferences 128

accommodation interactions 129
accountability for student learning 186, 187
adaptation process, multiple language versions of assessment 116–17
administration methods, in computer-based testing (CBT) 62
administrative perspective, student motivation 55–8
admissions 176
alternate responding 130
alternate test presentation 130–1
analysis of variance (ANOVA) 215
anchor items, sampling designs for students and items 11
ANOVA *see* analysis of variance

appropriateness and effectiveness, accommodating special needs 131–2
a priori judgment of examinees, standard setting 159–61
Arnold, Matthew 2
assessment design, development, and delivery 4–7
atypical response patterns 238–59; application example of PISA data (2003) 251–4, 258–9; application examples 249–51, 257–8; Bayesian methods 242, 244, 245; conditional maximum likelihood estimation method (CML) 245; dichotomous responses 239; estimation methods of item parameters 244–6; estimation of person parameters 248–9; expected a posteriori (EAP) estimation method 244; Fischer score 241–2; four-parameter logistic respons model (4PL) 239; item response theory (IRT) 238, 239; joint maximum likelihood estimation (JMLE) method 24; response patterns and estimation methods of ability levels 240–4; logistic models 239–46; marginal maximum likelihood (MML) 245; maximum likelihood a posteriori estimation method 242; Monte Carlo Markov chains 245–6; multidimensional disciplinary ability levels of students 238; multidimensional modeling 238, 254; multidimensional models of person-characteristic curves 247–8; Newton-Raphson method 241; person-characteristic curves 246; polytomous responses 239; Rasch model 238, 239; *R* source code for application example of PISA data (2003) 258–9; *R* source code for application examples 257–8; Social Sciences and Humanities Research Council of Canada 255; Warm's method 242–3
auxiliary tools in computer-based testing (CBT) 70

background questionnaires 27–42; classroom information needed for 32–3; community information needed for 33–4; defined 28; English language learners (ELLs) 29; final questionnaire 40; information needed for 29–34; language background 29; Ontario Secondary School Literacy Test (OSSLT) 28–9
balanced repeated replication 224
Bayesian methods 242, 244, 245
BEAR *see* Berkeley Evaluation and Assessment Research (BEAR) System
Berkeley Evaluation and Assessment Research (BEAR) System 23–4

bilingualism complexities 90
Binet, Alfred 1
Blais, Jean-Guy 238
Bloom's taxonomy for standard setting 156
Booklets in sampling designs for students and items 211
bookmark method in standard setting 161, 163–5, 172
bootstrapping estimation 224, 235–7
Briggs, Derek C. 186
Brochu, Pierre 238
Broomes, Orlena 27

Canada, student cognition measurement 14
Cantin, Hugo 260
CATs *see* computer-adaptive tests
CBT *see* computer-based testing
centralized versus decentralized models in scoring issues 144, 146–9, 150, 152
certification and licensure 155, 176
change as a fundamental concept in education 276, 288
Childs, Ruth A. 27
CIV *see* construct-irrelevant variance
classic test theory-based approach 118
classroom information needed for background questionnaires 32–3
closed-response items in scoring issues 143
cluster sampling 210
CMEC *see* Council of Ministers of Education Canada
cognition testing program examples 20–4; Berkeley Evaluation and Assessment Research (BEAR) System 23–4; College Board's SAT Reasoning Test 21; Programme for International Student Assessment-2003 (PISA) 22–3; *see also* student cognition measurement
cold-deck imputation methods in missing data 269–70
College Board's SAT Reasoning Test 21
community information needed for background questionnaires 33–4
complete case methods in missing data 266–7
complex person and item sampling 207–37; accommodating complex sampling designs of items in analyses 226–8; analysis of variance (ANOVA) 215; complex random sampling 209; confidence interval estimation 208; flow chart for analyzing complex survey data 229; hypothesis tests 208; impact of sampling design on estimation and inference 214–17; implications for items 217; implications for students 214–17; inferential statistics 208; interclass correlation coefficient (ICC) 215; latent characteristics 209; latent variables 209; measurement error 209; National Assessment of Educational Progress (NAEP) 208; New Jersey Assessment of Skills and Knowledge (NJ ASK) 208; Oregon Assessment of Knowledge and Skills (OAKS) 208; Pan-Canadian Assessment Program (PCAP) 208; plausible values methodology 226–8; population paramater estimates 214–15; a population parameter 208; positively or negatively biased 215; Programme for International Student Assessment (PISA) 208; Progress in International Reading Literacy Study (PIRLS) 208; psychometric models 209; psychometrics 209; a sample 208; sample statistic 208, 209; sampling and statistical inference 208; sampling distribution 208; sampling error 209; sampling variance of parameter estimates 215–17; School Achievement Indicators Program (SAIP) 208; simple example dataset (appendix) 231–4; Trends in International Mathematics and Science Study (TIMSS) 208; unbiased and efficient sample statistics 209; *see also* accommodating complex sampling designs of students
complex random sampling 209
complex sampling of items 210–11
complex sampling of students 209–10
composite index, value-added inferences 195
computer-adaptive tests (CATs) 63, 72–5; *see also* computer-based testing (CBT)
computer-administered exams 176
computer-based and computer-adaptive (CAT) framework, standard setting 170–1
computer-based testing (CBT) 62–84; administration methods 62; auxiliary tools 70; brief history of 63–4; computer-adaptive tests (CATs) 63, 72–5; computerized adaptive multistage tests 75–9; dashboard 68; dedicated commercial test centers 65–6; definition and background 62–3; designs for delivering CBT 71–2; future of 80–1; graphic user interfaces (GUIs) 67–8; innovative items 69; interfaces 67–8; Internet browser-based test delivery software 81; multiple computer labs 66–7; response-capturing components 69; security 81; semipassive components 60; technology-enhanced items 69; technology platforms 63, 64; templates 70–1; temporary testing sites 66; test at home (TAH) 67; test form list (TFL) 71–2; test-form quality control 79–80; testing environment 80–1; test item types 63, 67–8, 69–71; venues for 62, 64; virtualization 64
computer delivery, accommodating special needs 126
computerizd adaptive multistage tests 75–9
computer technology, English language learners (ELLs) academic assessment 98–9
conceptual issues, standard setting 154–5
conditional maximum likelihood estimation method (CML) 245
confidence interval estimation 208
confounding 190, 195
construct-irrelevant variance (CIV) 128–9
content assessment, English language learners (ELLs) academic assessment 93–4
content reviews, multiple language versions of assessment 117
contextual conditions, multiple language versions of assessment 111–12
contrasting groups model, standard setting 159–61
correcting bias in parameter estimates: design-based approaches for 218–22; model-based approaches for 222
correcting bias in standard error estimates: design-based approaches for 222–5; model-based approach for 226
Council of Ministers of Education Canada (CMEC) 144
counterfactual outcome 190
critical perspective, English language learners (ELLs) academic assessment 89
cut points, standard setting 160, 172

dashboard, in computer-based testing (CBT) 68
data-collection tools 263

Index

data-entry procedure, and missing data 264
dedicated commercial test centers, computer-based testing (CBT) 65–6
design-based approaches for correcting bias in parameter estimates 218–22
design-based approaches for correcting bias in standard error estimates 222–5
detecting guessing 48
developmental psychology 276
diagnosis, in missing data 264–5
dialect variation 97
dichotomous responses 239
dictionary and glossary provisions, English language learners (ELLs) academic assessment 98–9
DIF *see* differential item functioning
differential item functioning (DIF) 47, 118–19
dimensionality analyses 118
direct causal attributions 195–7
disproportionate sampling 210
diverse populations 87–9; *see also* English language learners (ELLs) academic assessment
domain definition of growth 279

educational interventions 190
educational policies 186
Educational Value-Added Assessment System (EVASS) approach 189–90
education policy decisions 1
ELLs *see* English language learners
English language learners (ELLs) academic assessment 87–109: accommodations in testing 98–100, 126; and background questionnaires 29; bilingualism complexities 90; computer technology 98–9; content assessment 93–4; critical perspective 89; definitions of ELLs 90–2; dialect variation 97; dictionary and glossary provisions 98–9; English proficiency assessment 92–3; evaluation of assessment system dimensions 100–3; extended time 98; first language and culture 93; future perspective 104–5; generalizability (G) theory 103; in globalization era 88; inclusion 93; international test comparisons 96–7; language bias 94–6; legal definitions 90; limitations of current practices 88; limited English proficient (LEP) definition 90, 91; linguagrams 90, 91; linguistically diverse populations 87–9; measurement error, sampling, and testing 92–6; National Assessment of Educational Progress (NAEP) 97; No Child Left Behind Act 90, 93; overgeneralization in test adaptation 96–100; population misspecification 90–2, 100, 102; probabilistic approaches 89, 100–3; randomness 100–1; sociolinguistics 89; STELLA 99; systemic perspective 89; teachers and 88; testing modeling 103; test review 94–6; test translation 96–7; validity of test scores 88, 89; vignette illustrations 100
English proficiency assessment 92–3
enlarged print 128
Ercikan, Kadriye 1, 110, 143
estimation methods of item parameters 244–6
estimation of person parameters 248–9
evidence-centered design, standard setting 155
expectancy-value theory of motivation 44–5

expected a posteriori (EAP) estimation method 244
expert reviews 117–18
explicit imputation methods in missing data 267–9
extended time 98, 129–30

falsification check 190, 191, 192
first language and culture 93
Fischer score 241–2
fixed-form assessment 210
flow chart for analyzing complex survey data 229
Foundation Skills Assessment Program 144–5
four-parameter logistic respons model 239
framework for improving research, policy, and practices, student motivation 58
Freedman, David 195

Gates Foundation, Measure of Effective Teaching 192–3
generalizability (G) theory 103
generalization from research 156
generalization in test adaptation, English language learners (ELLs) academic assessment 96–100
Getting Value out of Value-Added 188
global economic stage, and student cognition measurement 25
globalization era, and English language learners (ELLs) academic assessment 88
glossary provisions, English language learners (ELLs) academic assessment 98–9
Gorin, Joanna 20
grade-to-grade definition of growth 279–80
graphic user interfaces (GUIs) 67–8
growth definitions 279–80
growth prediction model (interindividual model) 287
guessing 47, 48
GUIs *see* graphic user interfaces
Gunderson-Bryden, Britta 143
Gustafson, Martha 87

Haggarty, Daphne 43
Hambleton and Zenisky model, online reporting resources 183–4
Hambleton, Ronald K. 175
hierarchical linear models (HLM) 282–3
HLM *see* hierarchical linear models
holistic judgment of performance items 165–6
home pages, online reporting resources 179, 182–3
hot-deck and cold-deck imputation methods in missing data 269–70
human capital investment, and student cognition measurement 14
hypothesis tests 208

ICC *see* interclass correlation coefficient
IEP *see* Individualized Education Plan
imputation methods in missing data 267–74; explicit methods 267–9; hot-deck and cold-deck methods 269–70; implicit methods 269–70; inter- and intrasubject methods 268–9; intersubject methods 267–8; intrasubject methods 268; multiple imputation methods 270–4; simple methods 267; *see also* missing data

inclusion, English language learners (ELLs) academic assessment 93
incomplete block or matrix sampling designs 211
Individualized Education Plan (IEP) 127, 177
inferential statistics 208
intended data uses, online reporting resources 175
interaction hypothesis 129
interactive results-oriented tools, online reporting resources 177–8, 180–1
interclass correlation coefficient (ICC) 215
interfaces, computer-based testing (CBT) 67–8
International Association for the Evaluation of Educational Achievement 2
international test comparisons, English language learners (ELLs) academic assessment 96–7
International Testing Commission (ITC) 111
Internet, online reporting resources 176
Internet browser-based test delivery software 81
intersubject imputation methods in missing data 267–8
interviews, as self-report measures of motivation 46
intrasubject imputation methods in missing data 268
IRT see item response test
ITC see International Testing Commission
item information summary sheet in standard setting 163
item nonresponse 47
item response test (IRT) in standard setting 161–2, 163
item response theory (IRT) 238, 239
item response time 46
item sampling see complex person and item sampling

jackknife estimates 223–4, 235–7
Jamgochian, Elisa 125
JMLE method see joint maximum likelihood estimation (JMLE) method
joint maximum likelihood estimation (JMLE) method 244
Jullien, Marc-Antoine 2
jurisdiction, multiple language versions of assessment 111

Kay, Joseph 2
Knowing What Students Know (Pellegrino, Chudowsky, and Glaser, 2001) 3

language background in background questionnaires 29
language bias, English language learners (ELLs) academic assessment 94–6
large-scale assessments: assessing diverse populations 5; assessment design development, and delivery 4–7; brief history of 1–4; defined 1; education policy decisions 1, 110; future of 7–8; key issues related to 4–7; psychometric modeling and statistical analysis 6–7; scoring, score reporting, and use of scores 5–6; *Standards for Educational and Psychological Testing* (1999) 1; training 137
latent characteristics 209
latent growth model (intraindividual model) 286–7
latent variables 209
legal accountability, standard setting 155
legal definitions, English language learners (ELLs) academic assessment 90

Leighton, Jacqueline P. 13
LEP see limited English proficient
likelihood function of response patterns and estimation methods of ability levels 240–4
limited English proficient (LEP) definition 90, 91
linearization 222
linguagrams 90, 91
linguistically diverse populations 87–9
linguistic reviews, multiple language versions of assessment 117
Lissitz, Robert W. 154
Liu, Yan 276
logistic models 239–46
logistic regression, multiple language versions of assessment 119
longitudinal assessment data 276–89; amount of change and rate of change 288; change as a fundamental concept in education 276, 288; data collected over more than two periods in time 282–7; data collected over two periods in time 280–1; developmental psychology 276; domain definition of growth 279; grade-to-grade definition of growth 279–80; growth definitions 279–80; growth prediction model (interindividual model) 287; hierarchical linear models (HLM) 282–3; latent growth model (intraindividual model) 286–7; measurement issues 277–80; measurement model 285–6; multiple-indicators latent growth model 284–7; program evaluation 276; research literature on 276–7, 287; and research question 288; standardization (transformation to z scores) 278–9; statistical analysis issues 280–7; structural equation models (SEM) 283; temporal measurement invariance 277–8; time-related change 276, 288; vertical scaling 279–80
low motivation impact on LSA results 48–50, 59
Luecht, Richard M. 62

Magis, David 238
Mann, Horace 2
marginal maximum likelihood (MML) method 245
matrix sampling designs 211
maximum likelihood a posteriori estimation method 242
measurement error 200, 209; at classroom or school level 197–8; English language learners (ELLs) 92–6; at student level 198
measurement issues in longitudinal assessment data 277–80
measurement model in longitudinal assessment data 285–6
measurement tools, in missing data 263
Measure of Effective Teaching (Gates Foundation) 192–3
measuring motivation 45–8, 58–9
mechanism identification, in missing data 265
minority groups, multiple language versions of assessment 116
misclassification errors, standard setting 160
Mislevy, Jessica L. 207
missing at random (MAR) data 262, 265
missing completely at random (MCAR) data 262, 265
missing data 260–75; calculation of the missing data ratio 264; complete case methods 266–7; data-collection

tools 263; data-entry procedure 264; definition/classification/mechanisms 261–2; diagnosis 264–5; measurement tools 263; mechanism identification 265; missing at random (MAR) 262, 265; missing completely at random (MCAR) 262, 265; model-based methods 274; not missing at random (NMAR) 262, 265; occasions missing 261; pilot survey 263; prevention of 262–4; questionnaire 263; reading problems 263; response rate 264; subjects missing 261; target population 263; time constraints 263; treatment 265–74; treatment methods example 265–6; unreached and omitted items 262; and validity of results 260; values missing 261; *see also* imputation methods in missing data
model-based approaches for correcting bias in parameter estimates 222
model-based approaches for correcting bias in standard error estimates 226
modifications of tests 126
modified Angoff procedure in standard setting 161, 162–3
Monte Carlo Markov chains 245–6
Motivated Strategies Learning Questionnaire 45
motivation theories 44–5, 58
multidimensional disciplinary ability levels of students 238
multidimensional modeling 238, 254
multidimensional models of person-characteristic curves 247–8
multiple computer labs, computer-based testing (CBT) 66–7
multiple imputation methods 270–4
multiple-indicators latent growth model 284–7
multiple language versions of assessment 110–24; adaptation process 116–17; challenges and solutions 116–20; classic test theory-based approach 118; content reviews 117; contextual conditions 111–12; current practices within Canadian jurisdictions 113–14; differential item functioning (DIF) methodologies 118–19; dimensionality analyses 118; expert reviews 117–18; guidelines for developing and using 111; identifying sources of DIF 119–20; International Testing Commission (ITC) 111; jurisdiction 111; linguistic reviews 117; logistic regression 119; minority groups 116; National Assessment of Educational Progress (NAEP) 110; Pan-Canadian Assessment Program (PCAP) 110; Program for International Student Assessment (PISA) 110; Progress in International Reading Literacy Study (PIRLS) 111; psychometric evidence 118; research review 112–13; shells or templates 116–17; simultaneous adaptation process 117; standardization index method 119; Standards for Educational and Psychological Testing 111; statistical approaches 119; student cognitive processes analysis 120; survey of practices in Canada 114–15; test adaptation 112; think-aloud protocols (TAPs) 120; Trends in International Mathematics and Science Study (TIMSS) 110; worldwide use of 111
multistage sampling 210

NAEP *see* National Assessment of Educational Progress
National Assessment of Educational Progress (NAEP) 32, 97, 110, 176, 208

National Center on Educational Outcomes (NCEO) 134, 136
National Educational Longitudinal Study of 1988 (NELS) 19
Nation at Risk, A (1983), United States 2
NCEO *see* National Center on Educational Outcomes
Nedelsky model in standard setting 161–2
NELS *see* National Educational Longitudinal Study of 1988
New Jersey Assessment of Skills and Knowledge (NJ ASK) 208
Newton-Raphson method 241
No Child Left Behind Act (2001), United States 2, 90, 93, 155
nondisclosure agreement in standard setting 167
not missing at random (NMAR) data 262, 265

occasions in missing data 261
Oliveri, Maria Elena 110, 143
omitted items in missing data 262
online reporting resources 175–85; categories of 176–7; computer-administered exams 176; developing score-reporting resources 183–4; Hambleton and Zenisky model 183–84; home pages 179, 182–83; individual education plan (IEP) 177; intended data uses 175; interactive results-oriented tools 177–8, 180–1; Internet 176; National Assessment of Educational Progress (NAEP) 176; overview of 176–9; programmatic/informational Web pages 178–9, 181–2; purpose of test 175; score reporting 175; stakeholders 175, 176; *Standards for Educational and Psychological Testing* 181–2; static, results-oriented Web pages 177, 179–80; test information 175–6; testing contexts 176; websites 176
Ontario Secondary School Literacy Test (OSSLT) 28–9
open-response items, scoring issues 143, 146
oral directions 126
oral presentation of test items 126
Oregon Assessment of Knowledge and Skills (OAKS) 208
Organisation for Economics Co-operation and Development (OECD) 2, 22
OSSLT *see* Ontario Secondary School Literacy Test
Otis, Arthur 1
oversampling students 210

PACP *see* Pan-Canadian Assessment Program
Pan-Canadian Assessment Program (PCAP) 110, 208
paper trail in standard setting 155
pattern marking 46–7
performance level descriptors (PLDs) in standard setting 155, 156–8, 172
performance level labels (PLLs) in standard setting 156
person-characteristic curves 246
person sampling *see* complex person and item sampling
Pharand, Sherri-Lynne 43
pilot survey 263
Pilot Twelve Country Study 2, 3
PIRLS *see* Progress in International Reading Literacy Study
PISA *see* Program for International Literacy Study
PLAP *see* Provincial Learning Assessment Program

plausible values methodology 226–8
polytomous responses 239
population misspecification, English language learners (ELLs) academic assessment 90–2, 100, 102
population parameter 208
population parameter estimates 214–15
prevention of missing data 262–4
primary sampling units (PSUs) 210
Principles for Fair Student Assessment Practices for Education in Canada 148
probabilistic approaches, English language learners (ELLs) academic assessment 89, 100–3
production function approach 188
proficiency growth summary (PGS), standard setting 157–8, 170, 172
program evaluation 276
programmatic/informational Web pages 178–9, 181–2
Programme for International Student Assessment (PISA) 2, 14, 22–3, 29, 110, 144, 208
Progress in International Reading Literacy Study (PIRLS) 29, 32, 111, 144, 208
provincial certification examinations 145
Provincial Learning Assessment Program (PLAP) 144
psychological testing 176
psychometric evidence, multiple language versions of assessment 118
psychometric modeling and statistical analysis 6–7
psychometric models 209
psychometric procedures, standard setting 154
psychometrics 209

questionnaires, as self-report measures of motivation 45–6

Race to the Top (RTTT) 170, 171
Raîche, Gilles 238
randomness, English language learners (ELLs) academic assessment 100–1
Rasch model 238, 239
rating consistency, scoring issues 146
reading problems, and missing data 263
regression, value-added inferences 195
reliability in standard setting 171–2
replication techniques 223
response-capturing components, computer-based testing (CBT) 69
response rate, in missing data 264
Reynolds Adolescent Depression Scale 46
Rousseau, Michel 1, 260
R source code for application example of PISA data (2003) 258–9
R source code for application examples 257–8
RTTT *see* Race to the Top
Ruberto, Lori 43
Rupp, André A. 207

Sáez, Leilani 125
SAIP *see* School Achievement Indicators Program
sample 208
sample statistic 208, 209

sampling designs for students and items 209–14; anchor items 11; booklets 211; cluster sampling 210; complex sampling of items 210–11; complex sampling of students 209–10; disproportionate sampling 210; fixed-form assessment 210; incomplete block or matrix sampling designs 211; motivation example 211–14; multistage sampling 210; oversampling students 210; primary sampling units (PSUs) 210; secondary sampling units (SSUs) 210; simple versus complex sampling (SRS) 209; stratification 209–10; ultimate sampling units (USUs) 210; *see also* complex person and item sampling
sampling distribution 208
sampling error 209
sampling variance of parameter estimates 215–17
SAS code for jackknife and bootstrapping techniques (appendix) 235–7
School Achievement Indicators Program (SAIP) 19, 31, 208
school evaluation 186, 187
score comparability 110–111; *see also* multiple language versions of assessments
score reporting, online reporting resources 175, 183–4
scoring issues 143–53; British Columbia 143; case study 144, 145–51; centralized versus decentralized models 144, 146–9, 150, 152; closed-response items 143; Council of Ministers of Education Canada (CMEC) 144; diverse models (case study) 149, 150–1; in educational achievement 146–9; Foundation Skills Assessment Program 144–5; open-response items 143, 146; overview of LSAs in British Columbia 144; *Principles for Fair Student Assessment Practices for Education in Canada* 148; provincial certification examinations 145; Provincial Learning Assessment Program (PLAP) 144; rating consistency 146; recommendations for changes 151–2; training scorers 149; uses of LSA scores 143
scoring, score reporting, and use of scores 5–6
secondary sampling units (SSUs) 210
security, computer-based testing (CBT) 81
self-report measures of motivation 45–6
semipassive components, computer-based testing (CBT) 60
shells or templates, multiple language versions of assessment 116–17
shoe leather, value-added inferences 193–7
Simon, Marielle 1, 110
simple example dataset (appendix) 231–4
simple versus complex sampling (SRS) 209
simultaneous adaptation process, multiple language versions of assessment 117
Snow cholera example 195–7
Snow, John 187, 195
Social Sciences Humanities Research Council of Canada (SSHRC) 13, 255
socioeconomic status (SES) 156
sociolinguistics 89
Solano-Flores, Guillermo 87
sorting, value-added inferences 190, 191
Spearman, Charles 1
special needs *see* accommodating special needs

SSUs *see* secondary sampling units
stability of value-added inferences 197–8
stakeholder groups 156, 175, 176
standard assessments 2
standardization (transformation to z scores) 278–9
standardization index method, multiple language versions of assessment 119
standard setting 154–74; background and history 154–6; Bloom's taxonomy 156; bookmark method 161, 163–5, 172; books and training materials 155–6; certification and licensure 155; computer-based and computer-adaptive (CAT) framework 170–1; conceptual issues 154–5; contrasting groups model 159–61; cut points 160, 172; evidence-centered design 155; expected future of 167, 169–71; generalization from research 156; holistic judgment of performance items 165–6; item information summary sheet 163; item response test (IRT) 161–2, 163; legal accountability 155; misclassification errors 160; modified Angoff procedure 161, 162–3; Nedelsky model 161–2; No Child Left Behind Act (2001), United States 155; nondisclosure agreement 167; paper trail 155; performance level descriptors (PLDs) 155, 156–8, 172; performance level labels (PLLs) 156; a priori judgment of examinees 159–61; proficiency growth summary (PGS) 157–8, 170, 172; psychometric procedures 154; Race to the Top (RTTT) 170, 171; reasons for using 155; reliability in 171–2; as research topic 156; socioeconomic status (SES) 156; stakeholder groups 156; standard-setting committee (the team) 166–7, 168, 169; subject matter experts (SMEs) 156; traditional standard-setting methods 159–66; validity 172
standard-setting committee (the team) 166–7, 168, 169
Standards for Educational and Psychological Testing (1999) 1, 111, 181–2
Stapelton, Laura M. 207
State Thinking Questionnaire 45–6
static, results-oriented Web pages 177, 179–80
statistical analysis issues in longitudinal assessment data 280–7
statistical approaches, multiple language versions of assessment 119
statistical modeling and direct causal attributions 195–7
STELLA, English language learners (ELLs) academic assessment 99
Stratification 209–10
structural equation models (SEM) 283
student cognition measurement 13–26; background 13–15; Canada 14; differential item functioning (DIF) 19; future considerations 25; global economic stage 25; human capital investment 14; National Educational Longitudinal Study of 1988 (NELS) 19; School Achievement Indicators Program (SAIP) 19; test philosophy 16–17; test specifications 18–20; traditional procedures for item development 15–20; United States 14; validity evidence foundation 17–18; *see also* cognition testing program examples
student cognitive processes analysis 120
student growth model versus value-added model 193–7
student information needed for background questionnaires 30–2

student motivation 43–61; administrative perspective 55–8; expectancy-value theory of motivation 44–5; framework for improving research, policy, and practices 58; future research agenda 58–9; impact of low motivation on LSA results 48, 59; measuring motivation 45–8, 58–9; minimizing impact of low motivation 48–50; motivation defined 44; proportion of students not motivated 48; self-report measures of motivation 45–6; student perspective 50–2; teacher perspective 52–5; theories of motivation 44–5, 58; *see also* test-taking behaviors as measures of motivation
student perspective, in student motivation 50–2
students with disabilities (SWDs) 126, 127; *see also* accommodating special needs
subject matter experts (SMEs) in standard setting 156
subjects in missing data 261
SWDs *see* students with disabilities
systemic perspective in English language learners (ELLs) academic assessment 89

TAH *see* test at home
target population, in missing data 263
teachers: classification of 192; and English language learners (ELLs) academic assessment 88; evaluation of 186, 187; perspective in student motivation 52–5
technology-enhanced items, computer-based testing (CBT) 69
technology platforms, computer-based testing (CBT) 63, 64
templates: computer-based testing (CBT) 70–1; multiple language versions of assessment 116–17
temporal measurement invariance 277–8
temporary testing sites, computer-based testing (CBT) 66
Terman, Lewis 1
test adaptation, multiple language versions of assessment 112
test at home (TAH), computer-based testing (CBT) 67
test form list (TFL), computer-based testing (CBT) 71–2
test-form quality control, computer-based testing (CBT) 79–80
test information, online reporting resources 175–6
testing contexts, online reporting resources 176
testing environment, computer-based testing (CBT) 80–1
test item types, computer-based testing (CBT) 63, 67–8, 69–71
test philosophy, student cognition measurement 16–17
test review, English language learners (ELLs) academic assessment 94–6
test scaling, value-added inferences 198–9
test specifications, student cognition measurement 18–20
test-taking behaviors as measures of motivation 46–8; detecting guessing 48; differential item functioning (DIF) 47; guessing 47; item nonresponse 47; item response time 46; pattern marking 46–7; *see also* student motivation
Test-Taking Motivation Questionnaire 46
test translation, English language learners (ELLs) academic assessment 96–7
TFL *see* test form list

think-aloud protocols (TAPs), multiple language versions of assessment 120
Tidal, Gerald 125
time constraints, in missing data 263
time-related change 276, 288
TIMSS *see* Trends in International Mathematics and Science Study
Tindal, Gerald 125
traditional procedures for item development, student cognition measurement 15–20
treatment, in missing data 265–74
Trends in International Mathematics and Science Study (TIMSS) 29, 96, 110, 208

UDA *see* universal design for assessments
ultimate sampling units (USUs) 210
unidimensionality 199–200
United States: Civil Rights Act 126; Individuals with Disabilities Act 126; *Nation at Risk, A* (1983) 2; No Child Left Behind Act (2001) 2, 90, 93, 155; student cognition measurement 14; testing accommodations 126
universal design for assessments (UDA) 134–6
unreached items in missing data 262

validity: English language learners (ELLs) academic assessment 88, 89; of measurement inferences 128; standard setting 172; value-added inferences 198
validity evidence foundation, student cognition measurement 17–18
value-added inferences 186–204; accountability for student learning 186, 187; classifications of teachers 192; Colorado example 193–5; composit index 195; confounding 190, 195; counterfactual outcome 190; educational interventions 190; educational policies 186; Educational Value-Added Assessment System (EVASS) approach 189–90; effects of teachers or schools on student achievement 190–3; falsification check 190, 191, 192; *Getting Value out of Value-Added* 188; implicit assumptions about LSAs 198–200; measurement error 200; measurement error at classroom or school level 197–8; measurement error at student level 198; Measure of Effective Teaching (Gates Foundation) 192–3; production function approach 188; regression 195; school evaluation 186, 187; shoe leather 193–7; Snow cholera example 195–7; sorting 190, 191; stability of 197–8; statistical modeling and direct causal attributions 195–7; student growth model versus value-added model 193–7; teacher evaluation 186, 187; technical limitations 187; test scaling 198–9; test validity 198; unidimensionality 199–200; value-added estimates or value-added indicators 188; value-added models (VAMs) 187–90; vertical linking 199
value-added models (VAMs) 187–90
Van Barneveld, Christina 43
venues for computer-based testing (CBT) 62, 64
vertical linking in value-added inferences 199
vertical scaling 279–80
vignette illustrations in English language learners (ELLs) academic assessment 100
virtualization, computer-based testing (CBT) 64

Warm's method 242–3
websites, online reporting resources 176
worldwide use, of multiple language versions of assessment 111
Wu, Amery D. 276

Zenisky, April L. 175
Zenisky model, online reporting resources 183–4
Zumbo, Bruno D. 276